Head First Kotlin

Wouldn't it be dreamy if there were a book on Kotlin that was easier to understand than the space shuttle flight manual? I guess it's just a fantasy...

Dawn Griffiths
David Griffiths

Beijing • Boston • Farnham • Sebastopol • Tokyo

Head First Kotlin

by Dawn Griffiths and David Griffiths

Published by O'Reilly Media, Inc., 1005 Gravenstein Highway North, Sebastopol, CA 95472.

O'Reilly Media books may be purchased for educational, business, or sales promotional use. Online editions are also available for most titles (*http://oreilly.com*). For more information, contact our corporate/institutional sales department: (800) 998-9938 or *corporate@oreilly.com*.

Series Creators: Kathy Sierra, Bert Bates

Editor: Jeff Bleiel

Cover Designer: Randy Comer

Production Editor: Kristen Brown

Production Services: Jasmine Kwityn

Indexer: Lucie Haskins

Head First logo: Eric Freeman

Page Viewers: Mum and Dad, Laura and Aisha

Printing History:

February 2019: First Edition.

Mum and Dad

Aisha and Laura

No `Duck` objects were harmed in the making of this book.

ISBN: 978-1-491-99669-0

[LSI]

[2021-01-22]

To the brains behind Kotlin for creating
such a great programming language.

Authors of Head First Kotlin

Dawn Griffiths has over 20 years experience working in the IT industry, working as a senior developer and senior software architect. She has written various books in the *Head First* series, including *Head First Android Development*. She also developed the animated video course *The Agile Sketchpad* with her husband, David, as a way of teaching key concepts and techniques in a way that keeps your brain active and engaged.

When Dawn's not writing books or creating videos, you'll find her honing her Tai Chi skills, reading, running, making bobbin lace, or cooking. She particularly enjoys spending time with her wonderful husband, David.

David Griffiths has worked as an Agile coach, a developer and a garage attendant, but not in that order. He began programming at age 12 when he saw a documentary on the work of Seymour Papert, and when he was 15, he wrote an implementation of Papert's computer language LOGO. Before writing *Head First Kotlin*, David wrote various other *Head First* books, including *Head First Android Development*, and created *The Agile Sketchpad* video course with Dawn.

When David's not writing, coding, or coaching, he spends much of his spare time traveling with his lovely wife—and coauthor—Dawn.

You can follow Dawn and David on Twitter at *https://twitter.com/HeadFirstKotlin*.

Table of Contents (Summary)

Table of Contents (the real thing)

Intro

Your brain on Kotlin. Here *you* are trying to *learn* something, while here your *brain* is, doing you a favor by making sure the learning doesn't *stick*. Your brain's thinking, "Better leave room for more important things, like which wild animals to avoid and whether naked snowboarding is a bad idea." So how *do* you trick your brain into thinking that your life depends on knowing how to code in Kotlin?

1 getting started

A Quick Dip

Kotlin is making waves.

From its first release, Kotlin has impressed programmers with its ***friendly syntax, conciseness, flexibility and power***. In this book, we'll teach you how to **build your own Kotlin applications**, and we'll start by getting you to build a basic application and run it. Along the way, you'll be introduced to some of Kotlin's basic syntax, such as *statements*, *loops* and *conditional branching*. Your journey has just begun...

Being able to choose which platform to compile your code against means that Kotlin code can run on servers, in the cloud, in browsers, on mobile devices, and more.

2 basic types and variables

Being a Variable

There's one thing all code depends on—variables.

So in this chapter, we're going to look under the hood, and show you ***how Kotlin variables really work***. You'll discover Kotlin's **basic types**, such as *Ints*, *Floats* and *Booleans*, and learn how the Kotlin compiler can **cleverly infer a variable's type from the value it's given**. You'll find out how to use **String templates** to construct complex Strings with very little code, and you'll learn how to create **arrays** to hold multiple values. Finally, you'll discover *why objects are so important to life in Kotlinville*.

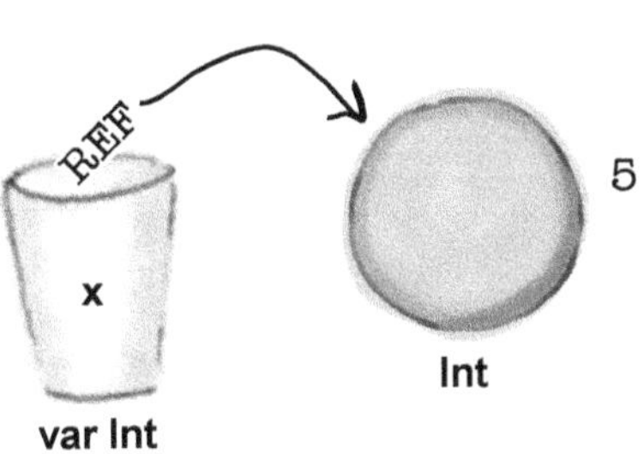

3 functions

Getting Out of Main

It's time to take it up a notch, and learn about functions.

So far, all the code you've written has been inside your application's *main* function. But if you want to write code that's **better organized** and **easier to maintain**, you need to know ***how to split your code into separate functions***. In this chapter, you'll learn *how to write functions* and *interact* with your application by building a game. You'll discover how to write compact ***single expression functions***. Along the way you'll find out how to ***iterate through ranges and collections*** using the powerful *for* loop.

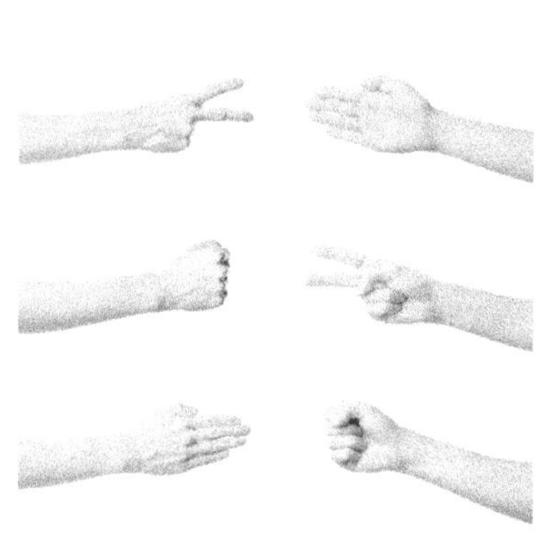

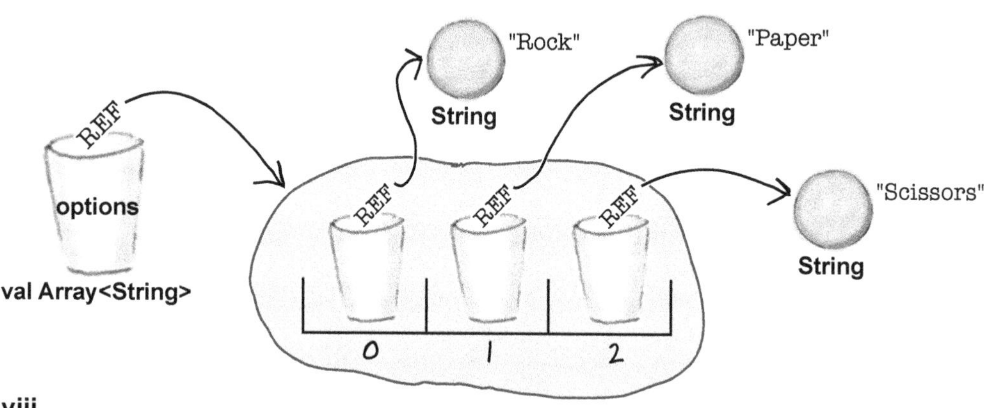

4 classes and objects

A Bit of Class

It's time we looked beyond Kotlin's basic types.

Sooner or later, you're going to want to use something *more* than Kotlin's basic types. And that's where ***classes*** come in. Classes are *templates* that allow you to **create your own types of objects**, and define their properties and functions. Here, you'll learn **how to design and define classes**, and how to use them to **create new types of objects**. You'll meet ***constructors***, ***initializer blocks***, ***getters*** and ***setters***, and you'll discover how they can be used to protect your properties. Finally, you'll learn how **data hiding is built into *all* Kotlin code**, saving you time, effort and a multitude of keystrokes.

One class

Dog
name
weight
breed
bark()

Many objects

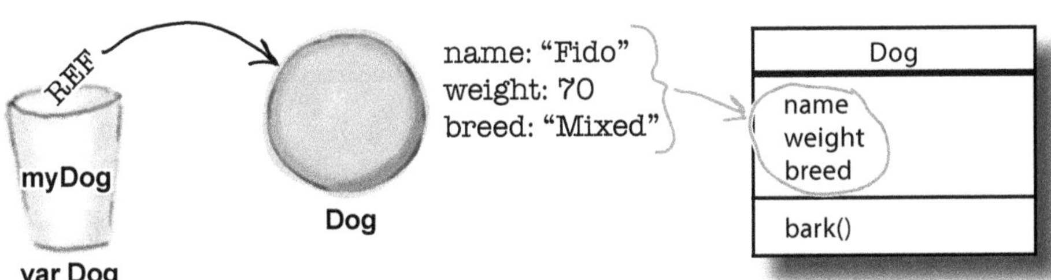

5 subclasses and superclasses

Using Your Inheritance

Ever found yourself thinking that an object's type would be perfect if you could just change a few things?

Well, that's one of the advantages of **inheritance**. Here, you'll learn how to create **subclasses**, and inherit the properties and functions of a **superclass**. You'll discover ***how to override functions and properties*** to make your classes behave the way *you* want, and you'll find out when this is (and isn't) appropriate. Finally, you'll see how inheritance helps you **avoid duplicate code**, and how to improve your flexibility with **polymorphism**.

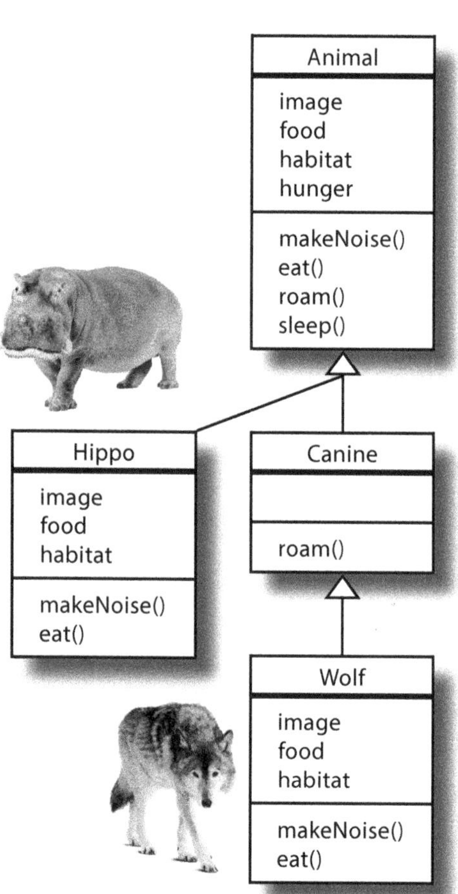

6 abstract classes and interfaces

Serious Polymorphism

A superclass inheritance hierarchy is just the beginning.

If you want to ***fully exploit polymorphism***, you need to design using **abstract classes** and **interfaces**. In this chapter, you'll discover how to use abstract classes to control which classes in your hierarchy ***can and can't be instantiated***. You'll see how they can force concrete subclasses to ***provide their own implementations***. You'll find out how to use interfaces to ***share behavior between independent classes***. And along the way, you'll learn the ins and outs of ***is***, ***as***, and ***when***.

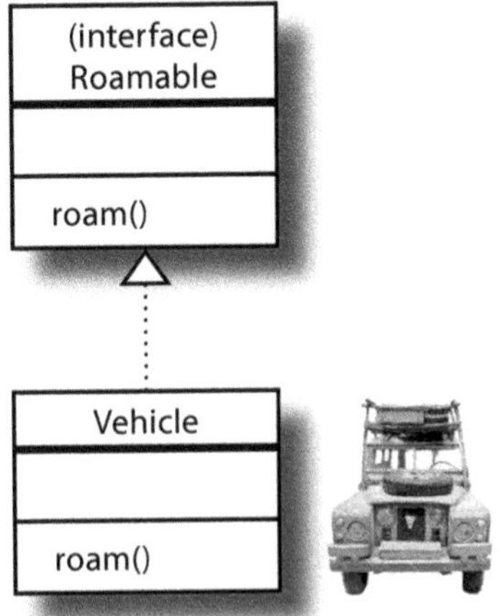

7 data classes

Dealing with Data

Nobody wants to spend their life reinventing the wheel. Most applications include classes whose main purpose is to *store data*, so to make your coding life easier, the Kotlin developers came up with the concept of a **data class**. Here, you'll learn how data classes enable you to write code that's ***cleaner and more concise*** than you ever dreamed was possible. You'll explore the data class ***utility functions***, and discover how to ***destructure a data object into its component parts***. Along the way, you'll find out how ***default parameter values*** can make your code more flexible, and we'll introduce you to **Any**, the *mother of all superclasses*.

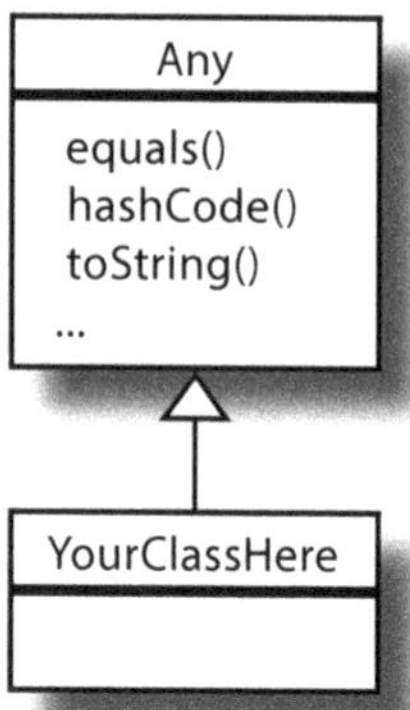

Data objects are considered equal if their properties hold the same values.

8 nulls and exceptions

Safe and Sound

Everybody wants to write code that's safe.

And the great news is that Kotlin was designed with *code-safety at its heart*. We'll start by showing you how Kotlin's use of **nullable types** means that you'll *hardly ever experience a NullPointerException during your entire stay in Kotlinville*. You'll discover how to make *safe calls*, and how Kotlin's **Elvis** operator stops you being *all shook up*. And when we're done with nulls, you'll find out how to **throw and catch exceptions** like a pro.

I'm gonna **TRY** this risky thing, and **CATCH** myself if I fail.

9 collections: Get Organized

Ever wanted something more flexible than an array?

Kotlin comes with a bunch of useful **collections** that give you more flexibility and greater control over how you ***store and manage groups of objects***. Want to keep a *resizeable list that you can keep adding to*? Want to *sort, shuffle or reverse its contents*? Want to *find something by name*? Or do you want something that will automatically *weed out duplicates* without you lifting a finger? If you want any of these things, or more, keep reading. It's all here...

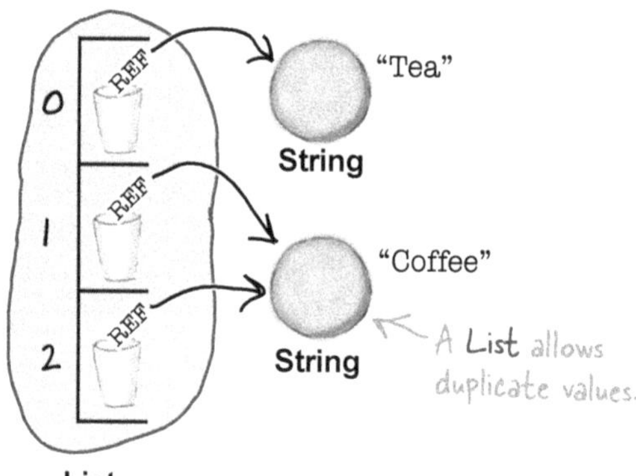

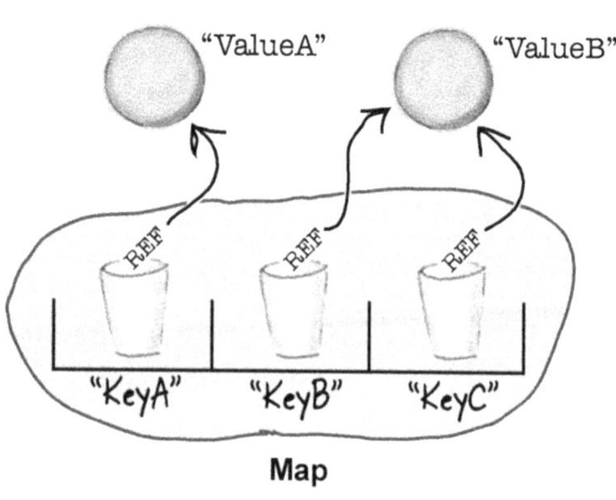

10 generics

Know Your Ins from Your Outs

Everybody likes code that's consistent.

And one way of writing consistent code that's less prone to problems is to use ***generics***. In this chapter, we'll look at how **Kotlin's collection classes use generics** to stop you from putting a Cabbage into a List<Seagull>. You'll discover when and how to ***write your own generic classes, interfaces and functions***, and how to **restrict a generic type** to a specific supertype. Finally, you'll find out ***how to use covariance and contravariance,*** putting **YOU** in control of your generic type's behavior.

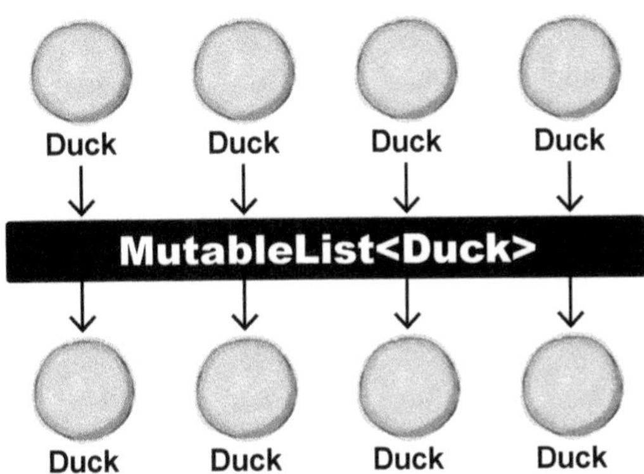

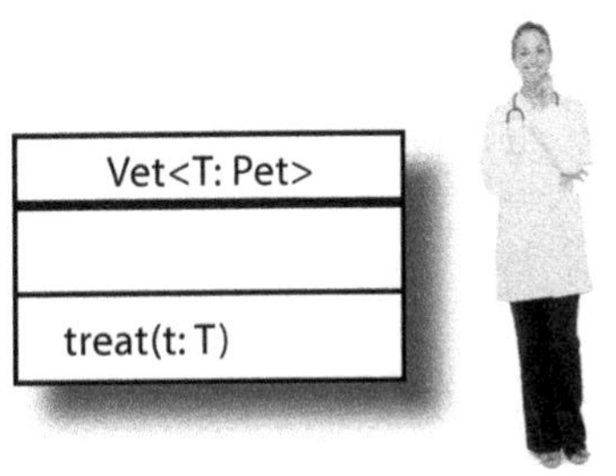

11 lambdas and higher-order functions

Treating Code Like Data

Want to write code that's even more powerful and flexible? If so, then you need **lambdas**. A *lambda*—or *lambda expression*—is a block of code that you can pass around just like an object. Here, you'll discover ***how to define a lambda***, ***assign it to a variable***, and then ***execute its code***. You'll learn about **function types**, and how these can help you write **higher-order functions** that use lambdas for their parameter or return values. And along the way, you'll find out how a little ***syntactic sugar can make your coding life sweeter***.

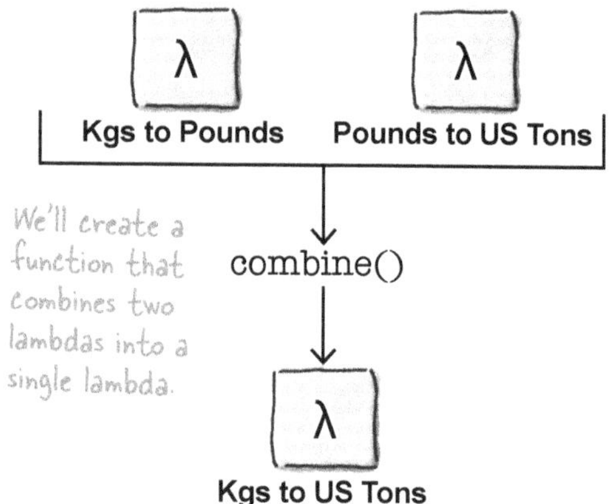

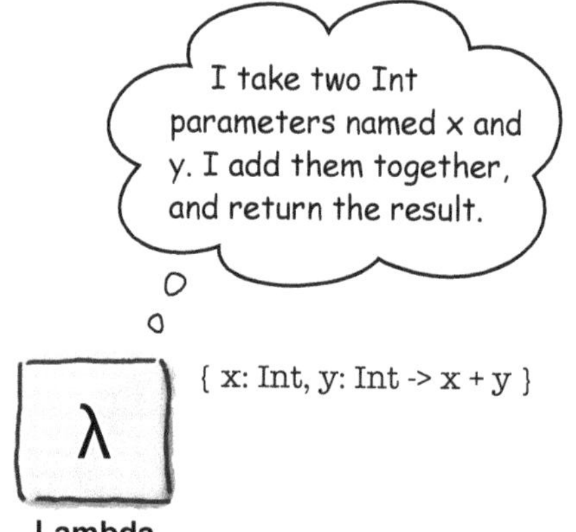

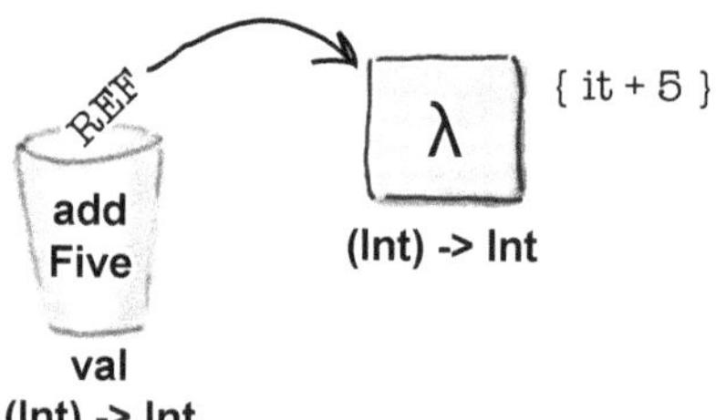

12 built-in higher-order functions

Power Up Your Code

Kotlin has an entire host of built-in higher-order functions. And in this chapter, we'll introduce you to some of the most useful ones. You'll meet the flexible ***filter family***, and discover how they can help you trim your collection down to size. You'll learn how to ***transform a collection using map***, ***loop through its items with forEach***, and how to ***group the items in your collection using groupBy***. You'll even use ***fold*** to perform complex calculations *using just one line of code*. By the end of the chapter, you'll be able to write code more **powerful than you ever thought possible**.

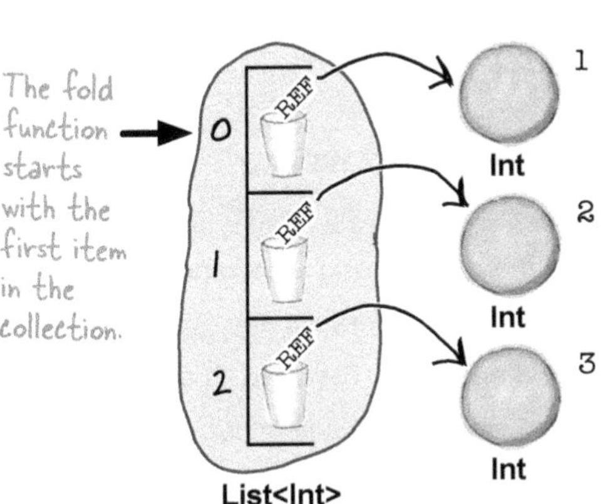

coroutines

Running Code in Parallel

Some tasks are best performed in the background.

If you want to *read data from a slow external server*, you probably don't want the rest of your code to hang around, waiting for the job to complete. In situations such as these, **coroutines are your new BFF**. Coroutines let you write code that's ***run asynchronously***. This means *less time hanging around*, a *better user experience*, and it can also *make your application more scalable*. Keep reading, and you'll learn the secret of how to talk to Bob, while simultaneously listening to Suzy.

Bam! Bam! Bam! Bam! Bam! Bam!
Tish! Tish!

This time, the toms and cymbals play in parallel.

testing

Hold Your Code to Account

Everybody knows that good code needs to work.

But each code change that you make runs the risk of introducing fresh bugs that stop your code from working as it should. That's why *thorough testing* is so important: it means you get to know about any problems in your code *before it's deployed to the live environment*. In this appendix, we'll discuss ***JUnit*** and ***KotlinTest***, two libraries which you can use to **unit test your code** so that you *always have a safety net*.

leftovers

The Top Ten Things (We Didn't Cover)

Even after all that, there's still a little more.

There are just a few more things we think you need to know. We wouldn't feel right about ignoring them, and we really wanted to give you a book you'd be able to lift without training at the local gym. Before you put down the book, **read through these tidbits**.

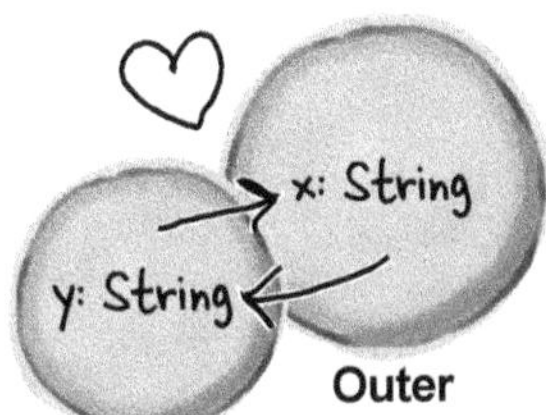

The Inner and Outer objects share a special bond. The Inner can use the Outer's variables, and vice versa.

how to use this book

Intro

I can't believe they put **that** in a Kotlin book.

In this section, we answer the burning question: "So why DID they put that in a book on Kotlin?"

Who is this book for?

If you can answer "yes" to all of these:

1. Have you done some programming?
2. Do you want to learn Kotlin?
3. Do you prefer actually doing things and applying the stuff you learn over listening to someone in a lecture rattle on for hours on end?

This is NOT a reference book. Head First Kotlin is a book designed for **learning**, not an encyclopedia of Kotlin facts.

this book is for you.

Who should probably back away from this book?

If you can answer "yes" to any of these:

1. Is your programming background limited to HTML only, with no scripting language experience?

   (If you've done anything with looping, or if/then logic, you'll do fine with this book, but HTML tagging alone might not be enough.)

2. Are you a kick-butt Kotlin programmer looking for a *reference* book?
3. Would you rather have your toenails pulled out by 15 screaming monkeys than learn something new? Do you believe a Kotlin book should cover *everything*, especially all the obscure stuff you'll never use, and if it bores the reader to tears in the process, then so much the better?

this book is ***not*** for you.

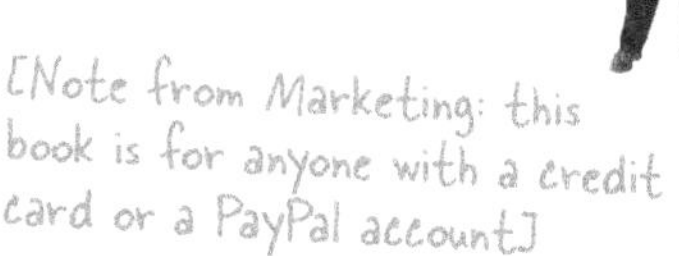

We know what you're thinking

"How can *this* be a serious Kotlin book?"

"What's with all the graphics?"

"Can I actually *learn* it this way?"

"Do I smell pizza?"

We know what your *brain* is thinking

Your brain craves novelty. It's always searching, scanning, *waiting* for something unusual. It was built that way, and it helps you stay alive.

So what does your brain do with all the routine, ordinary, normal things you encounter? Everything it *can* to stop them from interfering with the brain's *real* job—recording things that *matter*. It doesn't bother saving the boring things; they never make it past the "this is obviously not important" filter.

How does your brain *know* what's important? Suppose you're out for a day hike and a tiger jumps in front of you—what happens inside your head and body?

Neurons fire. Emotions crank up. *Chemicals surge.*

And that's how your brain knows…

This must be important! Don't forget it!

But imagine you're at home or in a library. It's a safe, warm, tiger-free zone. You're studying. Getting ready for an exam. Or trying to learn some tough technical topic your boss thinks will take a week, ten days at the most.

Just one problem. Your brain's trying to do you a big favor. It's trying to make sure that this *obviously* unimportant content doesn't clutter up scarce resources. Resources that are better spent storing the really *big* things. Like tigers. Like the danger of fire. Like how you should never have posted those party photos on your Facebook page. And there's no simple way to tell your brain, "Hey brain, thank you very much, but no matter how dull this book is, and how little I'm registering on the emotional Richter scale right now, I really *do* want you to keep this stuff around."

We think of a "Head First" reader as a learner.

So what does it take to *learn* something? First, you have to *get* it, then make sure you don't *forget* it. It's not about pushing facts into your head. Based on the latest research in cognitive science, neurobiology, and educational psychology, *learning* takes a lot more than text on a page. We know what turns your brain on.

Some of the Head First learning principles:

Make it visual. Images are far more memorable than words alone, and make learning much more effective (up to 89% improvement in recall and transfer studies). It also makes things more understandable. **Put the words within or near the graphics** they relate to, rather than on the bottom or on another page, and learners will be up to *twice* as likely to solve problems related to the content.

Use a conversational and personalized style. In recent studies, students performed up to 40% better on post-learning tests if the content spoke directly to the reader, using a first-person, conversational style rather than taking a formal tone. Tell stories instead of lecturing. Use casual language. Don't take yourself too seriously. Which would *you* pay more attention to: a stimulating dinner-party companion, or a lecture?

Get the learner to think more deeply. In other words, unless you actively flex your neurons, nothing much happens in your head. A reader has to be motivated, engaged, curious, and inspired to solve problems, draw conclusions, and generate new knowledge. And for that, you need challenges, exercises, and thought-provoking questions, and activities that involve both sides of the brain and multiple senses.

Get—and keep—the reader's attention. We've all had the "I really want to learn this, but I can't stay awake past page one" experience. Your brain pays attention to things that are out of the ordinary, interesting, strange, eye-catching, unexpected. Learning a new, tough, technical topic doesn't have to be boring. Your brain will learn much more quickly if it's not.

Touch their emotions. We now know that your ability to remember something is largely dependent on its emotional content. You remember what you care about. You remember when you *feel* something. No, we're not talking heart-wrenching stories about a boy and his dog. We're talking emotions like surprise, curiosity, fun, "what the...?" , and the feeling of "I rule!" that comes when you solve a puzzle, learn something everybody else thinks is hard, or realize you know something that "I'm more technical than thou" Bob from Engineering *doesn't*.

Metacognition: thinking about thinking

If you really want to learn, and you want to learn more quickly and more deeply, pay attention to how you pay attention. Think about how you think. Learn how you learn.

Most of us did not take courses on metacognition or learning theory when we were growing up. We were *expected* to learn, but rarely *taught* to learn.

But we assume that if you're holding this book, you really want to learn how to code in Kotlin. And you probably don't want to spend a lot of time. If you want to use what you read in this book, you need to *remember* what you read. And for that, you've got to *understand* it. To get the most from this book, or *any* book or learning experience, take responsibility for your brain. Your brain on *this* content.

The trick is to get your brain to see the new material you're learning as Really Important. Crucial to your well-being. As important as a tiger. Otherwise, you're in for a constant battle, with your brain doing its best to keep the new content from sticking.

So just how *DO* you get your brain to treat Kotlin like it was a hungry tiger?

There's the slow, tedious way, or the faster, more effective way. The slow way is about sheer repetition. You obviously know that you *are* able to learn and remember even the dullest of topics if you keep pounding the same thing into your brain. With enough repetition, your brain says, "This doesn't *feel* important to him, but he keeps looking at the same thing *over* and *over* and *over*, so I suppose it must be."

The faster way is to do ***anything that increases brain activity,*** especially different *types* of brain activity. The things on the previous page are a big part of the solution, and they're all things that have been proven to help your brain work in your favor. For example, studies show that putting words *within* the pictures they describe (as opposed to somewhere else in the page, like a caption or in the body text) causes your brain to try to makes sense of how the words and picture relate, and this causes more neurons to fire. More neurons firing = more chances for your brain to *get* that this is something worth paying attention to, and possibly recording.

A conversational style helps because people tend to pay more attention when they perceive that they're in a conversation, since they're expected to follow along and hold up their end. The amazing thing is, your brain doesn't necessarily *care* that the "conversation" is between you and a book! On the other hand, if the writing style is formal and dry, your brain perceives it the same way you experience being lectured to while sitting in a roomful of passive attendees. No need to stay awake.

But pictures and conversational style are just the beginning…

Here's what WE did:

We used ***pictures***, because your brain is tuned for visuals, not text. As far as your brain's concerned, a picture really *is* worth a thousand words. And when text and pictures work together, we embedded the text *in* the pictures because your brain works more effectively when the text is *within* the thing it refers to, as opposed to in a caption or buried in the body text somewhere.

We used ***redundancy***, saying the same thing in *different* ways and with different media types, and *multiple senses*, to increase the chance that the content gets coded into more than one area of your brain.

We used concepts and pictures in ***unexpected*** ways because your brain is tuned for novelty, and we used pictures and ideas with at least *some* ***emotional*** *content*, because your brain is tuned to pay attention to the biochemistry of emotions. That which causes you to *feel* something is more likely to be remembered, even if that feeling is nothing more than a little ***humor***, ***surprise***, or ***interest.***

We used a personalized, ***conversational style***, because your brain is tuned to pay more attention when it believes you're in a conversation than if it thinks you're passively listening to a presentation. Your brain does this even when you're *reading*.

We included ***activities***, because your brain is tuned to learn and remember more when you ***do*** things than when you *read* about things. And we made the exercises challenging-yet-doable, because that's what most people prefer.

We used ***multiple learning styles***, because *you* might prefer step-by-step procedures, while someone else wants to understand the big picture first, and someone else just wants to see an example. But regardless of your own learning preference, *everyone* benefits from seeing the same content represented in multiple ways.

We include content for ***both sides of your brain***, because the more of your brain you engage, the more likely you are to learn and remember, and the longer you can stay focused. Since working one side of the brain often means giving the other side a chance to rest, you can be more productive at learning for a longer period of time.

And we included ***stories*** and exercises that present ***more than one point of view,*** because your brain is tuned to learn more deeply when it's forced to make evaluations and judgments.

We included ***challenges***, with exercises, and by asking ***questions*** that don't always have a straight answer, because your brain is tuned to learn and remember when it has to *work* at something. Think about it—you can't get your *body* in shape just by *watching* people at the gym. But we did our best to make sure that when you're working hard, it's on the *right* things. That ***you're not spending one extra dendrite*** processing a hard-to-understand example, or parsing difficult, jargon-laden, or overly terse text.

We used ***people***. In stories, examples, pictures, etc., because, well, *you're* a person. And your brain pays more attention to *people* than it does to *things*.

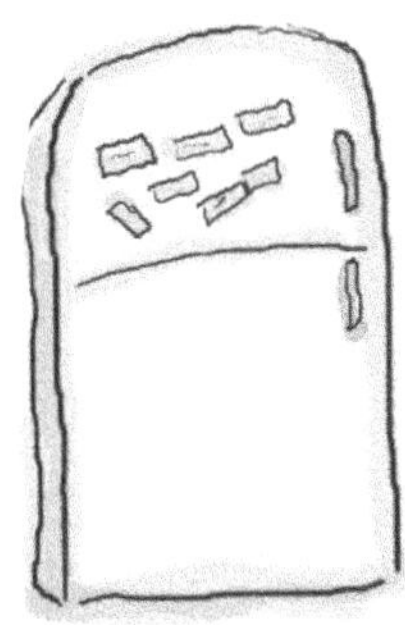

Here's what YOU can do to bend your brain into submission

So, we did our part. The rest is up to you. These tips are a starting point; listen to your brain and figure out what works for you and what doesn't. Try new things.

Cut this out and stick it on your refrigerator.

1. **Slow down. The more you understand, the less you have to memorize.**

   Don't just *read*. Stop and think. When the book asks you a question, don't just skip to the answer. Imagine that someone really *is* asking the question. The more deeply you force your brain to think, the better chance you have of learning and remembering.

2. **Do the exercises. Write your own notes.**

   We put them in, but if we did them for you, that would be like having someone else do your workouts for you. And don't just *look* at the exercises. **Use a pencil.** There's plenty of evidence that physical activity *while* learning can increase the learning.

3. **Read "There Are No Dumb Questions."**

   That means all of them. They're not optional sidebars, ***they're part of the core content!*** Don't skip them.

4. **Make this the last thing you read before bed. Or at least the last challenging thing.**

   Part of the learning (especially the transfer to long-term memory) happens *after* you put the book down. Your brain needs time on its own, to do more processing. If you put in something new during that processing time, some of what you just learned will be lost.

5. **Talk about it. Out loud.**

   Speaking activates a different part of the brain. If you're trying to understand something, or increase your chance of remembering it later, say it out loud. Better still, try to explain it out loud to someone else. You'll learn more quickly, and you might uncover ideas you hadn't known were there when you were reading about it.

6. **Drink water. Lots of it.**

   Your brain works best in a nice bath of fluid. Dehydration (which can happen before you ever feel thirsty) decreases cognitive function.

7. **Listen to your brain.**

   Pay attention to whether your brain is getting overloaded. If you find yourself starting to skim the surface or forget what you just read, it's time for a break. Once you go past a certain point, you won't learn faster by trying to shove more in, and you might even hurt the process.

8. **Feel something.**

   Your brain needs to know that this *matters*. Get involved with the stories. Make up your own captions for the photos. Groaning over a bad joke is *still* better than feeling nothing at all.

9. **Write a lot of code!**

   There's only one way to learn Kotlin: **write a lot of code**. And that's what you're going to do throughout this book. Coding is a skill, and the only way to get good at it is to practice. We're going to give you a lot of practice: every chapter has exercises that pose a problem for you to solve. Don't just skip over them—a lot of the learning happens when you solve the exercises. We included a solution to each exercise—don't be afraid to **peek at the solution** if you get stuck! (It's easy to get snagged on something small.) But try to solve the problem before you look at the solution. And definitely get it working before you move on to the next part of the book.

Read me

This is a learning experience, not a reference book. We deliberately stripped out everything that might get in the way of learning whatever it is we're working on at that point in the book. And the first time through, you need to begin at the beginning, because the book makes assumptions about what you've already seen and learned.

We assume you're new to Kotlin, but not to programming.

We assume that you've already done some programming. Maybe not a lot, but we'll assume you've already seen things like loops and variables in some other language. And unlike a lot of other Kotlin books, we don't assume that you already know Java.

We begin by teaching some basic Kotlin concepts, and then we start putting Kotlin to work for you right away.

We cover the fundamentals of Kotlin code in Chapter 1. That way, by the time you make it all the way to Chapter 2, you are creating programs that actually do something. The rest of the book then builds on your Kotlin skills, turning you from *Kotlin newbie* to *Kotlin ninja master* in very little time.

The redundancy is intentional and important.

One distinct difference in a Head First book is that we want you to *really* get it. And we want you to finish the book remembering what you've learned. Most reference books don't have retention and recall as a goal, but this book is about *learning*, so you'll see some of the same concepts come up more than once.

The code examples are as lean as possible.

We know how frustrating it is to wade through 200 lines of code looking for the two lines you need to understand. Most examples within this book are shown within the smallest possible context, so that the part you're trying to learn is clear and simple. So don't expect the code to be robust, or even complete. That's *your* assignment for after you finish the book, and it's all part of the learning experience.

The exercises and activities are NOT optional.

The exercises and activities are not add-ons; they're part of the core content of the book. Some of them are to help with memory, some are for understanding, and some will help you apply what you've learned. So don't skip the exercises! Your brain will thank you for it.

The Brain Power exercises don't have answers.

Not printed in the book, anyway. For some of them, there *is* no right answer, and for others, part of the learning experience is for *you* to decide if and when your answers are right. In some of the Brain Power exercises, you will find hints to point you in the right direction.

The technical review team

Technical reviewers:

Ingo Krotzky is a trained health information technician who has been working as a database programmer/software developer for contract research institutes.

Ken Kousen is the author of the books *Modern Java Recipes* (O'Reilly), *Gradle Recipes for Android* (O'Reilly) and *Making Java Groovy* (Manning), as well as O'Reilly video courses in Android, Groovy, Gradle, advanced Java and Spring. He is a regular speaker on the No Fluff, Just Stuff conference tour and a 2013 and 2016 JavaOne Rock Star, and has spoken at conferences all over the world. Through his company, Kousen I.T., Inc., he has taught software development training courses to thousands of students.

Acknowledgments

Our editor:

Heartfelt thanks to our awesome editor **Jeff Bleiel** for all his work and help. We've truly valued his trust, support, and encouragement. We've appreciated all the times he pointed out when things were unclear or needed a rethink, as it's led to us writing a much better book.

Jeff Bleiel

The O'Reilly team:

A big thank you goes to **Brian Foster** for his early help in getting *Head First Kotlin* off the ground; **Susan Conant**, **Rachel Roumeliotis** and **Nancy Davis** for their help smoothing the wheels; **Randy Comer** for designing the cover; the **early release team** for making early versions of the book available for download; and **Kristen Brown, Jasmine Kwityn, Lucie Haskins and the rest of the production team** for expertly steering the book through the production process, and for working so hard behind the scenes.

Friends, family and colleagues:

Writing a *Head First* book is always a rollercoaster, and we've truly valued the kindness and support of our friends, family and colleagues along the way. Special thanks go to **Jacqui**, **Ian**, **Vanessa**, **Dawn**, **Matt**, **Andy**, **Simon**, **Mum**, **Dad**, **Rob** and **Lorraine**.

The without-whom list:

Our awesome technical review team worked hard to give us their thoughts on the book, and we're so grateful for their input. They made sure that what we covered was spot on, and kept us entertained along the way. We think the book is much better as a result of their feedback.

Finally, our thanks to **Kathy Sierra** and **Bert Bates** for creating this extraordinary series of books, and for letting us into their brains.

O'Reilly

For almost 40 years, O'Reilly Media has provided technology and business training, knowledge, and insight to help companies succeed.

Our unique network of experts and innovators share their knowledge and expertise through books, articles, conferences, and our online learning platform. O'Reilly's online learning platform gives you on-demand access to live training courses, in-depth learning paths, interactive coding environments, and a vast collection of text and video from O'Reilly and 200+ other publishers.

For more information, please visit *http://oreilly.com*.

1 getting started

A Quick Dip

Kotlin is making waves.

From its first release, Kotlin has impressed programmers with its ***friendly syntax, conciseness, flexibility and power***. In this book, we'll teach you how to **build your own Kotlin applications**, and we'll start by getting you to build a basic application and run it. Along the way, you'll be introduced to some of Kotlin's basic syntax, such as *statements*, *loops* and *conditional branching*. Your journey has just begun...

Welcome to Kotlinville

Kotlin has been taking the programming world by storm. Despite being one of the youngest programming languages in town, many developers now view it as their language of choice. So what makes Kotlin so special?

Kotlin has many modern language features that make it attractive to developers. You'll find out about these features in more detail later in the book, but for now, here are some of the highlights.

It's crisp, concise and readable

Unlike some languages, Kotlin code is very concise, and you can perform powerful tasks in just one line. It provides shortcuts for common actions so that you don't have to write lots of repetitive boilerplate code, and it has a rich library of functions that you can use. And as there's less code to wade through, it's quicker to read, write and understand, leaving you more time to do other things.

You can use object-oriented AND functional programming

Can't decide whether to learn object-oriented or functional programming? Well, why not do both? Kotlin lets you create object-oriented code that uses classes, inheritance and polymorphism, just as you can in Java. But it also supports functional programming, giving you the best of both worlds.

The compiler keeps you safe

Nobody likes unsafe, buggy code, and Kotlin's compiler puts a lot of effort into making sure your code is as clean as possible, preventing many of the errors that can occur in other programming languages. Kotlin is statically typed, for example, so you can't perform inappropriate actions on the wrong type of variable and crash your code. And most of the time, you don't even need to explicitly specify the type yourself as the compiler can infer it for you.

Kotlin virtually eliminates the kinds of errors that regularly occur in other programming languages. That means safer, more reliable code, and less time spent chasing bugs.

So Kotlin is a modern, powerful and flexible programming language that offers many advantages. But that's not the end of the story.

You can use Kotlin nearly everywhere

Kotlin is so powerful and flexible that you can use it as a general-purpose language in many different contexts. This is because you can ***choose which platform to compile your Kotlin code against***.

Java Virtual Machines (JVMs)

Kotlin code can be compiled to JVM (Java Virtual Machine) bytecode, so you can use Kotlin practically anywhere that you can use Java. Kotlin is 100% interoperable with Java, so you can use existing Java libraries with it. If you're working on an application that contains a lot of old Java code, you don't have to throw all the old code away; your new Kotlin code will work alongside it. And if you want to use the Kotlin code you've written from inside Java, you can do so with ease.

Being able to choose which platform to compile your code against means that Kotlin code can run on servers, in the cloud, in browsers, on mobile devices, and more.

Android

Alongside other languages such as Java, Kotlin has first-class support for Android. Kotlin is fully supported in Android Studio, and you can make the most of Kotlin's many advantages when you develop Android apps.

Client-side and server-side JavaScript

You can also transpile—or translate and compile—Kotlin code into JavaScript, so that you can run it in a browser. You can use it to work with both client-side and server-side technology, such as WebGL or Node.js.

Native apps

If you want to write code that will run quickly on less powerful devices, you can compile your Kotlin code directly to native machine code. This allows you to write code that will run, for example, on iOS or Linux.

In this book, we're going to focus on creating Kotlin applications for JVMs, as this is the most straightforward way of getting to grips with the language. Afterwards, you'll be able to apply the knowledge you've gained to other platforms.

Even though we're building applications for Java Virtual Machines, you don't need to know Java to get the most out of this book. We're assuming you have some general programming experience, but that's it.

Let's dive in.

What we'll do in this chapter

In this chapter, we're going to show you how to build a basic Kotlin application. There are a number of steps we're going to go through to do this:

Create a new Kotlin project.
We'll start by installing IntelliJ IDEA (Community Edition), a free IDE that supports Kotlin application development. We'll then use the IDE to build a new Kotlin project:

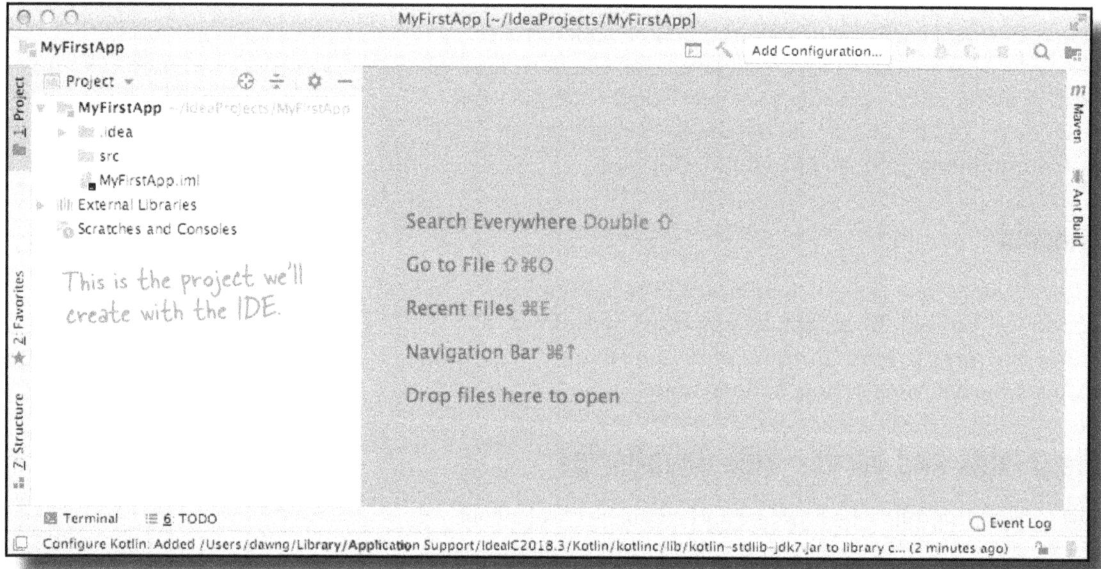

2. **Add a function that displays some text.**
We'll add a new Kotlin file to the project, then write a simple `main` function that will output the text "Pow!"

3. **Update the function to make it do more.**
Kotlin includes basic language structures such as statements, loops and conditional branching. We'll use these to change our function so that it does more.

4. **Try out code in the Kotlin interactive shell.**
Finally, we'll look at how to try out snippets of code in the Kotlin interactive shell (or REPL).

We'll install the IDE after you've tried the following exercise.

Sharpen your pencil

We know we've not taught you any Kotlin code yet, but see if you can guess what each line of code is doing. We've completed the first one to get you started.

```
val name = "Misty" ......Declare a variable named 'name' and give it a value of "Misty".
val height = 9 ..........

println("Hello") ..........
println("My cat is called $name") ..........
println("My cat is $height inches tall") ..........

val a = 6 ..........
val b = 7 ..........
val c = a + b + 10 ..........
val str = c.toString() ..........

val numList = arrayOf(1, 2, 3) ..........
var x = 0 ..........
while (x < 3) { ..........
    println("Item $x is ${numList[x]}")..........
    x = x + 1 ..........
} ..........

val myCat = Cat(name, height) ..........
val y = height - 3 ..........
if (y < 5) myCat.miaow(4) ..........

while (y < 8) { ..........
    myCat.play() ..........
    y = y + 1 ..........
} ..........
```

Sharpen your pencil Solution

We know we've not taught you any Kotlin code yet, but see if you can guess what each line of code is doing. We've completed the first one to get you started.

```
val name = "Misty"
```
Declare a variable named 'name' and give it a value of "Misty".

```
val height = 9
```
Declare a variable named 'height' and give it a value of 9.

```
println("Hello")
```
Prints "Hello" to the standard output.

```
println("My cat is called $name")
```
Prints "My cat is called Misty".

```
println("My cat is $height inches tall")
```
Prints "My cat is 9 inches tall".

```
val a = 6
```
Declare a variable named 'a' and give it a value of 6.

```
val b = 7
```
Declare a variable named 'b' and give it a value of 7.

```
val c = a + b + 10
```
Declare a variable named 'c' and give it a value of 23.

```
val str = c.toString()
```
Declare a variable named 'str' and give it a text value of "23".

```
val numList = arrayOf(1, 2, 3)
```
Create an array containing values of 1, 2 and 3.

```
var x = 0
```
Declare a variable named 'x' and give it a value of 0.

```
while (x < 3) {
```
Keep looping as long as x is less than 3.

```
    println("Item $x is ${numList[x]}")
```
Print the index and value of each item in the array.

```
    x = x + 1
```
Add 1 to x.

```
}
```
This is the end of the loop.

```
val myCat = Cat(name, height)
```
Declare a variable named 'myCat' and create a Cat object.

```
val y = height - 3
```
Declare a variable named 'y' and give it a value of 6.

```
if (y < 5) myCat.miaow(4)
```
If y is less than 5, the Cat should miaow 4 times.

```
while (y < 8) {
```
Keep looping as long as y is less than 8.

```
    myCat.play()
```
Make the Cat play.

```
    y = y + 1
```
Add 1 to y.

```
}
```
This is the end of the loop.

You are here.

Build application
Add function
Update function
Use REPL

Install IntelliJ IDEA (Community Edition)

The easiest way of writing and running Kotlin code is to use IntelliJ IDEA (Community Edition). This is a free IDE from JetBrains, the people who invented Kotlin, and it comes with everything you need to develop Kotlin applications, including:

A code editor
The code editor offers code completion to help you write Kotlin code, and formatting and color highlighting to make your code easier to read. It also gives you hints for improving your code.

Build tools
You can compile and run your code using quick and easy shortcuts.

Kotlin REPL
You have easy access to the Kotlin REPL, which lets you try out code snippets outside your main code.

Version control
IntelliJ IDEA interfaces with major version control systems such as Git, SVN, CVS and more

There are many more features too, all there to make your coding life easier.

To follow along with us in this book, you need to install IntelliJ IDEA (Community Edition). You can download the IDE here:

https://www.jetbrains.com/idea/download/index.html ← Make sure you choose the option to download the free Community Edition of IntelliJ IDEA.

Once you've installed the IDE, open it. You should see the IntelliJ IDEA welcome screen. You're ready to build your first Kotlin application.

This is the IntelliJ IDEA welcome screen. →

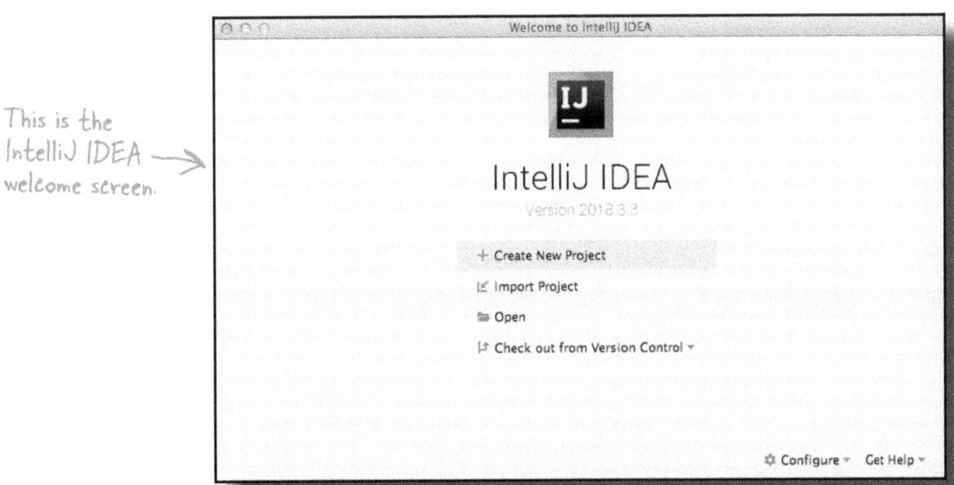

Let's build a basic application

Now that you've set up your development environment, you're ready to create your first Kotlin application. We're going to create a very simple application that will display the text "Pow!" in the IDE.

Whenever you create a new application in IntelliJ IDEA, you need to create a new project for it. Make sure you have the IDE open, and follow along with us.

1. Create a new project

The IntelliJ IDEA welcome screen gives you a number of options for what you want to do. We want to create a new project, so click on the option for "Create New Project".

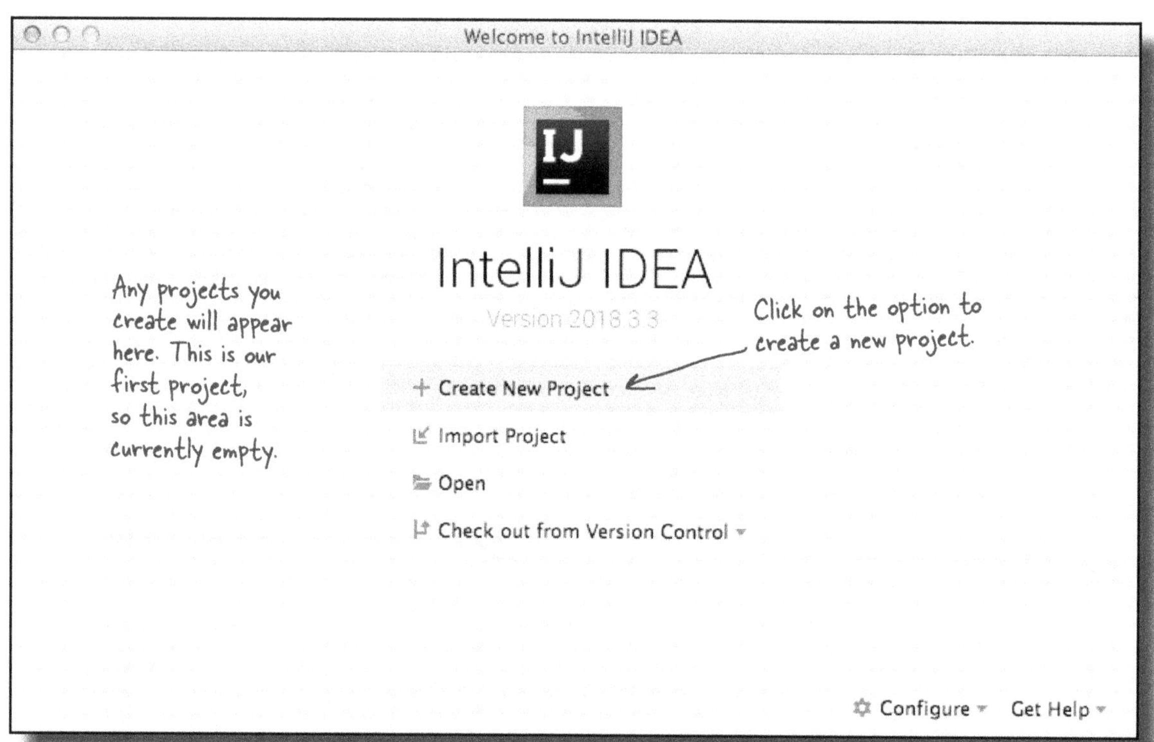

Building a basic application (continued)

2. Specify the type of project

Next, you need to tell IntelliJ IDEA what sort of project you want to create.

IntelliJ IDEA allows you to create projects for various languages and platforms, such as Java and Android. We're going to create a Kotlin project, so choose the option for "Kotlin".

You also need to specify which platform you want your Kotlin project to target. We're going to create a Kotlin application with a JVM target, so select the Kotlin/JVM option. Then click on the Next button.

There are other options too, but we're going to focus on creating applications that run against a JVM.

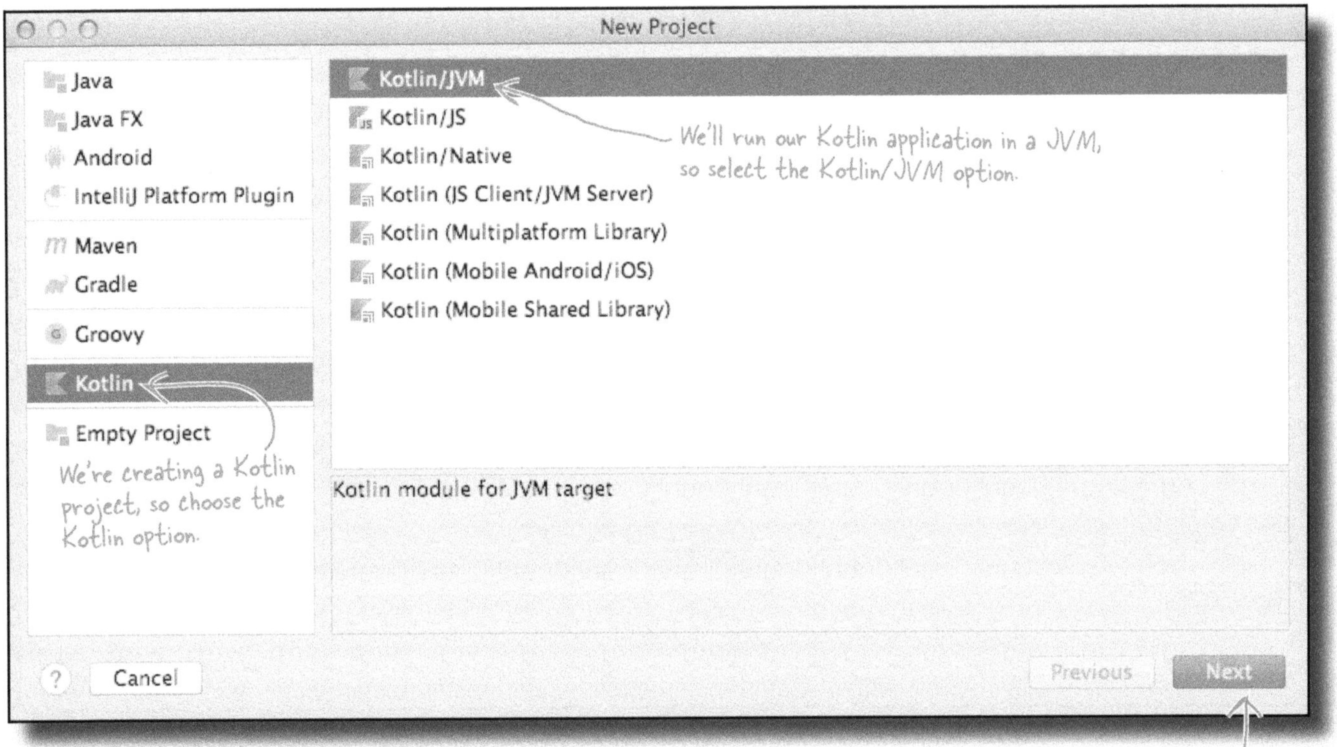

New Project

Java
Java FX
Android
IntelliJ Platform Plugin
Maven
Gradle
Groovy
Kotlin
Empty Project

Kotlin/JVM
Kotlin/JS
Kotlin/Native
Kotlin (JS Client/JVM Server)
Kotlin (Multiplatform Library)
Kotlin (Mobile Android/iOS)
Kotlin (Mobile Shared Library)

Kotlin module for JVM target

Cancel Previous Next

We'll run our Kotlin application in a JVM, so select the Kotlin/JVM option.

We're creating a Kotlin project, so choose the Kotlin option.

Click on the Next button to proceed to the next step.

Building a basic application (continued)

Build application
Add function
Update function
Use REPL

3. Configure the project

You now need to configure the project by saying what you want to call it, where you want to store the files, and what files should be used by the project. This includes which version of Java should be used by the JVM, and the library for the Kotlin runtime.

Name the project "MyFirstApp", and accept the rest of the defaults.

When you click on the Finish button, IntelliJ IDEA will create your project.

Name the project "MyFirstApp"

New Project
Project name: MyFirstApp
Project location: ~/IdeaProjects/MyFirstApp
Project SDK: 1.8 (java version "1.8.0_102") New...
Kotlin runtime
Accept the default values.
Use library: KotlinJavaRuntime Create...
Project level library KotlinJavaRuntime with 3 files will be created Configure...
More Settings
? Cancel Previous Finish

Click on the Finish button, and the IDE will create your project.

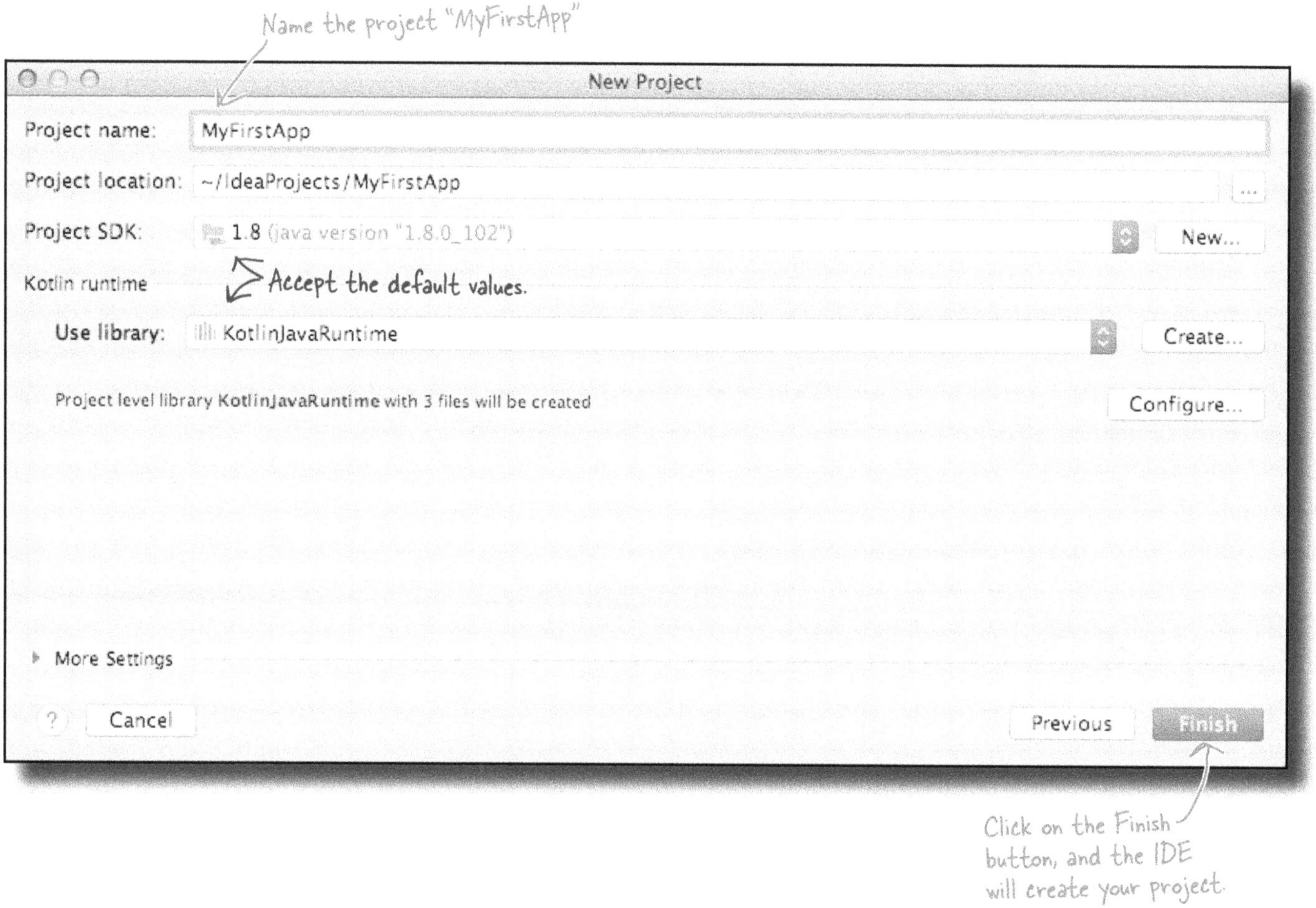

We've completed this step, so we've checked it.

- [x] **Build application**
- [ ] Add function
- [ ] Update function
- [ ] Use REPL

You've just created your first Kotlin project

After you've finished going through the steps to create a new project, IntelliJ IDEA sets up the project for you, then displays it. Here's the project that the IDE created for us:

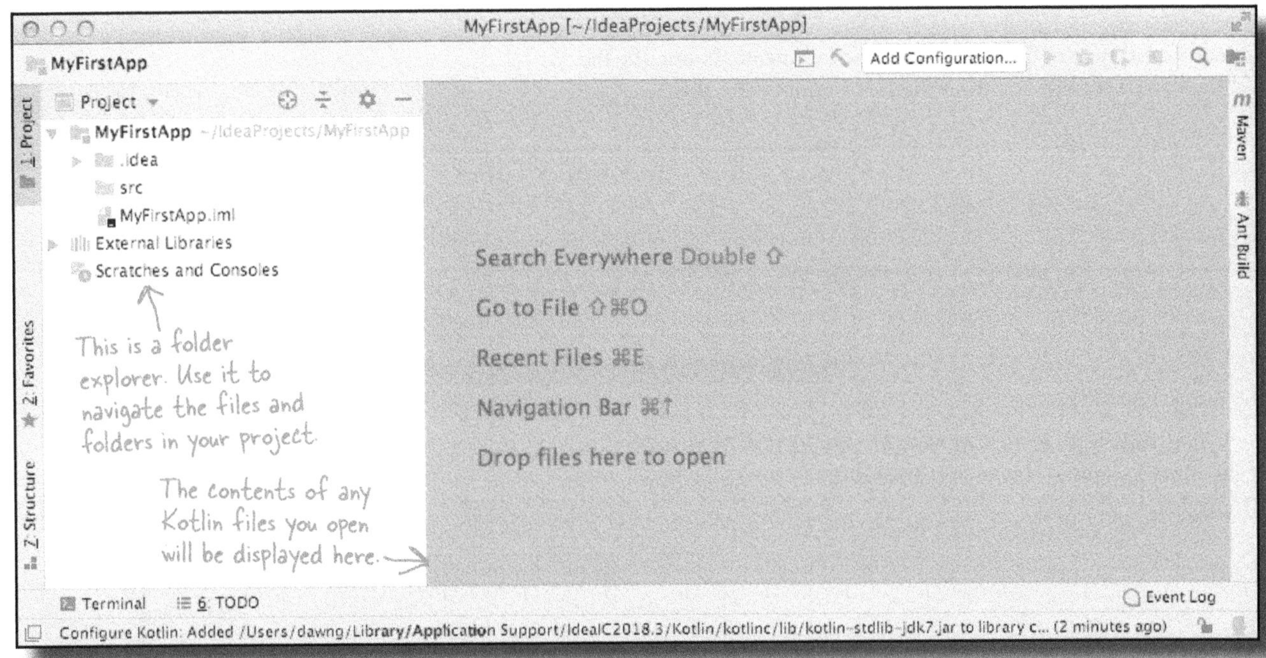

As you can see, the project features an explorer which you can use to navigate the files and folders that make up your project. IntelliJ IDEA creates this folder structure for you when you create the project.

The folder structure is comprised of configuration files that are used by the IDE, and some external libraries that your application will use. It also includes a *src* folder, which is used to hold your source code. You'll spend most of your time in Kotlinville working with the *src* folder.

The *src* folder is currently empty as we haven't added any Kotlin files yet. We'll do this next.

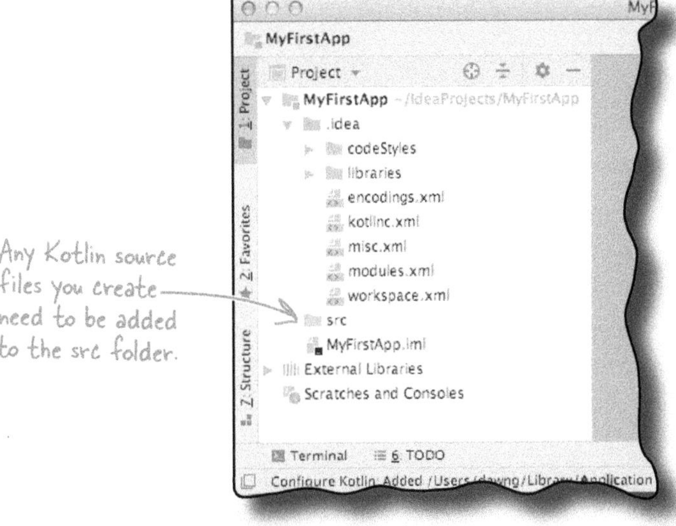

Add a new Kotlin file to the project

Build application
Add function
Update function
Use REPL

Before you can write any Kotlin code, you first need to create a Kotlin file to put it in.

To add a new Kotlin file to your project, highlight the *src* folder in IntelliJ IDEA's explorer, then click on the File menu and choose New → Kotlin File/Class. You will prompted for the name and type of Kotlin file you want to create. Name the file "App", and choose File from the Kind option, like this:

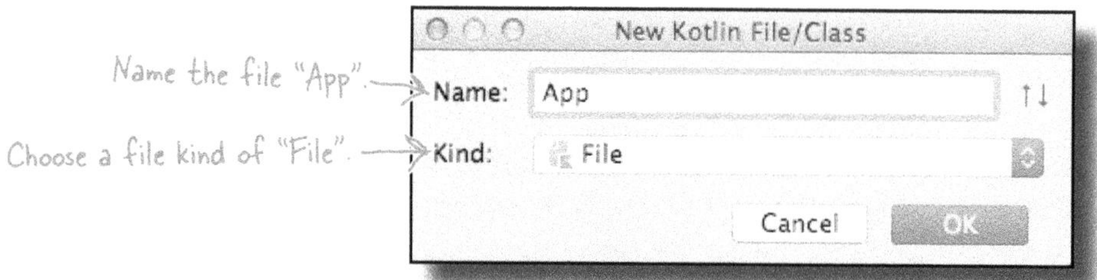

When you click on the OK button, IntelliJ IDEA creates a new Kotlin file named *App.kt*, and adds it to the *src* folder in your project:

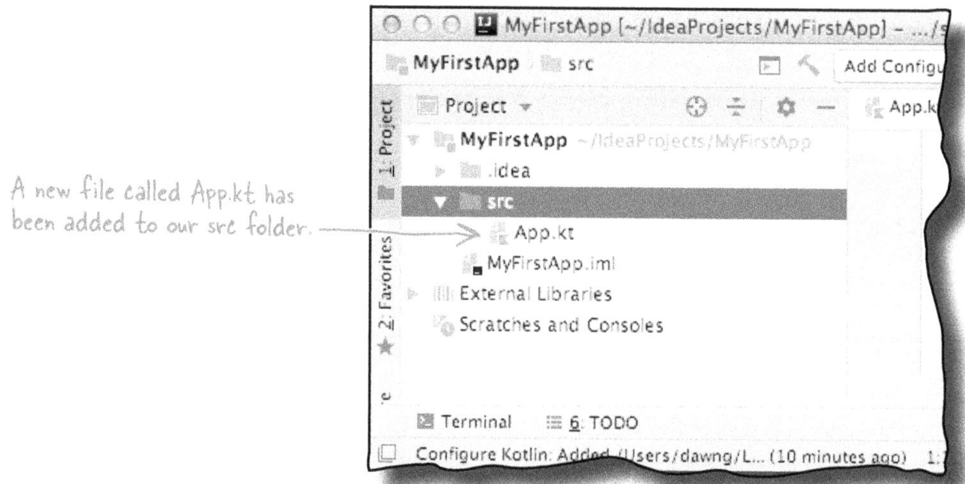

Next, let's look at the code we need to add to *App.kt* to get it to do something.

Anatomy of the main function

Build application
Add function
Update function
Use REPL

We're going to get our Kotlin code to display "Pow!" in the IDE's output window. We'll do this be adding a function to *App.kt*.

Whenever you write a Kotlin application, you *must* add a function to it called `main`, which starts your application. When you run your code, the JVM looks for this function, and executes it.

The `main` function looks like this:

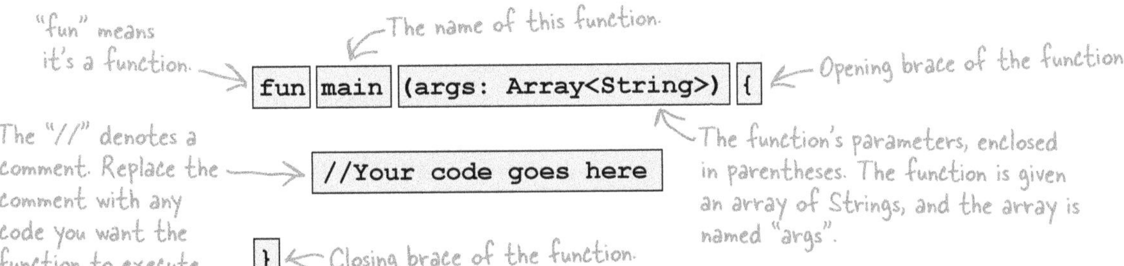

The function begins with the word **`fun`**, which is used to tell the Kotlin compiler that it's a function. You use the `fun` keyword for each new Kotlin function you create.

The `fun` keyword is followed by the name of the function, in this case **`main`**. Naming the function `main` means that it will be automatically executed when you run the application.

The code in the braces `()` after the function name tells the compiler what arguments (if any) the function takes. Here, the code `args: Array<String>` specifies that the function accepts an array of `String`s, and this array is named `args`.

You put any code you want to run between the curly braces `{}` of the `main` function. We want our code to print "Pow!" in the IDE, and we can do that using code like this:

```
fun main(args: Array<String>) {
    println("Pow!")
}
```

This says to print to the standard output. → `println`

The text you want to print. → `("Pow!")`

`println("Pow!")` prints a string of characters, or `String`, to the standard output. As we're running our code in an IDE, it will print "Pow!" in the IDE's output pane.

Now that you've seen what the function looks like, let's add it to our project.

If you're using Kotlin 1.2, or an earlier version, your `main` function *must* take the following form in order for it to start your application:

```
fun main(args: Array<String>) {
    //Your code goes here
}
```

From Kotlin1.3, however, you can omit `main`'s parameters so that the function looks like this:

```
fun main() {
    //Your code goes here
}
```

Through most of this book, we're going to use the longer form of the `main` function because this works for all versions of Kotlin.

Build application
Add function
Update function
Use REPL

Add the main function to App.kt

To add the `main` function to your project, open the file *App.kt* by double-clicking on it in IntelliJ IDEA's explorer. This opens the code editor, which you use to view and edit files:

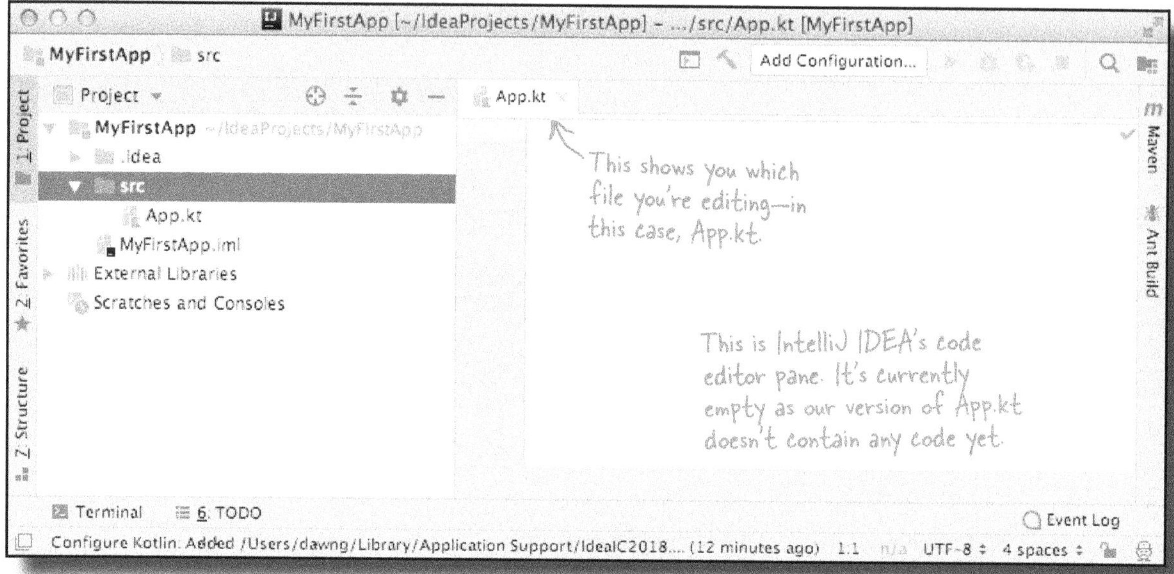

Then, update your version of *App.kt* so that it matches ours below:

```
fun main(args: Array<String>) {
    println("Pow!")
}
```

Let's try running our code to see what happens.

Q: Do I have to add a `main` function to every Kotlin file I create?

A: No. A Kotlin application might use dozens (or even hundreds) of files, but you may only have *one* with a `main` function—the one that starts the application running.

Test drive

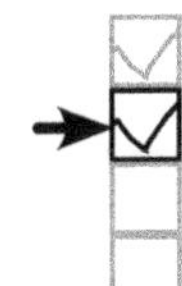

You run code in IntelliJ IDEA by going to the Run menu, and selecting the Run command. When prompted, choose the AppKt option. This builds the project, and runs the code.

After a short wait, you should see "Pow!" displayed in an output window at the bottom of the IDE like this:

Here's the output text in the IDE.

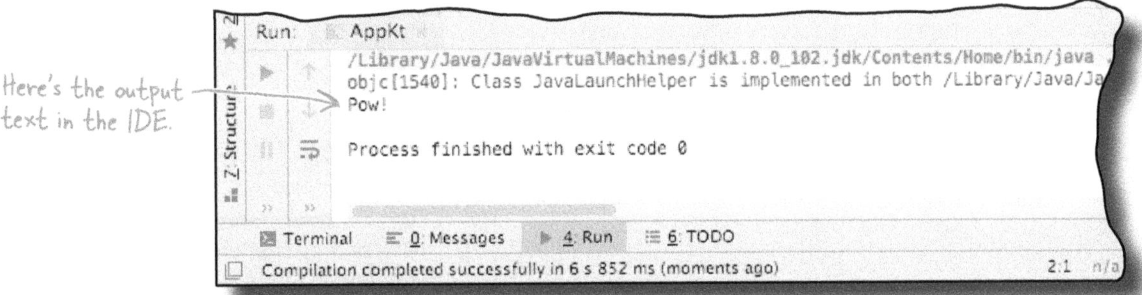

What the Run command does

When you use the Run command, IntelliJ IDEA goes through a couple of steps before it shows you the output of your code:

The IDE compiles your Kotlin source code into JVM bytecode. Assuming your code has no errors, compiling the code creates one or more class files that can run in a JVM. In our case, compiling *App.kt* creates a class file called *AppKt.class*.

It specifically compiles our source code into JVM bytecode because when we created the project, we selected the JVM option. Had we chosen to run it in another environment, the compiler would have compiled it into code for that environment instead.

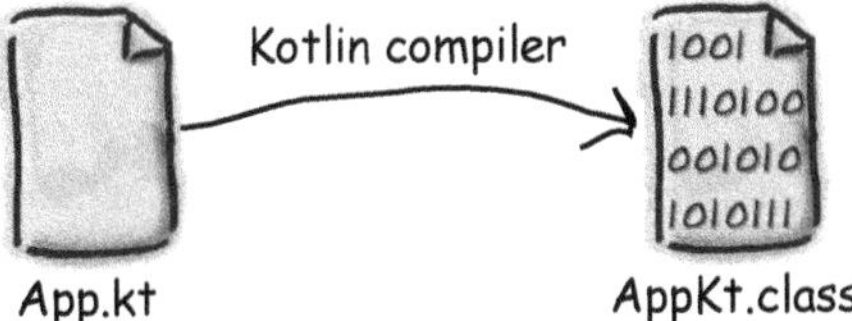

2 **The IDE starts the JVM and runs AppKt.class.** The JVM translates the *AppKt.class* bytecode into something the underlying platform understands, then runs it. This displays the `String` "Pow!" in the IDE's output window.

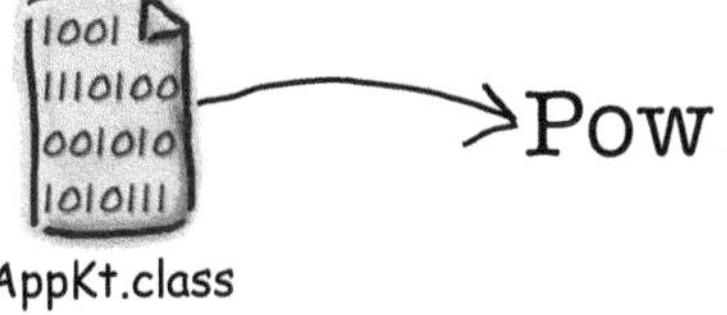

Now that we know our function works, let's look at how we can update it to make it do more.

What can you say in the main function?

Once you're inside the `main` function (or any other function, for that matter), the fun begins. You can say all the normal things that you say in most programming languages to make your application do something.

You can get your code to:

Do something (statements)

```
var x = 3
val name = "Cormoran"
x = x * 10
print("x is $x.")
//This is a comment
```

Do something again and again (loops)

```
while (x > 20) {
    x = x - 1
    print(" x is now $x.")
}
for (i in 1..10) {
    x = x + 1
    print(" x is now $x.")
}
```

Do something under a condition (branching)

```
if (x == 20) {
    println(" x must be 20.")
} else {
    println(" x isn't 20.")
}
if (name.equals("Cormoran")) {
    println("$name Strike")
}
```

We'll look at these in more detail over the next few pages.

Syntax Up Close

Here are some general syntax hints and tips for while you're finding your feet in Kotlinville:

* A single-lined comment begins with two forward slashes:

```
//This is a comment
```

* Most white space doesn't matter:

```
x          =          3
```

* Define a variable using `var` or `val`, followed by the variable's name. Use `var` for variables whose value you want to change, and `val` for ones whose value will stay the same. You'll learn more about variables in Chapter 2:

```
var x = 100
val serialNo = "AS498HG"
```

Loop and loop and loop...

Kotlin has three standard looping constructs: `while`, `do-while` and `for`. For now we'll just focus on `while`.

The syntax for `while` loops is relatively simple. So long as some condition is true, you do everything inside the loop *block*. The loop block is bounded by a pair of curly braces, and whatever you need to repeat needs to be inside that block.

If you just have one line of code in the loop block, you can omit the curly braces.

The key to a well-behaved `while` loop is its *conditional test*. A conditional test is an expression that results in a boolean value—something that is either *true* or *false*. As an example, if you say something like "While *isIceCreamInTub* is *true*, keep scooping" you have a clear boolean test. There is either ice cream in the tub, or there isn't. But if you say "While *Fred*, keep scooping", you don't have a real test. You need to change it to something like "While *Fred* is hungry, keep scooping" in order for it to make sense.

Simple boolean tests

You can do a simple boolean test by checking the value of a variable using a comparison operator. These include:

< (less than)

> (greater than)

== (equality) ← You use two equals signs to test for equality, not one.

<= (less than or equal to)

>= (greater than or equal to)

Notice the difference between the assignment operator (a single equals sign) and the equals operator (two equals signs).

Here's some example code that uses boolean tests:

```
var x = 4 //Assign 4 to x
while (x > 3) {
    //The loop code will run as x is greater than 3
    println(x)
    x = x - 1
}
var z = 27
while (z == 10) {
    //The loop code will not run as z is 27
    println(z)
    z = z + 6
}
```

A loopy example

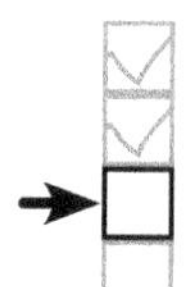

Build application
Add function
Update function
Use REPL

Let's update the code in *App.kt* with a new version of the `main` function. We'll update the `main` function so that it displays a message before the loop starts, each time it loops, and when the loop has ended.

Update your version of *App.kt* so that it matches ours below (our changes are in bold):

```
fun main(args: Array<String>) {
    println("Pow!")
    var x = 1
    println("Before the loop. x = $x.")
    while (x < 4) {
        println("In the loop. x = $x.")
        x = x + 1
    }
    println("After the loop. x = $x.")
}
```

Delete this line (`println("Pow!")`), as it's no longer needed.

This prints out the value of x.

MyFirstApp
src
App.kt

Let's try running the code.

Test drive

Run the code by going to the Run menu, and selecting the Run 'AppKt' command. The following text should appear in the output window at the bottom of the IDE:

```
Before the loop. x = 1.
In the loop. x = 1.
In the loop. x = 2.
In the loop. x = 3.
After the loop. x = 4.
```

Now that you've learned how `while` loops and boolean tests work, let's look at `if` statements.

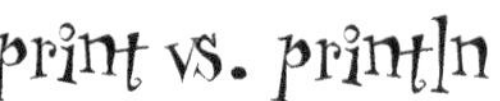

You've probably noticed us switching between **`print`** and **`println`**. What's the difference?

`println` inserts a *new* line (think of `println` as print new line) while **`print`** keeps printing to the *same* line. If you want each thing to print out on its own line, use `println`. If you want everything to stick together on the same line, use `print`.

Build application
Add function
Update function
Use REPL

Conditional branching

An `if` test is similar to the boolean test in a `while` loop except instead of saying "***while*** there's still ice cream..." you say "***if*** there's still ice cream..."

So that you can see how this works, here's some code that prints a `String` if one number is greater than another:

```
fun main(args: Array<String>) {
    val x = 3
    val y = 1
    if (x > y) {
        println("x is greater than y")
    }
    println("This line runs no matter what")
}
```

If you just have one line of code in the if block, you can leave out the curly braces.

This line is only executed if x is greater than y.

The above code executes the line that prints "*x* is greater than *y*" only if the condition (x is greater than y) is true. Regardless of whether it's true, though, the line that prints "This line runs no matter what" will run. So depending on the values of x and y, either one statement or two will print out.

We can also add an `else` to the condition, so that we can say somthing like, "*if* there's still ice cream, keep scooping, *else* (otherwise) eat the ice cream then buy some more".

Here's an updated version of the above code that includes an `else`:

```
fun main(args: Array<String>) {
    val x = 3
    val y = 1
    if (x > y) {
        println("x is greater than y")
    } else {
        println("x is not greater than y")
    }
    println("This line runs no matter what")
}
```

This line is only executed if the condition x > y is not met.

In most languages, that's pretty much the end of the story as far as using `if` is concerned; you use it to execute code *if* conditions have been met. Kotlin, however, takes things a step further.

Build application
Add function
Update function
Use REPL

Using if to return a value

In Kotlin, you can use `if` as an **expression**, so that it returns a value. It's like saying "*if* there's ice cream in the tub, return one value, else return a different value". You can use this form of `if` to write code that's more concise.

Let's see how this works by reworking the code you saw on the previous page. Previously, we used the following code to print a `String`:

```
if (x > y) {
    println("x is greater than y")
} else {
    println("x is not greater than y")
}
```

When you use if as an expression, you MUST include an else clause.

We can rewrite this using an `if` expression like so:

```
println(if (x > y) "x is greater than y" else "x is not greater than y")
```

The code:

```
if (x > y) "x is greater than y" else "x is not greater than y"
```

is the `if` expression. It first checks the `if`'s condition: `x > y`. If this condition is *true*, the expression returns the `String` "x is greater than y". Otherwise (`else`) the condition is *false*, and the expression returns the `String` "x is not greater than y" instead.

The code then prints the value of the `if` expression using `println`:

```
println(if (x > y) "x is greater than y" else "x is not greater than y")
```

If x is greater than y, the code prints "x is greater than y". If x is not greater than y, the code prints "x is not greater than y" instead.

So if `x` is greater than `y`, "x is greater than y" gets printed. If it's not, "x is not greater than y" gets printed instead.

As you can see, using an `if` expression in this way has the same effect as the code you saw on the previous page, but it's more concise.

We'll show you the code for the entire function on the next page.

- ☑ Build application
- ☑ Add function
- → ☐ **Update function**
- ☐ Use REPL

Update the main function

Let's update the code in *App.kt* with a new version of the `main` function that uses an `if` expression. Replace the code in your version of *App.kt* so that it matches ours below:

```
fun main(args: Array<String>) {
    var x = 1
    println("Before the loop. x = $x.")
    while (x < 4) {
        println("In the loop. x = $x.")
        x = x + 1
    }
    println("After the loop. x = $x.")
    val x = 3
    val y = 1
    println(if (x > y) "x is greater than y" else "x is not greater than y")
    println("This line runs no matter what")
}
```

Delete these lines.

Let's take the code for a test drive.

Test drive

Run the code by going to the Run menu, and selecting the Run 'AppKt' command. The following text should appear in the output window at the bottom of the IDE:

```
x is greater than y
This line runs no matter what
```

Now that you've learned how to use `if` for conditional branching and expressions, have a go at the following exercise.

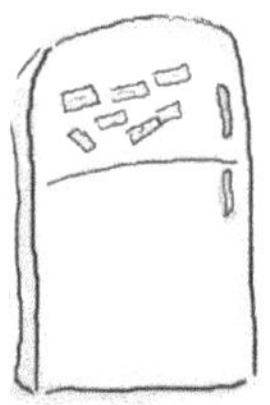

Code Magnets

Somebody used fridge magnets to write a useful new **main** function that prints the `String` "YabbaDabbaDo". Unfortunately, a freak kitchen whirlwind has dislodged the magnets. Can you piece the code back together again?

You won't need to use all of the magnets.

```
fun main(args: Array<String>) {
    var x = 1

    while (x < ........) {

        ............(if (x == ........) "Yab" else "Dab")

        ............("ba")

        x = x + 1
    }
    if (x == ........) println("Do")
}
```

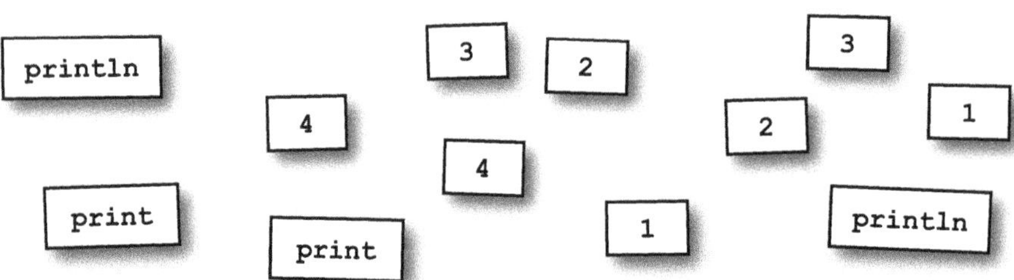

Answers on page 29.

Using the Kotlin interactive shell

We're nearly at the end of the chapter, but before we go, there's one more thing we want to introduce you to: the Kotlin interactive shell, or REPL. The REPL allows you to quickly try out snippets of code outside your main code.

REPL stands for Read-Eval-Print Loop, but nobody ever calls it that.

You open the REPL by going to the Tools menu in IntelliJ IDEA and choosing Kotlin → Kotlin REPL. This opens a new pane at the bottom of the screen like this:

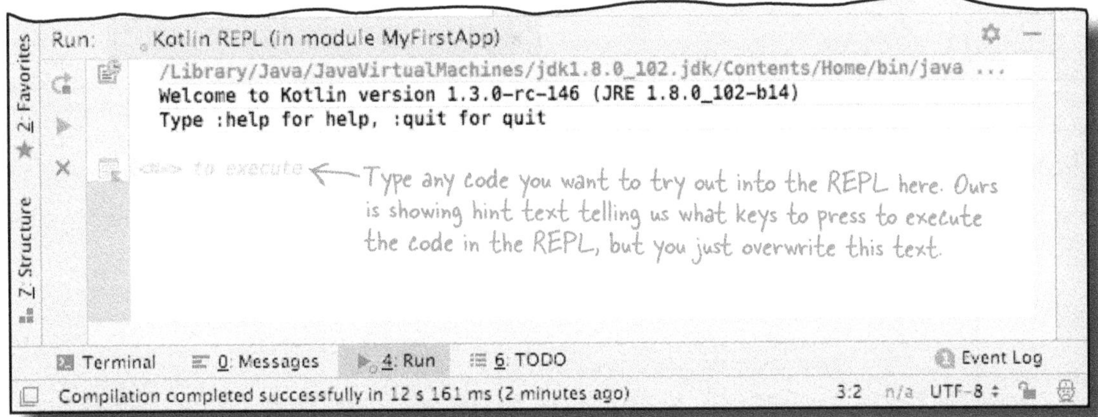

To use the REPL, simply type the code you want to try out into the REPL window. As an example, try adding the following:

```
println("I like turtles!")
```

Once you've added the code, execute it by clicking on the large green Run button on the left side of the REPL window After a pause, you should see the output "I like turtles!" in the REPL window:

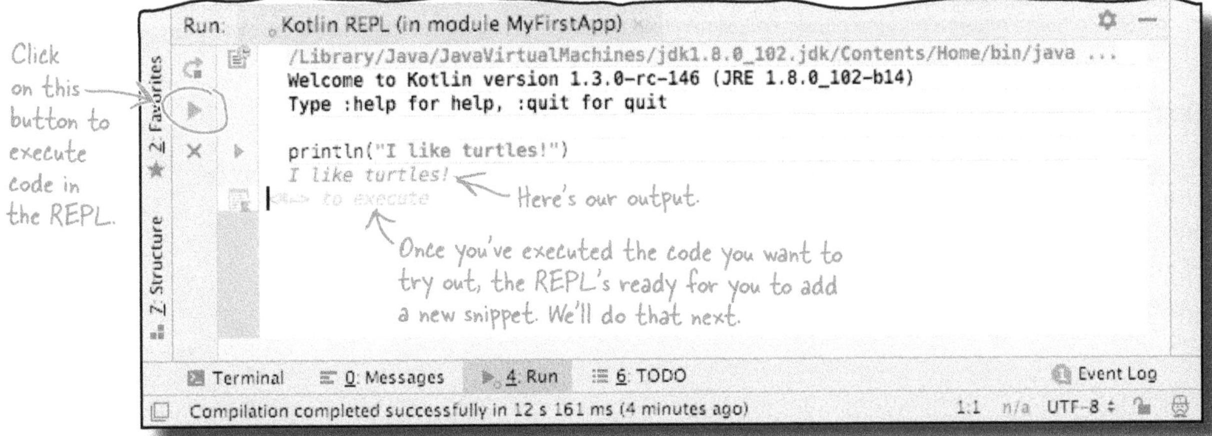

You can add multi-line code snippets to the REPL

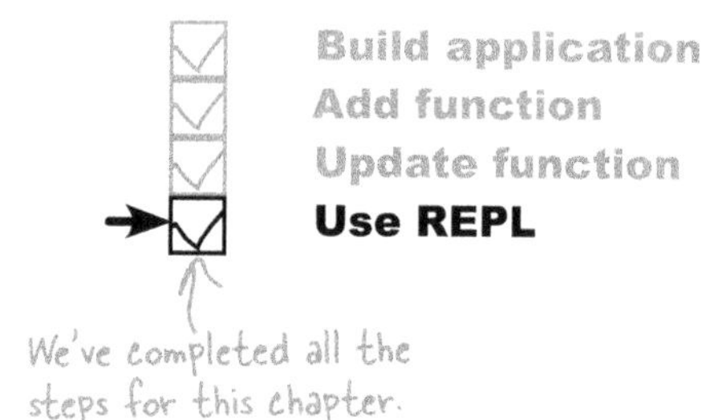

As well as adding single-line code snippets to the REPL, as we did on the previous page, you can try out code segments that take up multiple lines. As an example, try adding the following lines to the REPL window:

```
val x = 6
val y = 8
println(if (x > y) x else y)
```

This prints the larger of two numbers, x and y.

When you execute the code, you should see the output 8 in the REPL like this:

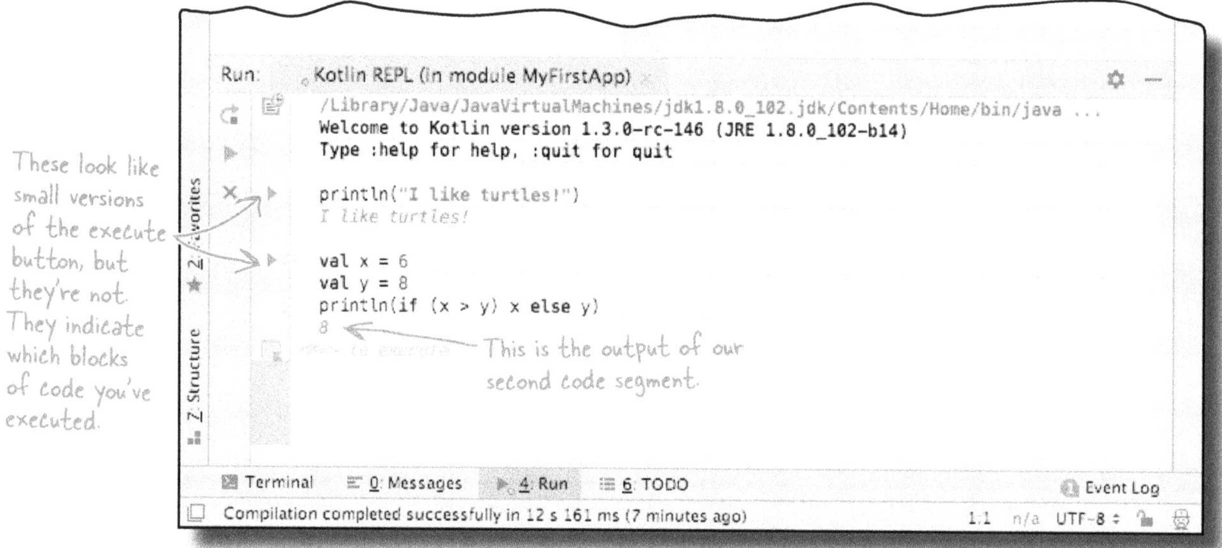

It's exercise time

Now that you've learned how to write Kotlin code and seen some of its basic syntax, have a go at the following exercises. Remember, if you're unsure, you can try out any code snippets in the REPL.

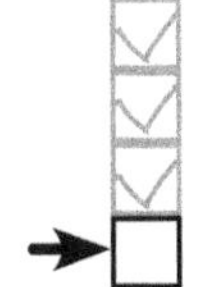

Build application
Add function
Update function
Use REPL

BE the Compiler

Each of the Kotlin files on this page represents a complete source file. Your job is to play like you're the compiler and determine whether each of these files will compile. If they won't compile, how would you fix them?

A

```
fun main(args: Array<String>) {
    var x = 1
    while (x < 10) {
        if (x > 3) {
            println("big x")
        }
    }
}
```

B

```
fun main(args: Array<String>) {
    val x = 10
    while (x > 1) {
        x = x - 1
        if (x < 3) println("small x")
    }
}
```

C

```
fun main(args: Array<String>) {
    var x = 10
    while (x > 1) {
        x = x - 1
        print(if (x < 3) "small x")
    }
}
```

BE the Compiler Solution

Each of the Kotlin files on this page represents a complete source file. Your job is to play like you're the compiler and determine whether each of these files will compile. If they won't compile, how would you fix them?

A

```
fun main(args: Array<String>) {
    var x = 1
    while (x < 10) {
        x = x + 1
        if (x > 3) {
            println("big x")
        }
    }
}
```

This will compile and run with no output, but without a line added to the program, it will run forever in an infinite "while" loop.

B

```
fun main(args: Array<String>) {
    val var x = 10
    while (x > 1) {
        x = x - 1
        if (x < 3) println("small x")
    }
}
```

This won't compile. x has been defined using val, which means that its value can't change. The code therefore can't update the value of x inside the "while" loop. To fix, change val to var.

C

```
fun main(args: Array<String>) {
    var x = 10
    while (x > 1) {
        x = x - 1
        print(if (x < 3) "small x" else "big x")
    }
}
```

This won't compile as it uses an if expression with no else clause. To fix, add the else clause.

Mixed Messages

A short Kotlin program is listed below. One block of the program is missing. Your challenge is to match the candidate block of code (on the left), with the output that you'd see if the block were inserted. Not all the lines of output will be used, and some lines of output may be used more than once. Draw lines connecting the candidate blocks of code with their matching output.

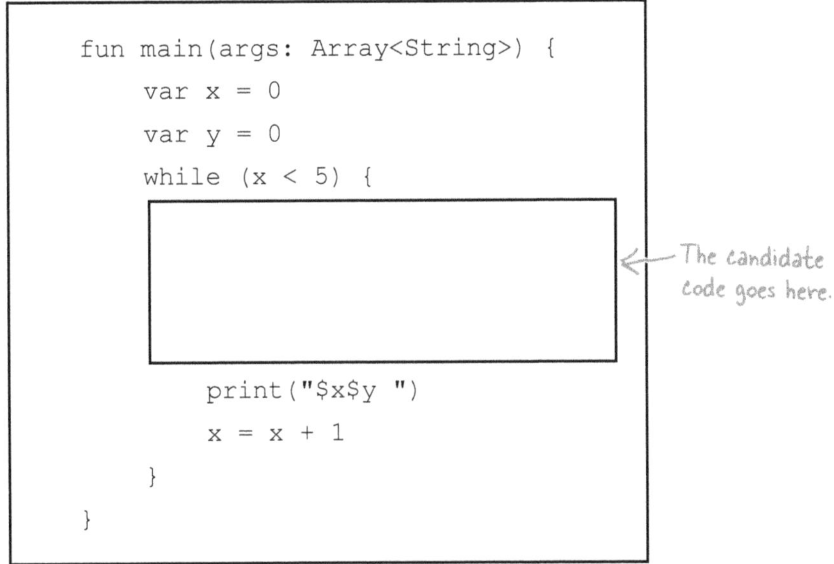

```
fun main(args: Array<String>) {
    var x = 0
    var y = 0
    while (x < 5) {
        [                    ]
        print("$x$y ")
        x = x + 1
    }
}
```


Match each candidate with one of the possible outputs.

Candidates:

```
y = x - y
```

```
y = y + x
```

```
y = y + 3
if (y > 4) y = y - 1
```

```
x = x + 2
y = y + x
```

```
if (y < 5) {
    x = x + 1
    if (y < 3) x = x - 1
}
y = y + 3
```

Possible output:

```
00 11 23 36 410
```

```
00 11 22 33 44
```

```
00 11 21 32 42
```

```
03 15 27 39 411
```

```
22 57
```

```
02 14 25 36 47
```

```
03 26 39 412
```

Mixed Messages Solution

A short Kotlin program is listed below. One block of the program is missing. Your challenge is to match the candidate block of code (on the left), with the output that you'd see if the block were inserted. Not all the lines of output will be used, and some lines of output may be used more than once. Draw lines connecting the candidate blocks of code with their matching output.

```
fun main(args: Array<String>) {
    var x = 0
    var y = 0
    while (x < 5) {
        [                    ]
        print("$x$y ")
        x = x + 1
    }
}
```

Candidates:

```
y = x - y
```

```
y = y + x
```

```
y = y + 3
if (y > 4) y = y - 1
```

```
x = x + 2
y = y + x
```

```
if (y < 5) {
    x = x + 1
    if (y < 3) x = x - 1
}
y = y + 3
```

Possible output:

```
00 11 23 36 410
```

```
00 11 22 33 44
```

```
00 11 21 32 42
```

```
03 15 27 39 411
```

```
22 57
```

```
02 14 25 36 47
```

```
03 26 39 412
```

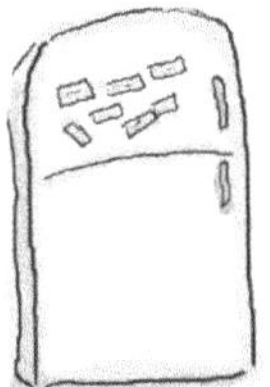

Code Magnets Solution

Somebody used fridge magnets to write a useful new **main** function that prints the `String` "YabbaDabbaDo". Unfortunately, a freak kitchen whirlwind has dislodged the magnets. Can you piece the code back together again?

You won't need to use all of the magnets.

```
fun main(args: Array<String>) {
    var x = 1

    while (x < 3 ) {

        print (if (x == 1 ) "Yab" else "Dab")

        print ("ba")

        x = x + 1
    }
    if (x == 3 ) println("Do")
}
```

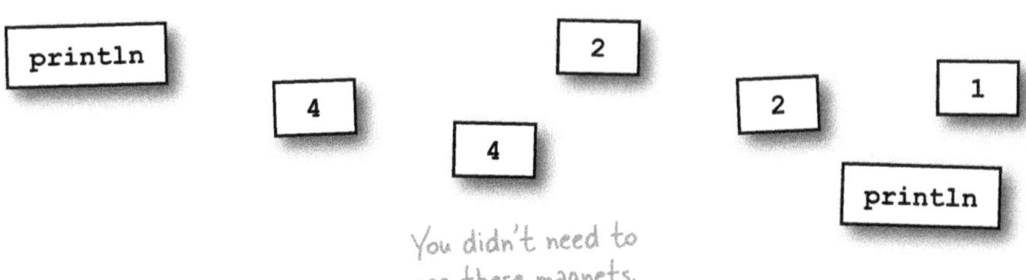

CHAPTER 1

Your Kotlin Toolbox

You've got Chapter 1 under your belt and now you've added Kotlin basic syntax to your toolbox.

You can download the full code for the chapter from https://tinyurl.com/HFKotlin.

BULLET POINTS

- Use `fun` to define a function.
- Every application needs a function named `main`.
- Use `//` to denote a single-lined comment.
- A `String` is a string of characters. You denote a `String` value by enclosing its characters in double quotes.
- Code blocks are defined by a pair of curly braces `{ }`.
- The assignment operator is *one* equals sign `=`.
- The equals operator uses *two* equals signs `==`.
- Use `var` to define a variable whose value may change.
- Use `val` to define a value whose value will stay the same.
- A `while` loop runs everything within its block so long as the conditional test is *true*.
- If the conditional test is *false*, the `while` loop code block won't run, and execution will move down to the code immediately after the loop block.
- Put a conditional test inside parentheses `( )`.
- Add conditional branches to your code using `if` and `else`. The `else` clause is optional.
- You can use `if` as an expression so that it returns a value. In this case, the `else` clause is mandatory.

2 basic types and variables

Being a Variable

There's one thing all code depends on—variables.

So in this chapter, we're going to look under the hood, and show you ***how Kotlin variables really work***. You'll discover Kotlin's **basic types**, such as *Ints*, *Floats* and *Booleans*, and learn how the Kotlin compiler can **cleverly infer a variable's type from the value it's given**. You'll find out how to use **String templates** to construct complex Strings with very little code, and you'll learn how to create **arrays** to hold multiple values. Finally, you'll discover *why objects are so important to life in Kotlinville*.

Your code needs variables

So far, you've learned how to write basic statements, expressions, `while` loops and `if` tests. But there's one key thing we need to look at in order to write great code: variables.

You've already seen how to declare variables using code like:

```
var x = 5
```

The code looks simple, but what's going on behind the scenes?

A variable is like a cup

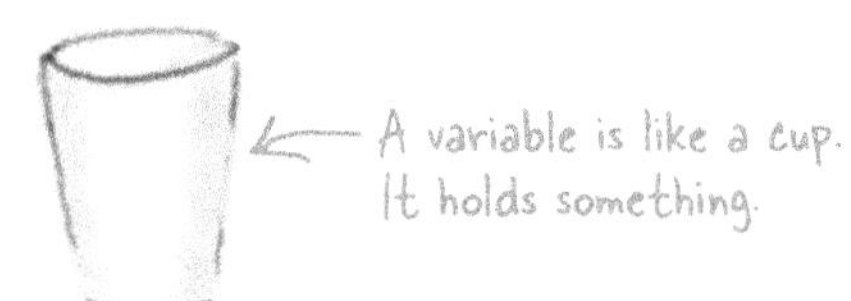

When you think of a variable in Kotlin, think of a cup. Cups come in many different shapes and sizes—big cups, small cups, the giant disposable cups that popcorn comes in at the movies—but they all have one thing in common: a cup holds something.

Declaring a variable is like ordering a drink from Starbucks. When you place your order, you tell the barista what type of drink you want, what name to shout out when it's ready, and even whether to use a fancy reusable cup instead of one that just gets thrown away. When you declare a variable using code like:

```
var x = 5
```

you're telling the Kotlin compiler what value the variable should have, what name to give it, and whether the variable can be reused for other values.

In order to create a variable, the compiler needs to know three things:

- **What the variable's name is.**
  This is so we can use that name in our code.
- **Whether or not the variable can be reused.**
  If we initially set your variable to 2, for example, can we later set it to 3? Or should it remain 2 forever?
- **What type of variable it is.**
  Is it an integer? A `String`? Or something more complex?

You've already seen how to name a variable, and how to use the `val` and `var` keywords to specify whether it can be reused for other values. But what about a variable's type?

What happens when you declare a variable

The compiler really cares about a variable's type so that it can prevent bizarre or dangerous operations that might lead to bugs. It won't let you assign the `String` "Fish" to an integer variable, for example, because it knows that it's inappropriate to perform mathematical operations on a `String`.

For this type-safety to work, the compiler needs to know the type of the variable. And the compiler can **infer the variable's type from the value that's assigned to it**.

Let's see how this works.

To create a variable, the compiler needs to know its name, type and whether it can be reused.

The value is transformed into an object...

When you declare a variable using code like:

```
var x = 5
```

the value you're assigning to the variable is used to create a new object. In this example, you're assigning the number 5 to a new variable named `x`. The compiler knows that 5 is an integer, and so the code creates a new `Int` object with a value of 5: ← We're going to look at some different types in more detail a couple of pages ahead.

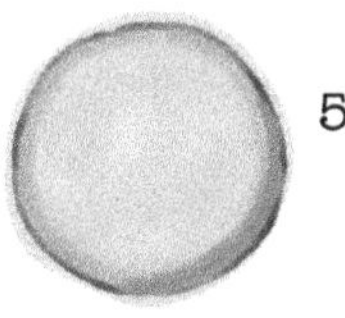

...and the compiler infers the variable's type from that of the object

The compiler then uses the type of the object for the type of the variable. In the above example, the object's type is `Int`, so the variable's type is `Int` as well. The variable stays this type forever.

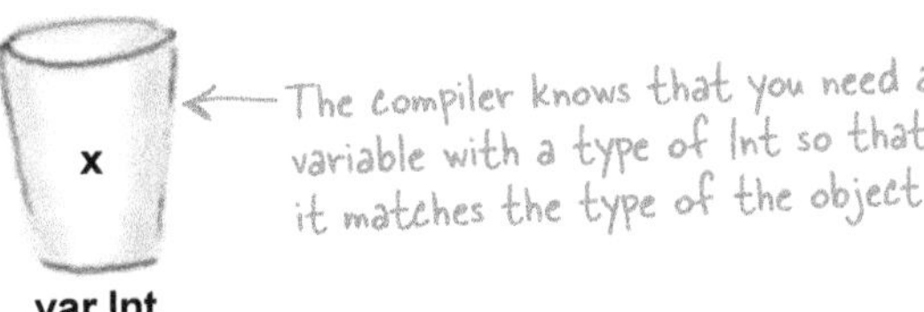

Next, the object is assigned to the variable. How does this happen?

The variable holds a reference to the object

When an object is assigned to a variable, **the object itself doesn't go into the variable**. A *reference* to the object goes into the variable instead:

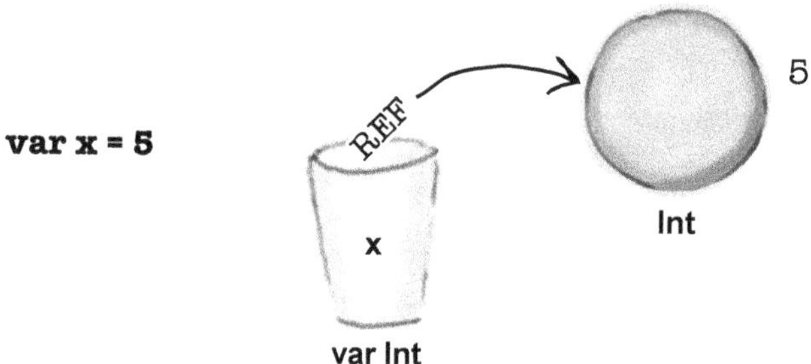

As the variable holds a reference to the object, this gives it access to the object.

val vs. var revisited

If you declare the variable using `val`, the reference to the object stays in the variable forever and can't be replaced. But if you use the `var` keyword instead, you can assign another value to the variable. As an example, if we use the code:

```
x = 6
```

to assign a value of 6 to `x`, this creates a new `Int` object with a value of 6, and puts a reference to it into `x`. This replaces the original reference:

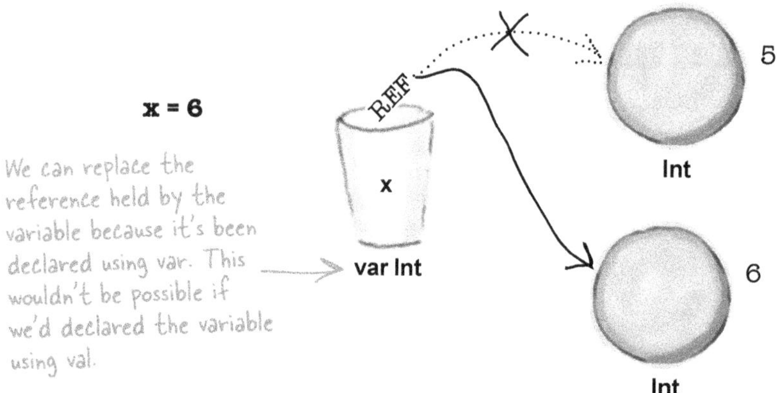

Now that you've seen what happens when you declare a variable, let's look at some of Kotlin's basic types for integers, floating points, booleans, characters and `Strings`.

Kotlin's basic types

Integers

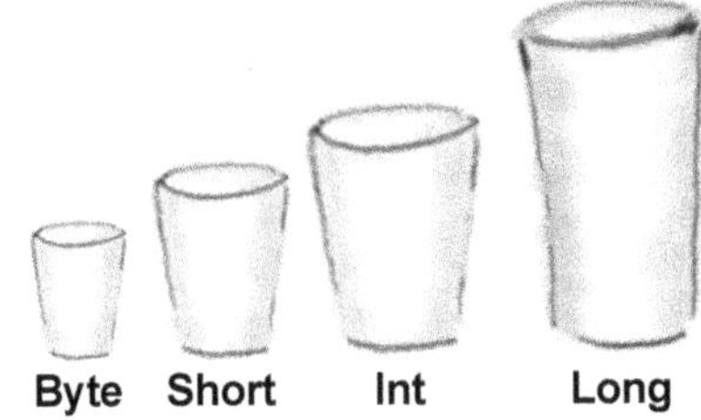

Kotlin has four basic integer types: **`Byte`**, **`Short`**, **`Int`** and **`Long`**. Each type can hold a fixed number of bits. `Byte`s can hold 8 bits, for example, so a `Byte` can hold integer values from -128 to 127. `Int`s, on the other hand, can hold 32 bits, so an `Int` can hold integer values from -2,147,483,648 to 2,147,483,647.

By default, if you declare a variable by assigning an integer to it using code like this:

```
var x = 1
```

you will create an object and variable of type `Int`. If the integer you assign is too large to fit into an `Int`, it will use a `Long` instead. You will also create a `Long` object and variable if you add an "L" to the end of the integer like this:

```
var hugeNumber = 6L
```

Here's a table showing the different integer types, their bit sizes and value ranges:

Type	Bits	Value range
Byte	8 bits	-128 to 127
Short	16 bits	-32768 to 32767
Int	32 bits	-2147483648 to 2147483647
Long	64 bits	-huge to (huge - 1)

Hexadecimal and Binary Numbers

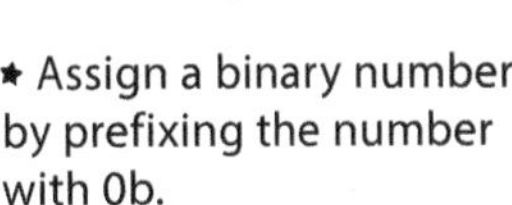

* Assign a binary number by prefixing the number with 0b.

```
x = 0b10
```

* Assign a hexadecimal number by prefixing the number with 0x.

```
y = 0xAB
```

* Octal numbers aren't supported.

Floating points

There are two basic floating-point types: **`Float`** and **`Double`**. `Float`s can hold 32 bits, whereas `Double`s can hold 64 bits.

By default, if you declare a variable by assigning a floating-point number to it using code like:

```
var x = 123.5
```

you will create an object and variable of type `Double`. If you add an "F" or "f" to the end of the number, a `Float` will get created instead:

```
var x = 123.5F
```

Booleans

`Boolean` variables are used for values that can either be `true` or `false`. You create a `Boolean` object and variable if you declare a variable using code like this:

```
var isBarking = true
var isTrained = false
```

Characters and Strings

There are two more basic types: **`Char`** and **`String`**.

`Char` variables are used for single characters. You create a `Char` variable by assigning a character in single quotes like this:

```
var letter = 'D'
```

`String` variables are used to hold multiple characters strung together. You create a `String` variable by assigning the characters enclosed in double quotes:

```
var name = "Fido"
```

Char variables are used for single characters. String variables are used for multiple characters strung together.

You said the compiler decides what the variable's type should be by looking at the type of value that's assigned to it. So how do I create a Byte or Short variable if the compiler assumes that small integers are Ints? And what if I want to define a variable before I know what value it should have?

In these situations, you need to explicitly declare the variable's type.

We'll look at how you do this next.

How to explicitly declare a variable's type

So far, you've seen how to create a variable by assigning a value to it, and letting the compiler infer the type from the value. But there are times when you need to *explicitly tell the compiler what type of variable you want to create.* You may want to use `Bytes` or `Shorts` instead of `Ints`, for example, because they are more efficient. Or you may want to declare a variable at the start of your code, and assign a value to it later on.

You explicitly declare a variable's type using code like this:

```
var smallNum: Short
```

By explicitly declaring a variable's type, you give the compiler just enough information to create the variable: its name, its type and whether it can be reused.

Instead of letting the compiler infer the variable's type from its value, you put a colon (`:`) after the variable's name, followed by the type you want it to be. So the above code is like saying "create a reusable variable named *smallNum*, and make sure it's a *Short*".

Similarly, if you want to declare a `Byte` variable, you use code like this:

```
var tinyNum: Byte
```

Declaring the type AND assigning a value

The above examples create variables without assigning values to them. If you want to explicitly declare a variable's type *and* assign a value to it, you can do that too. As an example, here's how you create a `Short` variable named `z`, and assign it a value of 6:

```
var z: Short = 6
```

This example creates a variable named `z` with a type of `Short`. The variable's value, 6, is small enough to fit into a `Short`, so a `Short` object with a value of 6 is created. A reference to the `Short` object is then put into the variable.

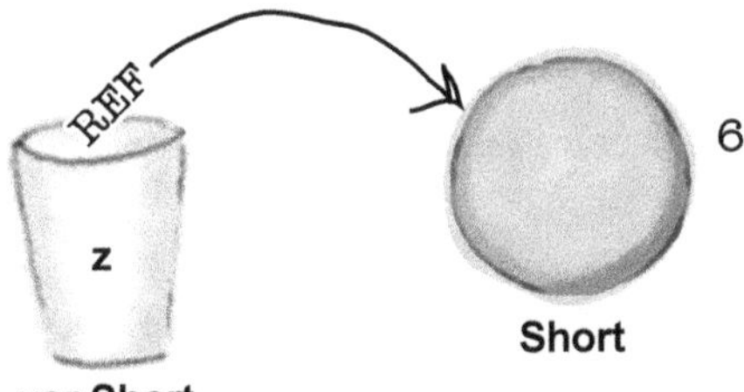

When you assign a value to a variable, you need to make sure that the value is compatible with the variable. We'll look at this in more detail on the next page.

Assigning an initial value to a variable is called initialization. You MUST initialize a variable before you use it, or you'll get a compiler error. The following code, for example, won't compile as x hasn't been been assigned a value:

```
var x: Int
var y = x + 6
```

x hasn't been assigned a value, so the compiler gets upset.

Use the right value for the variable's type

As we said earlier in the chapter, the compiler really cares about a variable's type so that it can stop you from performing inappropriate operations that may lead to bugs in your code. As an example, if you try to assign a floating-point number such as 3.12 to an integer variable, the compiler will refuse to compile your code. The following code, for example, won't work:

```
var x: Int = 3.12
```

The compiler realizes that 3.12 won't fit into an `Int` without some loss of precision (like, everything after the decimal point), so it refuses to compile the code.

Similarly, if you try put a large integer into a variable that's too small for it, the compiler will get upset. If you try to assign a value of 500 to a `Byte` variable, for example, you'll get a compiler error:

```
//This won't work
var tinyNum: Byte = 500
```

So in order to assign a literal value to a variable, you need to make sure that the value is compatible with the variable's type. This is particularly important when you want to assign the value of one variable to another. We'll look at this next.

The Kotlin compiler will only let you assign a value to a variable if the value and variable are compatible. If the value is too large or it's the wrong type, the code won't compile.

there are no Dumb Questions

Q: In Java, numbers are primitives, so a variable holds the actual number. Is that not the case with Kotlin?

A: No, it's not. In Kotlin, numbers are objects, and the variable holds a reference to the object, not the object itself.

Q: Why does Kotlin care so much about a variable's type?

A: Because it makes your code safer, and less prone to bugs. It might sound picky, but trust us, it's a good thing.

Q: In Java, you can treat `char` primitives as numbers. Can you do the same for `Chars` in Kotlin?

A: No, `Chars` in Kotlin are characters, not numbers. Repeat after us, Kotlin isn't Java.

Q: Can I name my variables anything I want?

A: No. The rules are a little flexible, but you can't, say, give your variable a name that's a reserved word. Naming your variable *while*, for example, is just asking for trouble. But the great news is that if you try and give a variable a name that's illegal, IntelliJ IDEA will immediately highlight it as a problem.

Assigning a value to another variable

When you assign the value of one variable to another, you need to make sure that their types are compatible. Let's see why by working through the following example:

```
var x = 5
var y = x
var z: Long = x
```

var x = 5

This creates an Int variable named x, and an Int object with a value of 5. x holds a reference to that object.

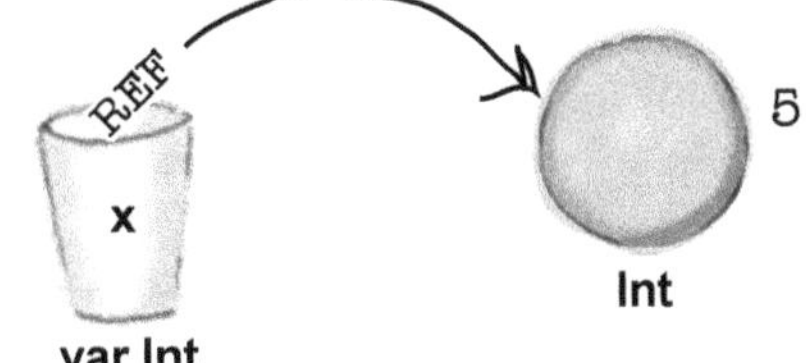

var y = x

The compiler sees that x is an Int object, so it knows that y must also have a type of Int. Rather than create a second Int object, the value of variable x is assigned to variable y. But what does this mean? It's like saying "Take the bits in x, make a copy of them, and stick that copy into y." **This means that both x and y contain references to the same object.**

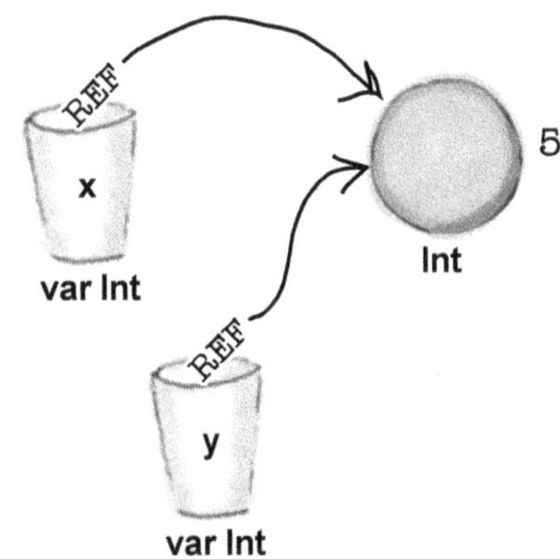

var z: Long = x

This line tells the compiler that you want to create a new Long variable, z, and assign it the value of x. But there's a problem. The x variable contains a reference to an Int object with a value of 5, not a Long object. We know that the object has a value of 5, and we know that 5 fits into a Long object. But because the z variable is a different type to the Int object, the compiler gets upset and refuses to compile the code.

So how do you assign the value of one variable to another if the variables are of different types?

We need to convert the value

Suppose you want to assign the value of an `Int` variable to a `Long`. The compiler won't let you assign the value directly as the two variables are different types; a `Long` variable can only hold a reference to a `Long` object, so the code won't compile if you try and assign an `Int` to it.

In order for the code to compile, you first have to convert the value to the right type. So if you want to assign the value of an `Int` variable to a `Long`, you first have to convert its value to a `Long`. And you do this using the `Int` object's *functions*.

An object has state and behavior

Being an object means that it has two things: **state** and **behavior**.

An object's *state* refers to the data that's associated with the object: its properties and values. A numeric object, for example, has a numeric value, such as 5, 42 or 3.12 (depending on the object's type). A `Char` object has a value that's a single character. A `Boolean` is either `true` or `false`.

An object's *behavior* describes the things the object can do, or that can be done to it. A `String` can be capitalized, for example. Numeric objects know how to perform basic math, and convert their value into an object of a different numeric type. The object's behavior is exposed through its functions.

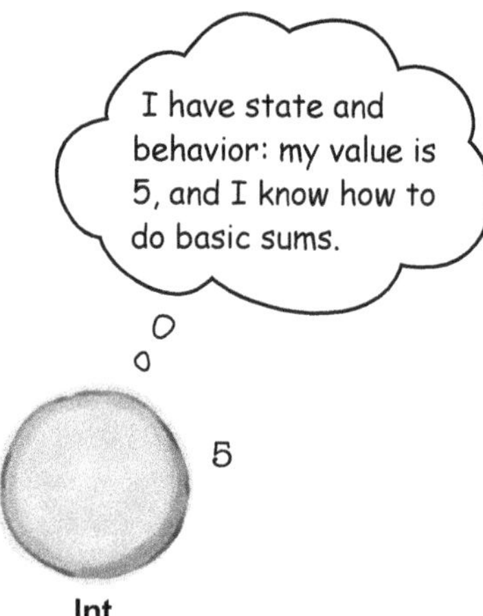

How to convert a numeric value to another type

In our example, we want to assign the value of an `Int` variable to a `Long`. Every numeric object has a function called `toLong()`, which takes the object's value, and uses it to create a new `Long` object. So if you want to assign the value of an `Int` variable to a `Long`, you use code like this:

```
var x = 5
var z: Long = x.toLong()
```

This is the dot operator.

The dot operator (`.`) allows you to call an object's functions. So `x.toLong()` is like saying "Go to the object that variable `x` has a reference to, and call its `toLong()` function".

We'll walk through what the code does on the next page.

Every numeric type has the following conversion functions: toByte(), toShort(), toInt(), toLong(), toFloat() and toDouble().

What happens when you convert a value

1 **var x = 5**

This creates an `Int` variable named `x`, and an `Int` object with a value of 5. `x` holds a reference to that object.

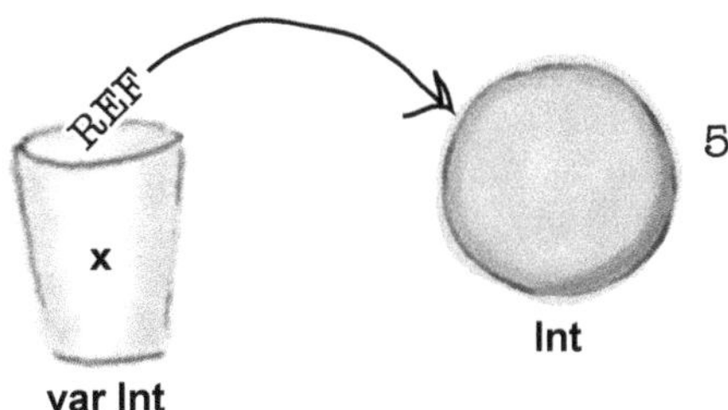

2 **var z: Long = x.toLong()**

This creates a new `Long` variable, `z`. The `toLong()` function on `x`'s object is called, and this creates a new `Long` object with a value of 5. A reference to the `Long` object gets put into the `z` variable.

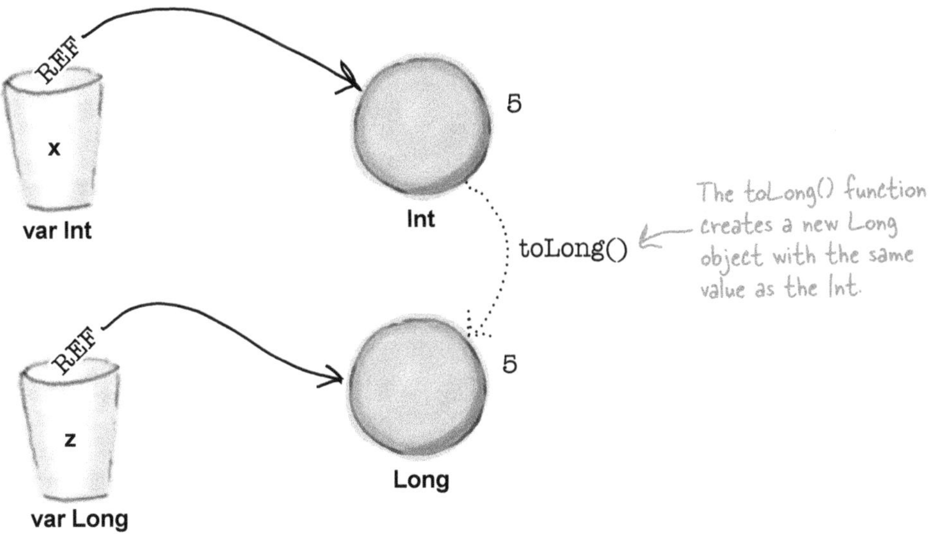

This approach works well if you want to convert a value into an object that's larger. But what if the new object is too small to contain the value?

Watch out for overspill

Trying to put a large value into a small variable is like trying to pour a bucket-load of coffee into a tiny teacup. Some of the coffee will fit into the cup, but some will spill out.

Suppose you want to put the value of a `Long` into an `Int`. As you saw earlier in the chapter, a `Long` can hold larger numbers than an `Int`.

If the `Long`'s value is within the range of values that an `Int` will hold, converting the value from a `Long` to an `Int` isn't a problem. As an example, converting a `Long` value of 42 to an `Int` will give you an `Int` with a value of 42:

```
var x = 42L
var y: Int = x.toInt()   //Value is 42
```

But if the `Long`'s value is too big for an `Int`, the compiler chops up the value, and you're left with some weird (but calculable) number. As an example, if you try to convert a `Long` value of 1234567890123 to an `Int`, your `Int` will have a value of 1912276171:

It involves signs, bits, binary and other geekery that we're not going into here. If you're really curious, however, search for "two's complement".

```
var x = 1234567890123
var y: Int = x.toInt()   //Value is 1912276171!
```

The compiler assumes this is deliberate, so the code compiles. And let's say you have a floating-point number, and you just want the whole number part of it. If you convert the number to an `Int`, the compiler will chop off everything after the decimal point:

```
var x = 123.456
var y: Int = x.toInt()   //Value is 123
```

The key thing is that when you're converting numeric values from one type to another, make sure the type is large enough for the value or you may get unexpected results in your code.

Now that you've seen how variables work and have some experience with Kotlin's basic types, have a go at the following exercise.

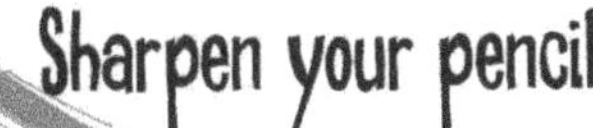

Sharpen your pencil

The following `main` function doesn't compile. Circle the lines that are invalid, and say why they stop the code from being compiled.

```
fun main(args: Array<String>) {

    var x: Int = 65.2

    var isPunk = true

    var message = 'Hello'

    var y = 7

    var z: Int = y

    y = y + 50

    var s: Short

    var bigNum: Long = y.toLong()

    var b: Byte = 2

    var smallNum = b.toShort()

    b = smallNum

    isPunk = "false"

    var k = y.toDouble()

    b = k.toByte()

    s = 0b10001

}
```

Sharpen your pencil Solution

The following `main` function doesn't compile. Circle the lines that are invalid, and say why they stop the code from being compiled.

```
fun main(args: Array<String>) {
    var x: Int = 65.2
    var isPunk = true
    var message = 'Hello'
    var y = 7
    var z: Int = y
    y = y + 50
    var s: Short
    var bigNum: Long = y.toLong()
    var b: Byte = 2
    var smallNum = b.toShort()
    b = smallNum
    isPunk = "false"
    var k = y.toDouble()
    b = k.toByte()
    s = 0b10001
}
```

- `var x: Int = 65.2` (circled) — 65.2 isn't a valid Int value.
- `var message = 'Hello'` (circled) — Single quotes are used to define Chars, which hold single characters.
- `b = smallNum` (circled) — smallNum is a Short, so its value can't be assigned to a Byte variable.
- `isPunk = "false"` (circled) — isPunk is a Boolean variable, so false shouldn't be enclosed in double quotes.

Store multiple values in an array

There's one more type of object we want to introduce you to—the array. Suppose you wanted to store the names of fifty ice cream flavors, or the bar codes of all the books in a library. To do that with variables would quickly get awkward. Instead, you can use an array.

Arrays are great if you want a quick and dirty group of things. They're easy to create, and you get fast access to each item in the array.

You can think of an array as being like a tray of cups, where each item in the array is a variable:

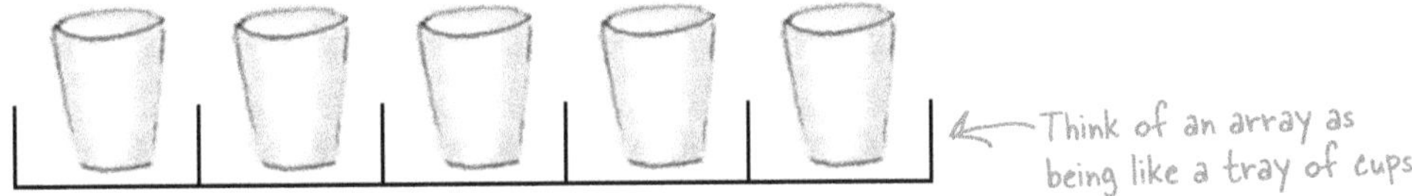

How to create an array

You create an array using the `arrayOf()` function. As an example, here's how you use the function to create an array with three items (the `Int`s 1, 2 and 3), and assign the array to a variable named `myArray`:

```
var myArray = arrayOf(1, 2, 3)
```

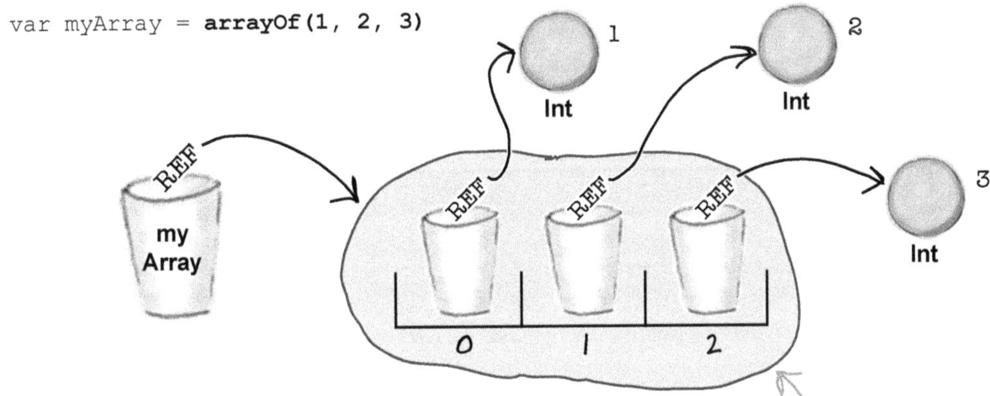

You can get the value of an item in the array by referencing the array variable with an index. As an example, here's how you print the value of the first item:

```
println(myArray[0])
```

And if you want to get the size of the array, use

```
myArray.size
```

On the next page, we'll put this together to write a serious business application—the Phrase-O-Matic.

Create the Phrase-O-Matic application

We're going to create a new application that generates useful marketing slogans.

First, create a new project in IntelliJ IDEA. To do this:

1. Open IntelliJ IDEA and choose "Create New Project" from the welcome screen. This starts the wizard you saw in Chapter 1.

2. When prompted, choose the options to create a Kotlin project that targets the JVM.

3. Name the project "PhraseOMatic", accept the rest of the defaults, and click on the Finish button.

4. When your new project appears in the IDE, create a new Kotlin file named *PhraseOMatic.kt* by highlighting the *src* folder, clicking on the File menu and choosing New → Kotlin File/Class. When prompted, name the file "PhraseOMatic", and choose File from the Kind option.

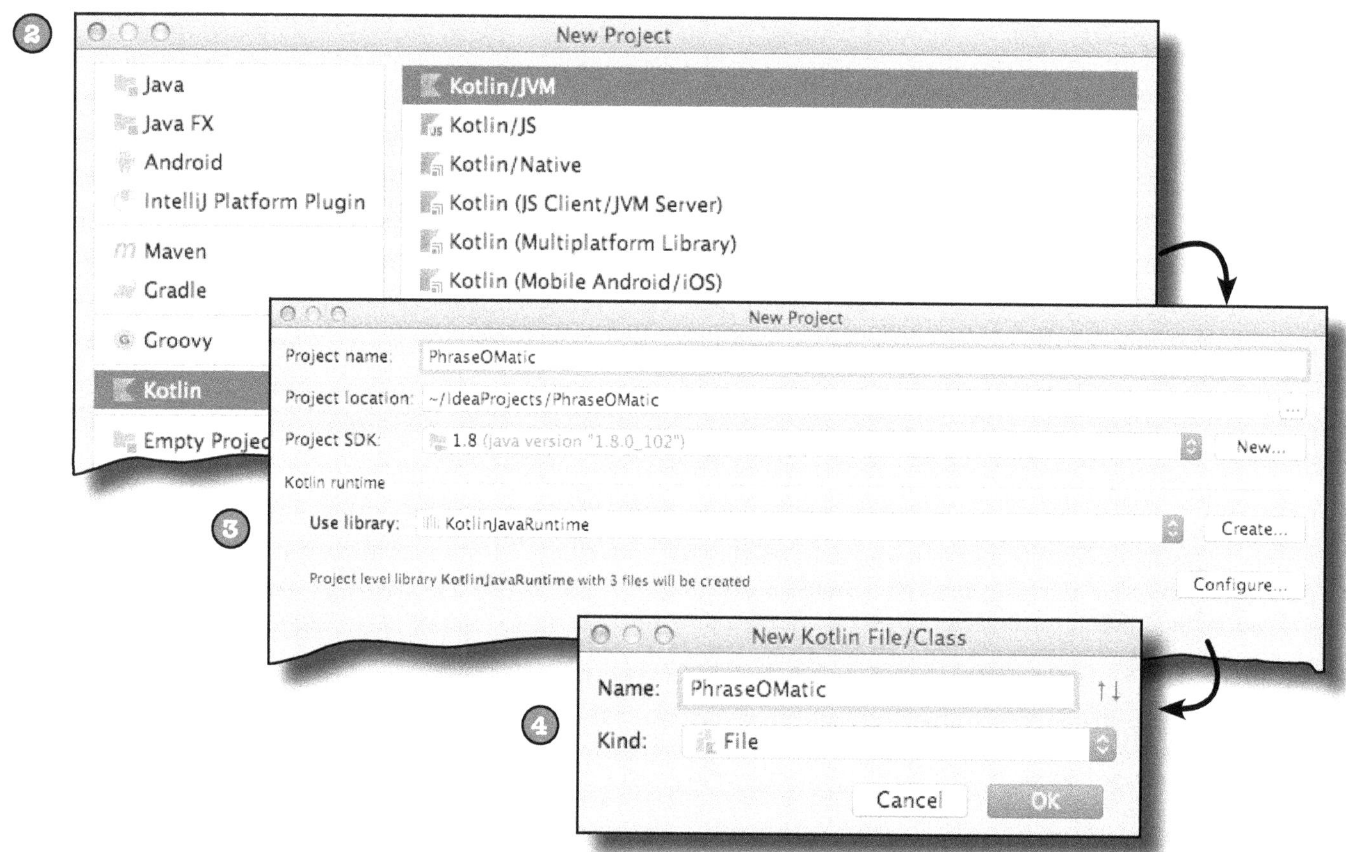

Add the code to PhraseOMatic.kt

The Phrase-O-Matic code consists of a `main` function that creates three arrays of words, randomly picks one word from each, and then joins them together. Add the code below to *PhraseOMatic.kt*:

```
fun main(args: Array<String>){
    val wordArray1 = arrayOf("24/7", "multi-tier", "B-to-B", "dynamic", "pervasive")
    val wordArray2 = arrayOf("empowered", "leveraged", "aligned", "targeted")
    val wordArray3 = arrayOf("process", "paradigm", "solution", "portal", "vision")

    val arraySize1 = wordArray1.size
    val arraySize2 = wordArray2.size
    val arraySize3 = wordArray3.size

    val rand1 = (Math.random() * arraySize1).toInt()
    val rand2 = (Math.random() * arraySize2).toInt()
    val rand3 = (Math.random() * arraySize3).toInt()

    val phrase = "${wordArray1[rand1]} ${wordArray2[rand2]} ${wordArray3[rand3]}"
    println(phrase)
}
```

PhraseOMatic
src
PhraseOMatic.kt

You've already seen what most of the code does, but there are a couple of lines we want to draw your attention to.

First, the line

```
val rand1 = (Math.random() * arraySize1).toInt()
```

generates a random number. `Math.random()` returns a random number between 0 and (almost) 1, so we have to multiply it by the number of items in the array. We then use `toInt()` to force the result to be an integer.

Finally, the line

```
val phrase = "${wordArray1[rand1]} ${wordArray2[rand2]} ${wordArray3[rand3]}"
```

uses a **String template** to pick three words and put them together. We'll look at `String` templates on the next page, and then we'll show you more stuff you can do with arrays.

We need a...

- multi-tier leveraged solution
- dynamic targeted vision
- 24/7 aligned paradigm
- B-to-B empowered portal

String Templates Up Close

String templates provide a quick and easy way of referring to a variable from inside a String.

To include the value of a variable inside a String, you prefix the variable name with a $. To include the value of an Int variable named x inside a String, for example, you would use:

```
var x = 42
var value = "Value of x is $x"
```

You can also use String templates to refer to an object's properties, or call its functions. In this case, you enclose the expression in curly braces. As an example, here's how you include an array's size in a String, and the value of its first item:

```
var myArray = arrayOf(1, 2, 3)
var arraySize = "myArray has ${myArray.size} items"
var firstItem = "The first item is ${myArray[0]}"
```

You can even use String templates to evaluate more complex expressions from inside a String. Here's how, for example, you would use an if expression to include different text depending on the size of the array myArray:

Notice how {}'s enclose the expression we want to evaluate inside the String.

```
var result = "myArray is ${if (myArray.size > 10) "large" else "small"}"
```

So String templates allow you to construct complex Strings with very little code.

there are no Dumb Questions

Q: Is Math.random() the standard way of getting a random number in Kotlin?

A: It depends which version of Kotlin you're using.

Before version 1.3, Kotlin didn't have a built-in way of generating its own random numbers. For applications running on a JVM, however, you could use the random() method from the Java Math library, as we have.

If you're using version 1.3 or above, you can use Kotlin's built-in Random functions instead. The following code, for example, uses Random's nextInt() function to generate a random Int:

```
kotlin.random.Random.nextInt()
```

In this book, we've decided to continue using Math.random() to generate random numbers, as this approach works with all versions of Kotlin running on the JVM.

The compiler infers the array's type from its values

You've seen how to create an array and access its items, so let's look at how you update its values.

Suppose you have an array of Ints named myArray:

```
var myArray = arrayOf(1, 2, 3)
```

If you want to update the second item so that it has a value of 15, you use code like the following:

```
myArray[1] = 15
```

But there's a catch: **the value has to be the right type**.

The compiler looks at the type of each item in the array, and infers what type of items the array should contain forever. In the above example, we've declared an array using Int values, so the compiler infers that the array can only hold Ints. If you try and put anything other than an Int into the array, your code won't compile:

```
myArray[1] = "Fido"  //This won't compile
```

Arrays hold items of a specific type. You can either let the compiler infer the type from the array's values, or explicitly define the type using Array<Type>.

How to explicitly define the array's type

Just as we did with other variables, you can explicitly define what type of items an array should hold. As an example, suppose you wanted to declare an array that holds Byte values. To do this, you would use code like the following:

```
var myArray: Array<Byte> = arrayOf(1, 2, 3)
```

The code Array<Byte> tells the compiler that you want to create an array that holds Byte variables. In general, simply specify the type of array you want to create by putting the type between the angle brackets (<>).

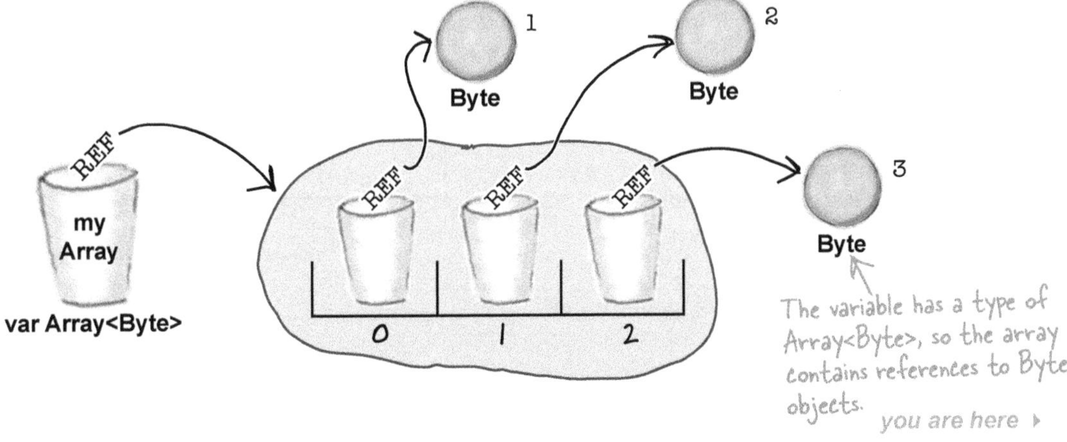

var means the variable can point to a different array

There's one final thing we need to look at: what effect `val` and `var` have when you declare an array.

As you already know, a variable holds a reference to an object. When you declare a variable using `var`, you can update the variable so that it holds a reference to a different object instead. If the variable holds a reference to an array, this means that you can update the variable so that it refers to a different array of the same type. As an example, the following code is perfectly valid and will compile:

```
var myArray = arrayOf(1, 2, 3)
myArray = arrayOf(4, 5)  <— This is a brand-new array.
```

Let's walk through what happens.

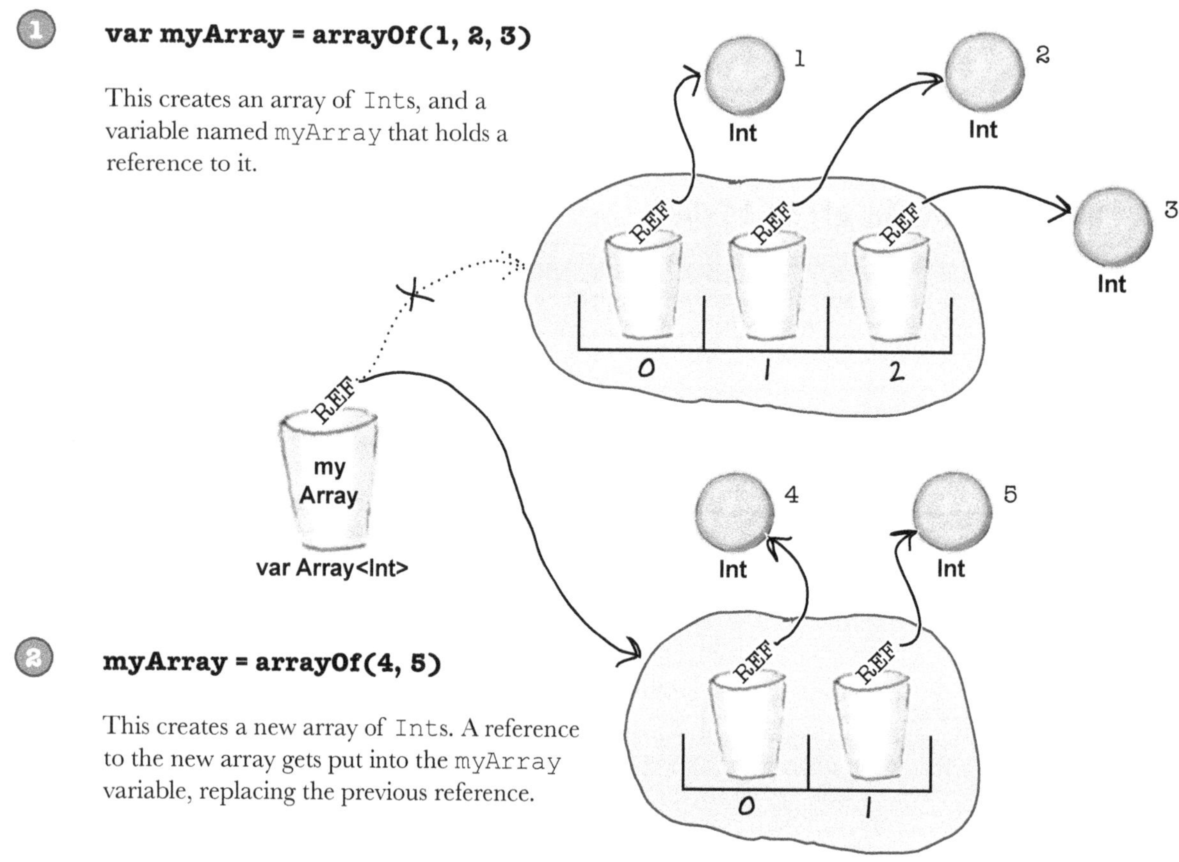

1. **var myArray = arrayOf(1, 2, 3)**

   This creates an array of `Ints`, and a variable named `myArray` that holds a reference to it.

2. **myArray = arrayOf(4, 5)**

   This creates a new array of `Ints`. A reference to the new array gets put into the `myArray` variable, replacing the previous reference.

So what happens if we use the variable using `val` instead?

val means the variable points to the same array forever...

When you declare an array using `val`, you can no longer update the variable so that it holds a reference to a different array. The following code, for example, won't compile:

```
val myArray = arrayOf(1, 2, 3)
myArray = arrayOf(4, 5, 6)
```

If you declare an array variable using val, you can't get it to refer to a different array.

Once the variable is assigned an array, it holds a reference to that array forever. But even though the variable maintains a reference to the same array, **the array itself can still be updated**.

Declaring a variable using val means that you can't reuse the variable for another object. You can, however, still update the object itself.

...but you can still update the variables in the array

When you declare a variable using `val`, you're telling the compiler that you want to create a variable that can't be reused for other values. But this instruction only applies to the variable itself. If the variable holds a reference to an array, the items in the array can still be updated.

As an example, suppose you have the following code:

```
val myArray = arrayOf(1, 2, 3)
myArray[2] = 6
```

This updates the third item in the array.

This creates a variable named `myArray` that holds a reference to an array of `Int`s. It's declared using `val`, so the variable must hold a reference to the same array for the duration of the program. The third item in the array is then successfully updated to 6, as the array itself can be updated:

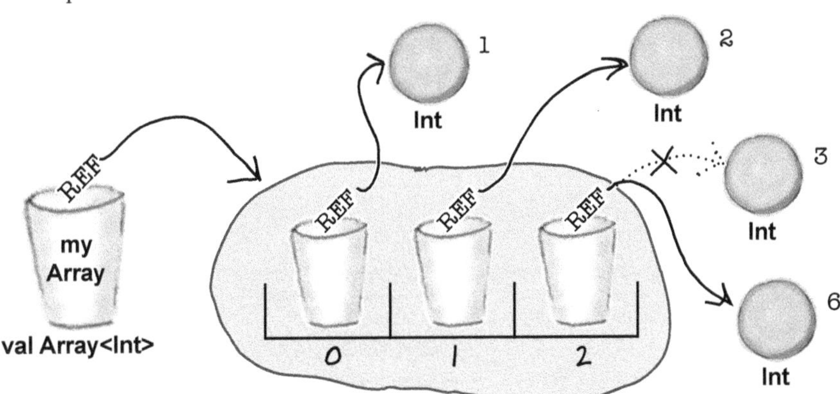

The array itself can still be updated, even though the variable is declared using val.

Now that you know how arrays work in Kotlinville, have a go at the following exercises.

BE the Compiler

Each of the Kotlin files on this page represents a complete source file. Your job is to play like you're the compiler and determine whether each of these files will compile and run without errors. If they won't, how would you fix them?

A

```
fun main(args: Array<String>) {

    val hobbits = arrayOf("Frodo", "Sam", "Merry", "Pippin")
    var x = 0

    while (x < 5) {
        println("${hobbits[x]} is a good Hobbit name")
        x = x + 1
    }

}
```

We want to print a line for each name in the hobbits array.

B

```
fun main(args: Array<String>) {

    val firemen = arrayOf("Pugh", "Pugh", "Barney McGrew", "Cuthbert", "Dibble", "Grub")
    var firemanNo = 0

    while (firemanNo < 6) {
        println("Fireman number $firemanNo is $firemen[firemanNo]")
        firemanNo = firemanNo + 1
    }

}
```

We want to print a line for each fireman in the firemen array.

Answers on page 55.

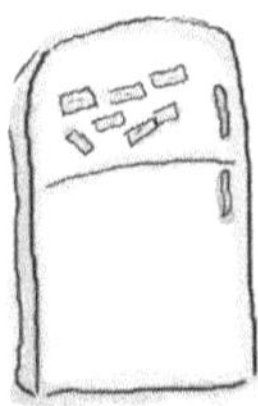

Code Magnets

A working Kotlin program is all scrambled up on the fridge. Can you reconstruct the code snippets to make a working Kotlin function that produces the following output:

```
Fruit = Banana
Fruit = Blueberry
Fruit = Pomegranate
Fruit = Cherry
```

```
fun main(args: Array<String>) {

}
```

The magnets need to go in this space.

```
var x = 0
x = x + 1
y = index[x]
while (x < 4) {
var y: Int
val index = arrayOf(1, 3, 4, 2)
}
println("Fruit = ${fruit[y]}")
val fruit = arrayOf("Apple", "Banana", "Cherry", "Blueberry", "Pomegranate")
```

Answers on page 56.

Mixed References

A short Kotlin program is listed below. When the line `//Do stuff` is reached, some objects and variables have been created. Your task is to determine which of the variables refer to which objects by the time the `//Do stuff` line is reached. Some objects may be referred to more than once. Draw lines connecting the variables to their objects.

```
fun main(args: Array<String>) {
    val x = arrayOf(0, 1, 2, 3, 4)
    x[3] = x[2]
    x[4] = x[0]
    x[2] = x[1]
    x[1] = x[0]
    x[0] = x[1]
    x[4] = x[3]
    x[3] = x[2]
    x[2] = x[4]
    //Do stuff
}
```

Variables:

Match each variable to its object.

Objects:

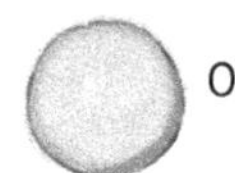

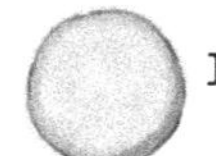

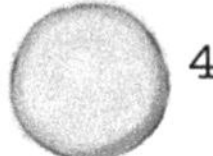

Answers on page 57.

BE the Compiler Solution

Each of the Kotlin files on this page represents a complete source file. Your job is to play like you're the compiler and determine whether each of these files will compile and run without errors. If they won't, how would you fix them?

A

```
fun main(args: Array<String>) {

    val hobbits = arrayOf("Frodo", "Sam", "Merry", "Pippin")
    var x = 0

    while (x < 4) {
        println("${hobbits[x]} is a good Hobbit name")
        x = x + 1
    }

}
```

The code compiles, but produces an error when it runs. Remember that arrays start with item 0, and end with item (size – 1).

B

```
fun main(args: Array<String>) {

    val firemen = arrayOf("Pugh", "Pugh", "Barney McGrew", "Cuthbert", "Dibble", "Grub")
    var firemanNo = 0

    while (firemanNo < 6) {
        println("Fireman number $firemanNo is ${firemen[firemanNo]}")
        firemanNo = firemanNo + 1
    }
}
```

You need curly braces around firemen[firemanNo] in order to print the name of each fireman.

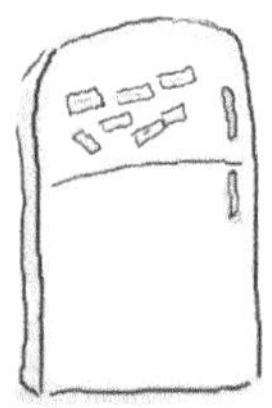

Code Magnets Solution

A working Kotlin program is all scrambled up on the fridge. Can you reconstruct the code snippets to make a working Kotlin function that produces the following output:

```
Fruit = Banana
Fruit = Blueberry
Fruit = Pomegranate
Fruit = Cherry
```

```
fun main(args: Array<String>) {

    val index = arrayOf(1, 3, 4, 2)
    val fruit = arrayOf("Apple", "Banana", "Cherry", "Blueberry", "Pomegranate")
    var x = 0
    var y: Int
    while (x < 4) {
        y = index[x]
        println("Fruit = ${fruit[y]}")
        x = x + 1
    }

}
```

A short Kotlin program is listed below. When the line `//Do stuff` is reached, some objects and variables have been created. Your task is to determine which of the variables refer to which objects by the time the `//Do stuff` line is reached. Some objects may be referred to more than once. Draw lines connecting the variables to their objects.

```
fun main(args: Array<String>) {
    val x = arrayOf(0, 1, 2, 3, 4)
    x[3] = x[2]  //x[3] is now 2
    x[4] = x[0]  //x[4] is now 0
    x[2] = x[1]  //x[2] is now 1
    x[1] = x[0]  //x[1] is now 0
    x[0] = x[1]  //x[1] is 0, so x[0] is still 0
    x[4] = x[3]  //x[3] is 2, so x[4] is now 2
    x[3] = x[2]  //x[2] is 1, so x[3] is now 1
    x[2] = x[4]  //x[4] is 2, so x[2] is now 2
    //Do stuff
}
```

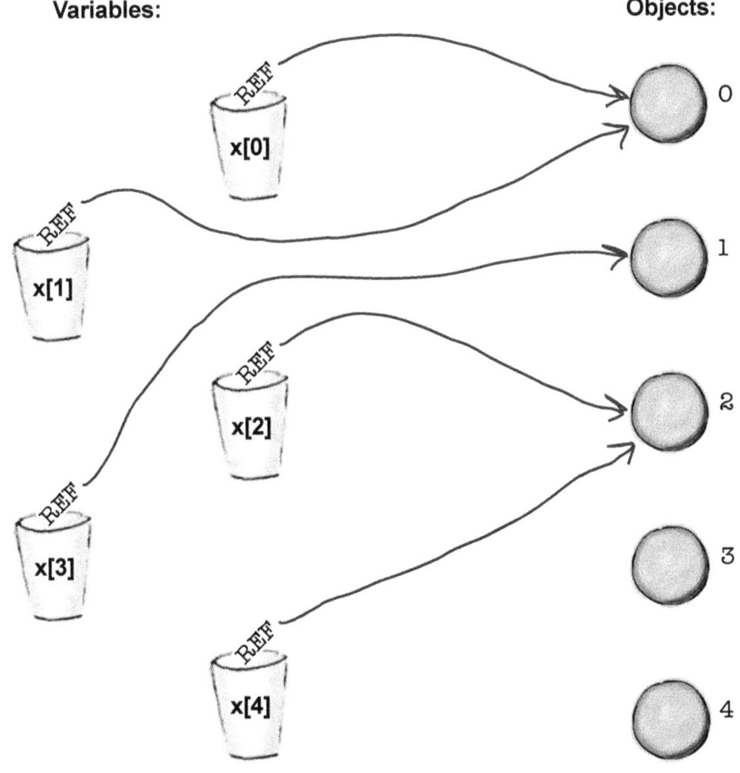

Your Kotlin Toolbox

You've got Chapter 2 under your belt and now you've added basic types and variables to your toolbox.

You can download the full code for the chapter from https://tinyurl.com/HFKotlin.

BULLET POINTS

- In order to create a variable, the compiler needs to know its name, its type, and whether it can be reused.
- If the variable's type isn't explicitly defined, the compiler infers it from its value.
- A variable holds a reference to an object.
- An object has state and behavior. Its behavior is exposed through its functions.
- Defining the variable with `var` means the variable's object reference can be replaced. Defining the variable with `val` means the variable holds a reference to the same object forever.
- Kotlin has a number of basic types: `Byte`, `Short`, `Int`, `Long`, `Float`, `Double`, `Boolean`, `Char` and `String`.
- Explicitly define a variable's type by putting a colon after the variable's name, followed by the type:
  ```
  var tinyNum: Byte
  ```
- You can only assign a value to a variable that has a compatible type.
- You can convert one numeric type to another. If the value won't fit into the new type, some precision is lost.
- Create an array using the `arrayOf` function:
  ```
  var myArray = arrayOf(1, 2, 3)
  ```
- Access an array's items using, for example, `myArray[0]`. The first item in an array has an index of 0.
- Get an array's size using `myArray.size`.
- The compiler infers the array's type from its items. You can explicitly define an array's type like this:
  ```
  var myArray: Array<Byte>
  ```
- If you define an array using `val`, you can still update the items in the array.
- `String` templates provide a quick and easy way of referring to a variable or evaluating an expression from inside a `String`.

3 functions

Getting Out of Main

It's time to take it up a notch, and learn about functions.

So far, all the code you've written has been inside your application's *main* function. But if you want to write code that's **better organized** and **easier to maintain**, you need to know ***how to split your code into separate functions***. In this chapter, you'll learn *how to write functions* and *interact* with your application by building a game. You'll discover how to write compact ***single expression functions***. Along the way you'll find out how to ***iterate through ranges and collections*** using the powerful *for* loop.

Let's build a game: Rock, Paper, Scissors

In all the code examples you've seen so far, we've added code to the application's `main` function. As you already know, this function launches your application as it's the function that gets executed when you run it.

This approach has worked well while we've been learning Kotlin's basic syntax, but most applications in the real-world *split the code across multiple functions*. This is because:

- **It makes your code more organized.**
  Instead of having all your code in one long `main` function, it's split into more manageable chunks. This makes the code much easier to read and understand.

- **It makes your code more reusable.**
  By splitting the code into separate functions, you can reuse it elsewhere.

There are other reasons too, but these are two of the most important.

Each function is a named section of code that performs a specific task. As an example, you could write a function named `max` that determines the highest value out of two values, and then call this function at various stages in your application.

In this chapter, we're going to take a closer look at how functions work by building a game of Rock, Paper, Scissors.

How the game will work

Goal: Make a guess that beats the computer's, and win!

Setup: When the application is launched, the game chooses Rock, Paper or Scissors at random. It then asks *you* to choose one of these options.

The rules: The game compares the two choices. If they are the same, the result is a draw. If the choices are different, however, the game determines the winner using the following rules:

Choices	Result
Scissors, Paper	The Scissors choice wins, as Scissors can cut Paper.
Rock, Scissors	The Rock choice wins, as Rock can blunt Scissors.
Paper, Rock	The Paper choice wins, as Paper can cover Rock.

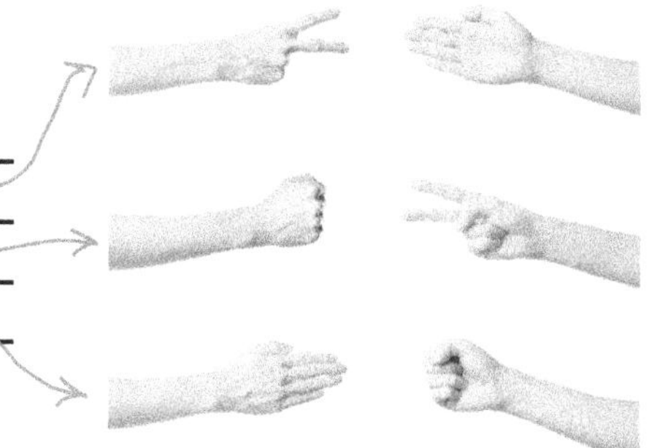

The game will be run in the IDE's output window.

A high-level design of the game

Before we start writing the code for the game, we need to draw up a plan of how it will work.

First, we need to figure out the general flow of the game. Here's the basic idea:

1. **You start the game.**
   The application randomly chooses one of the options: Rock, Paper or Scissors.

2. **The application asks for your choice.**
   You type your choice in the IDE's output window.

3. **The application validates your choice.**
   If you haven't chosen a valid option, it goes back to step 2, and asks you for another choice. The game does this repeatedly until you enter a valid option.

4. **The game displays the result.**
   It tells you what choices you and the application have made, and whether you've won, lost, or the result is a draw.

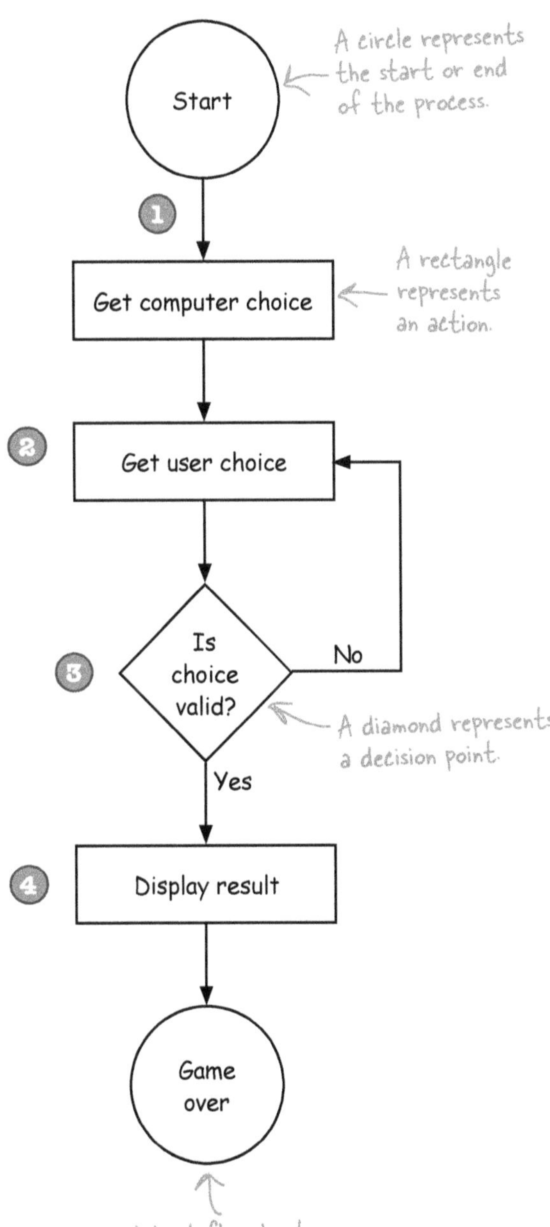

Now that we have a clearer idea of how the application will work, let's look at how we'll code it.

Here's what we're going to do

There are a number of steps we're going to go through to build the game:

1. **Get the game to choose an option.**
   We'll create a new function named `getGameChoice` which will choose one of "Rock", "Paper" or "Scissors" at random.

2. **Ask the user for their choice.**
   We'll do this by writing another new function named `getUserChoice`, and this will ask the user to enter their choice. We'll make sure they've entered a valid choice, and if they haven't, we'll keep asking them until they do.

```
Please enter one of the following: Rock Paper Scissors.
Errr... dunno
You must enter a valid choice.
Please enter one of the following: Rock Paper Scissors.
Paper
```

3. **Print the result.**
   We'll write a function named `printResult`, which will figure out whether the user won or lost, or whether the result is a tie. The function will then print the result.

```
You chose Paper. I chose Rock. You win!
```

Get started: create the project

We'll start by creating a project for the application. You do this in exactly the same way you did in previous chapters.

Create a new Kotlin project that targets the JVM, and name the project "Rock Paper Scissors". Then create a new Kotlin file named *Game.kt* by highlighting the *src* folder, clicking on the File menu and choosing New → Kotlin File/Class. When prompted, name the file "Game", and choose File from the Kind option.

Now that you've created the project, let's start writing some code.

Get the game to choose an option

The first thing we'll do is get the game to choose one of the options (Rock, Paper or Scissors) at random. Here's what we'll do:

1. **Create an array that contains the Strings "Rock", "Paper" and "Scissors".**
   We'll add this to the application's `main` function.

2. **Create a new getGameChoice function that will choose one of the options at random.**

3. **Call the getGameChoice function from the main function.**

We'll start by creating the array.

Create the Rock, Paper, Scissors array

We'll create the array using the `arrayOf` function, just as we did in the previous chapter. We'll add this code to the application's `main` function so that it gets created when the application launches. This also means that we'll be able to use it in the rest of the code we'll write later in the chapter.

To create the `main` function and add the array, update your version of *Game.kt* to match ours below:

```
fun main(args: Array<String>) {
    val options = arrayOf("Rock", "Paper", "Scissors")
}
```

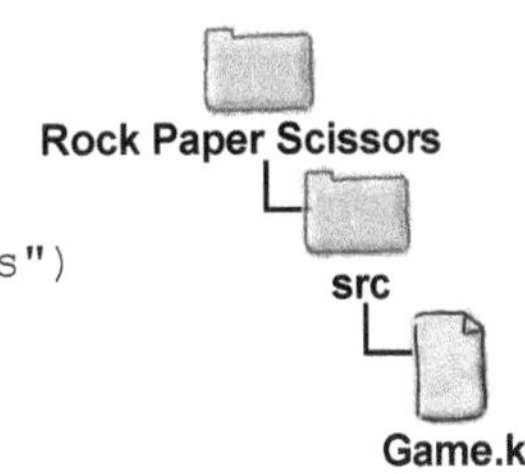

Now that we've created the array, we need to define the new `getGameChoice` function. Before we can do this, we need to understand more about how you create functions.

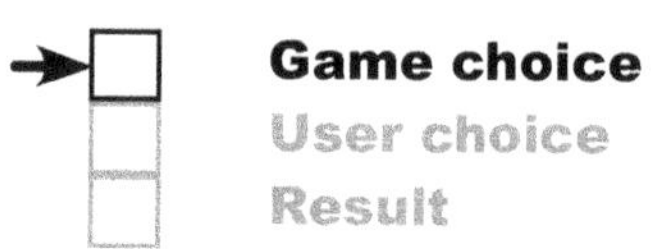

How you create functions

As you learned back in Chapter 1, you define new functions using the `fun` keyword, followed by the name of the function. As an example, if you wanted to create a new function named `foo`, you'd write code like this:

```
fun foo() {
    //Your code goes here
}
```

'fun' tells Kotlin that it's a function.

Once you've written the function, you can call it from elsewhere in your application:

```
fun main(args: Array<String>) {
    foo()
}
```

This runs a function named 'foo'.

You can send things to a function

Sometimes, a function needs extra information in order for it to perform a task. If you're writing a function to determine the highest of two values, for example, the function needs to know what these two values are.

You tell the compiler what values a function can accept by specifying one or more **parameters**. Each parameter must have a name and type.

As an example, here's how you specify that the `foo` function takes a single `Int` parameter named `param`:

```
fun foo(param: Int) {
    println("Parameter is $param")
}
```

You declare parameters inside the function's parentheses.

You can then call the function and pass it an `Int` value:

```
foo(6)
```

We're passing '6' to the foo function.

Note that **if a function has a parameter, you must pass it something**. And that something must be a value of the appropriate type. The following function call, for instance, won't work because the `foo` function accepts an `Int` value, not a `String`:

```
foo("Freddie")
```

We can't pass a String to foo as it only accepts an Int.

Parameters and Arguments

Depending on your programming background and personal preferences, you might use the term *arguments* or *parameters* for the values passed into a function. Although there are formal computer science distinctions that people who wear lab coats make, we have bigger fish to fry. *You* can call them whatever you like (arguments, parameters, donuts...) but we're doing it like this:

A function uses parameters. A caller passes it arguments.

Arguments are the things you pass into the functions. An *argument* (a value like 2 or "Pizza") lands face-down into a *parameter*. And a parameter is nothing more than a **local variable**: a variable with a name and type that's used inside the body of the function.

You can send more than one thing to a function

If you want your function to have multiple parameters, you separate them with commas when you declare them, and separate the arguments with commas when you pass them to the function. Most importantly, if a function has multiple parameters, you must pass arguments of the right type in the right order.

Calling a two-parameter function, and sending it two arguments

```
fun main(args: Array<String>) {
    printSum(5, 6)
}


fun printSum(int1: Int, int2: Int) {
    val result = int1 + int2
    println(result)
}
```

The arguments you pass land in the function in the same order you passed them. The first argument lands in the first parameter, the second argument lands in the second parameter, and so on.

You can pass arguments to a function so long as the argument type matches the parameter type

```
fun main(args: Array<String>) {
    val x: Int = 7
    val y: Int = 8
    printSum(x, y)
}


fun printSum(int1: Int, int2: Int) {
    val result = int1 + int2
    println(result)
}
```

Each argument you pass must be the same type as the parameter it lands in.

As well as passing values to a function, you can also get things back. Let's see how.

Game choice
User choice
Result

You can get things back from a function

If you want to get something back from a function, you need to declare it. As an example, here's how you declare that a function named max returns an Int value:

```
fun max(a: Int, b: Int): Int {
    val maxValue = if (a > b) a else b
    return maxValue
}
```

The : Int tells the compiler that the function returns an Int value.

You return a value using the 'return' keyword, followed by the value you're returning.

If you declare that a function returns a value, then you *must* return a value of the declared type. As an example, the following code is invalid becuase it returns a String instead of an Int:

```
fun max(a: Int, b: Int): Int {
    val maxValue = if (a > b) a else b
    return "Fish"
}
```

We've declared that the function returns an Int value, so the compiler will get upset if you try and return something else, like a String.

Functions with no return value

If you don't want your function to return a value, you can either omit the return type from the function declaration, or specify a return type of Unit. Declaring a return type of Unit means that the function returns no value. As an example, the following two function declarations are both valid, and do the same thing:

```
fun printSum(int1: Int, int2: Int) {
    val result = int1 + int2
    println(result)
}

fun printSum(int1: Int, int2: Int): Unit {
    val result = int1 + int2
    println(result)
}
```

The : Unit here means that the function returns no value. It's completely optional.

If you specify that your function has no return value, then you need to make sure that it doesn't return one. If you try to return a value in a function with no declared return type, or a return type of Unit, your code won't compile.

Game choice
User choice
Result

Functions with single-expression bodies

If you have a function whose body consists of a single expression, you can simplify the code by removing the curly braces and `return` statement from the function declaration. As an example, on the previous page, we showed you the following function to return the higher of two values:

```
fun max(a: Int, b: Int): Int {
    val maxValue = if (a > b) a else b
    return maxValue
}
```

The max function has a single expression in its body, which we then return.

The function returns the result of a single `if` expression, which means that we can rewrite the function like so:

```
fun max(a: Int, b: Int): Int = if (a > b) a else b
```

Use = to say what the function returns, and remove the {}'s.

And because the compiler can infer the function's return type from the `if` expression, we can make the code even shorter by omitting the `: Int`:

```
fun max(a: Int, b: Int) = if (a > b) a else b
```

The compiler knows that a and b are Ints, so it can work out the function's return type from the expression.

Create the getGameChoice function

Now that you've learned how to create functions, see if you can write the `getGameChoice` function for our Rock, Paper, Scissors game by having a go at the following exercise.

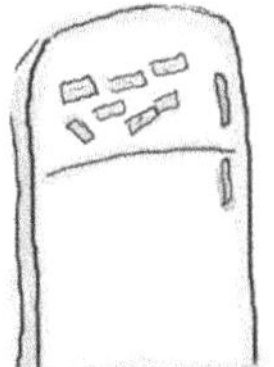

Code Magnets

The `getGameChoice` function will accept one parameter, an array of `String`s, and return one of the array's items. See if you can write the function using the magnets below.

```
fun getGameChoice(..............................) =
    optionsParam[..............................]
```

Magnets: `Array<String>`, `optionsParam:`, `(`, `.toInt()`, `.size`, `Math.random()`, `optionsParam`, `)`, `*`

Game choice
User choice
Result

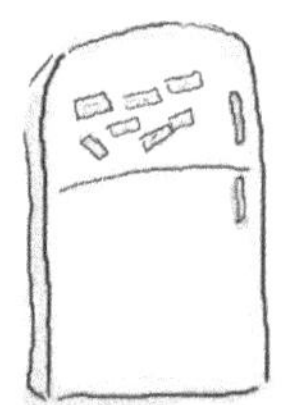

Code Magnets Solution

The `getGameChoice` function will accept one parameter, an array of `String`s, and return one of the array's items. See if you can write the function using the magnets below.

```
fun getGameChoice( optionsParam: Array<String> ) =
    optionsParam[ ( Math.random() * optionsParam .size ) .toInt() ]
```

The function has one parameter, an array of Strings.

Choose one of the array's items at random.

Add the getGameChoice function to Game.kt

Now that we know what the `getGameChoice` function looks like, let's add it to our application, and update our `main` function so that it calls the new function. Update your version of *Game.kt* so that it matches ours below (our changes are in bold):

```
fun main(args: Array<String>) {
    val options = arrayOf("Rock", "Paper", "Scissors")
    val gameChoice = getGameChoice(options)
}

fun getGameChoice(optionsParam: Array<String>) =
        optionsParam[(Math.random() * optionsParam.size).toInt()]
```

Call the getGameChoice function, passing it the options array.

You need to add the function.

Rock Paper Scissors
src
Game.kt

Now that we've added the `getGameChoice` function to our application, let's look at what's going on behind the scenes when the code runs.

Q: Can I return more than one value from a function?

A: A function can declare only one return value. But if you want to, say, return three `Int` values, then the declared type can be an array of `Int`s (`Array<Int>`). Put those `Int`s into the array, and pass it back.

Q: Do I have to do something with the return value of a function? Can I just ignore it?

A: Kotlin doesn't require you to acknowledge a return value. You might want to call a function with a return type, even though you don't care about the return value. In this case, you're calling the function for the work it does inside the function, rather than for what it returns. You don't have to assign or use the return value.

Behind the scenes: what happens

When the code runs, the following things happen:

val options = arrayOf("Rock", "Paper", "Scissors")

This creates an array of `Strings`, and a variable named `options` that holds a reference to it.

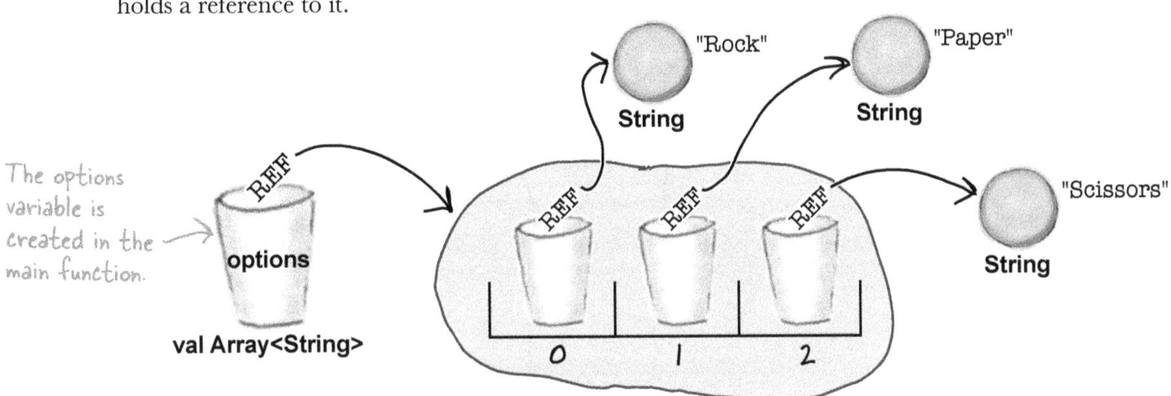

2 val gameChoice = **getGameChoice(options)**

The contents of the `options` variable get passed to the `getGameChoice` function. The `options` variable holds a reference to an array of `Strings`, so a copy of the reference gets passed to the `getGameChoice` function, and lands in its `optionsParam` parameter. This means that the `options` and `optionsParam` variables **both hold a reference to the same array**.

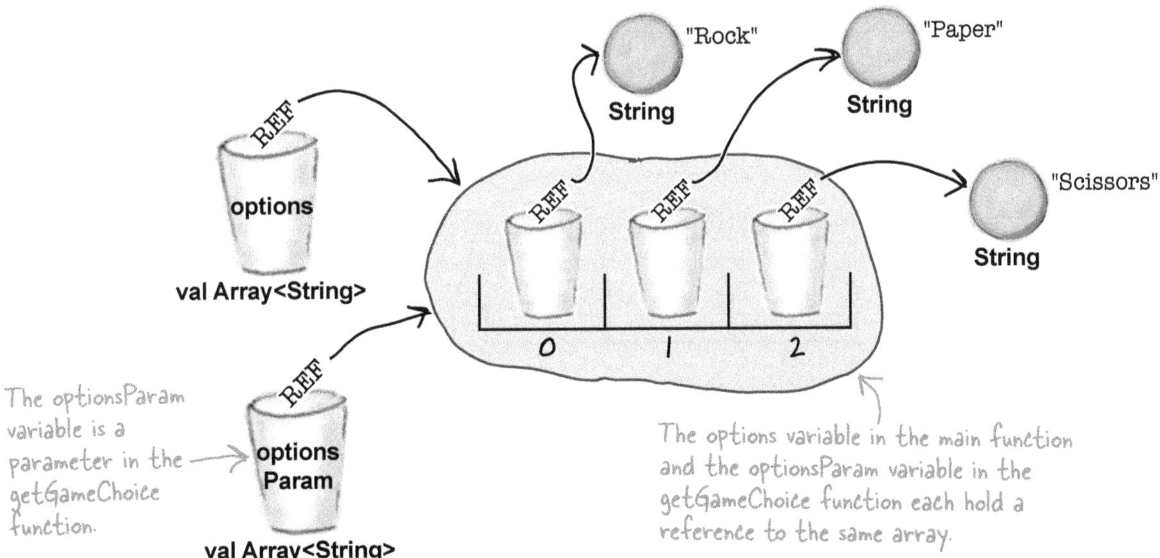

The story continues

3

```
fun getGameChoice(optionsParam: Array<String>) =
    optionsParam[(Math.random() * optionsParam.size).toInt()]
```

The `getGameChoice` function selects one of the `optionsParam`'s items at random (for example, the "Scissors" item). The function returns a reference to this item.

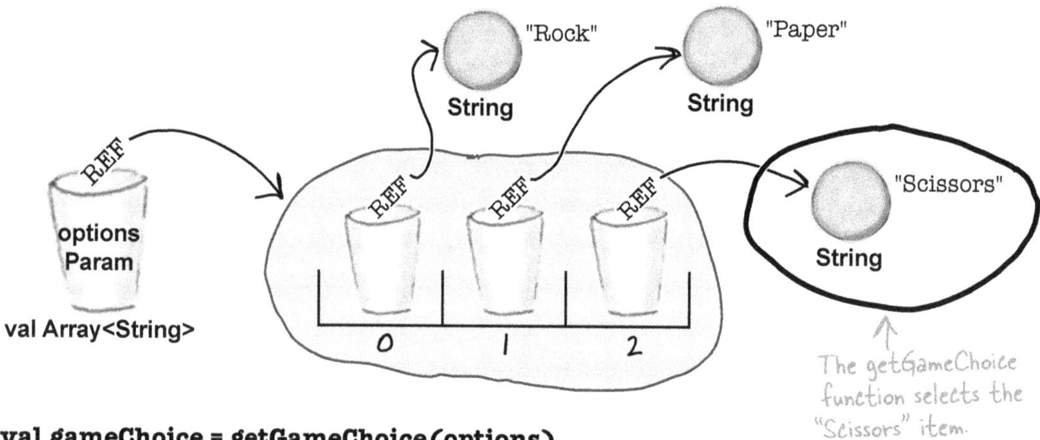

4

```
val gameChoice = getGameChoice(options)
```

This puts the reference returned by the `getGameChoice` function into a new variable named `gameChoice`. If, for example, the `getGameChoice` function returns a reference to the "Scissors" item of the array, this means that a reference to the "Scissors" object is put into the `gameChoice` variable.

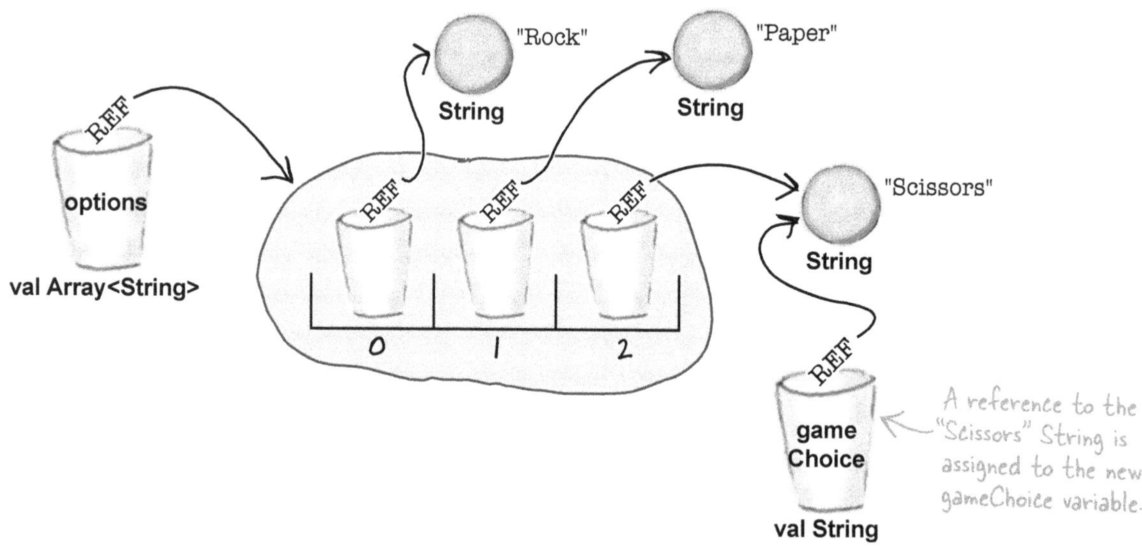

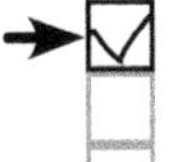

So when you pass a value to a function, you're really passing it a reference to an object. Does this mean you can make changes to the underlying object?

Yes, you can.

As an example, suppose you have the following code:

```
fun main(args: Array<String>) {
    val options = arrayOf("Rock", "Paper", "Scissors")
    updateArray(options)
    println(options[2])
}

fun updateArray(optionsParam: Array<String>) {
    optionsParam[2] = "Fred"
}
```

The `main` function creates an array containing the `Strings` "Rock", "Paper" and "Scissors". A reference to this array is passed to the `updateArray` function, which updates the third item of the array to "Fred". Finally, the `main` function prints the value of the array's third item, so it prints the text "Fred".

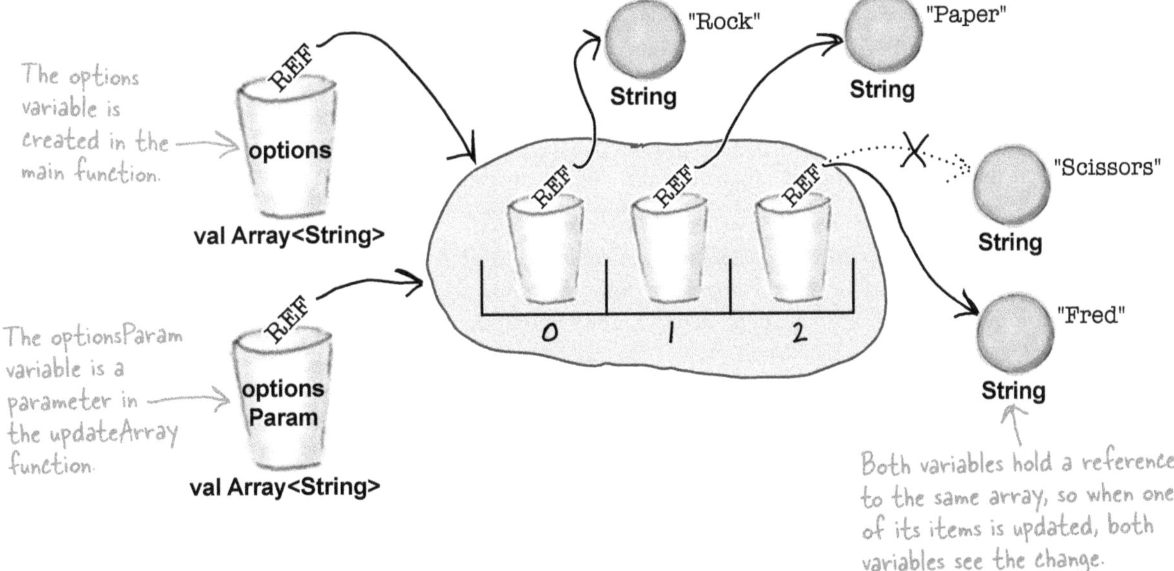

Local Variables Up Close

As we said earlier in the chapter, a local variable is one that's used inside the body of a function. They're declared within a function, and they're only visible inside that function. If you try to use a variable that's defined in another function, you'll get a compiler error, as in the example below:

```
fun main(args: Array<String>) {
    var x = 6
}

fun myFunction() {
    var y = x + 3
}
```

This code won't compile because myFunction can't see the x variable that's declared in main.

Any local variables must be initialized before they can be used. If you're using a variable for a function's return value, for example, you must initialize that variable or the compiler will get upset:

```
fun myFunction(): String {
    var message: String
    return message
}
```

You must initialize a variable if you want to use it as a function's return value, so this code won't compile.

Function parameters are virtually the same as local variables, as they only exist within the context of the function. They're always initialized, however, so you'll never get a compiler error telling you that a parameter variable might not have been initialized. This is because the compiler will give you an error message if you try to invoke a function without sending the arguments that the function needs; the compiler guarantees that functions are always called with arguments that match the parameters declared in the function, and the arguments are automatically assigned to the parameters.

Note that you can't assign a new value to any of a function's parameter variables. Behind the scenes, the parameter variables are created as local `val` variables that can't be reused for other values. The following code, for example, won't compile because we're trying to assign a new value to the function's parameter variable:

```
fun myFunction(message: String){
    message = "Hi!"
}
```

Parameter variables are treated as local variables created using val, so you can't reuse them for other values.

BE the Compiler

Here are three complete Kotlin functions. Your job is to play like you're the compiler and determine whether each of these functions will compile. If they won't compile, how would you fix them?

A

```
fun doSomething(msg: String, i: Int): Unit {
    if (i > 0) {
        var x = 0
        while (x < i) {
            println(msg)
            x = x + 1
        }
    }
}
```

B

```
fun timesThree(x: Int): Int {
    x = x * 3
    return x
}
```

C

```
fun maxValue(args: Array<Int>) {
    var max = args[0]
    var x = 1
    while (x < args.size) {
        var item = args[x]
        max = if (max >= item) max else item
        x = x + 1
    }
    return max
}
```

BE the Compiler Solution

Here are three complete Kotlin functions. Your job is to play like you're the compiler and determine whether each of these functions will compile. If they won't compile, how would you fix them?

A

```
fun doSomething(msg: String, i: Int): Unit {
    if (i > 0) {
        var x = 0
        while (x < i) {
            println(msg)
            x = x + 1
        }
    }
}
```

This will compile and run successfully. The function has a Unit return type, and this means that it has no return value.

B

```
fun timesThree(x: Int): Int {
    val y = x * 3
    return y
}
```

This won't compile, as you're assigning a new value to the function's parameter. You would also need to consider the function's return type, as multiplying an Int by three may result in a value that's too large for an Int value.

C

```
fun maxValue(args: Array<Int>): Int {
    var max = args[0]
    var x = 1
    while (x < args.size) {
        var item = args[x]
        max = if (max >= item) max else item
        x = x + 1
    }
    return max
}
```

This won't compile because the function needs to declare that it returns an Int value.

Game choice
User choice
Result

The getUserChoice function

Now that we've written the code to make the game choose an option, we can move onto the next step: getting the user's choice. We'll write a new function to do this called `getUserChoice`, which we'll call from the `main` function. We'll pass the `options` array to the `getUserChoice` function as a parameter, and we'll get it to return the user's choice (a `String`):

```
fun getUserChoice(optionsParam: Array<String>): String {
    //Code goes here
}
```

Let's go through what we need the `getUserChoice` function to do:

1. **Ask the user for their choice.**
   We'll loop through the items in the options array, and ask the user to type their choice into the output window.

2. **Read the user's choice from the output window.**
   After the user's entered their choice, we'll assign its value to a new variable.

3. **Validate the user's choice.**
   We'll check that the user has entered a choice, and that it's in the array. If the user has entered a valid choice, we'll get the function to return it. If they haven't, we'll keep asking until they do.

Let's start with the code to prompt the user for their choice.

Ask for the user's choice

To ask the user to input their choice of option, we'll make the `getUserChoice` function print the following message: "Please enter one of the following: Rock Paper Scissors."

One way of doing this would be to hard-code the message using the `println` function like this:

```
println("Please enter one of the following: Rock Paper Scissors.")
```

A more flexible approach, however, is to loop through each item in the `options` array, and print each item. This will be useful if we ever want to change any of the options.

You might want to play Rock, Paper, Scissors, Lizard, Spock instead.

Instead of using a `while` loop to do this, we're going to use a new type of loop called a `for` loop. Let's see how it works.

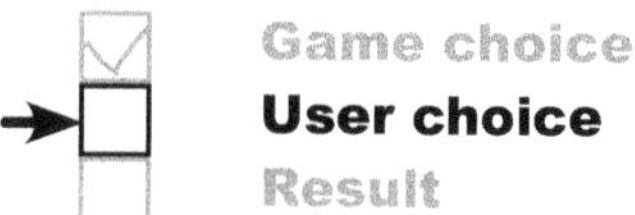

How for loops work

A **for** loop is useful in situations where you want to loop through a fixed range of numbers, or through every item in an array (or some other type of collection—we'll look at collections in Chapter 9). Let's look at how you do this.

Looping through a range of numbers

Suppose you wanted to loop through a range of numbers, from 1 to 10. You've already seen how to do this kind of thing using a `while` loop:

```
var x = 1
while (x < 11) {
    //Your code goes here
    x = x + 1
}
```

But it's much cleaner, and requires fewer lines of code, if you use a `for` loop instead. Here's the equivalent code:

```
for (x in 1..10) {
    //Your code goes here
}
```

It's like saying "for each number between 1 and 10, assign the number to a variable named *x*, and run the body of the loop".

To loop through a range of numbers, you first specify a name for the variable the loop should use. In the above case, we've named the variable `x`, but you can use any valid variable name. The variable gets created when the loop runs.

You specify the range of values using the `..` operator. In the case above, we've used a range of `1..10`, so the code loops through the numbers 1 through to 10. At the beginning of each loop, it assigns the current number to the variable (in our case `x`).

Just like a `while` loop, if the loop body consists of a single statement, you can omit the curly braces. As an example, here's how you would use a `for` loop to print the numbers 1 to 100:

```
for (x in 1..100) println(x)
```

Note that the `..` operator includes the end number in its range. If you wanted to exclude it, you would replace the `..` operator with `until`. As an example, the following code prints the numbers from 1 to 99, and excludes 100:

```
for (x in 1 until 100) println(x)
```

Math Shortcuts

The increment operator ++ adds 1 to a variable. So:

```
x++
```

is a shortcut for:

```
x = x + 1
```

Similarly, the decrement operator -- subtracts 1 from a variable. Use:

```
x--
```

as a shortcut for:

```
x = x - 1
```

If you want to add a number other than 1 to a variable, you can use the += operator. So:

```
x += 2
```

does the same as:

```
x = x + 2
```

Similarly, you can use -=, *= and /= as shortcuts for subtraction, multiplication and division.

While loops run while a given condition is true.

For loops run over a range of values or items.

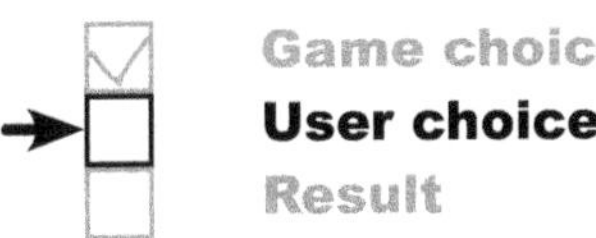

How for loops work (continued)

Use downTo to reverse the range

If you want to loop through a range of numbers in reverse order, you use **downTo** instead of `..` or `until`. As an example, you'd use the following code to print the numbers from 15 down to 1:

```
for (x in 15 downTo 1) println(x)
```

Using downTo instead of .. loops through the numbers in reverse order.

Use step to skip numbers in the range

By default, the `..` operator, `until` and `downTo` step through the range one number at a time. If you want, you can increase the size of the step using `step`. As an example, the following code prints alternate numbers from 1 to 100:

```
for (x in 1..100 step 2) println(x)
```

Looping through the items in an array

You can also use a `for` loop to iterate through the items in an array. In our case, for example, we want to loop through the items in an array named `options`. To do this, we can use a `for` loop in this format:

```
for (item in optionsParam) {
    println("$item is an item in the array")
}
```

This loops through each item in an array named optionsParam.

You can also loop through an array's indices using code like this:

```
for (index in optionsParam.indices) {
    println("Index $index has item ${optionsParam[index]}")
}
```

You can even simplify the above loop by returning the array's index *and* value as part of the loop:

```
for ((index, item) in optionsParam.withIndex()) {
    println("Index $index has item $item")
}
```

This loops through each item in the array. It assigns the item's index to the index variable, and the item itself to the item variable.

Now that you know how `for` loops work, let's write the code that will ask the user to enter one of "Rock, "Paper" or "Scissors".

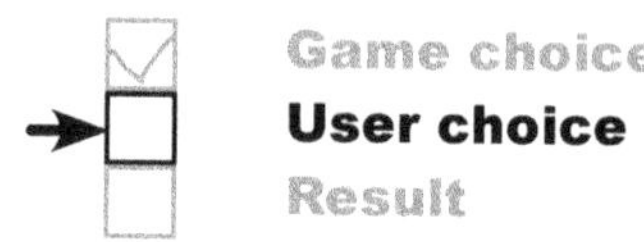

Ask the user for their choice

We're going to use a `for` loop to print the text "Please enter one of the following: Rock Paper Scissors." Here's the code that will do this; we'll update *Game.kt* later in the chapter when we've finished writing the `getUserChoice` function:

```
fun getUserChoice(optionsParam: Array<String>): String {
    //Ask the user for their choice
    print("Please enter one of the following:")
    for (item in optionsParam) print(" $item")
    println(".")
}
```

This prints the value of each item in the array.

Use the readLine function to read the user's input

After we've asked the user to enter their choice, we need to read their response. We'll do this by calling the **`readLine()`** function:

```
val userInput = readLine()
```

The `readLine()` function reads a line of input from the standard input stream (in our case, the output window in the IDE). It returns a `String` value, the text entered by the user.

If the input stream for your application has been redirected to a file, the `readLine()` function returns `null` if the end of file has been reached. `null` means that it has no value, or that it's missing.

You'll find out a lot more about null values in Chapter 8 but for now, this is all you need to know about them.

Here's an updated version of the `getUserChoice` function (we'll add it to our application when we've finished writing it):

We'll update the getUserChoice function a few pages ahead.

```
fun getUserChoice(optionsParam: Array<String>): String {
    //Ask the user for their choice
    print("Please enter one of the following:")
    for (item in optionsParam) print(" $item")
    println(".")
    //Read the user input
    val userInput = readLine()
}
```

This reads the user's input from the standard input stream. In our case, this is the output window in the IDE.

Next, we need to validate the user input to make sure they've entered an appropriate choice. We'll do that after you've had a go at the following exercise.

A short Kotlin program is listed below. One block of the program is missing. Your challenge is to match the candidate block of code (on the left), with the output that you'd see if the block were inserted. Not all the lines of output will be used, and some lines of output may be used more than once. Draw lines connecting the candidate blocks of code with their matching output.

```
fun main(args: Array<String>) {
    var x = 0
    var y = 20
    for(outer in 1..3) {
        for (inner in 4 downTo 2) {
            [                    ]
            y++
            x += 3
        }
        y -= 2
    }
    println("$x $y")
}
```

The candidate code goes here.

Match each candidate with one of the possible outputs.

Candidates:

```
x += 6
```

```
x--
```

```
y = x + y
```

```
y = 7
```

```
x = x + y
y = x - 7
```

```
x = y
y++
```

Possible output:

```
4286 4275
```

```
27 23
```

```
27 6
```

```
81 23
```

```
27 131
```

```
18 23
```

```
35 32
```

```
3728 3826
```

Mixed Messages Solution

A short Kotlin program is listed below. One block of the program is missing. Your challenge is to match the candidate block of code (on the left), with the output that you'd see if the block were inserted. Not all the lines of output will be used, and some lines of output may be used more than once. Draw lines connecting the candidate blocks of code with their matching output.

```
fun main(args: Array<String>) {
    var x = 0
    var y = 20
    for(outer in 1..3) {
        for (inner in 4 downTo 2) {
            [                    ]
            y++
            x += 3
        }
        y -= 2
    }
    println("$x $y")
}
```

The candidate code goes here.

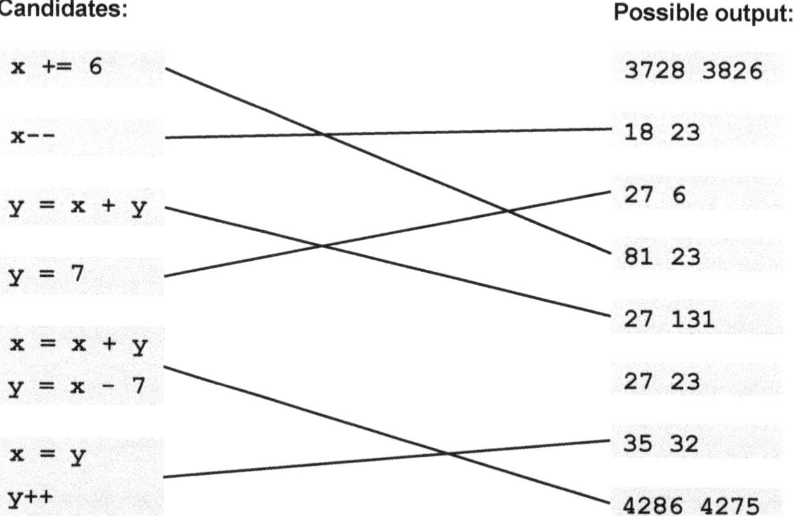

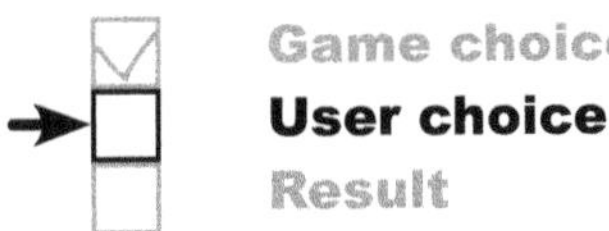

We need to validate the user's input

The final code we need to write for the `getUserChoice` function needs to validate the user's input to make sure they've entered a valid option. The code needs to do the following:

1. **Check that the user input isn't null.**
   As we said earlier, the `readLine()` function returns a null value if it's reading a line from a file, and it's at the end of the file. Even though this isn't the case in our situation, we still need to check that the user input isn't `null` in order to keep the compiler sweet.

2. **Check whether the user's choice is in the options array.**
   We can do this using the `in` operator that you saw when we discussed `for` loops.

3. **Loop until the user enters a valid choice.**
   We want to loop until a condition is met (the user enters a valid option), so we'll use a `while` loop for this.

You're already familiar with most of the code needed to do this, but to write code that's more concise, we're going to use some boolean expressions that are more powerful than the ones you've seen before. We'll discuss these next, and after that we'll show you the full code for the `getUserChoice` function.

'And' and 'Or' operators (&& and ||)

Let's say you're writing code to choose a new phone, with lots of rules about which phone to select. You might, say, want to limit the price range so that it's between $200 and $300. To do this, you use code like this:

```
if (price >= 200 && price <= 300) {
    //Code to choose the phone
}
```

The `&&` means "and". It evaluates to `true` if **both** sides of the `&&` are true. When the code gets run, Kotlin first evaluates the left side of the expression. If this is false, Kotlin doesn't bother evaluating the right side. As one side of the expression is false, this means that the entire expression must be false. ← This is sometimes referred to as short-circuiting.

If you want to use an "or" expression instead, you use the `||` operator:

```
if (price <= 10 || price >= 1000) {
    //Phone is too cheap or too expensive
}
```

This expression evaluates to `true` if **either** side of the `||` is true. This time, Kotlin doesn't evaluate the right side of the expression if the left side is true.

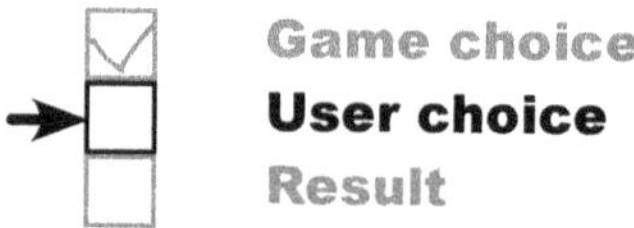

Not equals (!= and !)

Suppose you wanted to run code for all phones except one model. To do this, you'd use code like the following:

```
if (model != 2000) {
    //Code that runs if model is not 2000
}
```

The != means "is not equal to".

Similarly, you can use ! to indicate "not". As an example, the following loop runs while the isBroken variable is not true:

```
while (!isBroken) {
    //Code that runs if the phone is not broken
}
```

Use parentheses to make your code clear

Boolean expressions can get really big and complicated:

```
if ((price <= 500 && memory >= 16) ||
    (price <= 750 && memory >= 32) ||
    (price <= 1000 && memory >= 64)) {
    //Do something appropriate
}
```

If you want to get really technical, you might wonder about the precedence of these operators. Instead of becoming an expert in the arcane world of precedence, we recommend that you use parentheses to make your code clearer.

Now that you've seen some more powerful boolean expressions, we'll show you the remaining code for the getUserChoice function, and add it to the application.

Game choice
User choice
Result

Add the getUserChoice function to Game.kt

Below is the revised code for the application, including the complete `getUserChoice` function. Update your version of *Game.kt* so that it matches ours (our changes are in bold):

```
fun main(args: Array<String>) {
    val options = arrayOf("Rock", "Paper", "Scissors")
    val gameChoice = getGameChoice(options)
    val userChoice = getUserChoice(options)
}

fun getGameChoice(optionsParam: Array<String>) =
        optionsParam[(Math.random() * optionsParam.size).toInt()]

fun getUserChoice(optionsParam: Array<String>): String {
    var isValidChoice = false
    var userChoice = ""
    //Loop until the user enters a valid choice
    while (!isValidChoice) {
        //Ask the user for their choice
        print("Please enter one of the following:")
        for (item in optionsParam) print(" $item")
        println(".")
        //Read the user input
        val userInput = readLine()
        //Validate the user input
        if (userInput != null && userInput in optionsParam) {
            isValidChoice = true
            userChoice = userInput
        }
        //If the choice is invalid, inform the user
        if (!isValidChoice) println("You must enter a valid choice.")
    }
    return userChoice
}
```

Call the getUserChoice function.

We'll use the isValidChoice variable to indicate whether the user has entered a valid choice.

Keep looping until isValidChoice is true.

Check that the user input isn't null, and that it's in the options array.

If the user input is OK, we can stop looping.

If the user input is invalid, we'll keep looping.

Rock Paper Scissors
src
Game.kt

Let's take the code for a test drive, and see what happens when it runs.

Test drive

Game choice
User choice
Result

Run your code by going to the Run menu, and selecting the Run 'GameKt' command. When the IDE's output window opens, you'll be asked to enter one of "Rock", "Paper" or "Scissors":

```
Please enter one of the following: Rock Paper Scissors.
```

When you enter an invalid option and hit the Return key, you're asked to enter an option that's valid. This is repeated until you enter one of "Rock", "Paper" or "Scissors", at which point the program ends.

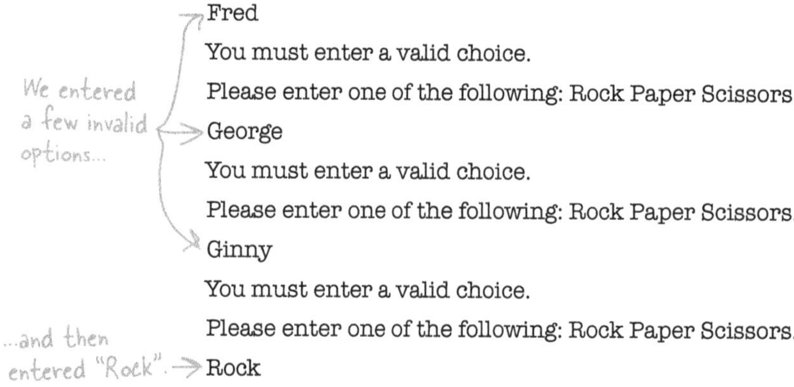

We need to print the results

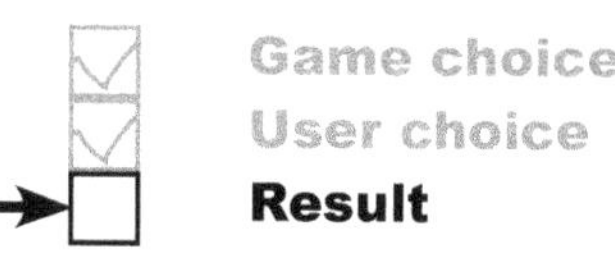

The final thing we need our application to do is print the results. As a reminder, if the user and the game make the same choice, the result is a tie. If the choices are different, however, the game determines the winner using the following rules:

Choices	Result
Scissors, Paper	The Scissors choice wins, as Scissors can cut Paper.
Rock, Scissors	The Rock choice wins, as Rock can blunt Scissors.
Paper, Rock	The Paper choice wins, as Paper can cover Rock.

We'll print the results in a new function named `printResult`. We'll call this function from `main`, and pass it two parameters: the user's choice and the game's choice.

Before we show you the code for the function, see if you can figure it out for yourself by having a go at the following exercise.

Pool Puzzle

Your **job** is to take code snippets from the pool and place them into the blank lines in the `printResult` function. You may **not** use the same code snippet more than once, and you won't need to use all the snippets. Your **goal** is to print the choices made by the user and the game, and say who won.

```
fun printResult(userChoice: String, gameChoice: String) {
    val result: String
    //Figure out the result
    if (userChoice........gameChoice) result = "Tie!"
    else if ((userChoice........"Rock"........gameChoice........"Scissors")........
            (userChoice........"Paper"........gameChoice........"Rock") ........
            (userChoice........"Scissors"........gameChoice........"Paper")) result = "You win!"
    else result = "You lose!"
    //Print the result
    println("You chose $userChoice. I chose $gameChoice. $result")
}
```

Note: each thing from the pool can only be used once!

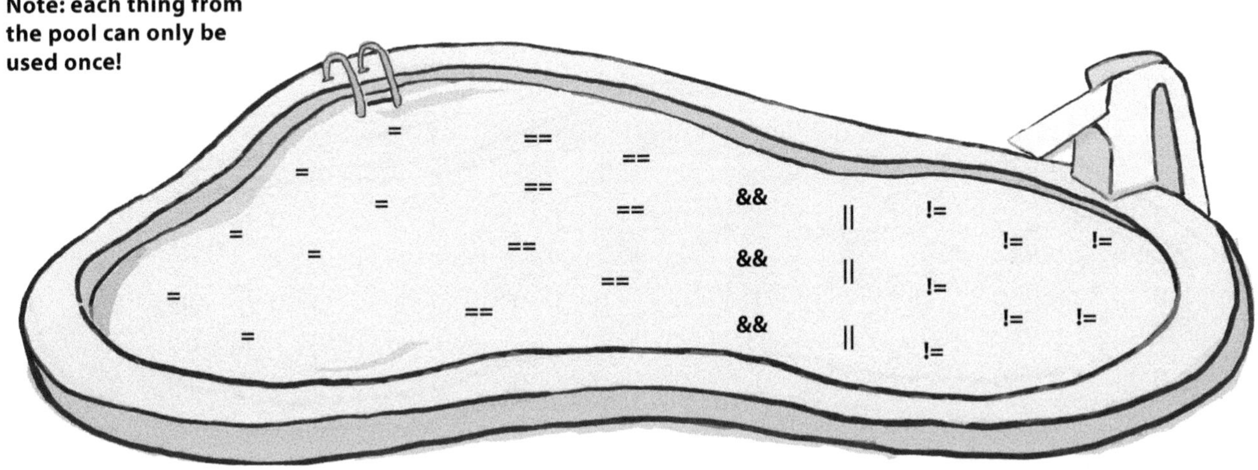

Pool Puzzle Solution

Your **job** is to take code snippets from the pool and place them into the blank lines in the `printResult` function. You may **not** use the same code snippet more than once, and you won't need to use all the snippets. Your **goal** is to print the choices made by the user and the game, and say who won.

```
fun printResult(userChoice: String, gameChoice: String) {
    val result: String
    //Figure out the result
    if (userChoice == gameChoice) result = "Tie!"
    else if ((userChoice == "Rock" && gameChoice == "Scissors") ||
            (userChoice == "Paper" && gameChoice == "Rock") ||
            (userChoice == "Scissors" && gameChoice == "Paper")) result = "You win!"
    else result = "You lose!"
    //Print the result
    println("You chose $userChoice. I chose $gameChoice. $result")
}
```

If the user and the game chose the same option, the result is a tie.

If any of these combos are true, the user wins.

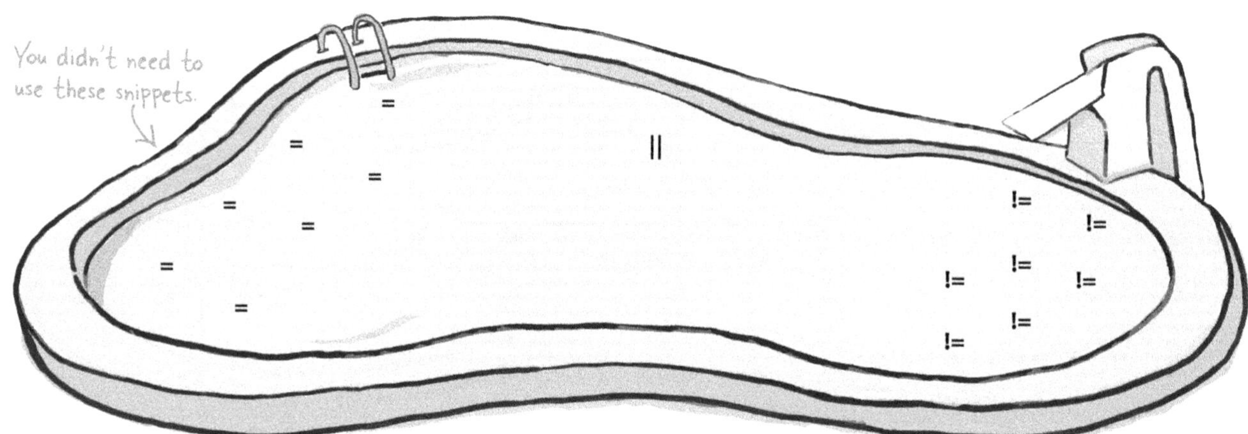

Game choice
User choice
Result

Add the printResult function to Game.kt

We need to add the `printResult` function to *Game.kt*, and call it from the `main` function. Here's the code: update your version of the code so that it matches ours (our changes are in bold):

```
fun main(args: Array<String>) {
    val options = arrayOf("Rock", "Paper", "Scissors")
    val gameChoice = getGameChoice(options)
    val userChoice = getUserChoice(options)
    printResult(userChoice, gameChoice)   <-- Call the printResult function from main.
}

fun getGameChoice(optionsParam: Array<String>) =
        optionsParam[(Math.random() * optionsParam.size).toInt()]

fun getUserChoice(optionsParam: Array<String>): String {
    var isValidChoice = false
    var userChoice = ""
    //Loop until the user enters a valid choice
    while (!isValidChoice) {
        //Ask the user for their choice
        print("Please enter one of the following:")
        for (item in optionsParam) print(" $item")
        println(".")
        //Read the user input
        val userInput = readLine()
        //Validate the user input
        if (userInput != null && userInput in optionsParam) {
            isValidChoice = true
            userChoice = userInput
        }
        //If the choice is invalid, inform the user
        if (!isValidChoice) println("You must enter a valid choice.")
    }
    return userChoice
}
```

Rock Paper Scissors
src
Game.kt

The code continues on the next page.

The Game.kt code continued

```
fun printResult(userChoice: String, gameChoice: String) {
    val result: String
    //Figure out the result
    if (userChoice == gameChoice) result = "Tie!"
    else if ((userChoice == "Rock" && gameChoice == "Scissors") ||
            (userChoice == "Paper" && gameChoice == "Rock") ||
            (userChoice == "Scissors" && gameChoice == "Paper")) result = "You win!"
    else result = "You lose!"
    //Print the result
    println("You chose $userChoice. I chose $gameChoice. $result")
}
```

You need to add this function.

Rock Paper Scissors
src
Game.kt

That's all the code we need for our application. Let's see what happens when we run it.

Test drive

When we run the code, the IDE's output window opens, enter one of "Rock", "Paper" or "Scissors" (we're choosing "Paper"):

```
Please enter one of the following: Rock Paper Scissors.
Paper
You chose Paper. I chose Rock. You win!
```

The application prints our choice, the option selected by the game, and the result.

Q: I entered an option of "paper" but the game told me I'd entered an invalid option. Why's that?

A: It's because you entered a lowercase `String`, instead of one that starts with an initial capital letter. The game requires you to enter one of "Rock", "Paper" or "Scissors", and it doesn't recognize "paper" as one of the options.

Q: Can I get Kotlin to ignore the case? Can I capitalize the user input before checking whether it's in the array?

A: Kotlin includes `toLowerCase`, `toUpperCase` and `capitalize` functions to create a lowercase, uppercase or capitalized version of a `String`. As an example, here's how you would use the `capitalize` function to capitalize the first letter of the `String` named `userInput`:

```
userInput = userInput.capitalize()
```

So you could convert the user input to an appropriate format before checking if it matches any of the values in the array.

Your Kotlin Toolbox

You've got Chapter 3 under your belt and now you've added functions to your toolbox.

You can download the full code for the chapter from https://tinyurl.com/HFKotlin.

BULLET POINTS

- Use functions to organize your code and make it more reusable.
- A function can have parameters, so you can pass more than one value to it.
- The number and type of values you pass to the function must match the order and type of the parameters declared by the function.
- A function can return a value. You must define the type of value (if any) it returns.
- A `Unit` return type means that the function doesn't return anything.
- Choose `for` loops over `while` loops when you know how many times you want to repeat the loop code.
- The `readLine()` function reads a line of input from the standard input stream. It returns a `String` value, the text entered by the user.
- If the input stream has been redirected to a file and the end of the file has been reached, the `readLine()` function returns `null`. `null` means it has no value, or it's missing.
- `&&` means "and". `||` means "or". `!` means "not".

4 classes and objects

A Bit of Class

It's time we looked beyond Kotlin's basic types.

Sooner or later, you're going to want to use something *more* than Kotlin's basic types. And that's where ***classes*** come in. Classes are *templates* that allow you to **create your own types of objects**, and define their properties and functions. Here, you'll learn **how to design and define classes**, and how to use them to **create new types of objects**. You'll meet ***constructors***, ***initializer blocks***, ***getters*** and ***setters***, and you'll discover how they can be used to protect your properties. Finally, you'll learn how **data hiding is built into *all* Kotlin code**, saving you time, effort and a multitude of keystrokes.

Object types are defined using classes

So far, you've learned how to create and use variables from Kotlin's basic types, such as numbers, `Strings` and arrays. You know, for example, that when you write the code:

```
var x = 6
```

this creates an `Int` object with a value of 6, and a reference to the object is assigned to a new variable named `x`:

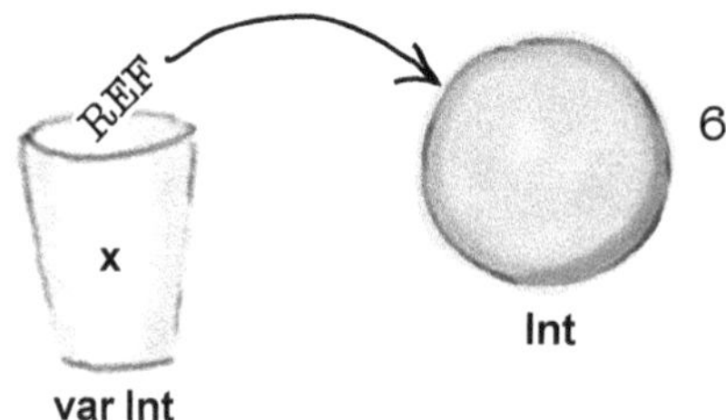

Behind the scenes, these types are defined using **classes**. A class is a template that defines what properties and functions are associated with objects of that type. When you create an `Int` object, for example, the compiler checks the `Int` class and sees that it requires an integer value, and has functions such as `toLong` and `toString`.

You can define your own classes

If you want your application to deal with types of objects that Kotlin doesn't have, you can define your own types by writing new classes. If you're building an application that records information about dogs, for example, you might want to define a `Dog` class so that you can create your own `Dog` objects, and record the name, weight and breed of each dog:

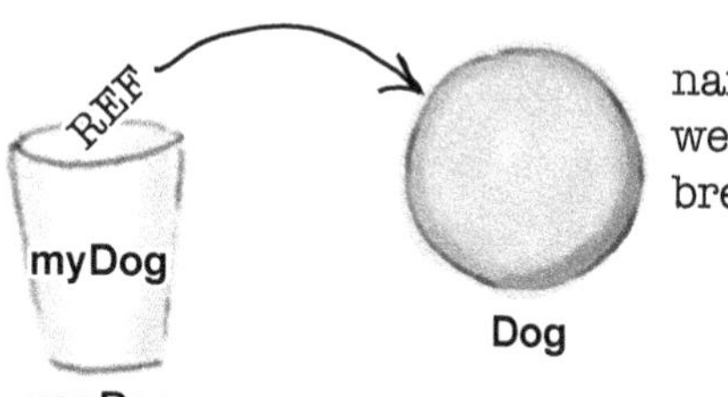

name: "Fido"
weight: 70
breed: "Mixed"

This is the Dog class. It tells the compiler that a Dog has a name, weight and breed, and a bark function.

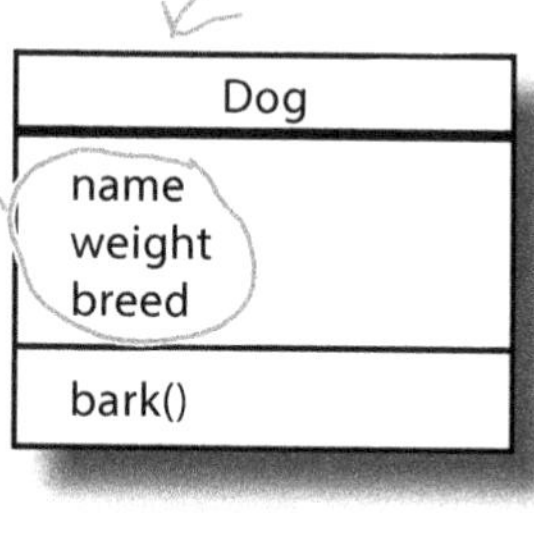

So how do you go about defining a class?

How to design your own classes

When you want to define your own class, you need to think about the objects that will be created from that class. You need to consider:

- **The things each object knows about itself.**
- **The things each object can do.**

The things an object knows about itself are its **properties**. They represent an object's state (the data), and each object of that type can have unique values. A `Dog` class, for example, might have `name`, `weight` and `breed` properties. A `Song` class might have `title` and `artist` properties.

The things an object can do are its **functions**. They determine an object's behavior, and may use the object's properties. The `Dog` class, for example, might have a `bark` function, and the `Song` class might have a `play` function.

Here are some examples of classes with their properties and functions:

The things an object knows about itself are its properties.

The things an object can do are its functions.

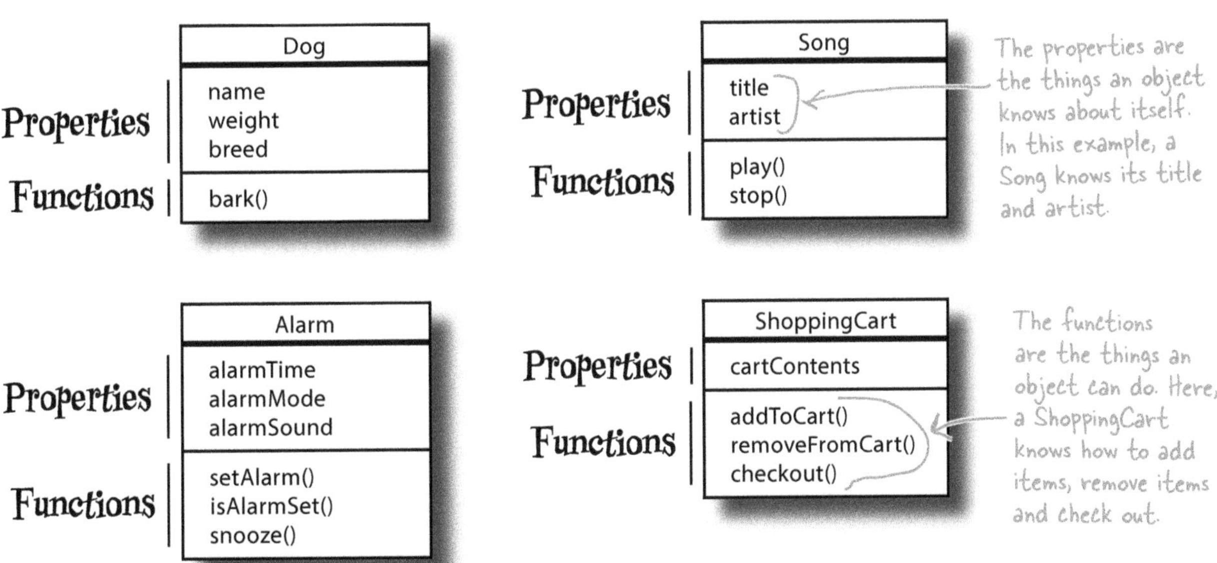

When you know what properties and functions your class should have, you're ready to write the code to create it. We'll look at this next.

Let's define a Dog class

We're going to create a Dog class that we can use to create Dog objects. Each Dog will have a name, weight and breed, so we'll use these for the class properties. We'll also define a bark function so that the size of the Dog's bark depends on its weight.

Here's what our Dog class code looks like:

"class" means it's a class.

The name of the class.

The class properties.

Opening brace of the class.

```
class Dog (val name: String, var weight: Int, val breed: String) {
    fun bark() {
        println(if (weight < 20) "Yip!" else "Woof!")
    }
}
```

The bark function.

Closing brace of the class.

Dog
name weight breed
bark()

The code:

```
class Dog(val name: String, var weight: Int, val breed: String) {
    ...
}
```

defines the name of the class (Dog), and the properties that the Dog class has. We'll take a closer look at what's going on behind the scenes a few pages ahead, but for now, all you need to know is that the above code defines the name, weight and breed properties—and when the Dog object is created, values are assigned to these properties.

You define any class functions in the class body (inside the curly braces { }). We're defining a bark function, so the code looks like this:

A function that's defined inside a class is called a member function. It's sometimes called a method.

```
class Dog(val name: String, var weight: Int, val breed: String) {
    fun bark() {
        println(if (weight < 20) "Yip!" else "Woof!")
    }
}
```

This is just like the functions you saw in the previous chapter. The only difference is that it's defined inside the Dog class body.

Now that you've seen the code for the Dog class, let's look at how you use it to create a Dog object.

How to create a Dog object

You can think of a class as a template for an object, as it tells the compiler how to make objects of that particular type. It tells the compiler what properties each object should have, and each object made from that class can have its own values. Each `Dog` object, for example, would have `name`, `weight` and `breed` properties, with each `Dog` having its own values.

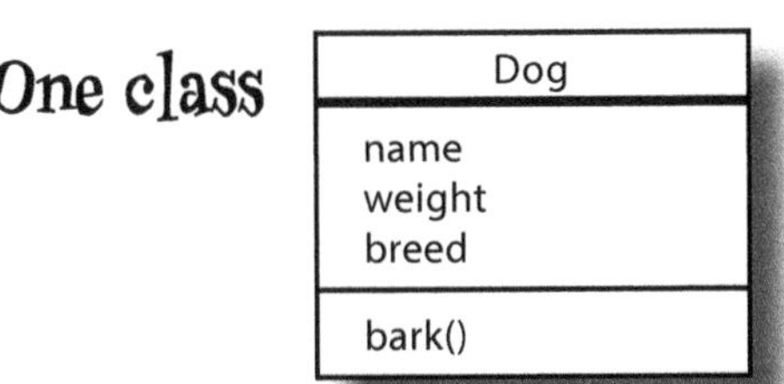

We're going to use the `Dog` class to create a `Dog` object, and assign it to a new variable named `myDog`. Here's the code:

```
var myDog = Dog("Fido", 70, "Mixed")
```

You create a Dog by passing it arguments for the three properties.

The code passes three arguments to the `Dog` object. These match the properties we defined in the `Dog` class: the `Dog`'s `name`, `weight` and `breed`:

```
class Dog(val name: String, var weight: Int, val breed: String) {
    ...
}
```

When the code runs, it creates a new `Dog` object, and the arguments are used to assign values to the `Dog`'s properties. In our case, for example, we're creating a new `Dog` object where the `name` property is "Fido", the `weight` property is 70 pounds, and the `breed` property is "Mixed":

Now that you've seen how to create a new `Dog` object, let's look at how you access its properties and functions.

How to access properties and functions

Once you've created an object, you can access its properties using the dot operator (`.`). If you wanted to print a `Dog`'s `name`, for example, you would use code like this:

```
var myDog = Dog("Fido", 70, "Mixed")
println(myDog.name)
```

myDog.name is like saying "go to myDog, and get its name".

You can also update any properties that you have defined using the `var` keyword. As an example, here's how you would update the `Dog`'s `weight` property to 75 pounds:

```
myDog.weight = 75
```

Go to myDog, and set its weight to 75.

Note that the compiler won't let you update any properties that you've defined using the `val` keyword. If you try to do so, you'll get a compiler error.

You can also use the dot operator to call an object's functions. If you wanted to call the `Dog`'s `bark` function, for example, you would use the following code:

```
myDog.bark()
```

Go to myDog, and call its bark function.

What if the Dog is in a Dog array?

You can also add any objects you create to an array. If you wanted to create an array of `Dog`s, for example, you would use code like this:

```
var dogs = arrayOf(Dog("Fido", 70, "Mixed"), Dog("Ripper", 10, "Poodle"))
```

This code creates two Dog objects, and adds them to an array<Dog> array named dogs.

This defines a variable named `dogs`, and as it's an array that you're populating with `Dog` objects, the compiler makes its type `array<Dog>`. Two `Dog` objects are then added to the array.

You can still access the properties and functions of each `Dog` object in the array. As an example, suppose you wanted to update the second `Dog`'s `weight` and make it `bark`. To do this, you would get a reference to the second item in the `dogs` array using `dogs[1]`, and then use the dot operator to access the `Dog`'s `weight` property and `bark` function:

```
dogs[1].weight = 15
dogs[1].bark()
```

The compiler knows that dogs[1] is a Dog object, so you can access the Dog's properties and call its functions.

This is like saying "get the second object from the *dogs* array, change its weight to 15 pounds, and make it bark."

Create a Songs application

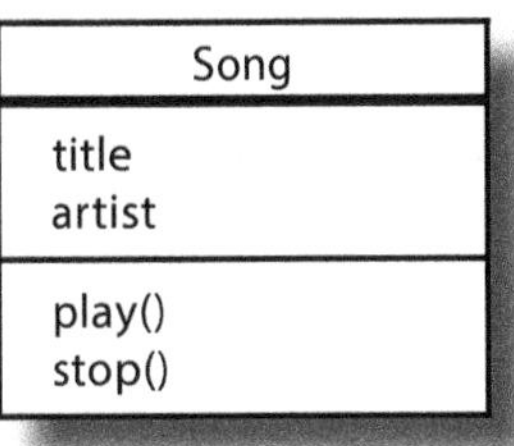

Before we go any further into how classes work, we're going to give you some more class practice by creating a new Songs project. We'll add a `Song` class to the project, and create and use some `Song` objects.

Create a new Kotlin project that targets the JVM, and name the project "Songs". Then create a new Kotlin file named *Songs.kt* by highlighting the *src* folder, clicking on the File menu and choosing New → Kotlin File/Class. When prompted, name the file "Songs", and choose File from the Kind option.

Next, add the following code to *Songs.kt*:

```
class Song(val title: String, val artist: String) {
    fun play() {
        println("Playing the song $title by $artist")
    }

    fun stop() {
        println("Stopped playing $title")
    }
}

fun main(args: Array<String>) {
    val songOne = Song("The Mesopotamians", "They Might Be Giants")
    val songTwo = Song("Going Underground", "The Jam")
    val songThree = Song("Make Me Smile", "Steve Harley")
    songTwo.play()
    songTwo.stop()
    songThree.play()
}
```

Define title and artist properties.

Add play and stop functions.

Create three Songs.

Play songTwo, stop it, then play songThree.

Songs
src
Songs.kt

Test drive

When we run the code, the following text gets printed in the IDE's output window:

```
Playing the song Going Underground by The Jam
Stopped playing Going Underground
Playing the song Make Me Smile by Steve Harley
```

Now that you've seen how to define a class and use it to create objects, let's dive into the mysterious world of object creation.

The miracle of object creation

When you declare and assign an object, there are three main steps:

1. **Declare a variable.**

```
var myDog = Dog("Fido", 70, "Mixed")
```

2. **Create an object.**

```
var myDog = Dog("Fido", 70, "Mixed")
```

3. **Link the object to the variable by assigning a reference.**

```
var myDog = Dog("Fido", 70, "Mixed")
```

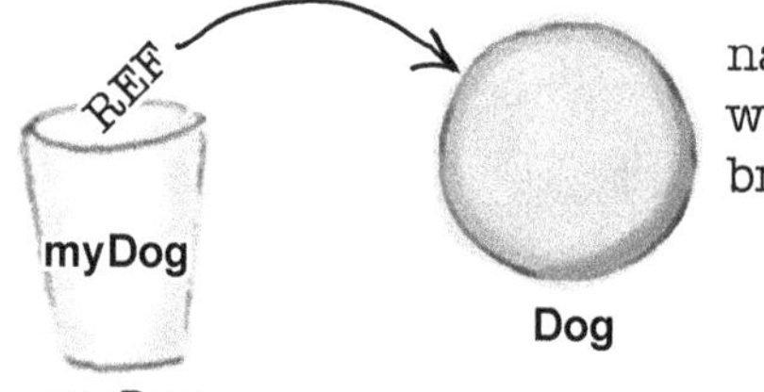

The big miracle happens at step two—when the object is created. There's a lot going on behind the scenes, so let's take a closer look.

How objects are created

When we define an object using code like:

```
var myDog = Dog("Fido", 70, "Mixed")
```

It **looks** like we're calling a function named Dog because of the parentheses.

it *looks* like we're calling a function named `Dog`. But even though it looks and feels a lot like a function, it's not. Instead, we're calling the `Dog` **constructor**.

A constructor contains the code that's needed to initialize an object. It runs before the object can be assigned to a reference, which means that you get a chance to step in, and do things to make the object ready for use. Most people use constructors to define an object's properties and assign values to them.

Each time you create a new object, the constructor for that object's class is invoked. So when you run the code:

```
var myDog = Dog("Fido", 70, "Mixed")
```

the `Dog` class constructor gets called.

A constructor runs when you instantiate an object. It's used to define properties and initialize them.

What the Dog constructor looks like

When we created our `Dog` class, we included a constructor; it's the parentheses and the code in between in the class header:

```
class Dog(val name: String, var weight: Int, val breed: String) {
    ...
}
```

This code (including the parentheses) is the class constructor. Technically, it's called the **primary** constructor.

The `Dog` constructor defines three properties—`name`, `weight` and `breed`. Each `Dog` has these properties, and when the `Dog` gets created, the constructor assigns a value to each property. This initializes the state of each `Dog`, and ensures that it's set up correctly.

Let's take a look at what happens behind the scenes when the `Dog` constructor gets called.

Behind the scenes: calling the Dog constructor

Let's go through what happens when we run the code:

```
var myDog = Dog("Fido", 70, "Mixed")
```

1. **The system creates an object for each argument that's passed to the Dog constructor.**
It creates a `String` with a value of "Fido", an `Int` with a value of 70, and a `String` with a value of "Mixed".

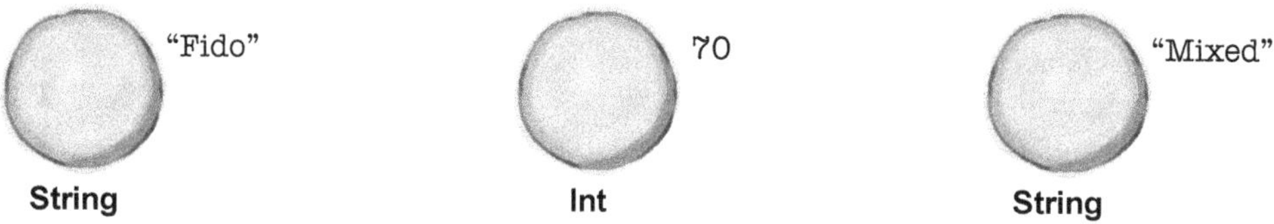

2. **The system allocates the space for a new Dog object, and the Dog constructor gets called.**

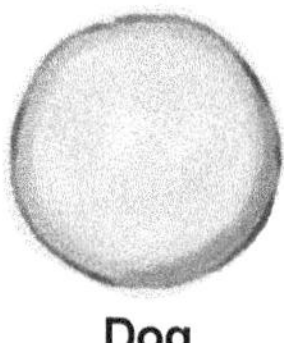

3. **The Dog constructor defines three properties: name, weight and breed.**
Behine the scenes, **each property is a variable**. A variable of the appropriate type is created for each property, as defined in the constructor.

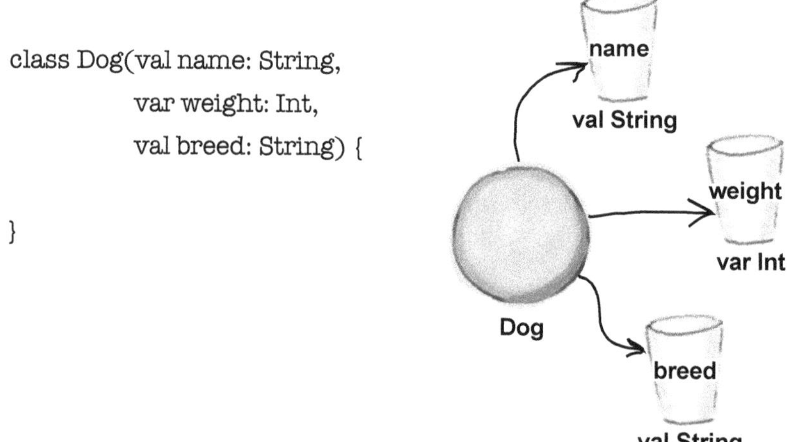

The story continues...

4 **Each of the Dog's property variables is assigned a reference to the appropriate value object.**

The `name` property, for example, is assigned a reference to the "Fido" `String` object, and so on.

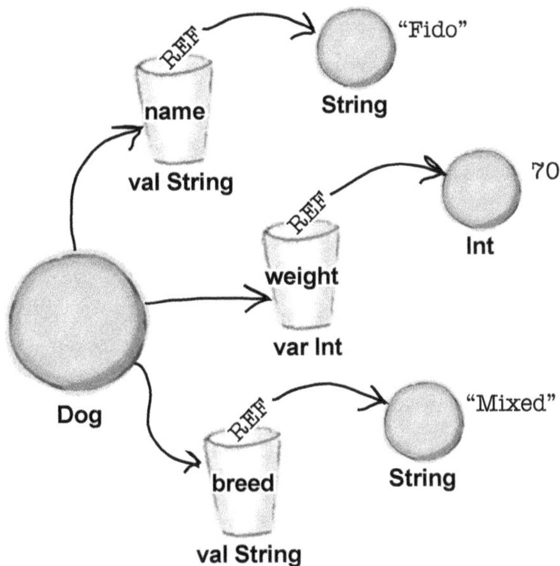

5 **Finally, a reference to the Dog object is assigned to a new Dog variable named myDog.**

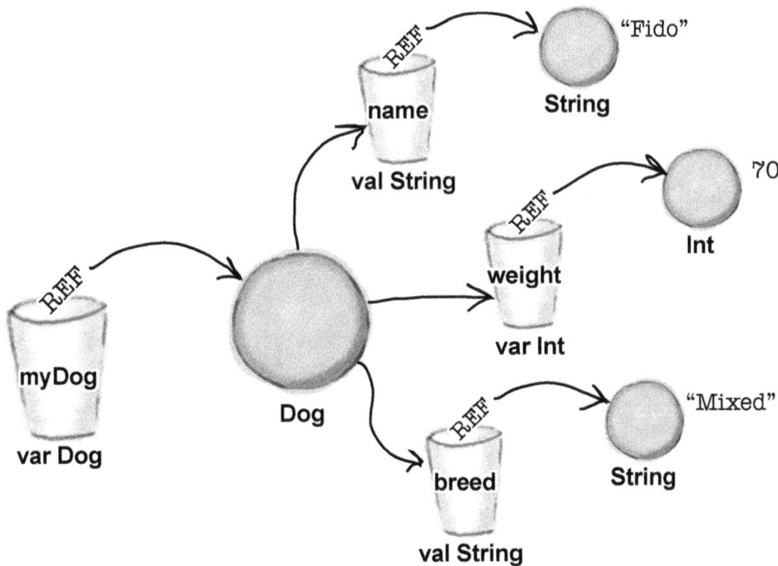

That's right—a property is a variable that's local to the object.

This means that everything you've already learned about variables applies to properties. If you define a property using the `val` keyword, for example, this means that you can't assign a new value to it. You can, however, update any properties that have been defined using `var`.

In our example, we're using `val` to define the `name` and `breed` properties, and `var` to define the `weight`:

```
class Dog(val name: String, var weight: Int, val breed: String) {
    ...
}
```

This means that we can only update the `Dog`'s `weight` property, and not the `Dog`'s `name` or `breed`.

there are no Dumb Questions

Q: Does the constructor allocate the memory for the object that's being created?

A: No, the system does. The constructor initializes the object, so it makes sure that the object's properties are created and that they're assigned their initial values. All memory is managed by the system.

Q: Can I define a class without defining a constructor?

A: Yes, you can. You'll find out how this works later in the chapter.

An object is sometimes known as an <u>instance</u> of a particular class, so its properties are sometimes called <u>instance variables</u>.

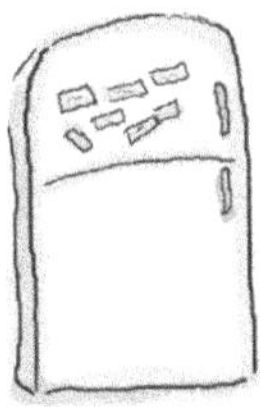

Code Magnets

Somebody used fridge magnets to write a noisy new **DrumKit** class, and a `main` function that prints the following output:

ding ding ba-da-bing!

bang bang bang!

ding ding ba-da-bing!

Unfortunately, the magnets have got scrambled. Can you piece the code back together again?

```
class DrumKit(var hasTopHat: Boolean, var hasSnare: Boolean) {

}

fun main(args: Array<String>) {

}
```

You need to put the magnets in these boxes.

Magnets:

```
println("ding ding ba-da-bing!")
{
d.hasSnare =
fun playSnare()
val d = DrumKit(true, true)
(hasSnare)
fun playTopHat()
}
(hasTopHat)
}
{
if
d.playTopHat()
d.playSnare()
d.playTopHat()
d.playSnare()
if
false
println("bang bang bang!")
```

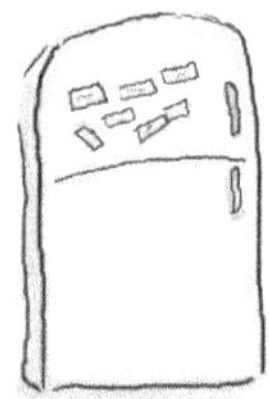

Code Magnets Solution

Somebody used fridge magnets to write a noisy new **DrumKit** class, and a `main` function that prints the following output:

ding ding ba-da-bing!
bang bang bang!
ding ding ba-da-bing!

Unfortunately, the magnets have got scrambled. Can you piece the code back together again?

```
class DrumKit(var hasTopHat: Boolean, var hasSnare: Boolean) {

    fun playTopHat() {
        if (hasTopHat) println("ding ding ba-da-bing!")
    }

    fun playSnare() {
        if (hasSnare) println("bang bang bang!")
    }
}
```

The playTopHat function prints some text if the hasTopHat property is true.

The playSnare function prints some text if the hasSnare property is true.

```
fun main(args: Array<String>) {
    val d = DrumKit(true, true)
    d.playTopHat()
    d.playSnare()
    d.hasSnare = false
    d.playTopHat()
    d.playSnare()
}
```

Create a DrumKit variable.

hasTopHat and hasSnare are both true, so playTopHat and playSnare both print text.

Setting the hasSnare property to false means that only the playTopHat function prints text.

Going deeper into properties

So far you've seen how to define a property by including it in the class constructor, and how doing so assigns a value to that property when the constructor is called. But what if you need to do something a little different? What if you want to validate a value before assigning it to a property? Or what if you want to initialize a property with a generic default value so that you don't need to add it to the class constructor?

To find out how you can do this kind of thing, we need to take a closer look at constructor code.

Behind the scenes of the Dog constructor

As you already know, our current `Dog` constructor code defines three properties for the `name`, `weight` and `breed` of each `Dog` object, and assigns a value to each one when the `Dog` constructor is called:

```
class Dog(val name: String, var weight: Int, val breed: String) {
    ...
}
```

You can do this so concisely because the constructor code uses a shortcut for performing this kind of task. When the Kotlin language was developed, the brains behind it felt that defining and initializing properties was such a common action that it was worth making the syntax to do it very concise and simple.

If you were to perform the same action without using the shortcut, here's what the code would look like:

The constructor parameters no longer have val and var prefixes, so the constructor no longer creates properties for them.

```
class Dog(name_param: String, weight_param: Int, breed_param: String) {
    val name = name_param
    var weight = weight_param
    val breed = breed_param

    ...
}
```

The properties are defined in the class body instead.

Dog
name weight breed
bark()

Here, the three constructor parameters—`name_param`, `weight_param` and `breed_param`—have no `val` and `var` prefixes, which means that they no longer define properties. They are plain old parameters, just like the ones you see in function definitions. The `name`, `weight` and `breed` properties are instead defined in the main body of the class. Each one is assigned the value of the associated constructor parameter.

So how does this allow us to do more with our properties?

Flexible property initialization

Defining properties in the main body of the class gives you a lot more flexibility than adding them to the constructor, as it means that you no longer have to initialize each one with a parameter value.

Dog
name weight breed activities
bark()

Suppose that you wanted to assign a default value to a property without including it in the constructor. You might, for example, want to add an `activities` property to the `Dog` class, and initialize it with a default array containing a value of "Walks". Here's the code to do this:

```
class Dog(val name: String, var weight: Int, val breed: String) {
    var activities = arrayOf("Walks")
    ...
}
```

Each Dog object that's created will have an activities property. It's initial value will be an array containing a value of "Walks".

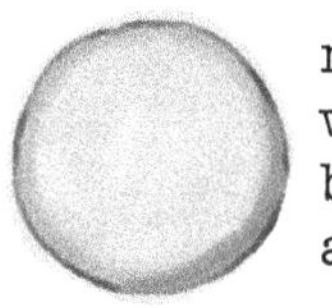

Alternatively, you might want to tweak the value of a constructor parameter before assigning it to a property. You might, for example, want to record an uppercase `String` for the `breed` property instead of the value that's passed to the constructor. To do this, you would use the `toUpperCase` function to create an uppercase version of the `String`, which you would then assign to the `breed` property like this:

```
class Dog(val name: String, var weight: Int, breed_param: String) {
    var activities = arrayOf("Walks")
    val breed = breed_param.toUpperCase()
    ...
}
```

This takes the value of breed_param, makes it uppercase, and assigns it to the breed property.

Initializing a property in this way works well if you want to assign a simple value or expression to it. But what if you need to do something more complex?

How to use initializer blocks

If you need to initialize a property to something more complex than a simple expression, or if there's extra code you want to run when each object is created, you can use one or more **initializer blocks**. Initializer blocks are executed when the object is initialized, immediately after the constructor is called, and they're prefixed with the **init** keyword. Here's an example of an initializer block that prints a message whenever a Dog object is initialized:

```
class Dog(val name: String, var weight: Int, breed_param: String) {
    var activities = arrayOf("Walks")
    val breed = breed_param.toUpperCase()

    init {
        println("Dog $name has been created.")
    }

    ...
}
```

This is an initializer block. It contains the code that you want to runs when the Dog object is initialized.

Dog
name weight breed activities
bark()

Your class can have multiple initializer blocks. Each one runs in the order in which it appears in the class body, interleaved with any property initializers. Here's an example of some code with multiple initializer blocks:

```
class Dog(val name: String, var weight: Int, breed_param: String) {

    init {
        println("Dog $name has been created.")
    }

    var activities = arrayOf("Walks")
    val breed = breed_param.toUpperCase()

    init {
        println("The breed is $breed.")
    }

    ...
}
```

The properties defined in the constructor are created first.

This initializer block runs next.

These properties are created after the first initializer block has finished.

The second initializer block runs after the properties have been created.

As you've seen, there are various ways in which you can initialize your variables. But is it necessary?

You MUST initialize your properties

Back in Chapter 2, you learned that every variable you declare in a function must be initialized before it can be used. This also applies to any properties you define in a class: **you must initialize properties before you try to use them**. This is so important that if you declare a property without initializing it in either the property declaration or the initializer block, the compiler will get very upset and refuse to compile your code. The following code, for example, won't compile because we've added a new property named `temperament` which hasn't been initialized:

```
class Dog(val name: String, var weight: Int, breed_param: String) {
    var activities = arrayOf("Walks")
    val breed = breed_param.toUpperCase()
    var temperament: String   // The temperament property hasn't been initialized, so the code won't compile.

    ...
}
```

Nearly all of the time, you'll be able to assign default values to your properties. In the above example, for instance, your code will compile if you initialize the `temperament` property to `""`:

```
var temperament = ""   // This initializes the temperament property with an empty String.
```

Q: In Java, you don't have to initialize the variables that you declare inside a class. Is there a way of not initializing class properties in Kotlin?

A: If you're completely certain that you can't assign an initial value to a property when you call the class constructor, you can prefix it with **`lateinit`**. This tells the compiler that you're aware that the property hasn't been initialized yet, and you'll handle it later. If you wanted to mark the *temperament* property for late initialization, for example, you'd use:

```
lateinit var temperament: String
```

Doing so allows the compiler to compile your code. In general, however, we strongly encourage you to initialize your properties.

Q: What happens if I try to use a property value before it's been initialized?

A: If you don't initialize a property before you try and use it, you'll get a runtime error when you run the code.

Q: Can I use `lateinit` with any type of property?

A: You can only use `lateinit` with properties defined using `var`, and you can't use it with any of the following types: `Byte`, `Short`, `Int`, `Long`, `Double`, `Float`, `Char` or `Boolean`. This is down to how these types are treated when the code runs in the JVM. This means that properties of any of these types must be initialized when the property is defined, or in an initializer block.

Empty Constructors Up Close

If you want to be able to quickly create objects without passing values for any of its properties, you can define a class with no constructor.

Suppose, for example, that you wanted to quickly create Duck objects. To do this, you could define a Duck class without a constructor like this:

```
class Duck {  <- There's no () after the name of the class, so the class has no defined constructor.

    fun quack() {
        println("Quack! Quack! Quack!")
    }
}
```

When you define a class with no constructor, the compiler secretly writes one for you. It adds an *empty constructor* (a constructor with no parameters) to your compiled code. So when you compile the above Duck class, the compiler treats it as though you'd written the following code:

```
class Duck() {

    fun quack() {
        println("Quack! Quack! Quack!")
    }
}
```

This is an empty constructor: a constructor with no parameters. Behind the scenes, whenever you define a class with no constructor, the compiler adds an empty constructor to your compiled code.

This means that in order to create a Duck object, you use the code:

```
var myDuck = Duck()  <- Creates a Duck variable named myDuck, and assigns it a reference to a Duck object.
```

and not:

```
var myDuck = Duck  <- This code won't compile.
```

The compiler has created an empty constructor for the Duck class on your behalf, so this means that you *must* call the empty constructor in order to instantiate the Duck.

BE the Compiler

Each of the Kotlin files on this page represents a complete source file. Your job is to play like you're the compiler and determine whether each of these files will compile. If they won't compile, how would you fix them?

A

```
class TapeDeck {
    var hasRecorder = false

    fun playTape() {
        println("Tape playing")
    }

    fun recordTape() {
        if (hasRecorder) {
            println ("Tape recording")
        }
    }
}

fun main(args: Array<String>) {
    t.hasRecorder = true
    t.playTape()
    t.recordTape()
}
```

B

```
class DVDPlayer(var hasRecorder: Boolean) {

    fun recordDVD() {
        if (hasRecorder) {
            println ("DVD recording")
        }
    }
}

fun main(args: Array<String>) {
    val d = DVDPlayer(true)
    d.playDVD()
    d.recordDVD()
}
```

Answers on page 119.

How do you validate property values?

Earlier in the chapter, you learned how to directly get or set a property's value using the dot operator. You already know, for example, that you can print the Dog's name using:

```
println(myDog.name)
```

and that you can set its weight to 75 pounds using:

```
myDog.weight = 75
```

But in the hands of the wrong person, allowing direct access to all our properties in this way can be quite a dangerous weapon. Because what's to prevent someone writing the following code:

```
myDog.weight = -1
```

Cripes.

A Dog with negative weight would be a Bad Thing.

To stop this kind of thing from happening, we need some way of validating a value before it's assigned to a property.

The solution: custom getters and setters

If you want to tweak a property's return value, or validate a value before it gets assigned to a property, you can write your own **getters and setters**.

Getters and setters let you, well, get and set property values. A getter's sole purpose in life is to send back a return value, the value of whatever it is that particular getter is supposed to be getting. And a setter lives and breathes for the chance to take an argument value, and use it to set the value of a property.

If you're into being all formal about it, you might prefer to call them accessors and mutators instead.

Writing custom getters and setters lets you protect your property values, and they give you more control over what values are returned or assigned. We'll show you how they work by adding two new things to our Dog class:

- **A custom getter to return the Dog's weight in kilograms.**
- **A custom setter to validate a proposed value for the Dog's weight before we assign it.**

Let's start by creating a custom getter to return the Dog's weight in kilograms.

How to write a custom getter

In order to add a custom getter that will allow us to return the Dog's weight in kilograms, we're going to do two things: add a new property to the Dog class named weightInKgs, and write a custom getter for it which will return the appropriate value. Here's the code to do both these things:

```
class Dog(val name: String, var weight: Int, breed_param: String) {
    var activities = arrayOf("Walks")
    val breed = breed_param.toUpperCase()
    val weightInKgs: Double
        get() = weight / 2.2
    ...
}
```

This code adds a new weightInKgs property with a custom getter. The getter takes the value of the weight parameter, and divides it by 2.2 to get the weight in kilograms.

Dog
name weight breed activities weightInKgs
bark()

The line:

```
get() = weight / 2.2
```

defines the getter. It's a no parameter function named **get** that you add to the property. You add it to the property by writing it immediately below the property declaration. Its return type **must** match that of the property whose value you want to return or the code won't compile. In the above example, the weightInKgs property is a Double, so the property's getter must also return a Double.

Technically, getters and setters are optional parts of the property declaration.

Each time you ask for the value of a property using code like:

```
myDog.weightInKgs
```

the property's getter gets called. The above code, for example, calls the getter for the weightInKgs property. The getter uses the Dog's weight property to calculate the Dog's weight in kilograms, and returns the result.

Note that in this example, we didn't need to initialize the weightInKgs property because its value is derived in the getter. Each time the property's value is required, the getter is called, which figures out the value that should be returned.

Now that you know how to add a custom getter, let's look at how you add a custom setter by adding one to the weight property.

there are no Dumb Questions

Q: Couldn't we have written a normal function to return the weight in kilograms?

A: We could, but sometimes it's useful to create a new property with a getter instead. Many frameworks, for example, let you bind a GUI component to a property, so creating a new property in this sort of situation can make your coding life a lot easier.

How to write a custom setter

We're going to add a custom setter to the weight property so that the weight can only be updated to a value greater than 0. To do this, we need to move the weight property definition from the constructor to the class body, and then add the setter to the property. Here's the code to do that:

```
class Dog(val name: String, weight_param: Int, breed_param: String) {
    var activities = arrayOf("Walks")
    val breed = breed_param.toUpperCase()
    var weight = weight_param
        set(value) {
            if (value > 0) field = value
        }
    ...
}
```

This code adds a custom setter to the weight property. The setter means that the value of the weight property will only get updated to a value greater than 0.

The following code defines the setter:

```
set(value) {
    if (value > 0) field = value
}
```

A setter is a function named **set** that's added to the property by writing it beneath the property declaration. A setter has one parameter—usually named value—which is the proposed new value of the property.

In the above example, the value of the weight property is only updated if the value parameter is greater than 0. If you try and update the weight property to a value that's less than or equal to 0, the setter stops the property from being updated.

The setter updates the value of the weight property by means of the **field** identifier. field refers to the property's backing field, which you can think of as being a reference to the underlying value of the property. Using field in your getters and setters in place of the property name is important, as it stops you getting stuck in an endless loop. When the following setter code runs, for example, the system tries to update the weight property, which results in the setter being called again... and again... and again:

```
var weight = weight_param
    set(value) {
        if (value > 0) weight = value
    }
```

Don't do this! You'll get stuck in an endless loop. Use field instead.

A property's setter runs each time you try to set a property's value. The following code, for example, calls the weight property's setter, passing it a value of 75:

myDog.weight = 75

Data Hiding Up Close

As you've seen over the past few pages, writing custom getters and setters means that you can protect your properties from misuse. A custom getter lets you control what value is returned when the property value is requested, and a custom setter lets you validate a value before asigning it to a property.

Behind the scenes, the compiler secretly creates getters and setters for all properties that don't already have one. If a property is defined using `val`, the compiler adds a getter, and if a property is defined using `var`, the compiler adds both a getter and a setter. So when you write the code:

A val property doesn't need a setter because once it's been initialized, its value can't be updated.

```
var myProperty: String
```

the compiler secretly adds the following getters and setters when the code is compiled:

```
var myProperty: String
    get() = field
    set(value) {
        field = value
    }
```

This means that whenever you use the dot operator to get or set a property's value, behind the scenes **its always the property's getter or setter that gets called**.

So why does the compiler do this?

Adding a getter and setter to every property means that there's a standard way of accessing that property's value. The getter handles any requests to get the value, and the setter handles any requests to set it. So if you want to change your mind about how these requests are implemented, you can do so without breaking anybody else's code.

Removing direct access to a property's value by wrapping it in getters and setters is known as data hiding.

The full code for the Dogs project

We're nearly at the end of the chapter, but before we go, we thought we'd show you the entire code for the Dogs project.

Create a new Kotlin project that targets the JVM, and name the project "Dogs". Then create a new Kotlin file named *Dogs.kt* by highlighting the *src* folder, clicking on the File menu and choosing New → Kotlin File/Class. When prompted, name the file "Dogs", and choose File from the Kind option.

Next, add the following code to *Dogs.kt*:

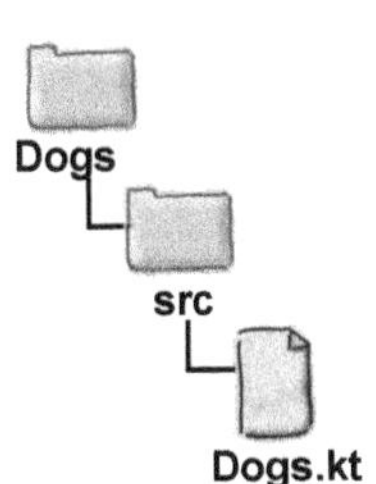


```
class Dog(val name: String,
          weight_param: Int,
          breed_param: String) {

    init {
        print("Dog $name has been created. ")
    }

    var activities = arrayOf("Walks")
    val breed = breed_param.toUpperCase()

    init {
        println("The breed is $breed.")
    }

    var weight = weight_param
        set(value) {
            if (value > 0) field = value
        }

    val weightInKgs: Double
        get() = weight / 2.2

    fun bark() {
        println(if (weight < 20) "Yip!" else "Woof!")
    }
}
```

The code continued...

Dogs
src
Dogs.kt

```
fun main(args: Array<String>) {
    val myDog = Dog("Fido", 70, "Mixed")
    myDog.bark()
    myDog.weight = 75
    println("Weight in Kgs is ${myDog.weightInKgs}")
    myDog.weight = -2
    println("Weight is ${myDog.weight}")
    myDog.activities = arrayOf("Walks", "Fetching balls", "Frisbee")
    for (item in myDog.activities) {
        println("My dog enjoys $item")
    }

    val dogs = arrayOf(Dog("Kelpie", 20, "Westie"), Dog("Ripper", 10, "Poodle"))
    dogs[1].bark()
    dogs[1].weight = 15
    println("Weight for ${dogs[1].name} is ${dogs[1].weight}")
}
```

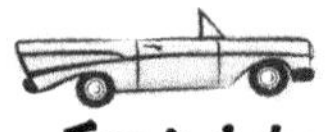

Test drive

When we run the code, the following text gets printed in the IDE's output window:

```
Dog Fido has been created. The breed is MIXED.
Woof!
Weight in Kgs is 34.090909090909086
Weight is 75
My dog enjoys Walks
My dog enjoys Fetching balls
My dog enjoys Frisbee
Dog Kelpie has been created. The breed is WESTIE.
Dog Ripper has been created. The breed is POODLE.
Yip!
Weight for Ripper is 15
```

Pool Puzzle

Your **job** is to take code snippets from the pool and place them into the blank lines in the code. You may **not** use the same code snippet more than once, and you won't need to use all the snippets. Your **goal** is to create the code that will produce the output listed.

The code needs to produce this output.

Rectangle 0 has area 15. It is not a square.
Rectangle 1 has area 36. It is a square.
Rectangle 2 has area 63. It is not a square.
Rectangle 3 has area 96. It is not a square.

```
class Rectangle(var width: Int, var height: Int) {
    val isSquare: Boolean
        ..........(width == height)

    val area: Int
        ..........(width * height)
}

fun main(args: Array<String>) {
    val r = arrayOf(Rectangle(1, 1), Rectangle(1, 1),
                    Rectangle(1, 1), Rectangle(1, 1))
    for (x in 0.......) {
        .......width = (x + 1) * 3
        .......height = x + 5
        print("Rectangle $x has area ${..................}. ")
        println("It is ${if (..................) "" else "not "}a square.")
    }
}
```

Note: each thing from the pool can only be used once!

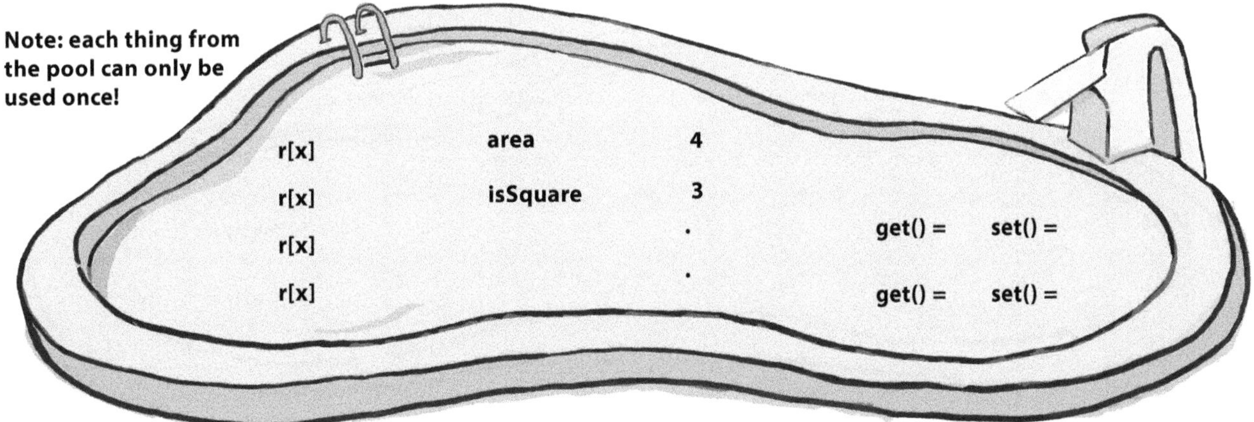

Pool Puzzle Solution

Your **job** is to take code snippets from the pool and place them into the blank lines in the code. You may **not** use the same code snippet more than once, and you won't need to use all the snippets. Your **goal** is to create the code that will produce the output listed.

```
Rectangle 0 has area 15. It is not a square.
Rectangle 1 has area 36. It is a square.
Rectangle 2 has area 63. It is not a square.
Rectangle 3 has area 96. It is not a square.
```

```
class Rectangle(var width: Int, var height: Int) {
    val isSquare: Boolean
        get() = (width == height)
    val area: Int
        get() = (width * height)
}

fun main(args: Array<String>) {
    val r = arrayOf(Rectangle(1, 1), Rectangle(1, 1),
                    Rectangle(1, 1), Rectangle(1, 1))
    for (x in 0..3) {
        r[x].width = (x + 1) * 3
        r[x].height = x + 5
        print("Rectangle $x has area ${r[x].area}. ")
        println("It is ${if (r[x].isSquare) "" else "not "}a square.")
    }
}
```

This is a getter that says whether a rectangle is square.

This is a getter that calculates the rectangle's area.

The r array has 4 items, so we'll loop from index 0 to index 3.

Set the width and height of the rectangle.

Print the rectangle's area.

Print whether or not the rectangle is a square.

You didn't need to use these snippets.

4

set() =

set() =

BE the Compiler Solution

Each of the Kotlin files on this page represents a complete source file. Your job is to play like you're the compiler and determine whether each of these files will compile. If they won't compile, how would you fix them?

A

```
class TapeDeck {
    var hasRecorder = false

    fun playTape() {
        println("Tape playing")
    }

    fun recordTape() {
        if (hasRecorder) {
            println ("Tape recording")
        }
    }
}

fun main(args: Array<String>) {
    val t = TapeDeck()
    t.hasRecorder = true
    t.playTape()
    t.recordTape()
}
```

This won't compile because you need to create a TapeDeck object before you can use it.

```
class DVDPlayer(var hasRecorder: Boolean) {

    fun playDVD() {
        println("DVD playing")
    }

    fun recordDVD() {
        if (hasRecorder) {
            println ("DVD recording")
        }
    }
}

fun main(args: Array<String>) {
    val d = DVDPlayer(true)
    d.playDVD()
    d.recordDVD()
}
```

This won't compile because the DVDPlayer class needs to have a playDVD function.

CHAPTER 4

Your Kotlin Toolbox

You've got Chapter 4 under your belt and now you've added classes and objects to your toolbox.

You can download the full code for the chapter from https://tinyurl.com/HFKotlin.

BULLET POINTS

- Classes let you define your own types.
- A class is a template for an object. One class can create many objects.
- The things an object knows about itself are its properties. The things an object can do are its functions.
- A property is a variable that's local to the class.
- The `class` keyword defines a class.
- Use the dot operator to access an object's properties and functions.
- A constructor runs when you initialize an object.
- You can define a property in the primary constructor by prefixing a parameter with `val` or `var`. You can define a property outside the constructor by adding it to the class body.
- Initializer blocks run when an object is initialized.
- You must initialize each property before you use its value.
- Getters and setters let you get and set property values.
- Behind the scenes, the compiler adds a default getter and setter to every property.

5 subclasses and superclasses

Ever found yourself thinking that an object's type would be perfect if you could just change a few things?

Well, that's one of the advantages of **inheritance**. Here, you'll learn how to create **subclasses**, and inherit the properties and functions of a **superclass**. You'll discover ***how to override functions and properties*** to make your classes behave the way *you* want, and you'll find out when this is (and isn't) appropriate. Finally, you'll see how inheritance helps you **avoid duplicate code**, and how to improve your flexibility with **polymorphism**.

Inheritance helps you avoid duplicate code

When you develop larger applications with multiple classes, you need to start thinking about **inheritance**. When you design with inheritance, you put common code in one class, and then allow other more specific classes to inherit this code. When you need to modify the code, you only have to update it in one place, and the changes are reflected in all the classes that inherit that behavior.

The class that contains the common code is called the **superclass**, and the classes that inherit from it are called **subclasses.**

A superclass is sometimes called a base class, and a subclass is sometimes called a derived class. In this book, we're sticking with superclass and subclass.

An inheritance example

Suppose you have two classes named `Car` and `ConvertibleCar`.

The `Car` class includes the properties and functions required to create a generic car, such as `make` and `model` properties, and functions named `accelerate`, `applyBrake` and `changeTemperature`.

The `ConvertibleCar` class is a subclass of the `Car` class, so it automatically inherits all the `Car` properties and functions. But the `ConvertibleCar` class can also add new functions and properties of its own, and override the things it inherits from the `Car` superclass:

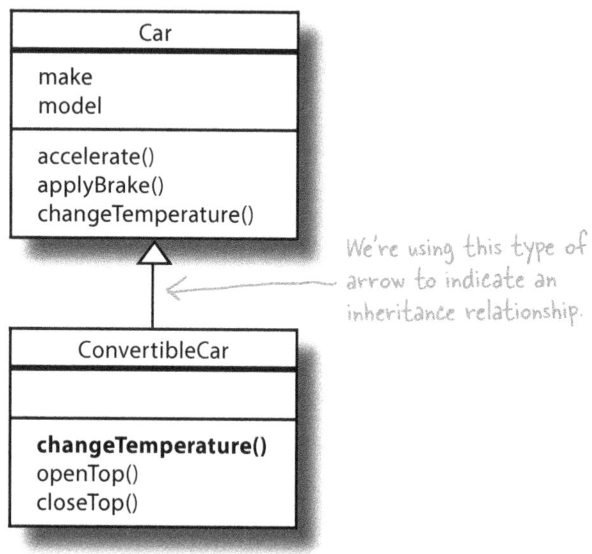

The `ConvertibleCar` class adds two extra functions named `openTop` and `closeTop`. It also overrides the `changeTemperature` function so that if the car gets too cold when the roof is open, it closes the roof.

A superclass contains common properties and functions that are inherited by one or more subclasses.

A subclass can include extra properties and functions, and can override the things that it inherits.

What we're going to do

In this chapter, we're going to teach you how to design and code an inheritance class hierarchy. We're going to do this in three stages:

1. **Design an animal class hierarchy.**
   We'll take a bunch of animals, and design an inheritance structure for them. We'll take you through a set of general steps for designing with inheritance which you can then apply to your own projects.

2. **Write the code for (part of) the animal class hierarchy.**
   Once we've designed the inheritance, we'll write the code for some of the classes.

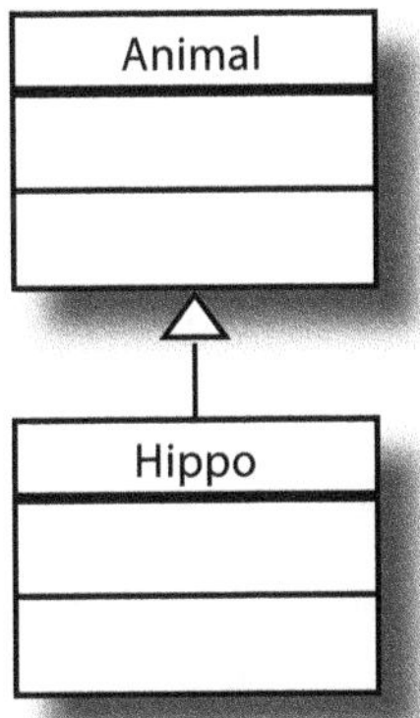

3. **Write code that uses the animal class hierarchy.**
   We'll look at how to use the inheritance structure to write more flexible code.

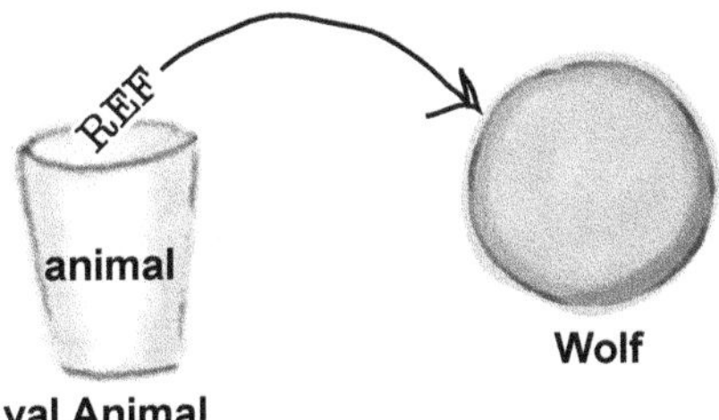

We'll start by designing the animal inheritance structure.

Design an animal class inheritance structure

Design classes
Build classes
Use classes

Imagine you've been asked to design the class structure for an animal simulation program that lets the user add a bunch of different animals to an environment to see what happens.

We're not going to code the whole application, we're mostly interested in the class design.

We know *some* of the types of animal that will be included in the application, but not all. Each animal will be represented by an object, and it will do whatever it is that each particular type of animal is programmed to do.

We want to be able to add new kinds of animals to the application later on, so it's important that our class design is flexible enough to accommodate this.

Before we start thinking about specific animals, we need to figure out the characteristics that are common to all the animals. We can then build these characteristics into a superclass that all the animal subclasses can inherit from.

We're going to guide you through the general steps for designing a class inheritance hierarchy. This is the first step.

Look for attributes and behaviors that the objects have in common.

Look at these types of animal. What do they have in common?

This helps you to abstract out attributes and behaviors that can be added to the superclass.

- → ☐ **Design classes**
- ☐ Build classes
- ☐ Use classes

Use inheritance to avoid duplicate code in subclasses

We're going to add some common properties and functions to an **`Animal`** superclass so that they can be inherited by each of the animal subclasses. This isn't meant to be an exhaustive list, but it's enough for you to get the general idea.

We'll have four **properties**:

`image`: The file name representing an image of this animal.

`food`: The type of food this animal eats, such as meat or grass.

`habitat`: The animal's primary habitat, such as woodland, savannah or water.

`hunger` : An Int representing the hunger level of the animal. It changes depending on when (and how much) the animal eats.

And four **functions**:

`makeNoise()`: Lets the animal make a noise.

`eat()`: What the animal does when it encounters its preferred food source.

`roam()`: What the animal does when it's not eating or sleeping.

`sleep()`: Makes the animal take a nap.

2 **Design a superclass that represents the common state and behavior.**

We'll put properties and functions common to all the animals into a new superclass named `Animal`. All of the animal subclasses will inherit these properties and functions.

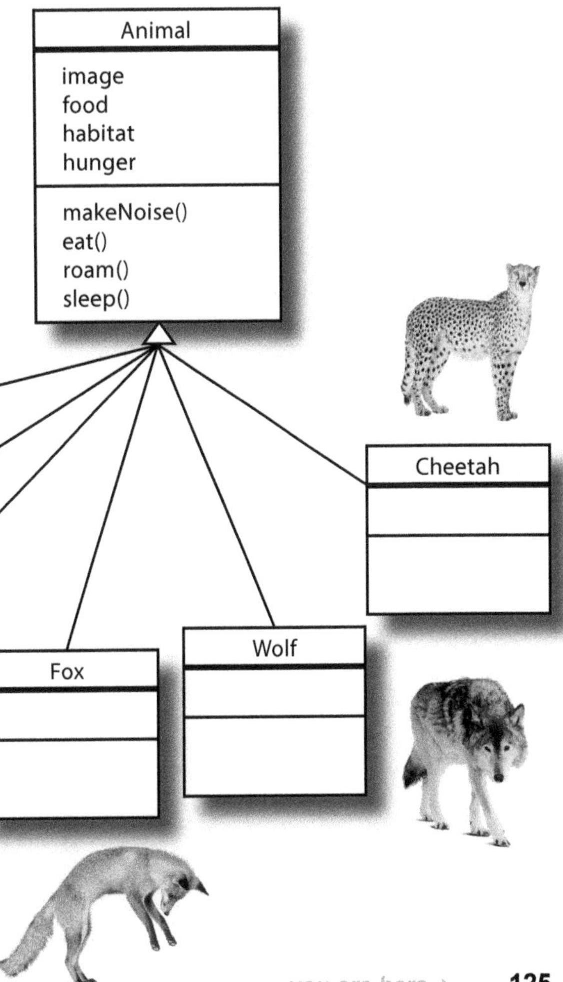

What should the subclasses override?

Next, we need to think about which properties and functions the animal subclasses should override. We'll start with the properties.

The animals have different property values...

The `Animal` superclass has properties named `image`, `food`, `habitat` and `hunger`, and all of these properties are inherited by the animal subclasses.

All of our animals look different, live in different habitats, and have different dietary requirements. This means that we can override the `image`, `food` and `habitat` properties so that they're initialized in a different way for each type of animal. We can initialize the `Hippo` `habitat` property with a value of "water", for example, and set the `Lion`'s `food` property to "meat".

3 **Decide if a subclass needs default property values or function implementations that are specific to that subclass.** In this example, we'll override the `image`, `food` and `habitat` properties, and the `makeNoise` and `eat` functions.

...and different function implementations

Each animal subclass inherits functions named `makeNoise`, `eat`, `roam` and `sleep` from the `Animal` superclass. So which of these functions can we override?

Lions roar, wolves howl and hippos grunt. All of the animals make different noises, which means that we should override the `makeNoise` function in each animal subclass. Each subclass will still include a `makeNoise` function, but the implementation of this function will vary from animal to animal.

Similarly, each animal eats, but *how* it eats can vary. A hippo grazes on grass, for example, while a cheetah hunts meat. To accommodate these different eating habits, we'll override the `eat` function in each animal subclass.

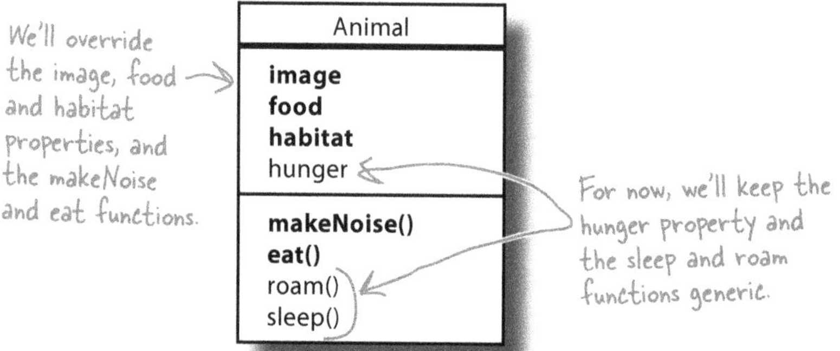

We can group some of the animals

The class hierarchy is starting to shape up. We have each subclass overriding a bunch of properties and functions, so that there's no mistaking a wolf's howl for a hippo's grunt.

But there's more that we can do. When you design with inheritance, you can build a whole **hierarchy of classes** that inherit from each other, starting with the topmost superclass and working down. In our example, we can look at the animal subclasses, and see if two or more can be grouped together in some way, and given code that's common to only that group. A wolf and fox are both types of canine, for example, so there may be common behavior that we can abstract out into a `Canine` class. Similarly, a lion, cheetah and lynx are all types of feline, so it might be helpful to add a new `Feline` class.

Look for more opportunities to abstract out properties and functions by finding two or more subclasses with common behavior.

When we look at our subclasses, we see that we have two canines, three felines and a hippo (which is neither).

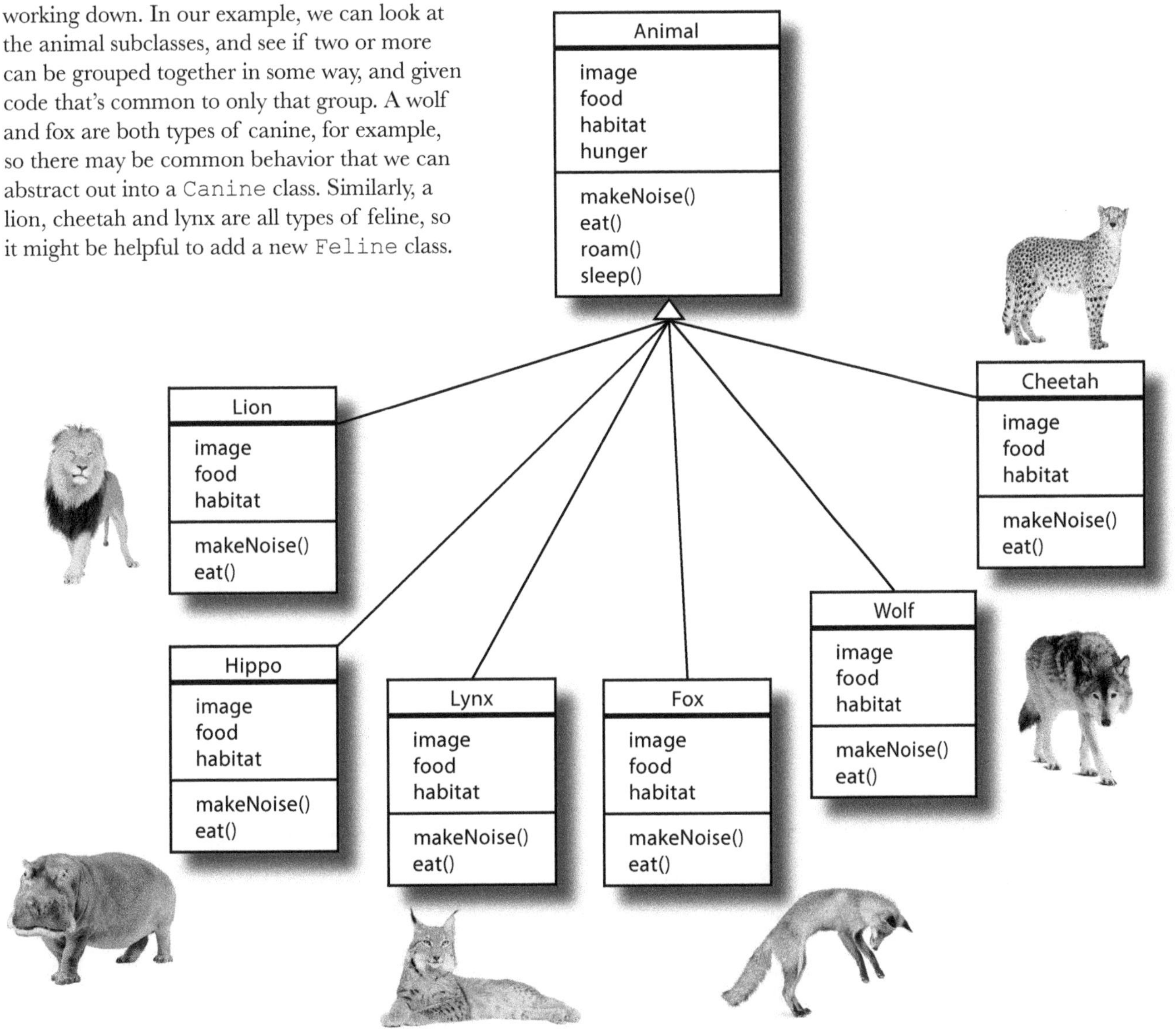

Animal
image
food
habitat
hunger
makeNoise()
eat()
roam()
sleep()

Lion
image
food
habitat
makeNoise()
eat()

Cheetah
image
food
habitat
makeNoise()
eat()

Hippo
image
food
habitat
makeNoise()
eat()

Lynx
image
food
habitat
makeNoise()
eat()

Fox
image
food
habitat
makeNoise()
eat()

Wolf
image
food
habitat
makeNoise()
eat()

Add Canine and Feline classes

Design classes
Build classes
Use classes

Animals already have an organizational hierarchy, so we can reflect this in our class design at the level that makes most sense. We'll use the biological families to organize the animals by adding `Canine` and `Feline` classes to our class hierarchy. The `Canine` class will contain properties and functions common to canines such as wolves and foxes, and the `Feline` class will contain the properties and functions that cats such as lions, cheetahs and lynx have in common.

Each subclass can also define its own properties and functions, but here we're just concentrating on the animals' commonality.

5 **Complete the class hierarchy.**
We'll override the `roam` function in both the `Canine` and `Feline` classes because these groups of animal tend to roam in ways that are similar enough for the simulation program. We'll let the `Hippo` class continue to use the generic `roam` function it inherits from `Animal`.

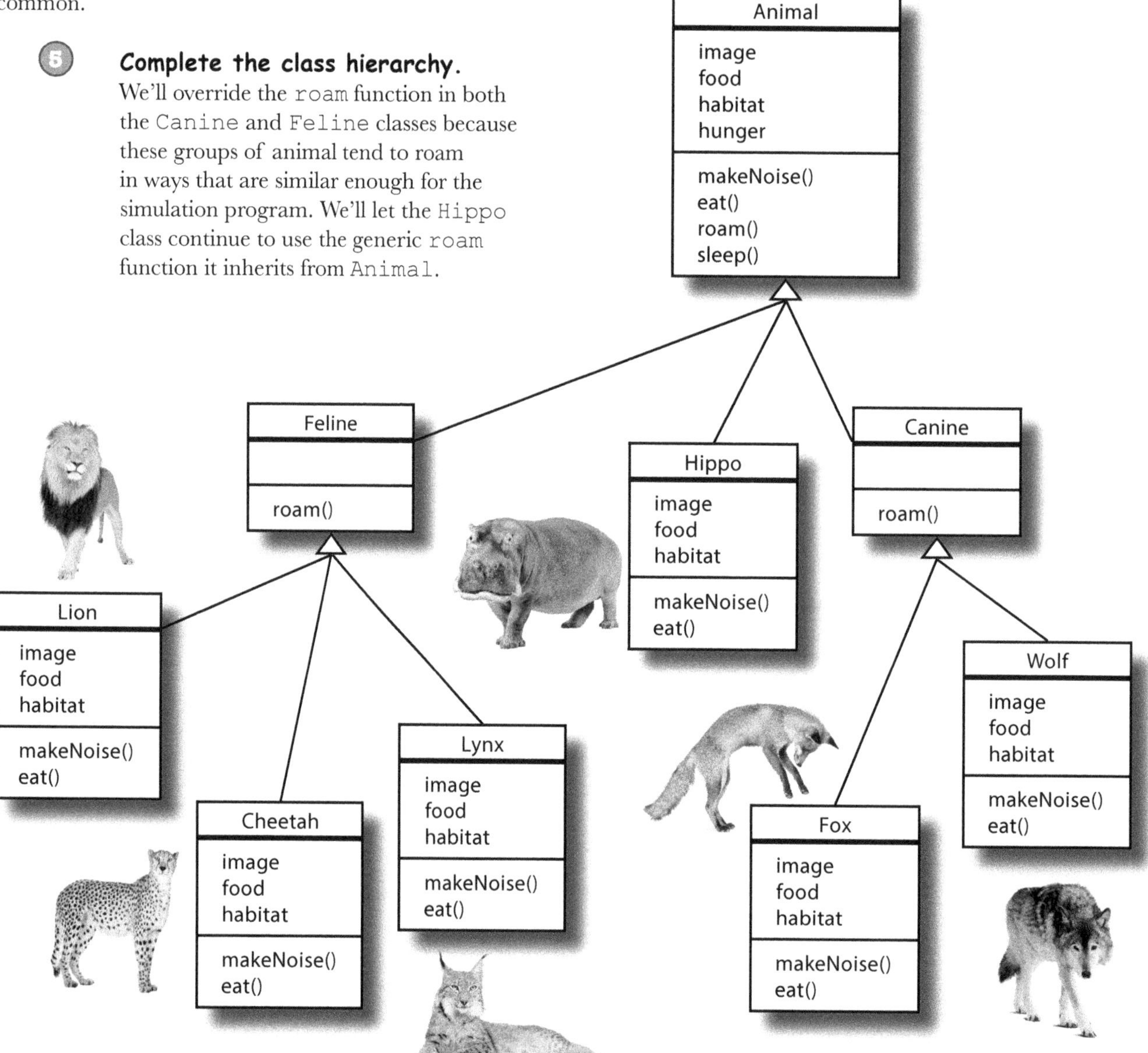

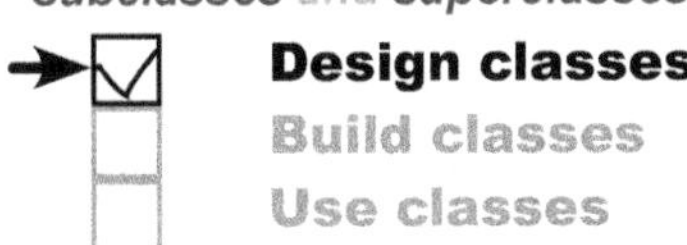

Use IS-A to test your class hierarchy

When you're designing a class hierarchy, you can test if one thing should be a subclass of another by applying the **IS-A** test. Simply ask yourself: "Does it make sense to say type X IS-A type Y?" If it does, then both classes should probably live in the same inheritance hierarchy, as the chances are, they have the same or overlapping behaviors. If it *doesn't* make sense, then you know that you need to think again.

There's more to it than this, but it's a good guideline for now. We'll look at more class design issues in the next chapter.

It makes sense, for example, for us to say "a Hippo IS-A Animal". A hippo is a type of animal, so the `Hippo` class can sensibly be a subclass of `Animal`.

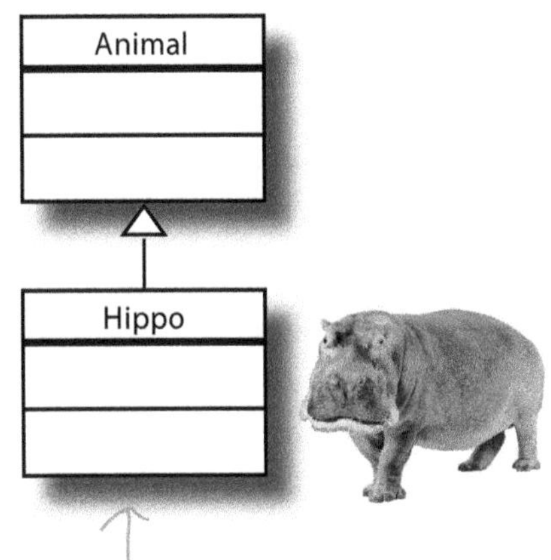

It makes sense to say "a Hippo IS-A Animal", so Hippo can sensibly be a subclass of Animal.

Keep in mind that the IS-A relationship implies that if `X` IS-A `Y`, then `X` can do anything that a `Y` can do (and possibly more), so the IS-A test works in only one direction. It doesn't make sense, for example, to say that "an `Animal` IS-A `Hippo`" because an animal is not a type of hippo.

Use HAS-A to test for other relationships

If the IS-A test fails for two classes, they may still be related in some way.

Suppose, for example, that you have two classes named `Fridge` and `Kitchen`. Saying "a Fridge IS-A Kitchen" makes no sense, and neither does "a Kitchen IS-A Fridge." But the two classes are still related, just not through inheritance.

`Kitchen` and `Fridge` are joined by a **HAS-A** relationship. Does it make sense to say "a Kitchen HAS-A Fridge"? If yes, then it means that the `Kitchen` class has a `Fridge` property. In other words, `Kitchen` includes a reference to a `Fridge`, but `Kitchen` is not a subclass of `Fridge`, and vice versa.

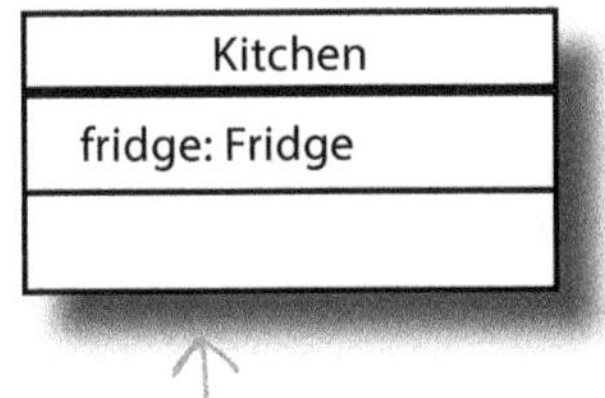

Fridge
size: Int
openDoor()
closeDoor()

Kitchen HAS-A Fridge, so there's a relationship. But neither class is a subclass of the other.

The IS-A test works anywhere in the inheritance tree

Design classes
Build classes
Use classes

If your inheritance tree is well-designed, the IS-A test should make sense when you ask *any* subclass if it IS-A any of its supertypes.

If class `B` is a subclass of class `A`, class `B` IS-A class `A`. **This is true anywhere in the inheritance tree.** If class `C` is a subclass of `B`, **class `C` passes the IS-A test for both `B` and `A`.**

With an inheritance tree like the one shown here, you're always allowed to say "Wolf is a subclass of Animal", or "Wolf IS-A Animal". It makes no difference if `Animal` is the superclass of the superclass of `Wolf`. **As long as `Animal` is somewhere in the inheritance hierarchy above `Wolf`, `Wolf` IS-A `Animal` will always be true.**

The structure of the `Animal` inheritance tree tells the world:

"Wolf IS-A Canine, so Wolf can do anything a Canine can do. And Wolf IS-A Animal, so Wolf can do anything an Animal can do."

It makes no difference if `Wolf` overrides some of the functions in `Animal` or `Canine`. As far as the code is concerned, a `Wolf` can do those functions. How `Wolf` does them, or in which class they're overridden, makes no difference. A `Wolf` can `makeNoise`, `eat`, `roam` and `sleep` because `Wolf` is a subclass of `Animal`.

Now that you've seen how to design a class hierarchy, have a go at the following exercise. After that, you'll learn how to code the `Animal` class hierarchy.

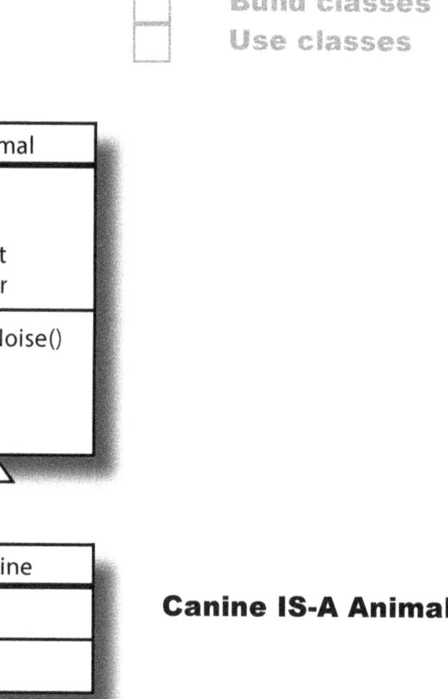

Canine IS-A Animal

Wolf IS-A Canine

Wolf IS-A Animal

Watch it!

Don't use inheritance if the IS-A test fails, just so that you can reuse code from another class.

As an example, suppose you added special voice activation code to an Alarm class, which you want to reuse in a Kettle class. A Kettle is not a specific type of Alarm, so Kettle should not be a subclass of Alarm. Instead, consider creating a separate VoiceActivation class that all voice activation objects can take advantage of using a HAS-A relationship. (You'll see more design options in the next chapter.)

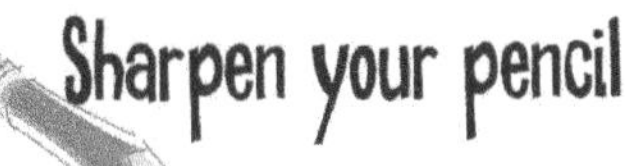

Below is a table containing a list of class names. Your job is to figure out the relationships that make sense, and say what the superclasses and subclasses are for each class. Then draw an inheritance tree for the classes.

Class	Superclasses	Subclasses
Person		
Musician		
RockStar		
BassPlayer		
ConcertPianist		

Sharpen your pencil Solution

Below is a table containing a list of class names. Your job is to figure out the relationships that make sense, and say what the superclasses and subclasses are for each class. Then draw an inheritance tree for the classes.

Class	Superclasses	Subclasses
Person		Musician, RockStar, BassPlayer, ConcertPianist
Musician	Person	RockStar, BassPlayer, ConcertPianist
RockStar	Musician, Person	
BassPlayer	Musician, Person	
ConcertPianist	Musician, Person	

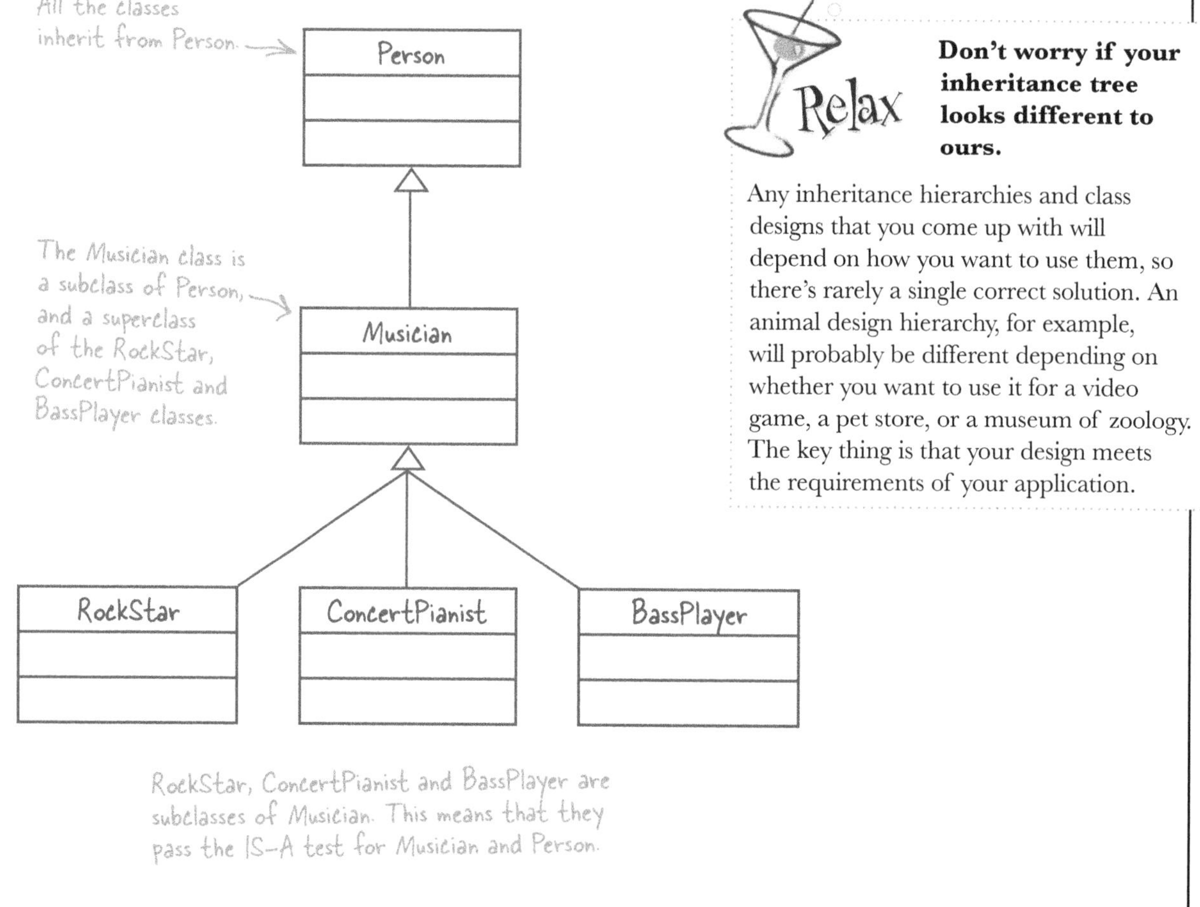

Relax

Don't worry if your inheritance tree looks different to ours.

Any inheritance hierarchies and class designs that you come up with will depend on how you want to use them, so there's rarely a single correct solution. An animal design hierarchy, for example, will probably be different depending on whether you want to use it for a video game, a pet store, or a museum of zoology. The key thing is that your design meets the requirements of your application.

Design classes
Build classes
Use classes

We'll create some Kotlin animals

Now that we've designed an animal class hierarchy, let's write the code for it.

First, create a new Kotlin project that targets the JVM, and name the project "Animals". Then create a new Kotlin file named *Animals.kt* by highlighting the *src* folder, clicking on the File menu and choosing New → Kotlin File/Class. When prompted, name the file "Animals", and choose File from the Kind option.

We'll add a new class named `Animal` to the project, which will provide the default code for creating a generic animal. Here's the code—update your version of *Animals.kt* to match ours:

Animal
image food habitat hunger
makeNoise() eat() roam() sleep()

```
class Animal {
    val image = ""
    val food = ""
    val habitat = ""
    var hunger = 10

    fun makeNoise() {
        println("The Animal is making a noise")
    }

    fun eat() {
        println("The Animal is eating")
    }

    fun roam() {
        println("The Animal is roaming")
    }

    fun sleep() {
        println("The Animal is sleeping")
    }
}
```

The Animal class has properties named image, food, habitat and hunger.

We've defined default implementations of the makeNoise, eat, roam and sleep functions.

Animals
src
Animals.kt

Now that we have an `Animal` class, we need to tell the compiler that we want to use it as a superclass.

Declare the superclass and its properties and functions as open

Before a class can be used as a superclass, you have to explicitly tell the compiler that this is allowed. You do this by prefixing the name of the class—and any properties or functions you want to override—with the keyword **open**. This tells the compiler that you've designed the class to be a superclass, and that you're happy for the properties and functions you've declared as open to be overridden.

In our class hierarchy, we want to be able to use Animal as a superclass, and override most of its properties and functions. Here's the code to allow us to do that—update your version of *Animals.kt* to reflect our changes (in bold):

To use a class as a superclass, it must be declared as open. Everything you want to override must also be open.

```
open class Animal {
    open val image = ""
    open val food = ""
    open val habitat = ""
    var hunger = 10

    open fun makeNoise() {
        println("The Animal is making a noise")
    }

    open fun eat() {
        println("The Animal is eating")
    }

    open fun roam() {
        println("The Animal is roaming")
    }

    fun sleep() {
        println("The Animal is sleeping")
    }
}
```

We want to use the class as a superclass, so we need to declare it open.

We want to override the image, food and habitat properties, so we've prefixed each one with open.

We've declared the makeNoise, eat and roam functions as open because we'll override them in our subclasses.

Animal
image **food** **habitat** hunger
makeNoise() **eat()** **roam()** sleep()

Animals
src
Animals.kt

Now that we've declared the Animal superclass as open, along with all the properties and functions we want to override, we can start creating animal subclasses. Let's see how to do this by writing the code for the Hippo class.

How a subclass inherits from a superclass

To make a class inherit from another, you add a colon (`:`) to the class header followed by the name of the superclass. This makes the class a subclass, and gives it all the properties and functions of the class it inherits from.

In our case, we want the `Hippo` class to inherit from the `Animal` superclass, so we use the following code:

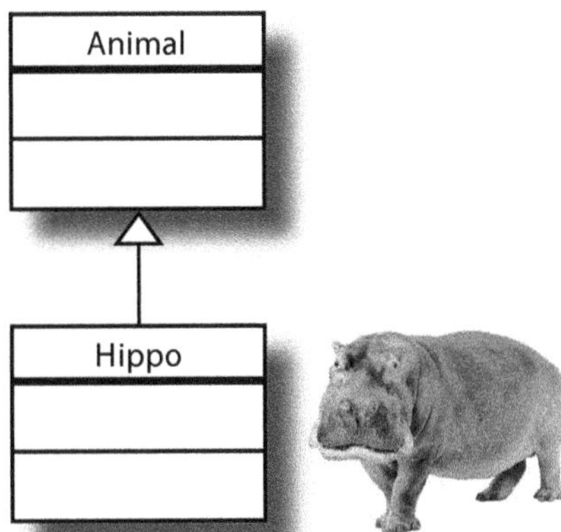


```
class Hippo : Animal() {
    //Hippo code goes here
}
```

This is like saying "class Hippo is a subtype of class Animal". We'll add the Hippo class to our code a few pages ahead.

The `Animal()` after the `:` calls the `Animal`'s constructor. This ensures that any `Animal` initialization code—such as assigning values to properties—gets to run. Calling the superclass constructor is mandatory: **if the superclass has a primary constructor, then you *must* call it in the subclass header or your code won't compile**. And even if you haven't explicitly added a constructor to your superclass, remember that the compiler automatically creates an empty one for you when the code gets compiled.

We didn't add a constructor to our Animal class, so the compiler added an empty one when it compiled the code. This constructor is called using Animal().

If the superclass constructor includes parameters, you must pass values for these parameters when you call the constructor. As an example, suppose you have a `Car` class that has two parameters in its constructor named `make` and `model`:

```
open class Car(val make: String, val model: String) {
    //Code for the Car class
}
```

The Car constructor defines two properties: make and model.

To define a subclass of `Car` named `ConvertibleCar`, you would have to call the `Car` constructor in the `ConvertibleCar` class header, passing in values for the `make` and `model` parameters. In this situation, you would normally add a constructor to the subclass that asks for these values, and then pass them to the superclass constructor, as in the example below:

The ConvertibleCar constructor has two parameters: make_param and model_param. It passes the values of these parameters to the Car constructor, which initializes the make and model properties.

```
class ConvertibleCar(make_param: String,
                     model_param: String) : Car(make_param, model_param) {
    //Code for the ConvertibleCar class
}
```

Now that you know how to declare a superclass, let's look at how you override its properties and functions. We'll start with the properties.

How (and when) to override properties

You override a property that's been inherited from a superclass by adding the property to the subclass, and prefixing it with the **`override`** keyword.

In our example, we want to override the `image`, `food` and `habitat` properties that the `Hippo` class inherits from the `Animal` superclass so that they're initialized with values that are specific to the `Hippo`. Here's the code to do that:

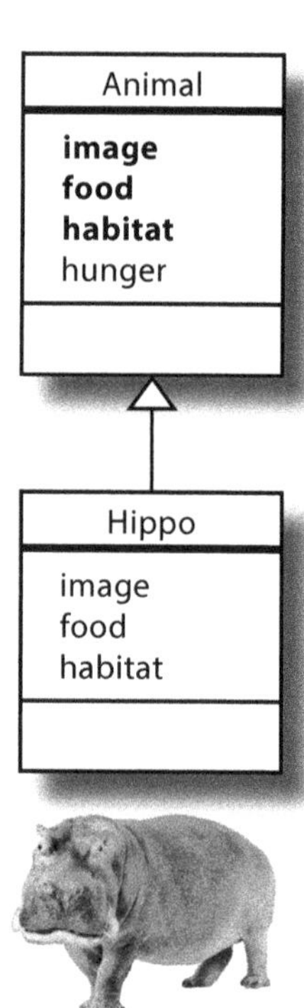


```
class Hippo : Animal() {
    override val image = "hippo.jpg"
    override val food = "grass"
    override val habitat = "water"
}
```

We'll add the Hippo class to our project a few pages ahead.

This overrides the image, food and habitat properties from the Animal class.

In this example, we've overridden the three properties in order to initialize each with a different value to the superclass. This is because each property is defined in the `Animal` superclass using `val`.

As you learned on the previous page, when a class inherits from a superclass, you have to call the superclass constructor; this is so that it can run its initialization code, including creating its properties and initializing them. This means that **if you define a property in the superclass using `val`, you *must* override it in the subclass if you want to assign a different value to it**.

If a superclass property has been defined using `var`, you don't need to override it in order to assign a new value to it, as `var` variables can be reused for other values. You can instead assign it a new value in the subclass's initializer block, as in this example:

```
open class Animal {
    var image = ""
    ...
}

class Hippo : Animal() {
    init {
        image = "hippo.jpg"
    }
    ...
}
```

Here, image is defined using var, and initialized with "".

We're using the Hippo's initializer block to assign a new value to the image property. In this case, there was no need to override the property.

Overriding properties lets you do more than assign default values

So far, we've only discussed how you can override a property to initialize it with a different value to the superclass, but this isn't the only way in which overriding properties can help your class design:

- **You can override a property's getter and setter.**
  In the previous chapter, you learned how to add custom getters and setters to properties. If you want a property to have a different getter or setter to the one it inherits from the superclass, you can define new ones by overriding the property and adding the getter and setter to the subclass.

- **You can override a val property in the superclass with a var property in the subclass.**
  If a property in the superclass has been defined using `val`, you can override it with a `var` property in the subclass. To do this, simply override the property and declare it to be a `var`. Note that this only works one way; if you try to override a `var` property with a `val`, the compiler will get upset and refuse to compile your code.

- **You can override a property's type with one of the superclass version's subtypes.**
  When you override a property, its type must match the type of the superclass version of the property, or be one of its subtypes.

Now that you know how to override properties, and when you should do it, let's look at how you override functions.

there are no Dumb Questions

Q: Can I override a property that's been defined in the superclass constructor?

A: Yes. Any properties you define in the class constructor can be prefixed with `open` or `override`, so you can overide properties that have been defined in the superclass constructor.

Q: Why do I have to prefix classes, properties and functions with `open` if I want to override them? You don't in Java.

A: In Kotlin, you can only inherit from superclasses and override their properties and functions if they've been prefixed with `open`. This is the opposite way round to how it works in Java.

In Java, classes are open by default, and you use `final` to stop other classes inheriting from them or overriding their instance variables and methods.

Q: Why does Kotlin take the opposite approach to Java?

A: Because the `open` prefix makes it much more explicit as to which classes have been designed to be used as superclasses, and which properties and functions can be overridden. This approach corresponds to one of the principles from Joshua Bloch's book *Effective Java*: "Design and document for inheritance or else prohibit it."

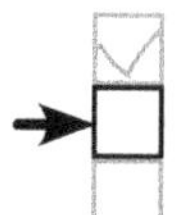

How to override functions

You override a function in a similar way to how you override a property: by adding the function to the subclass, prefixed with `override`.

In our example, we want to override the `makeNoise` and `eat` functions in the `Hippo` subclass so that the actions they perform are specific to the `Hippo`. Here's the code to do that:

```
class Hippo : Animal() {
    override val image = "hippo.jpg"
    override val food = "grass"
    override val habitat = "water"

    override fun makeNoise() {
        println("Grunt! Grunt!")
    }

    override fun eat() {
        println("The Hippo is eating $food")
    }
}
```

We'll add the Hippo class to our project a couple of pages ahead.

We're overriding the makeNoise and eat functions so that their implementations are Hippo-specific.

Animal
image food habitat hunger
makeNoise() eat() roam() sleep()

Hippo
image food habitat
makeNoise() eat()

Grunt! Grunt!

The rules for overriding functions

When you override a function, there are two rules that you must follow:

- **The function parameters in the subclass must match those in the superclass.**
  So if, for example, a function in the superclass takes three `Int` arguments, the overridden function in the subclass must also take three `Int` arguments or the code won't compile.

- **The function return types must be compatible.**
  Whatever the superclass function declares as a return type, the overriding function must return either the same type, or a subclass type. A subclass type is guaranteed to do anything its superclass declares, so it's safe to return a subclass where the superclass is expected.

You'll find out more about using a subclass in place of a superclass later in the chapter.

In our `Hippo` code above, the functions we're overriding have no parameters and no return types. This matches the function definitions in the superclass, so they follow the rules for overriding functions.

An overridden function or property stays open...

As you learned earlier in the chapter, if you want to override a function or property, you have to declare it `open` in the superclass. What we *didn't* tell you is that the function or property *stays* open in each of its subclasses, even if it's overridden, so you don't have to declare it as `open` further down the tree. The code for the following class hierarchy, for example, is valid:

```
open class Vehicle {
    open fun lowerTemperature() {
        println("Turn down temperature")
    }
}

open class Car : Vehicle() {
    override fun lowerTemperature() {
        println("Turn on air conditioning")
    }
}

class ConvertibleCar : Car() {
    override fun lowerTemperature() {
        println("Open roof")
    }
}
```

The Vehicle class defines an open lowerTemperature() function.

The lowerTemperature() function remains open in the Car subclass, even though we're overriding it...

...which means that we can override it again in the ConvertibleCar class.

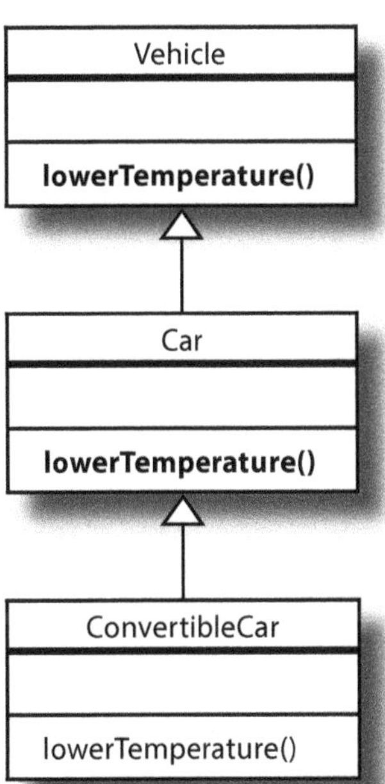

...until it's declared final

If you want to stop a function or property from being overridden further down the class hierarchy, you can prefix it with **`final`**. If, for example, you wanted to prevent subclasses of the `Car` class from overriding the `lowerTemperature` function, you would use the following code:

```
open class Car : Vehicle() {
    final override fun lowerTemperature() {
        println("Turn on air conditioning")
    }
}
```

Declaring the function as final in the Car class means that it can no longer be overridden in any of Car's subclasses.

Now that you know how to inherit properties and functions from a superclass and override them, let's add the `Hippo` code to our project.

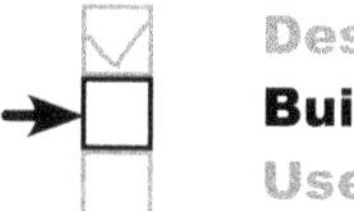

Add the Hippo class to the Animals project

We want to add the Hippo class code to the Animals project, so update your code in *Animals.kt* so that it matches ours below (our changes are in bold):

```
open class Animal {
    open val image = ""
    open val food = ""
    open val habitat = ""
    var hunger = 10

    open fun makeNoise() {
        println("The Animal is making a noise")
    }

    open fun eat() {
        println("The Animal is eating")
    }

    open fun roam() {
        println("The Animal is roaming")
    }

    fun sleep() {
        println("The Animal is sleeping")
    }
}

class Hippo : Animal() {
    override val image = "hippo.jpg"
    override val food = "grass"
    override val habitat = "water"

    override fun makeNoise() {
        println("Grunt! Grunt!")
    }

    override fun eat() {
        println("The Hippo is eating $food")
    }
}
```

The Animal class hasn't changed.

The Hippo class is a subclass of Animal.

The Hippo subclass overrides these properties and functions.

Animals
src
Animals.kt

Animal
image food habitat hunger
makeNoise() eat() roam() sleep()

Hippo
image food habitat
makeNoise() eat()

Now that you've seen how to create the Hippo class, see if you can create the Canine and Wolf classes in the following exercise.

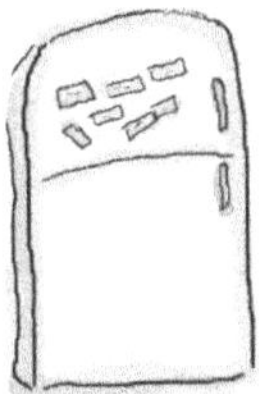

Code Magnets

See if you can rearrange the magnets below to create the Canine and Wolf classes.

The Canine class is a subclass of Animal, and overrides its roam function.

The Wolf class is a subclass of Canine, and overrides the image, food and habitat properties, and the makeNoise and eat functions, from the Animal class.

You won't need to use all of the magnets.

```
........ class Canine ............ {

    ........ fun ........ {

        println("The ........ is roaming")
    }
}

class Wolf ............ {

    ........ val image = "wolf.jpg"

    ........ val food = "meat"

    ........ val habitat = "forests"


    ........ fun makeNoise() {

        println("Hooooowl!")
    }


    ........ fun eat() {

        println("The Wolf is eating $food")
    }
}
```

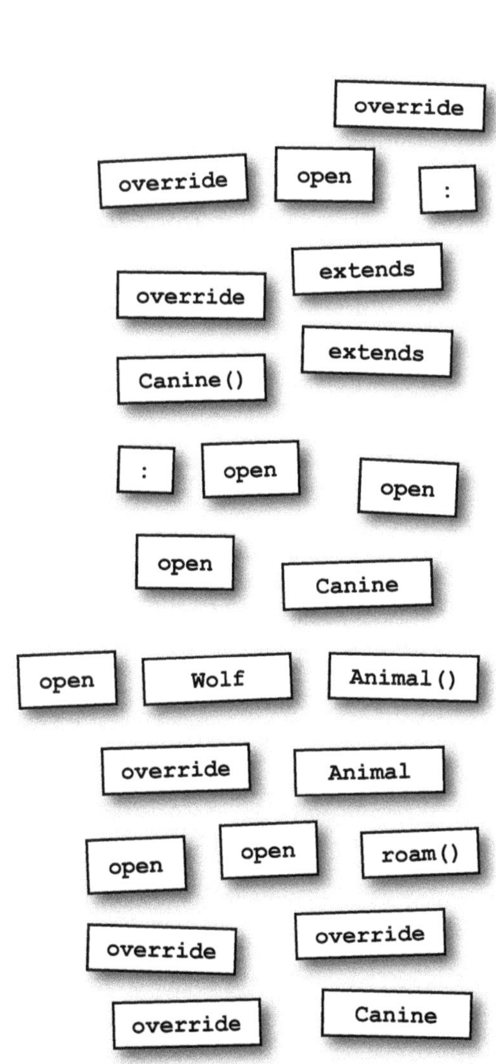

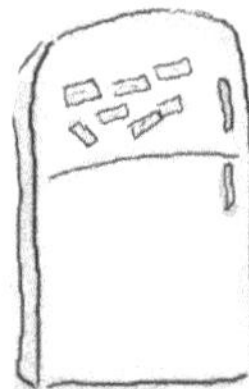

Code Magnets Solution

See if you can rearrange the magnets below to create the Canine and Wolf classes.

The Canine class is a subclass of Animal, and overrides its roam function.

The Wolf class is a subclass of Canine, and overrides the image, food and habitat properties, and the makeNoise and eat functions, from the Animal class.

You won't need to use all of the magnets.

```
open class Canine : Animal() {
    override fun roam() {
        println("The Canine is roaming")
    }
}

class Wolf : Canine() {
    override val image = "wolf.jpg"
    override val food = "meat"
    override val habitat = "forests"

    override fun makeNoise() {
        println("Hooooowl!")
    }

    override fun eat() {
        println("The Wolf is eating $food")
    }
}
```

Canine is a subclass of Animal. It's declared open so that we can use it as a superclass for the Wolf class.

Override the roam() function.

Wolf is a subclass of Canine.

Override these properties.

Override these two functions.

You didn't need to use these magnets.

open | extends | extends | open | open | open | Canine | Wolf | Animal | open | open | override

Add the Canine and Wolf classes

Now that you've created the `Canine` and `Wolf` classes, let's add them to the Animals project. Update the code in *Animals.kt* to add these two classes (our changes are shown below in bold):

```
open class Animal {
    ...
}

class Hippo : Animal() {
    ...
}

open class Canine : Animal() {
    override fun roam() {
        println("The Canine is roaming")
    }
}

class Wolf : Canine() {
    override val image = "wolf.jpg"
    override val food = "meat"
    override val habitat = "forests"

    override fun makeNoise() {
        println("Hooooowl!")
    }

    override fun eat() {
        println("The Wolf is eating $food")
    }
}
```

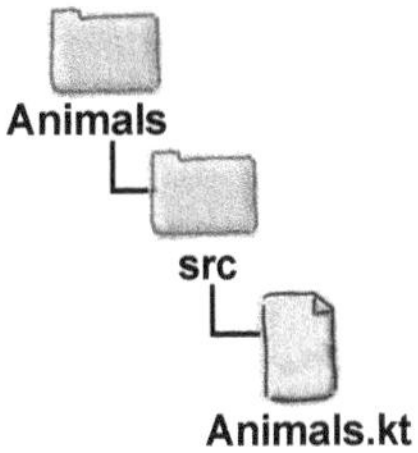

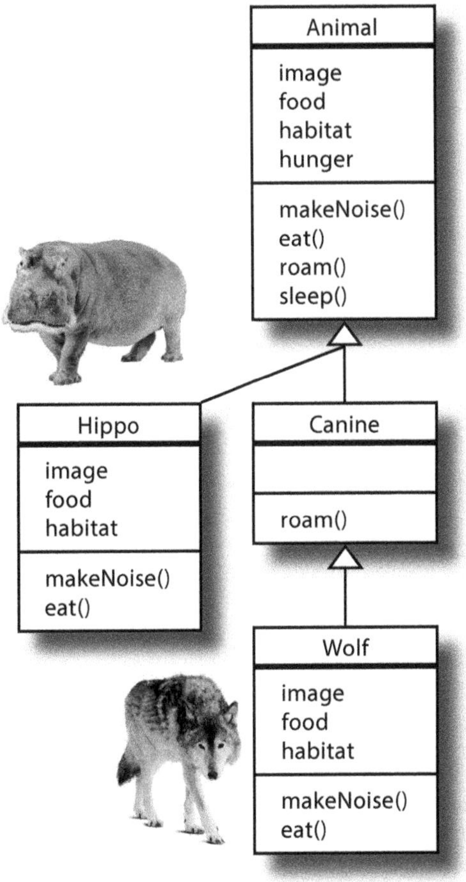

We've not changed the code for the Animal or Hippo classes.

Add the Canine class...

...and also the Wolf class.

Animals
src
Animals.kt

Animal
image food habitat hunger
makeNoise() eat() roam() sleep()

Hippo
image food habitat
makeNoise() eat()

Canine
roam()

Wolf
image food habitat
makeNoise() eat()

Next, we'll look at what happens when we create a `Wolf` object and call some of its functions.

Which function is called?

The `Wolf` class has four functions: one inherited from `Animal`, one inherited from `Canine` (which is an overridden version of a function in the `Animal` class), and two overridden in the `Wolf` class. When you create a `Wolf` object and assign it to a variable, you can use the dot operator on that variable to invoke each of the four functions. But which version of those functions gets called?

When you call a function on an object reference, you're calling **the most specific version of the function for that object type**: the one that's lowest on the inheritance tree.

When you call a function on a `Wolf` object, for example, the system first looks for the function in the `Wolf` class. If the system finds the function in this class, it executes the function. If the function *isn't* defined in the `Wolf` class, however, the system walks up the inheritance tree to the `Canine` class. If the function is defined here, the system executes it, and if it's not, the system continues up the tree. The system continues to walk up the class hierarchy until it finds a match for the function.

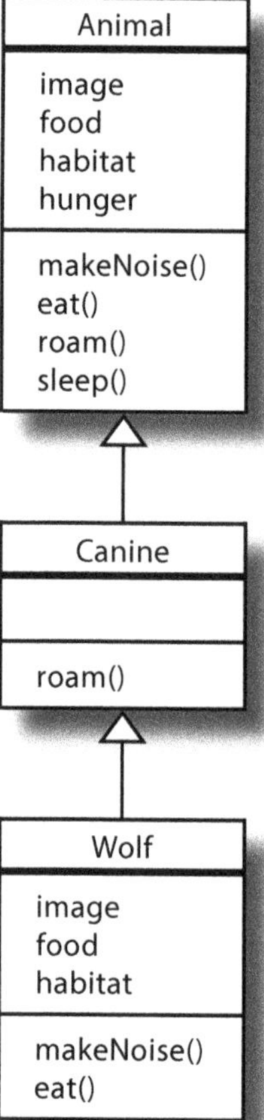

To see this in action, imagine that you decide to create a new `Wolf` object and call its `makeNoise` function. The system looks for the function in the `Wolf` class, and as the function has been overridden in this class, the system executes this version:

```
val w = Wolf()
w.makeNoise()
```

Calls the makeNoise() function defined in the Wolf class.

What if you then decide to call the `Wolf`'s `roam` function? This function isn't overridden in the `Wolf` class, so the system looks for it in the `Canine` class instead. As it's been overridden here, the system uses this version.

```
w.roam()
```

Calls the function in the Canine class.

Finally, suppose you call the `Wolf`'s `sleep` function. The system looks for the function in the `Wolf` class, and as it hasn't been overridden here, the system walks up the inheritance tree to the `Canine` class. The function hasn't been overridden in this class either, so the system uses the version that's in `Animal`.

```
w.sleep()
```

Calls the function in the Animal class.

Inheritance guarantees that all subclasses have the functions and properties defined in the superclass

When you define a set of properties and functions in a superclass, you're guaranteeing that all its subclasses also have these properties and functions. In other words, you define a common protocol, or contract, for a set of classes that are related by inheritance.

The `Animal` class, for example, establishes a common protocol for all animal subtypes that says "any *Animal* has properties named *image*, *food*, *habitat* and *hunger*, and functions named *makeNoise*, *eat*, *roam* and *sleep*":

When we say "any Animal", we mean the Animal class, or any subclass of Animal.

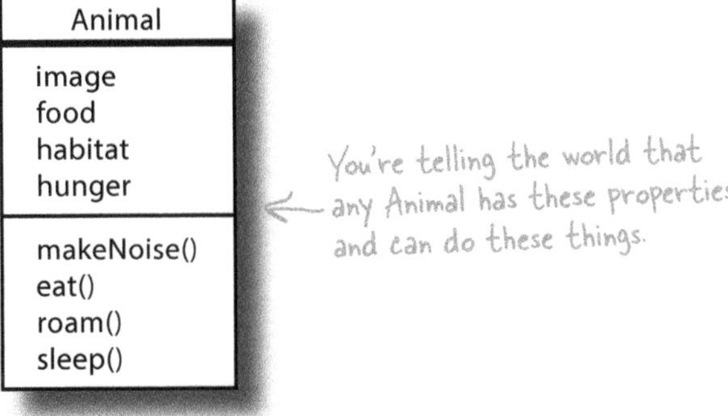

Any place where you can use a superclass, you can use one of its subclasses instead

When you define a supertype for a group of classes, **you can use any subclass in place of the superclass it inherits from**. So when you declare a variable, any object that's a subclass of the variable's type can be assigned to it. The following code, for example, defines an `Animal` variable, and assigns it a reference to a `Wolf` object. The compiler knows that a `Wolf` is a type of `Animal`, so the code compiles:

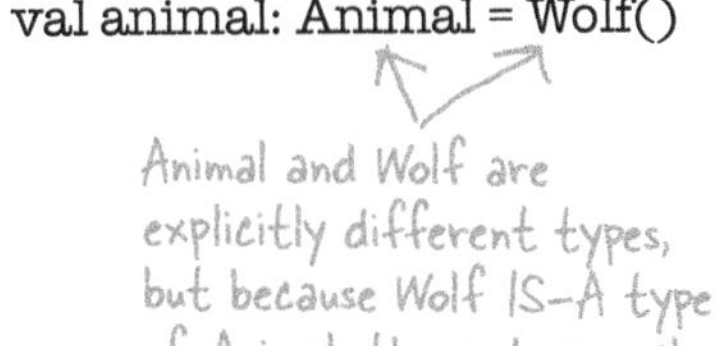

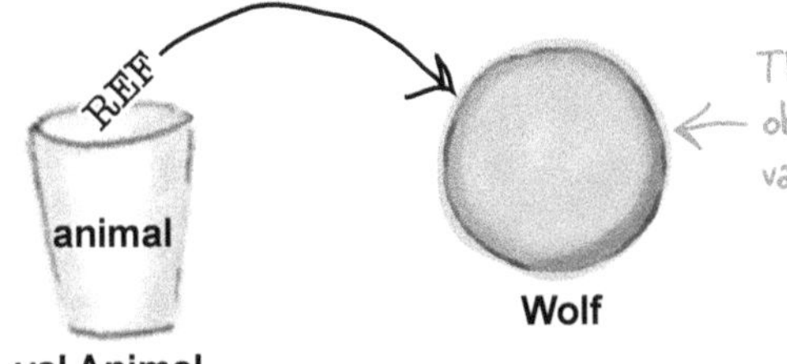

When you call a function on the variable, it's the object's version that responds

As you already know, if you assign an object to a variable, you can use the variable to access the object's functions. This is still the case if the variable is a supertype of the object.

Suppose, for example, that you assign a `Wolf` object to an `Animal` variable and call its `eat` function using code like this:

```
val animal: Animal = Wolf()
animal.eat()
```

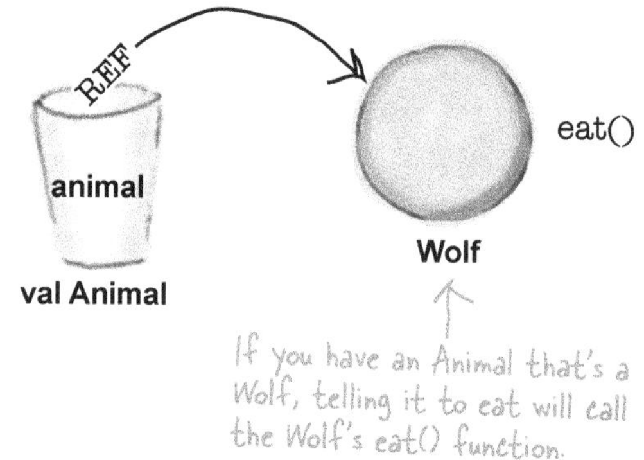

If you have an Animal that's a Wolf, telling it to eat will call the Wolf's eat() function.

When the `eat` function gets called, it's the version that's in the `Wolf` class that responds. The system knows that the underlying object is a `Wolf`, so it gets to respond in a `Wolf`-like way.

You can also create an array of different types of animal, and get each one to behave in its own way. As each animal is a subclass of `Animal`, we can simply add each one to an array, and call functions on each item in the array:

```
val animals = arrayOf(Hippo(),
                      Wolf(),
                      Lion(),
                      Cheetah(),
                      Lynx(),
                      Fox())
```

The compiler spots that these are all types of Animal, so it creates an array of type Array<Animal>.

```
for (item in animals) {
    item.roam()
    item.eat()
}
```

This loops through the animals, and calls the roam() and eat() functions of each one. Each animal responds in a way that's appropriate to its type.

So designing with inheritance means that you can write flexible code in the safe knowledge that each object will do the right thing when its functions are called.

But that's not the end of the story.

You can use a supertype for a function's parameters and return type

If you can declare a variable of a supertype (say, `Animal`), and assign a subclass object to it (say, `Wolf`), what do you think might happen when you use a subtype as an argument to a function?

Suppose, for example, that we create a `Vet` class with a function named `giveShot`:

```
class Vet {
    fun giveShot(animal: Animal) {
        //Code to do something medical to the Animal that it won't like
        animal.makeNoise()
    }
}
```

The Vet's giveShot function has an Animal parameter.

giveShot calls the Animal's makeNoise function

Vet
giveShot()

The `Animal` parameter can take any `Animal` type as the argument. So when the `Vet`'s `giveShot` function is called, it executes the `Animal`'s `makeNoise` function, and whatever type of `Animal` it is will respond:

```
val vet = Vet()
val wolf = Wolf()
val hippo = Hippo()
vet.giveShot(wolf)
vet.giveShot(hippo)
```

Wolf and Hippo are both types of Animal, so you can pass Wolf and Hippo objects as arguments to the giveShot function.

So if you want other types of animal to work with the `Vet` class, all you have to do is make sure that each one is a subclass of the `Animal` class. The `Vet`'s `giveShot` function will still work, even though it was written without any knowledge of any new `Animal` subtypes the `Vet` may be working on.

Being able to use one type of object in a place that explicitly expects a different type is called **polymorphism**. It's the ability to provide different implementations for functions that have been inherited from somewhere else.

We'll show you the full code for the Animals project on the next page.

Polymorphism means "many forms". It allows different subclasses to have different implementations of the same function.

The updated Animals code

Here's an updated version of *Animals.kt* that includes the `Vet` class and a `main` function. Update your version of the code to match ours below (our changes are in bold):

```
open class Animal {
    open val image = ""
    open val food = ""
    open val habitat = ""
    var hunger = 10

    open fun makeNoise() {
        println("The Animal is making a noise")
    }

    open fun eat() {
        println("The Animal is eating")
    }

    open fun roam() {
        println("The Animal is roaming")
    }

    fun sleep() {
        println("The Animal is sleeping")
    }
}

class Hippo: Animal() {
    override val image = "hippo.jpg"
    override val food = "grass"
    override val habitat = "water"

    override fun makeNoise() {
        println("Grunt! Grunt!")
    }

    override fun eat() {
        println("The Hippo is eating $food")
    }
}

open class Canine: Animal() {
    override fun roam() {
        println("The Canine is roaming")
    }
}
```

We've not changed any of the code on this page.

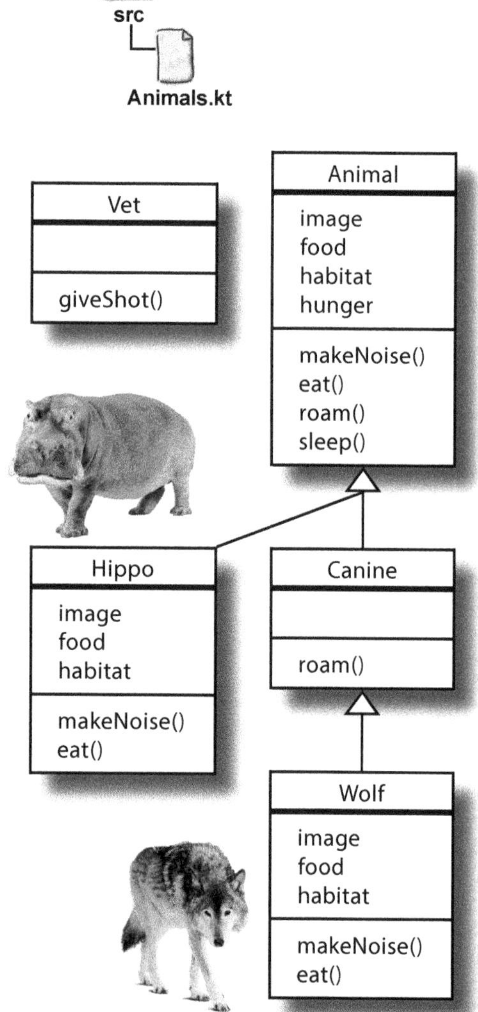

The code continues on the next page.

The code continued...

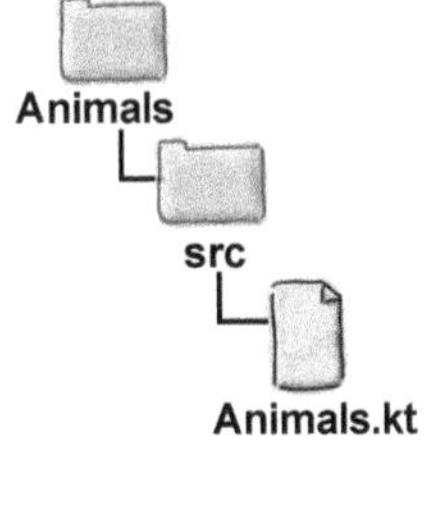


```
class Wolf: Canine() {
    override val image = "wolf.jpg"
    override val food = "meat"
    override val habitat = "forests"

    override fun makeNoise() {
        println("Hooooowl!")
    }

    override fun eat() {
        println("The Wolf is eating $food")
    }
}

class Vet {
    fun giveShot(animal: Animal) {
        //Code to do something medical
        animal.makeNoise()
    }
}

fun main(args: Array<String>) {
    val animals = arrayOf(Hippo(), Wolf())
    for (item in animals) {
        item.roam()
        item.eat()
    }

    val vet = Vet()
    val wolf = Wolf()
    val hippo = Hippo()
    vet.giveShot(wolf)
    vet.giveShot(hippo)
}
```

Add the Vet class.

Add the main function.

Loop through an array of Animals.

Call the Vet's giveShot function, passing in two Animal subtypes.

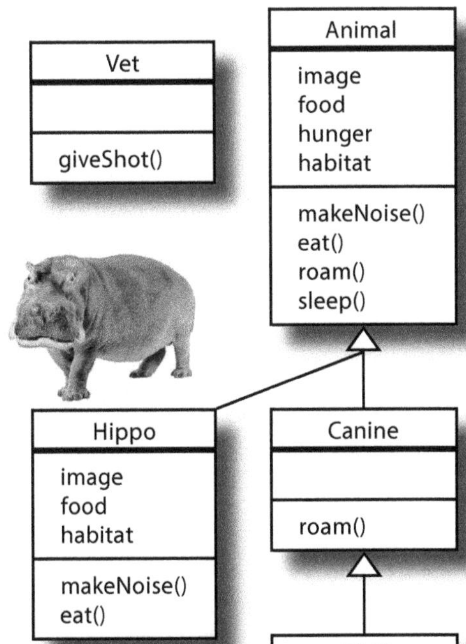

Test drive

When we run the code, the following text gets printed in the IDE's output window:

```
The Animal is roaming
The Hippo is eating grass
The Canine is roaming
The Wolf is eating meat
Hooooowl!
Grunt! Grunt!
```

Hippo inherits the Animal's roam function.

Wolf inherits the Canine's roam function.

Each Animal makes its own noise when the Vet's giveShot function runs.

there are no Dumb Questions

Q: Why does Kotlin let me override a `val` property with a `var`?

A: Back in Chapter 4, we said that when you create a `val` property, the compiler secretly adds a getter for it. And when you create a `var` property, the compiler adds both a getter and a setter.

When you override a `val` property with a `var`, you're effectively asking the compiler to add an extra setter to the property in the subclass. This is valid, so the code compiles.

Q: Can I override a `var` property with a `val`?

A: No. If you try to override a `var` property with a `val`, your code won't compile.

When you define a class hierarchy, you're guaranteeing that you can do the same things to a subclass that you can do to a superclass. And if you try to override a `var` property with a `val`, you're telling the compiler that you no longer want to be able to update a property's value. This breaks the common protocol between the superclass and its subtypes, so the code won't compile.

Q: You said that when you call a function on a variable, the system walks up the inheritance hierarchy looking for a match. What happens if the system doesn't find one?

A: You don't have to worry about the system not finding a matching function.

The compiler guarantees that a particular function is callable for a specific variable type, but it doesn't care from which class that function comes from at runtime. If we were to call the `sleep` function on a `Wolf`, for example, the compiler checks that the `sleep` function exists, but it doesn't care that the function is defined in (and inherited from) class `Animal`.

Remember that if a class *inherits* a function, it *has* the function. Where the inherited function is defined makes no difference to the compiler. But at runtime, the system will always pick the right one, the most specific version of the function for that particular object.

Q: Can a subclass have more than one direct superclass?

A: No. Multiple inheritance isn't allowed in Kotlin, so each subclass can have only one direct superclass. We'll look at this in more detail in Chapter 6.

Q: When I override a function in a subclass, the function parameter types must be the same. Can I define a function that has the same name as the one in the superclass but with different parameter types?

A: Yes, you can. You can define multiple functions with the same name, just so long as the parameter types are different. This is called *overloading* (not overriding) and it has nothing to do with inheritance.

We'll look at overloading functions in Chapter 7.

Q: Can you explain polymorphism again?

A: Sure. Polymorphism is the ability to use any subtype object in place of its supertype. As different subclasses can have different implementations of the same function, it allows each object to respond to function calls in the way that's most appropriate for each object.

You'll find out more ways in which you can take advantage of polymorphism in the next chapter.

BE the Compiler

The code on the left represents a source file. Your job is to play like you're the compiler and say which of the A-B pairs of functions on the right would compile and produce the required output when inserted into the code on the left. The A function fits into class Monster, and the B function fits into class Vampyre.

Output:

The code needs to produce this output.

Fancy a bite?
Fire!
Aargh!

This is the code.

```
open class Monster {

  A

}

class Vampyre : Monster() {
```

```
}

class Dragon : Monster() {
    override fun frighten(): Boolean {
        println("Fire!")
        return true
    }
}

fun main(args: Array<String>) {
    val m = arrayOf(Vampyre(),
                    Dragon(),
                    Monster())
    for (item in m) {
        item.frighten()
    }
}
```

These are the pairs of functions.

1A
```
open fun frighten(): Boolean {
    println("Aargh!")
    return true
}
```

1B
```
override fun frighten(): Boolean {
    println("Fancy a bite?")
    return false
}
```

2A
```
fun frighten(): Boolean {
    println("Aargh!")
    return true
}
```

2B
```
override fun frighten(): Boolean {
    println("Fancy a bite?")
    return true
}
```

3A
```
open fun frighten(): Boolean {
    println("Aargh!")
    return false
}
```

3B
```
fun beScary(): Boolean {
    println("Fancy a bite?")
    return true
}
```

BE the Compiler Solution

The code on the left represents a source file. Your job is to play like you're the compiler and say which of the A-B pairs of functions on the right would compile and produce the required output when inserted into the code on the left. The A function fits into class Monster, and the B function fits into class Vampyre.

Output:

Fancy a bite?
Fire!
Aargh!

```
open class Monster {

    (A)

}

class Vampyre : Monster() {

    (B)

}

class Dragon : Monster() {
    override fun frighten(): Boolean {
        println("Fire!")
        return true
    }
}

fun main(args: Array<String>) {
    val m = arrayOf(Vampyre(),
                    Dragon(),
                    Monster())
    for (item in m) {
        item.frighten()
    }
}
```

1A

```
open fun frighten(): Boolean {
    println("Aargh!")
    return true
}
```

This code compiles and produces the correct output

1B

```
override fun frighten(): Boolean {
    println("Fancy a bite?")
    return false
}
```

2A

```
fun frighten(): Boolean {
    println("Aargh!")
    return true
}
```

This code won't compile because the frighten() function in the Monster class isn't open.

2B

```
override fun frighten(): Boolean {
    println("Fancy a bite?")
    return true
}
```

3A

```
open fun frighten(): Boolean {
    println("Aargh!")
    return false
}
```

This compiles but it produces incorrect output as Vampyre doesn't override frighten().

3B

```
fun beScary(): Boolean {
    println("Fancy a bite?")
    return true
}
```

Your Kotlin Toolbox

You've got Chapter 5 under your belt and now you've added superclasses and subclasses to your toolbox.

You can download the full code for the chapter from https://tinyurl.com/HFKotlin.

BULLET POINTS

- A superclass contains common properties and functions that are inherited by one or more subclasses.
- A subclass can include extra properties and functions that aren't in the superclass, and can override the things it inherits.
- Use the IS-A test to verify that your inheritance is valid. If `X` is a *subclass* of `Y`, then `X` *IS-A* `Y` must make sense.
- The IS-A relationship works in only one direction. A `Hippo` is an `Animal`, but not all `Animal`s are `Hippo`s.
- If class `B` is a subclass of class `A`, and class `C` is a subclass of class `B`, class `C` passes the IS-A test for both `B` and `A`.
- Before you can use a class as a superclass, you must declare it `open`. You must also declare any properties and functions you want to override as `open`.
- Use `:` to specify a subclass's superclass.
- If the superclass has a primary constructor, then you must call it in the subclass header.
- Override properties and functions in the subclass by prefixing them with `override`. When you override a property, its type must be compatible with that of the superclass property. When you override a function, its parameter list must stay the same, and its return type must be compatible with that of the superclass.
- Overridden functions and properties stay open until they're declared `final`.
- When a function is overridden in a subclass, and that function is invoked on an instance of the subclass, the overridden version of the function is called.
- Inheritance guarantees that all subclasses have the functions and properties defined in the superclass.
- You can use a subclass in any place where the superclass type is expected.
- Polymorphism means "many forms". It allows different subclasses to have different implementations of the same function.

6 abstract classes and interfaces

Serious Polymorphism

A superclass inheritance hierarchy is just the beginning.

If you want to ***fully exploit polymorphism***, you need to design using **abstract classes** and **interfaces**. In this chapter, you'll discover how to use abstract classes to control which classes in your hierarchy ***can and can't be instantiated***. You'll see how they can force concrete subclasses to ***provide their own implementations***. You'll find out how to use interfaces to ***share behavior between independent classes***. And along the way, you'll learn the ins and outs of ***is***, ***as,*** and ***when***.

The Animal class hierarchy revisited

In the previous chapter, you learned how to design an inheritance hierarchy by creating the class structure for a bunch of animals. We abstracted out the common properties and functions into an `Animal` superclass, and overrode some of the properties and functions in the `Animal` subclasses so that we'd have subclass-specific implementations where we thought it was appropriate.

By defining the common properties and functions in the `Animal` superclass, we're establishing a common protocol for all `Animal`s, which makes the design nice and flexible. We can write code using `Animal` variables and parameters so that any `Animal` subtype (including ones we didn't know about at the time we wrote our code) can be used at runtime.

Here's a reminder of the class structure:

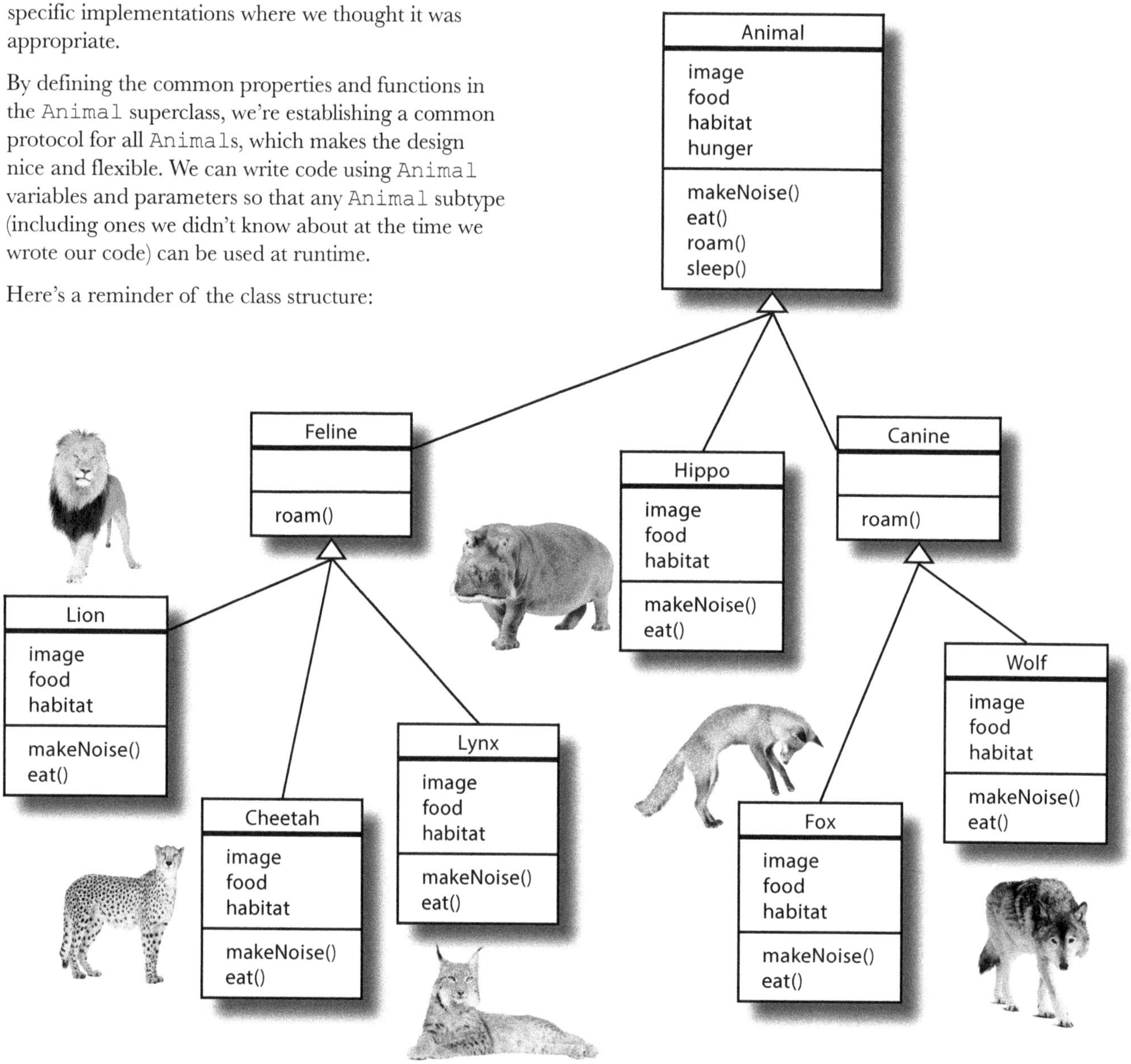

Animal
image
food
habitat
hunger
makeNoise()
eat()
roam()
sleep()

Feline
roam()

Hippo
image
food
habitat
makeNoise()
eat()

Canine
roam()

Lion
image
food
habitat
makeNoise()
eat()

Cheetah
image
food
habitat
makeNoise()
eat()

Lynx
image
food
habitat
makeNoise()
eat()

Fox
image
food
habitat
makeNoise()
eat()

Wolf
image
food
habitat
makeNoise()
eat()

Some classes shouldn't be instantiated

The class structure, however, needs some improvement. It makes sense for us to create new `Wolf`, `Hippo` or `Fox` objects, but the inheritance hierarchy also allows us to create generic `Animal` objects. This is a Bad Thing because we can't say what an `Animal` looks like, what it eats, what sort of noise it makes, and so on.

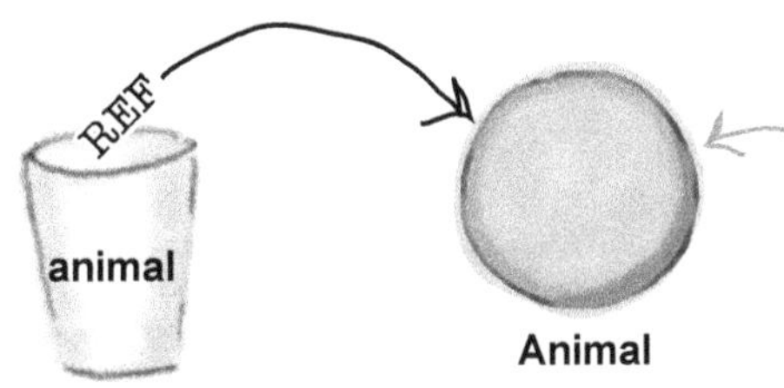

We know what Wolf, Hippo and Fox objects look like, but what about an Animal object? Does it have fur? Does it have legs? And how does it eat and roam?

How do we deal with this? We need an `Animal` class for inheritance and polymorphism, but we only want to be able to instantiate the less abstract subclasses of `Animal`, not `Animal` itself. We want to be able to create `Hippo`, `Wolf` and `Fox` objects, but not `Animal` objects.

Declare a class as abstract to stop it from being instantiated

If you want to prevent a class from being instantiated, you can mark the class as **abstract** by prefixing it with the `abstract` keyword. Here's how, for example, you turn `Animal` into an abstract class:

```
abstract class Animal {
    ...
}
```

Prefix class with "abstract" to make it an abstract class.

Being an abstract class means that nobody can create any objects of that type, even if you've defined a constructor for it. You can still use that abstract class as a declared variable type, but you don't have to worry about somebody creating objects of that type—the compiler stops it from happening:

```
var animal: Animal
animal = Wolf()
animal = Animal()
```

This line won't compile because you can't create Animal objects.

If a superclass is marked as abstract, you don't need to declare that it's open.

Think about the `Animal` class hierarchy. Which classes do you think should be declared abstract? In other words, which classes do you think shouldn't be instantiated?

Abstract or concrete?

In our `Animal` class hierarchy, there are three classes that need to be declared abstract: `Animal`, `Canine` and `Feline`. While we need these classes for inheritance, we don't want anyone to be able to create objects of these types.

A class that's not abstract is called **concrete**, so that leaves `Hippo`, `Wolf`, `Fox`, `Lion`, `Cheetah` and `Lynx` as the concrete subclasses.

In general, whether a class should be abstract or concrete depends on the context of your application. A `Tree` class, for example, might need to be abstract in a tree nursery application where the differences between an `Oak` and a `Maple` really matter. But if you were designing a golf simulation, `Tree` might be a concrete class because the application doesn't need to distinguish between different types of tree.

We're marking the Animal, Canine and Feline classes as abstract by giving each one a gray background.

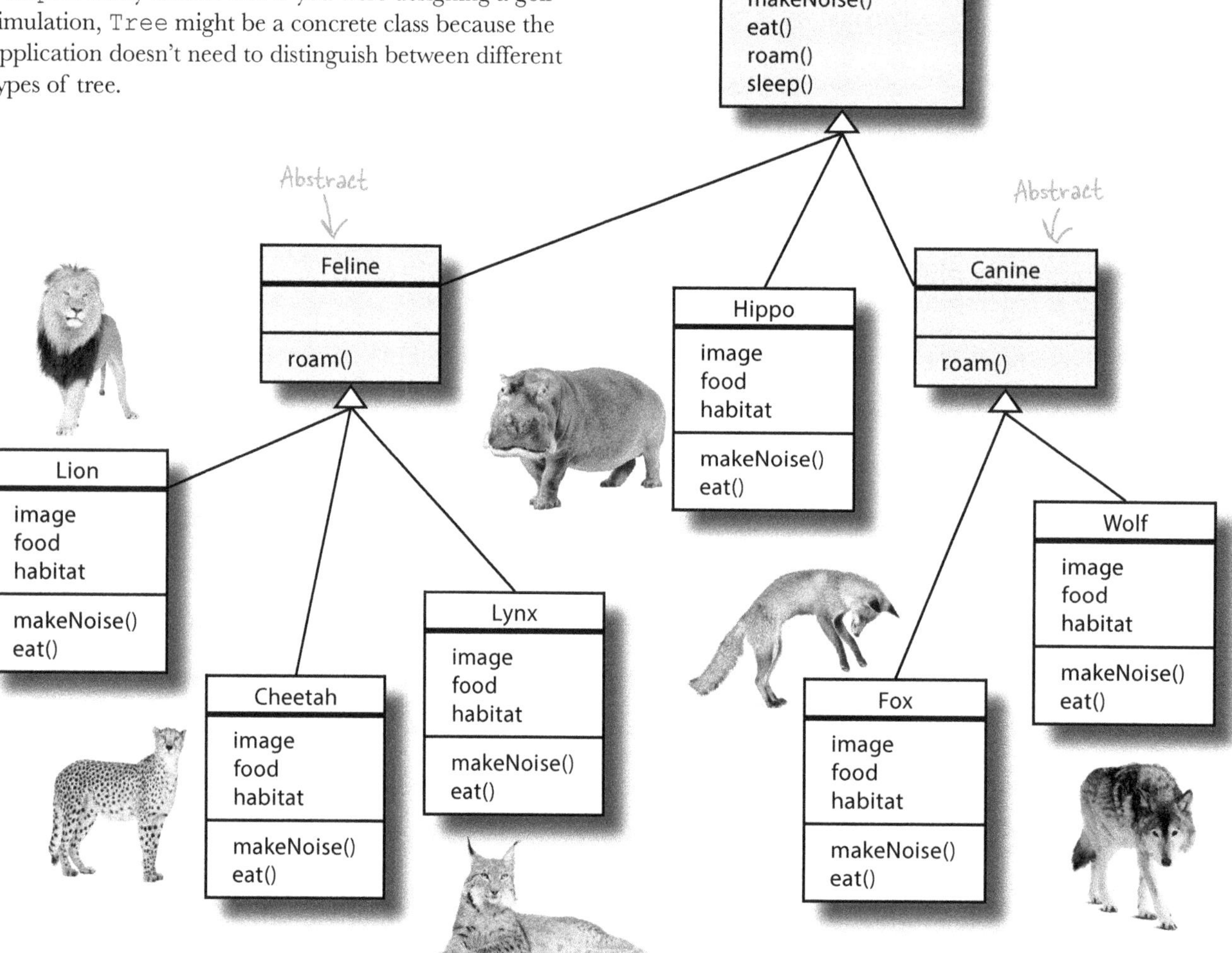

An abstract class can have abstract properties and functions

In an abstract class, you can choose to mark properties and functions as abstract. This is useful if the class has behaviors that don't make sense unless they're implemented by a more specific subclass, and you can't think of a generic implementation that might be useful for subclasses to inherit.

Let's see how this works by considering what properties and functions we should mark as abstract in the `Animal` class.

We can mark three properties as abstract

When we created the `Animal` class, we decided to initialize the `image`, `food` and `habitat` properties with generic values and override them in the animal-specific subclasses. This was because there was no value we could assign to these properties that would have been useful to the subclasses.

Because these properties have generic values that must be overridden, we can mark each one as abstract by prefixing it with the `abstract` keyword. Here's the code to do that:

```
abstract class Animal {
    abstract val image: String
    abstract val food: String
    abstract val habitat: String
    var hunger = 10
    ...
}
```

Here, we've marked the image, food and habitat properties as abstract

Animal

image
food
habitat
hunger

...

Notice that in the above code, we haven't initialized any of the abstract properties. If you try to initialize an abstract property, or define a custom getter or setter for it, the compiler will refuse to compile your code. This is because by marking a property as abstract, you've decided that there's no useful initial value it can have, and no useful implementation for a custom getter or setter.

Now that we know what properties we can mark as abstract, let's consider the functions.

An abstract class can contain abstract and non-abstract properties and functions. It's possible for an abstract class to have no abstract members.

Abstract properties and functions don't need to be marked as open.

The Animal class has two abstract functions

The `Animal` class defines two functions—`makeNoise` and `eat`—that are overridden in every concrete subclass. As these two functions are always overridden and there's no implementation we can provide that would help the subclasses, we can mark the `makeNoise` and `eat` functions as abstract by prefixing each one with the `abstract` keyword. Here's the code to do this:

```
abstract class Animal {
    ...
    abstract fun makeNoise()

    abstract fun eat()

    open fun roam() {
        println("The Animal is roaming")
    }

    fun sleep() {
        println("The Animal is sleeping")
    }
}
```

Animal
image food habitat hunger
makeNoise() eat() roam() sleep()

In the above code, neither of the abstract functions have function bodies. This is because when you mark a function as abstract, you're telling the compiler that there's no useful code you can write for the function body.

If you try to add a body to an abstract function, the compiler will get upset and refuse to compile your code. The following code, for example, won't compile because there are curly braces after the function definition:

```
abstract fun makeNoise() {}
```

The curly braces form an empty function body, so the code won't compile.

In order for the code to compile, you must remove the curly braces so that the code looks like this:

```
abstract fun makeNoise()
```

As the abstract function no longer has a function body, the code compiles.

Watch it!

If you mark a property or function as abstract, you must mark the class as abstract too.

If you put even one abstract property or function in a class, you have to mark the class as abstract or your code won't compile.

Abstract properties and functions define a common protocol so that you can use polymorphism.

Inheritable function implementations (functions with actual bodies) are useful to put in a superclass *when it makes sense*. And in an abstract class, it often *doesn't* make sense because you may not be able to come up with any generic code that the subclasses would find useful.

Abstract functions are useful because even though they don't contain any actual function code, they define the protocol for a group of subclasses which you can use for polymorphism. As you learned in the previous chapter, polymorphism means that when you define a supertype for a group of classes, you can use any subclass in place of the superclass it inherits from. It gives you the ability to use a superclass type as a variable type, function argument, return type or array type, as in the following example:

```
val animals = arrayOf(Hippo(),
                      Wolf(),
                      Lion(),
                      Cheetah(),
                      Lynx(),
                      Fox())

for (item in animals) {
    item.roam()
    item.eat()
}
```

Create an array of different Animal objects.

Each Animal in the array responds in its own way.

This means that you can add new subtypes (such as a new `Animal` subclass) to your application without having to rewrite or add new functions to deal with those new types.

Now that you've seen how (and when) to mark classes, properties and functions as abstract, let's see how you implement them.

How to implement an abstract class

You declare that a class inherits from an abstract superclass in the same way that you say that a class inherits from a normal superclass: by adding a colon to the class header followed by the name of the abstract class. Here's how, for example, you say that the `Hippo` class inherits from the abstract `Animal` class:

```
class Hippo : Animal() {
    ...
}
```

Just like when you inherit from a normal superclass, you must call the abstract class constructor in the subclass header.

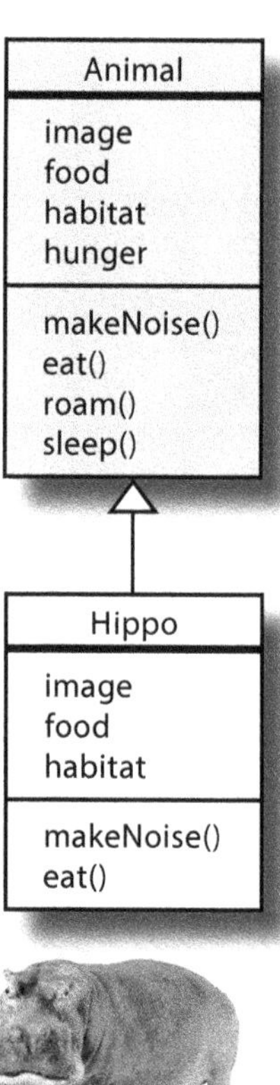

You implement abstract properties and functions by overriding each one and providing an implementation. This means that you need to initialize any abstract properties, and you need to provide a body for any abstract functions.

In our example, the `Hippo` class is a concrete subclass of `Animal`. Here's the code for the `Hippo` class that implements the `image`, `food` and `habitat` properties, along with the `makeNoise` and `eat` functions:

```
class Hippo : Animal() {
    override val image = "hippo.jpg"
    override val food = "grass"
    override val habitat = "water"

    override fun makeNoise() {
        println("Grunt! Grunt!")
    }

    override fun eat() {
        println("The Hippo is eating $food")
    }
}
```

You implement abstract properties and functions by overriding them. This is the same as if the superclass was concrete.

When you implement abstract properties and functions, you must follow the same rules for overriding that you use for overriding normal properties and functions:

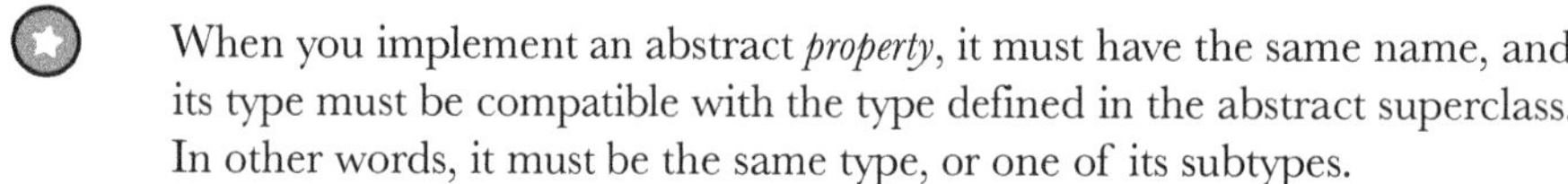

- When you implement an abstract *property*, it must have the same name, and its type must be compatible with the type defined in the abstract superclass. In other words, it must be the same type, or one of its subtypes.

- When you implement an abstract *function*, it must have the same function signature (name and arguments) as the function that's defined in the abstract superclass. Its return type must be compatible with the declared return type.

You MUST implement all abstract properties and functions

The first **concrete** class in the inheritance tree below the abstract superclass *must* implement all abstract properties and functions. In our class hierarchy, for example, the `Hippo` class is a direct concrete subclass of `Animal`, so it must implement all the abstract properties and functions defined in the `Animal` class in order for the code to compile.

With **abstract** subclasses, you have a choice: you can either implement the abstract properties and functions, or pass the buck to its subclasses. If both `Animal` and `Canine` are abstract, for example, the `Canine` class can either implement the abstract properties and functions from `Animal`, or say nothing about them and leave them for its subclasses to implement.

Any abstract properties and functions that aren't implemented in `Canine` must be implemented in its concrete subclasses, like `Wolf`. And if the `Canine` class were to define any new abstract properties and functions, the `Canine` subclasses would have to implement these too.

Now that you've learned about abstract classes, properties and functions, let's update the code in our `Animal` hierarchy.

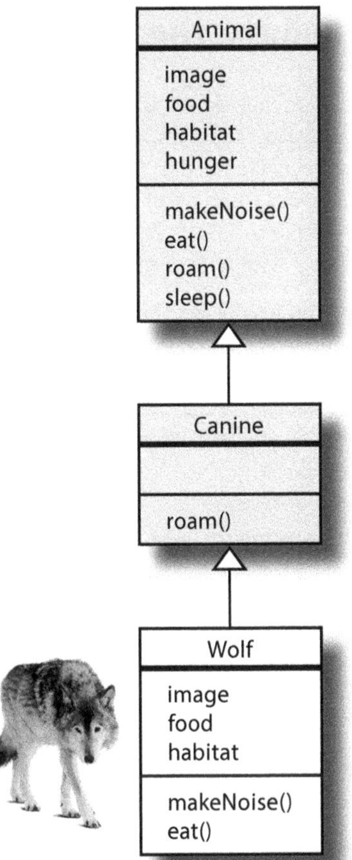

there are no Dumb Questions

Q: Why must the first concrete class implement all the abstract properties and functions it inherits?

A: Every property and function in a concrete class must be implemented so that the compiler knows what to do when they're accessed.

Only abstract classes can have abstract properties or functions. If a class has any properties or functions that are marked as abstract, the entire class must be abstract.

Q: I want to define a custom getter and setter for an abstract property. Why can't I?

A: When you mark a property as abstract, you're telling the compiler that the property has no useful implementation that would help its subclasses. If the compiler sees that an abstract property has some sort of implementation, such as a custom getter or setter, or an initial value, the compiler gets confused and won't compile the code.

When a subclass inherits from an abstract superclass, the subclass can still define its own functions and properties.

Let's update the Animals project

In the previous chapter, we wrote the code for the `Animal`, `Canine`, `Hippo`, `Wolf` and `Vet` classes, and added these to the Animals project. We need to update this code so that we make the `Animal` and `Canine` classes abstract. We'll also make the `image`, `food` and `habitat` properties in the `Animal` class abstract, along with its `makeNoise` and `eat` functions.

Open the Animals project that you created in the previous chapter, and then update your version of the code in file *Animals.kt* so that it matches ours below (our changes are in bold):

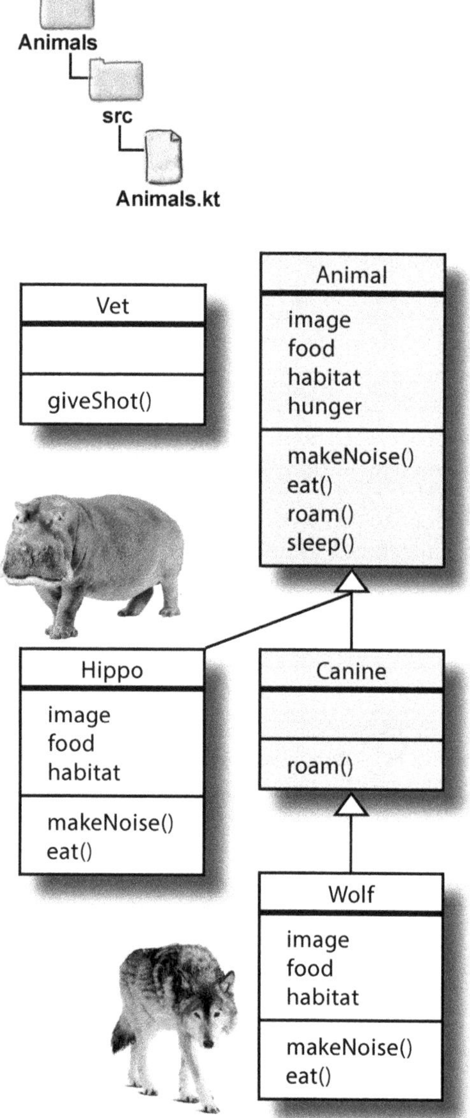

Mark the Animal class as abstract instead of open.

Mark these properties as abstract...

...and also these two functions.

```
abstract open class Animal {
    abstract open val image: String = ""
    abstract open val food: String = ""
    abstract open val habitat: String = ""
    var hunger = 10

    abstract open fun makeNoise() {
        println("The Animal is making a noise")
    }

    abstract open fun eat() {
        println("The Animal is eating")
    }

    open fun roam() {
        println("The Animal is roaming")
    }

    fun sleep() {
        println("The Animal is sleeping")
    }
}
```

(In the listing, `open`, the `= ""` initializers, the function bodies' braces and the `println` lines of `makeNoise()` and `eat()` are struck through.)

The code continues on the next page.

The code continued...

```
class Hippo : Animal() {
    override val image = "hippo.jpg"
    override val food = "grass"
    override val habitat = "water"

    override fun makeNoise() {
        println("Grunt! Grunt!")
    }

    override fun eat() {
        println("The Hippo is eating $food")
    }
}

abstract open class Canine : Animal() {
    override fun roam() {
        println("The Canine is roaming")
    }
}

class Wolf : Canine() {
    override val image = "wolf.jpg"
    override val food = "meat"
    override val habitat = "forests"

    override fun makeNoise() {
        println("Hooooowl!")
    }

    override fun eat() {
        println("The Wolf is eating $food")
    }
}
```

Mark the Canine class as abstract. (The word "open" is crossed out.)

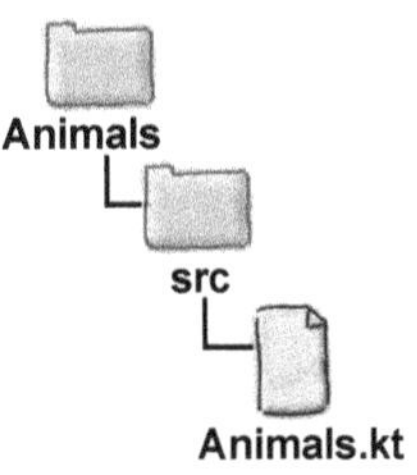

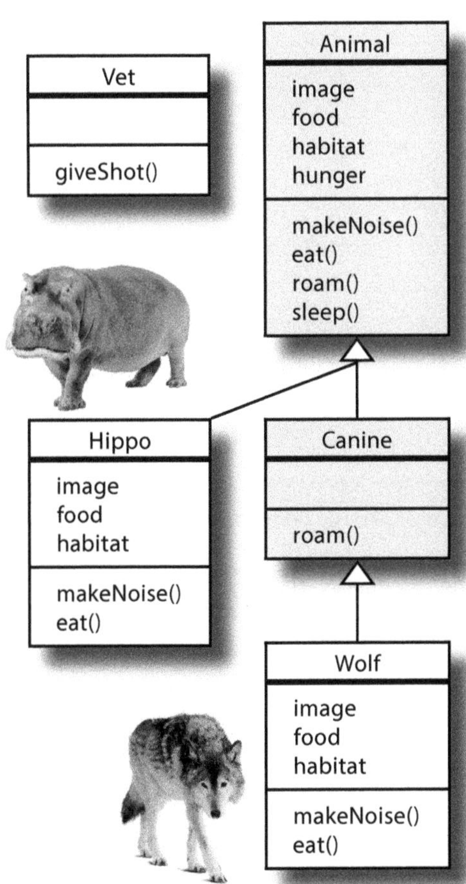

The code continues on the next page.

The code continued...

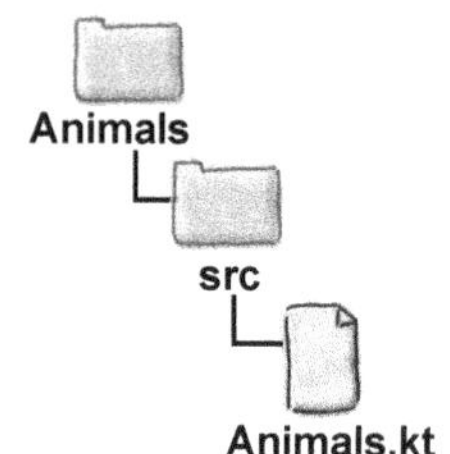


```
class Vet {
    fun giveShot(animal: Animal) {
        //Code to do something medical
        animal.makeNoise()
    }
}

fun main(args: Array<String>) {
    val animals = arrayOf(Hippo(), Wolf())
    for (item in animals) {
        item.roam()
        item.eat()
    }

    val vet = Vet()
    val wolf = Wolf()
    val hippo = Hippo()
    vet.giveShot(wolf)
    vet.giveShot(hippo)
}
```

We've not changed any of the code on this page.

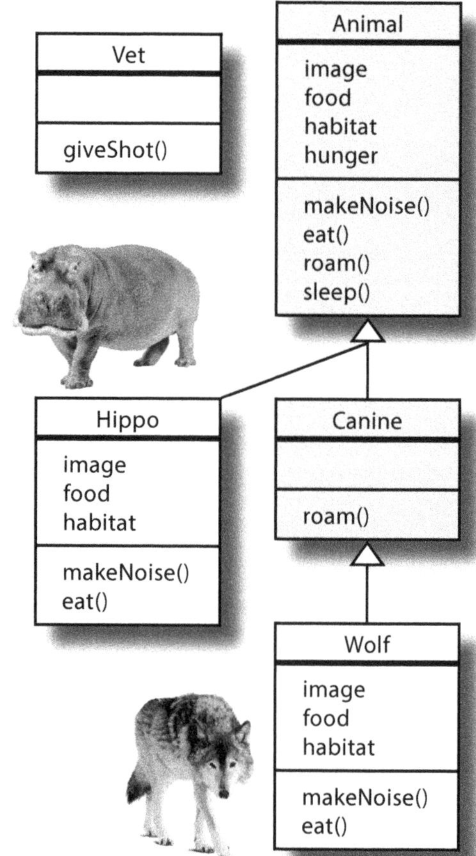

Let's take the code for a test drive to see what happens.

Test drive

Run your code. The following text gets printed in the IDE's output window as before, but now we're using abstract classes to control which classes can be instantiated.

```
The Animal is roaming
The Hippo is eating grass
The Canine is roaming
The Wolf is eating meat
Hooooowl!
Grunt! Grunt!
```

Pool Puzzle

Your **job** is to take code snippets from the pool and place them into the blank lines in the code. You may **not** use the same code snippet more than once, and you won't need to use all the snippets. Your **goal** is to create the code that matches the class inheritance hierarchy shown below.

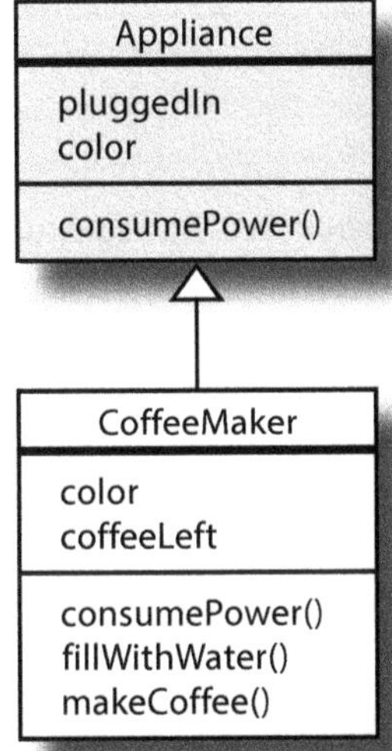


```
.......... class Appliance {
    var pluggedIn = true
    .......... val color: String

    .......... fun ..................
}

class CoffeeMaker : .................... {
    ..........val color = ""
    var coffeeLeft = false

    ..........fun .................. {
        println("Consuming power")
    }

    fun fillWithWater() {
        println("Fill with water")
    }

    fun makeCoffee() {
        println("Make the coffee")
    }
}
```

Note: each thing from the pool can only be used once!

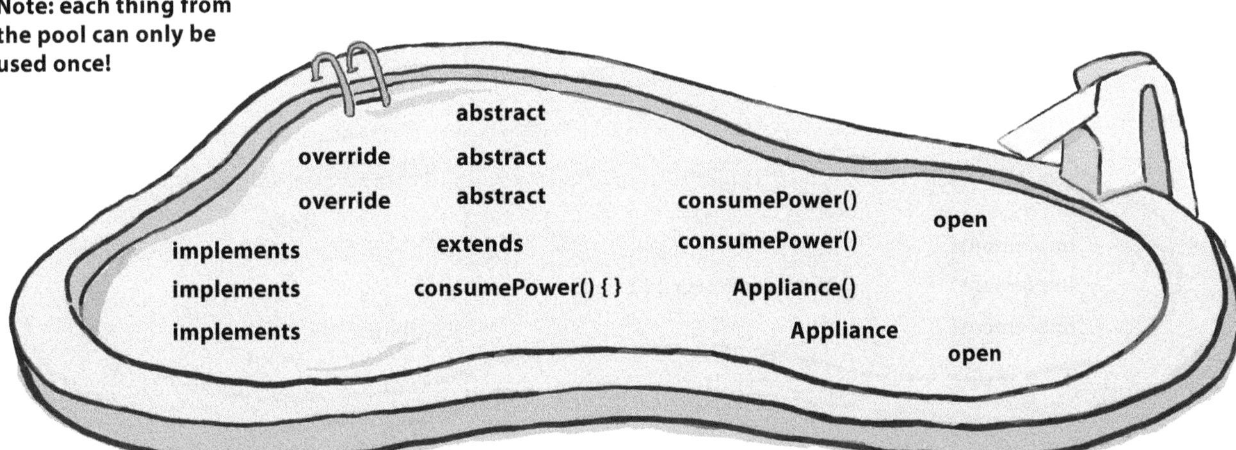

Pool Puzzle Solution

Your **job** is to take code snippets from the pool and place them into the blank lines in the code. You may **not** use the same code snippet more than once, and you won't need to use all the snippets. Your **goal** is to create the code that matches the class inheritance hierarchy shown below.

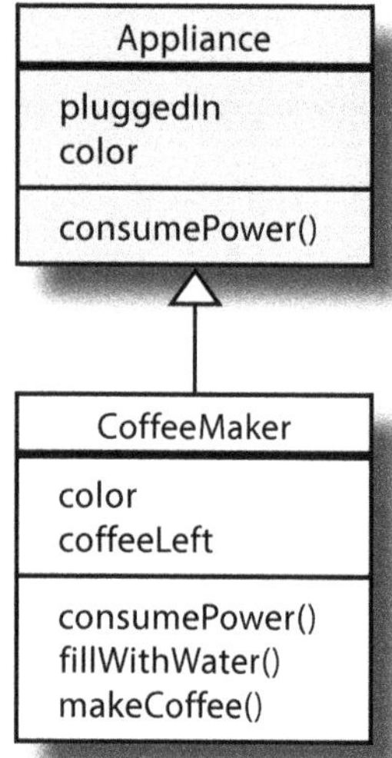

Mark the Appliance class as abstract, along with the color property and the consumePower() function.

```
abstract class Appliance {
    var pluggedIn = true
    abstract val color: String

    abstract fun consumePower()
}
```

CoffeeMaker inherits from Appliance.

Override the color property.

Override the consumePower() function.

```
class CoffeeMaker : Appliance() {
    override val color = ""
    var coffeeLeft = false

    override fun consumePower() {
        println("Consuming power")
    }

    fun fillWithWater() {
        println("Fill with water")
    }

    fun makeCoffee() {
        println("Make the coffee")
    }
}
```

You didn't need to use these snippets.

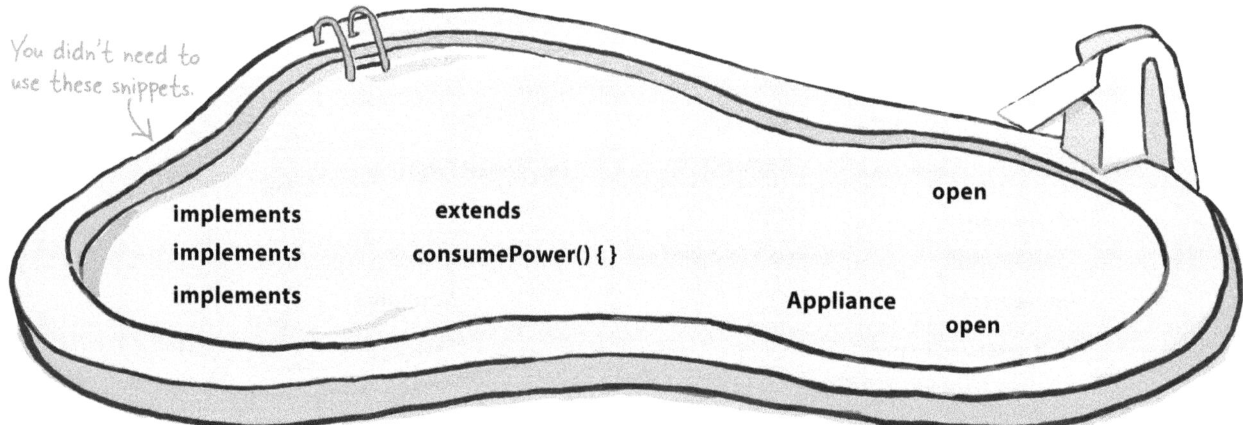

Independent classes can have common behavior

So far, you've learned how to create an inheritance hierarchy using a mix of abstract superclasses and concrete subclasses. This approach helps you to avoid writing duplicate code, and it means that you can write flexible code that benefits from polymorphism. But what if you want to include classes in your application that share *some* of the behavior defined in the inheritance hierarchy, but not all?

Suppose, for example, that we want to add a `Vehicle` class to our animal simulation application that has one function: `roam`. This would allow us to create `Vehicle` objects that can roam around the animals environment.

It would be useful if the `Vehicle` class could somehow implement the `Animal`'s `roam` function, as this would mean that we could use polymorphism to create an array of objects that can roam, and call functions on each one. But the `Vehicle` class doesn't belong in the `Animal` superclass hierarchy as it fails the IS-A test: saying "a Vehicle IS-A Animal" makes no sense, and neither does saying "an Animal IS-A Vehicle".

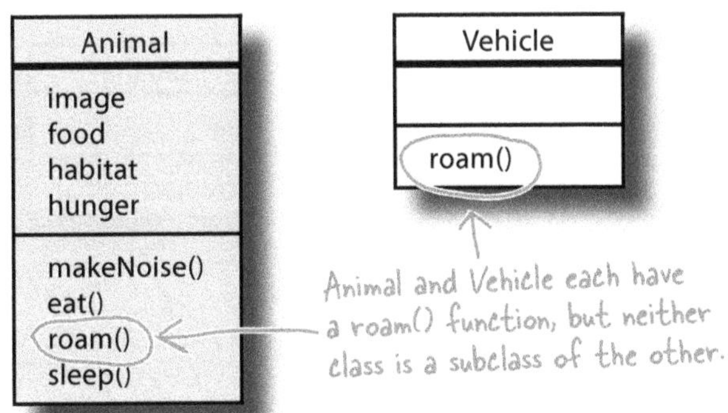

If two classes fail the IS-A test, this indicates that they probably don't belong in the same superclass hierarchy.

When you have independent classes that exhibit common behavior, you can model this behavior using an **interface**. So what's an interface?

An interface lets you define common behavior OUTSIDE a superclass hierarchy

Interfaces are used to define a protocol for common behavior so that you can benefit from polymorphism without having to rely on a strict inheritance structure. Interfaces are similar to abstract classes in that they can't be instantiated, and they can define abstract or concrete functions and properties, but there's one key difference: **a class can implement multiple interfaces, but can only inherit from a single direct superclass**. So using interfaces can provide the same benefits as using abstract classes, but with more flexibility.

Let's see how this works by adding an interface named `Roamable` to our application, which we'll use to define roaming behavior. We'll implement this interface in the `Animal` and `Vehicle` classes.

We'll start by defining the `Roamable` interface.

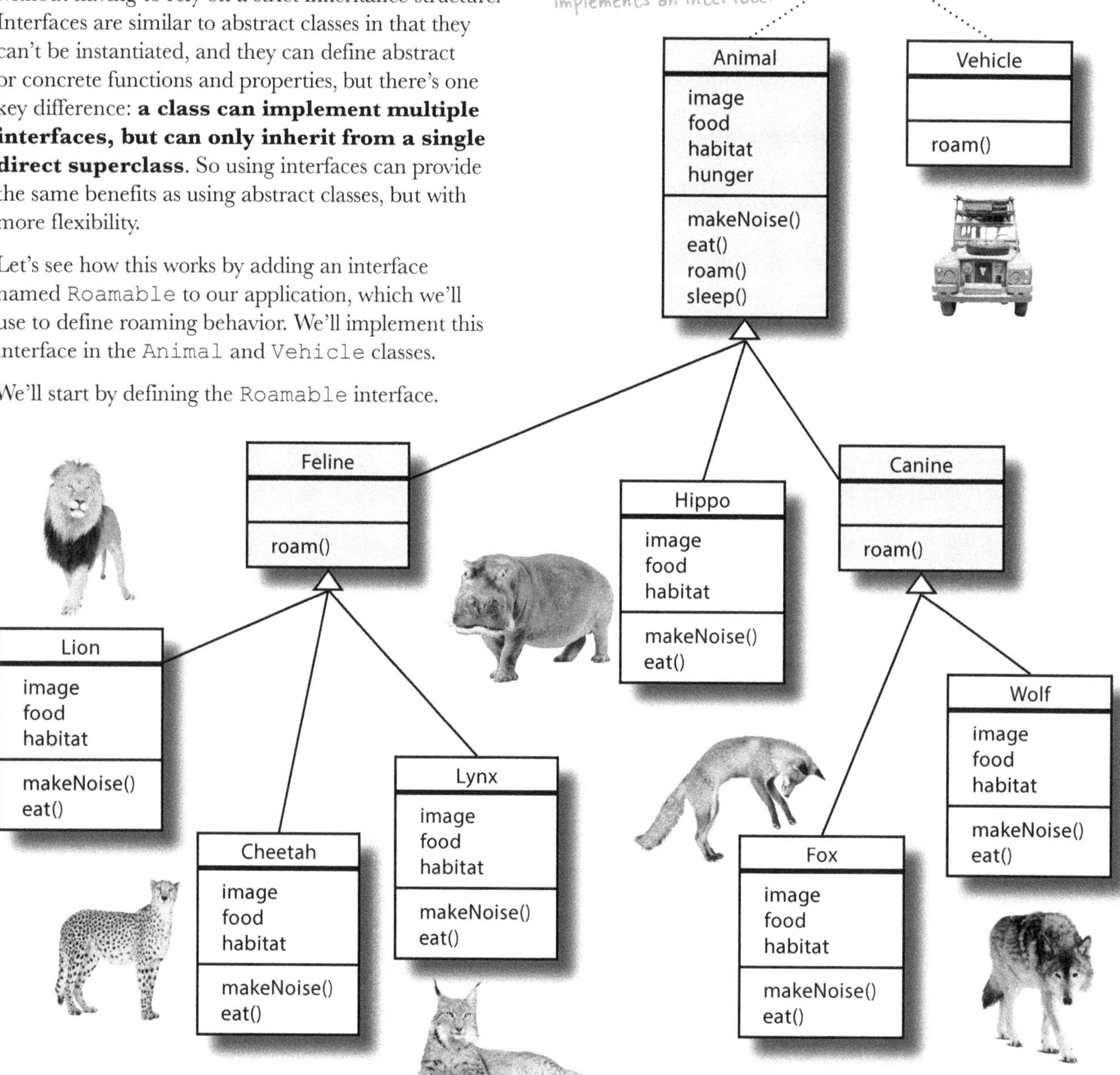

Let's define the Roamable interface

We're going to create a `Roamable` interface that we can use to provide a common protocol for roaming behavior. We'll define an abstract function named `roam` that the `Animal` and `Vehicle` classes will need to implement (you'll see the code for these classes later).

Here's what our `Roamable` interface code looks like (we'll add it to our Animals project a few pages ahead):

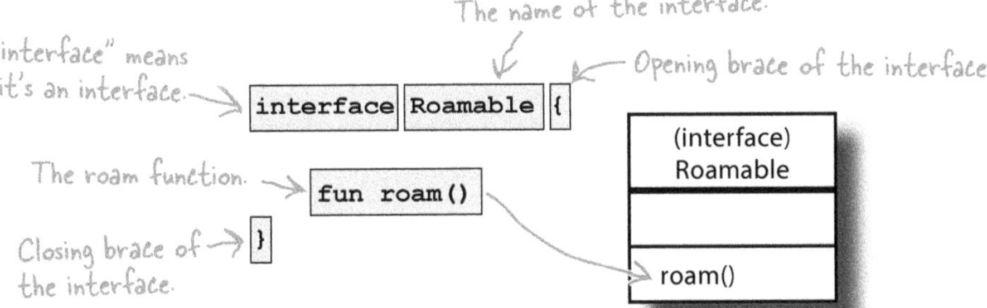

Interface functions can be abstract or concrete

You add functions to interfaces by including them in the interface body (inside the curly braces { }). In our example, we're defining an abstract function named `roam`, so the code looks like this:

```
interface Roamable {
    fun roam()    <— This is how you define an abstract function in an interface.
}
```

When you add an abstract function to an interface, there's no need to prefix the function name with the `abstract` keyword, as you would if you were adding an abstract function to an abstract class. With an interface, the compiler automatically infers that a function with no body must be abstract, so you don't have to mark it as such.

You can also add concrete functions to interfaces by providing the function with a body. The following code, for example, provides a concrete implementation for the `roam` function:

```
interface Roamable {
    fun roam() {
        println("The Roamable is roaming")    <— To add a concrete function to an interface, simply give it a body.
    }
}
```

As you can see, you define functions in an interface in a similar way to how you define functions in an abstract class. So what about properties?

How to define interface properties

You add a property to an interface by including it in the interface body. This is the *only* way in which you can define an interface property, as unlike abstract classes, **interfaces can't have constructors**. Here's how, for example, you would add an abstract Int property to the Roamable interface named `velocity`:

```
interface Roamable {
    val velocity: Int
}
```

Just as with abstract functions, there's no need to prefix an abstract property with the abstract keyword.

(interface)
Roamable

velocity

Unlike properties in abstract classes, properties that are defined in an interface can't store state, and therefore can't be initialized. You can, however, return a value for a property by defining a custom getter using code like this:

```
interface Roamable {
    val velocity: Int
        get() = 20
}
```

This returns a value of 20 whenever the property is accessed. But you can still override the property in any class that implements the interface.

Another restriction is that interface properties **don't have backing fields**. You learned in Chapter 4 that a backing field provides a reference to the underlying value of a property, so you can't, say, define a custom setter that updates a property's value like this:

```
interface Roamable {
    var velocity: Int
        get() = 20
        set(value) {
            field = value
        }
}
```

If you try to write code like this in an interface, it won't compile. This is because you can't use the "field" keyword in an interface, so you can't update the underlying value of the property.

You, however, define a setter so long as it doesn't try and reference the property's backing field. The following code, for example, is valid:

```
interface Roamable {
    var velocity: Int
        get() = 20
        set(value) {
            println("Unable to update velocity")
        }
}
```

This code compiles because you're not using the field keyword. But it won't update the underlying value of the property.

Now that you've learned how to define an interface, let's see how to implement one.

Declare that a class implements an interface...

You mark that a class implements an interface in a similar way to how you mark that a class inherits from a superclass: by adding a colon to the class header followed by the name of the interface. Here's how, for example, you declare that the `Vehicle` class implements the `Roamable` interface:

```
class Vehicle : Roamable {
    ...
}
```

This is like saying "The Vehicle class implements the Roamable interface".

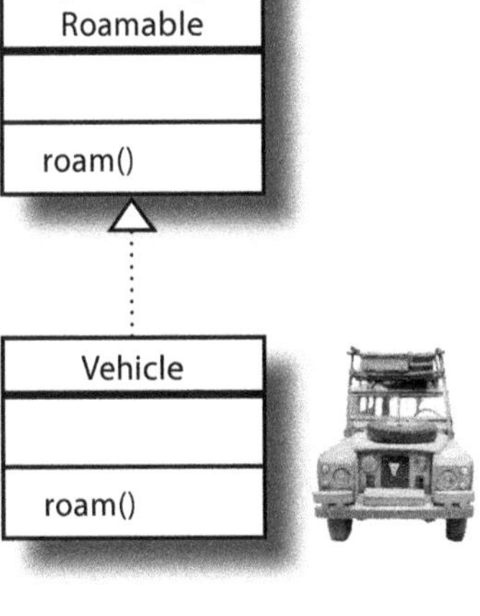

Unlike when you declare that a class inherits from a superclass, you don't put parentheses after the interface name. This is because the parentheses are only needed in order to call the superclass constructor, and interfaces don't have constructors.

...then override its properties and functions

Declaring that a class implements an interface gives the class all the properties and functions that are in that interface. You can override any of these properties and functions, and you do this in exactly the same way that you would override properties and functions inherited from a superclass. The following code, for example, overrides the `roam` function from the `Roamable` interface:

```
class Vehicle : Roamable {
    override fun roam() {
        println("The Vehicle is roaming")
    }
}
```

This code overrides the roam() function that the Vehicle class inherits from the Roamable interface.

Just like abstract superclasses, any concrete classes that implement the interface *must* have a concrete implementation for any abstract properties and functions. The `Vehicle` class, for example, directly implements the `Roamable` interface, so it must implement all the abstract properties and functions defined in this interface in order for the code to compile. If the class that implements the interface is abstract, however, the class can either implement the properties and functions itself, or pass the buck to its subclasses.

Note that a class that implements an interface can still define its own properties and functions. The `Vehicle` class, for example, could define its own `fuelType` property and still implement the `Roamable` interface.

Earlier in the chapter, we said that a class could implement multiple interfaces. Let's see how.

Concrete classes can't contain abstract properties and functions, so they must implement all of the abstract properties and functions that they inherit.

How to implement multiple interfaces

You declare that a class (or interface) implements multiple interfaces by adding each one to the class header, separating each one with a comma. Suppose, for example, that you have two interfaces named A and B. You would declare that a class named X implements both interfaces using the code:

```
class X : A, B {
    ...
}
```

Class X implements the A and B interfaces.

A class can also inherit from a superclass in addition to implementing one or more interfaces. Here's how, for example, you specify that class Y implements interface A, and inherits from class C:

```
class Y : C(), A {
    ...
}
```

Class Y inherits from class C, and implements interface A.

If a class inherits multiple implementations of the same function or property, the class must provide its own implementation, or specify which version of the function or property it should use. If, for example, the A and B interfaces both include a concrete function named myFunction, and the X class implements both interfaces, the X class must provide an implementation of myFunction so that the compiler knows how to handle a call to this function:

```
interface A {
    fun myFunction() { println("from A") }
}

interface B {
    fun myFunction() { println("from B") }
}

class X : A, B {
    override fun myFunction() {
        super<A>.myFunction()
        super<B>.myFunction()
        //Extra code specific to class X
    }
}
```

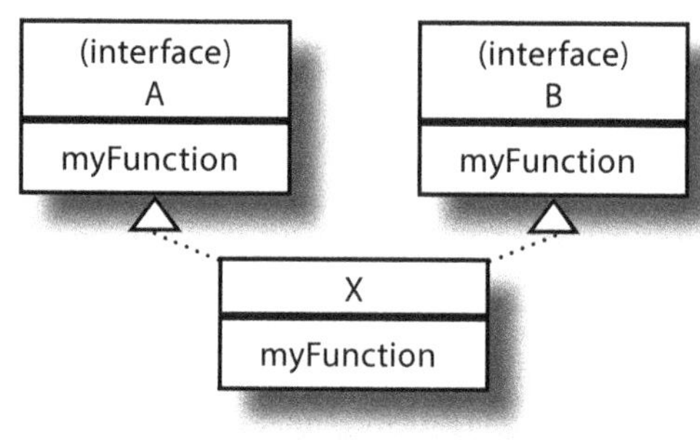

super<A> refers to the superclass (or interface) named A. So super<A>.myFunction() calls the version of myFunction that's defined in A.

This code calls the version of myFunction defined in A, then the version defined in B. It then runs code that's specific to class X.

How do you know whether to make a class, a subclass, an abstract class, or an interface?

Unsure whether you should create a class, abstract class or interface? Then the following tips should help you out:

- Make a class with no superclass when your new class doesn't pass the IS-A test for any other type.
- Make a subclass that inherits from a superclass when you need to make a more specific version of a class and need to override or add new behaviors.
- Make an abstract class when you want to define a template for a group of subclasses. Make the class abstract when you want to guarantee that nobody can make objects of that type.
- Make an interface when you want to define common behavior, or a role that other classes can play, regardless of where these classes are in the inheritance tree.

Roses are red,
Violets are blue,
Inherit from one,
But implement two.

A Kotlin class can have only one parent (superclass), and that parent class defines who you are. But you can implement multiple interfaces, and those interfaces define the roles that you can play.

Now that you've seen how to define and implement interfaces, let's update the code for our Animals project.

there are no Dumb Questions

Q: Are there any naming conventions for interfaces?

A: Nothing is enforced, but because interfaces specify behavior, words ending in *-ible* or *-able* are often used; they give a name to what something *does*, rather than what it *is*.

Q: Why don't interfaces and abstract classes need to be marked as open?

A: Interfaces and abstract classes live to be implemented or inherited from. The compiler knows this, so behind the scenes, every interface and abstract class is implicitly open, even if it isn't marked as such.

Q: You said that you can override any of the properties and functions that are defined in an interface. Don't you mean that you can override any of its *abstract* properties and functions?

A: No. With an interface, you can override any of its properties and functions. So even if a function in an interface has a concrete implementation, you can still override it.

Q: Can an interface inherit from a superclass?

A: No, but it *can* implement one or more interfaces.

Q: When should I define a concrete implementation for a function, and when should I leave it abstract?

A: You normally provide a concrete implementation if you can think of one that would be helpful to anything that inherits it.

If you *can't* think of a helpful implementation, you would normally leave it abstract as this forces any concrete subclasses to provide their own implementation.

Update the Animals project

We'll add a new `Roamable` interface and `Vehicle` class to our project. The `Vehicle` class will implement the `Roamable` interface, and so will the abstract `Animal` class.

Update your version of the code in file *Animals.kt* so that it matches ours below (our changes are in bold):

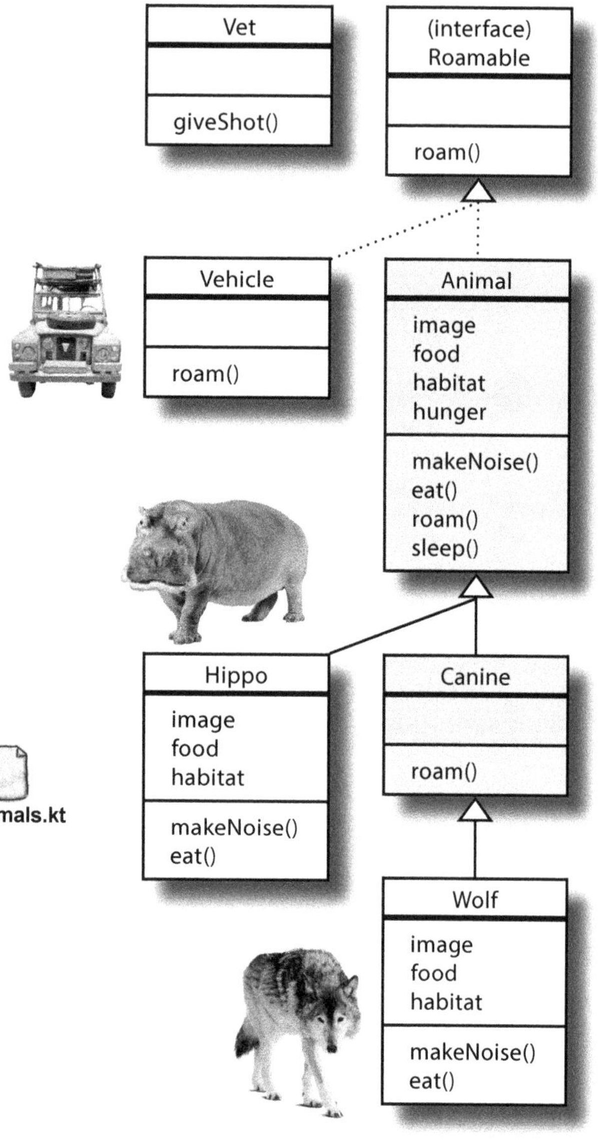

Add the Roamable interface with an abstract function named roam().

The Animal class needs to implement the Roamable interface.

Override the roam() function from the Roamable interface.

```
interface Roamable {
    fun roam()
}

abstract class Animal : Roamable {
    abstract val image: String
    abstract val food: String
    abstract val habitat: String
    var hunger = 10

    abstract fun makeNoise()

    abstract fun eat()

    override fun roam() {
        println("The Animal is roaming")
    }

    fun sleep() {
        println("The Animal is sleeping")
    }
}
```

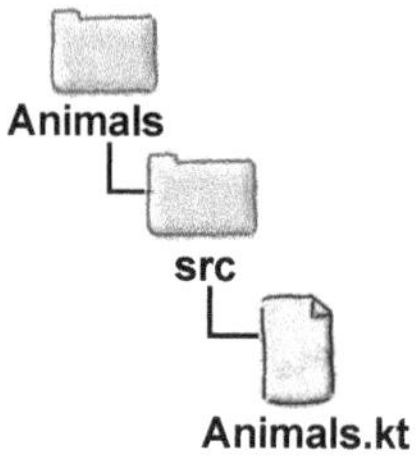

Animals
src
Animals.kt

Vet
giveShot()

(interface) Roamable
roam()

Vehicle
roam()

Animal
image
food
habitat
hunger
makeNoise()
eat()
roam()
sleep()

Hippo
image
food
habitat
makeNoise()
eat()

Canine
roam()

Wolf
image
food
habitat
makeNoise()
eat()

The code continues on the next page.

The code continued...

```
class Hippo : Animal() {
    override val image = "hippo.jpg"
    override val food = "grass"
    override val habitat = "water"

    override fun makeNoise() {
        println("Grunt! Grunt!")
    }

    override fun eat() {
        println("The Hippo is eating $food")
    }
}

abstract class Canine : Animal() {
    override fun roam() {
        println("The Canine is roaming")
    }
}

class Wolf : Canine() {
    override val image = "wolf.jpg"
    override val food = "meat"
    override val habitat = "forests"

    override fun makeNoise() {
        println("Hooooowl!")
    }

    override fun eat() {
        println("The Wolf is eating $food")
    }
}
```

We've not updated any of the code on this page.

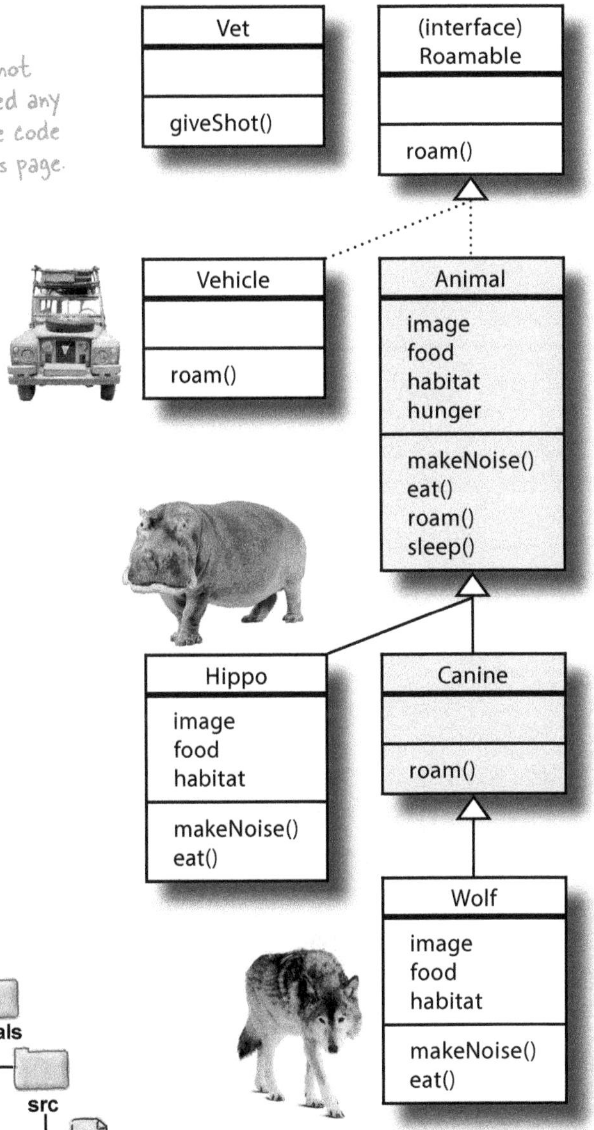

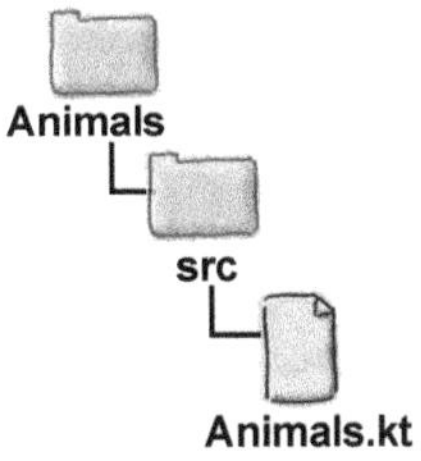

Vet: giveShot()

(interface) Roamable: roam()

Vehicle: roam()

Animal: image, food, habitat, hunger; makeNoise(), eat(), roam(), sleep()

Hippo: image, food, habitat; makeNoise(), eat()

Canine: roam()

Wolf: image, food, habitat; makeNoise(), eat()

Animals / src / Animals.kt

The code continues on the next page.

The code continued...

```
class Vehicle : Roamable {    ← Add the Vehicle class.
    override fun roam() {
        println("The Vehicle is roaming")
    }
}

class Vet {
    fun giveShot(animal: Animal) {
        //Code to do something medical
        animal.makeNoise()
    }
}

fun main(args: Array<String>) {
    val animals = arrayOf(Hippo(), Wolf())
    for (item in animals) {
        item.roam()
        item.eat()
    }

    val vet = Vet()
    val wolf = Wolf()
    val hippo = Hippo()
    vet.giveShot(wolf)
    vet.giveShot(hippo)
}
```


Let's see what happens when we take our code for a test drive.

Test drive

Run your code. Text gets printed in the IDE's output window as before, but now the `Animal` class uses the `Roamable` interface for its roaming behavior.

We still need to use `Vehicle` objects in our main function, but first, have a go at the following exercise.

```
The Animal is roaming
The Hippo is eating grass
The Canine is roaming
The Wolf is eating meat
Hooooowl!
Grunt! Grunt!
```

On the left you'll find sets of class diagrams. Your job is to turn these into valid Kotlin declarations. We did the first one for you.

Diagram:

1
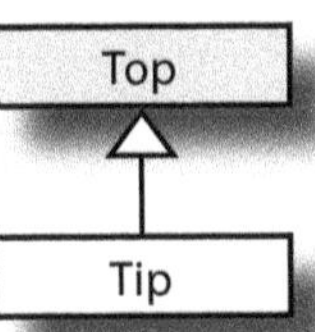

2
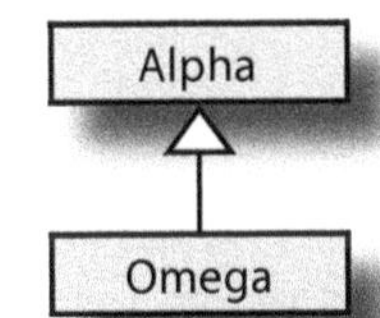

3
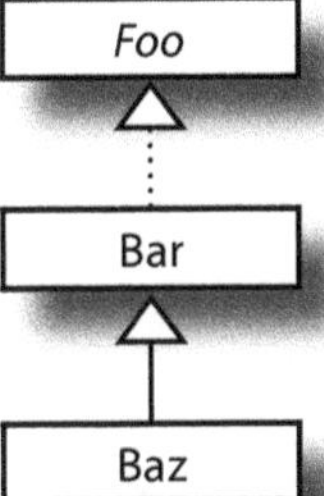

4
Foo
Bar
Baz

5
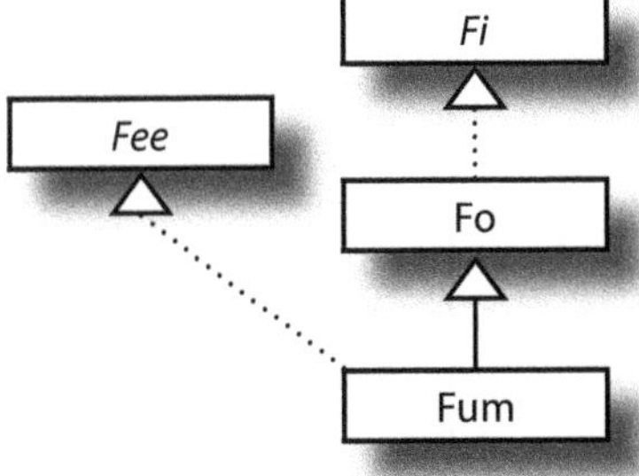

Declaration:

1
```
open class Click { }
class Clack : Click() { }
```

2

3

4

5

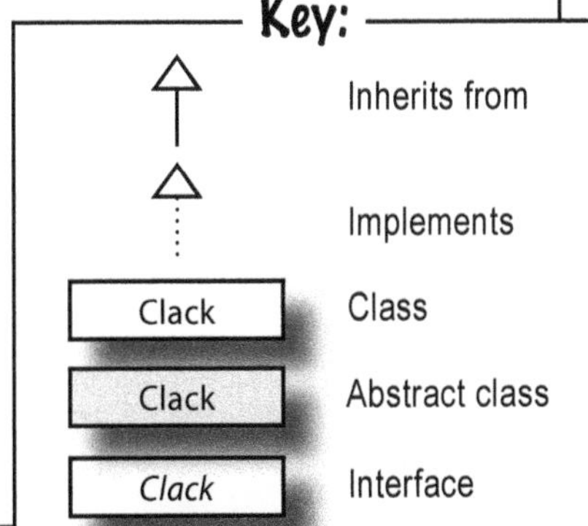

Exercise Solution

On the left you'll find sets of class diagrams. Your job is to turn these into valid Kotlin declarations. We did the first one for you.

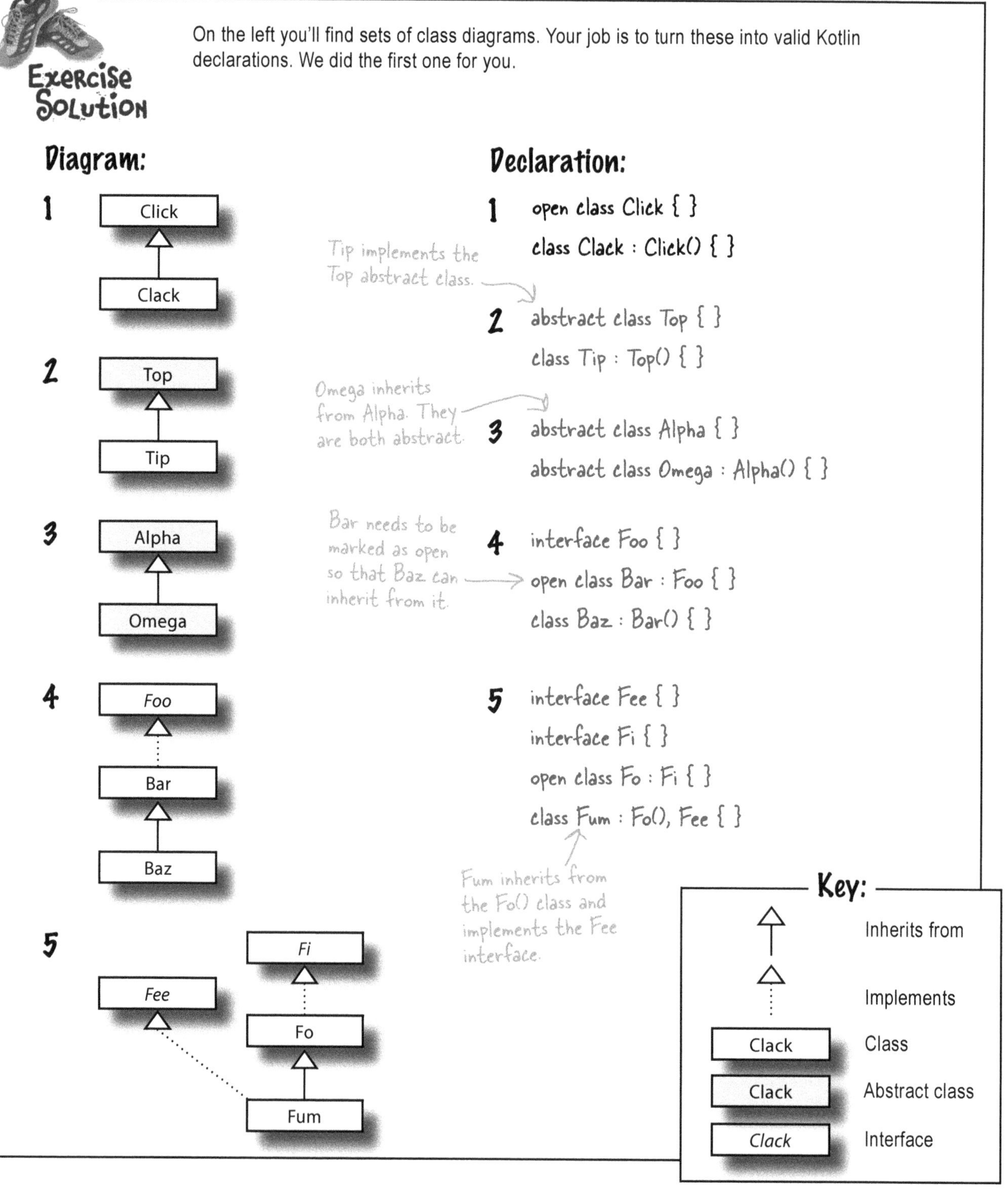

Interfaces let you use polymorphism

You already know that using interfaces means that your code can benefit from polymorphism. You can, for example, use polymorphism to create an array of `Roamable` objects, and call each object's `roam` function:

```
val roamables = arrayOf(Hippo(), Wolf(), Vehicle())
for (item in roamables) {
    item.roam()
}
```

This line creates an array of Roamable objects.

As the roamables array holds Roamable objects, this means that the item variable is of type Roamable.

REF
item
var Roamable

But what if you don't just want to access functions and properties defined in the `Roamable` interface? What if you want to call each `Animal`'s `makeNoise` function too? You can't just use:

```
item.makeNoise()
```

because `item` is a variable of type `Roamable`, so it doesn't recognize the `makeNoise` function.

Access uncommon behavior by checking an object's type

You can access behavior that's not defined by a variable's type by first using the **`is`** operator to check the type of the underlying object. If the underlying object is of the appropriate type, the compiler then lets you access behavior that's appropriate for that type. The following code, for example, checks whether the object referred to by an `Animal` variable is a `Wolf`, and if so, calls the `eat` function:

```
val animal: Animal = Wolf()
if (animal is Wolf) {
    animal.eat()
}
```

The compiler knows that the object is a Wolf, so calls its eat() function.

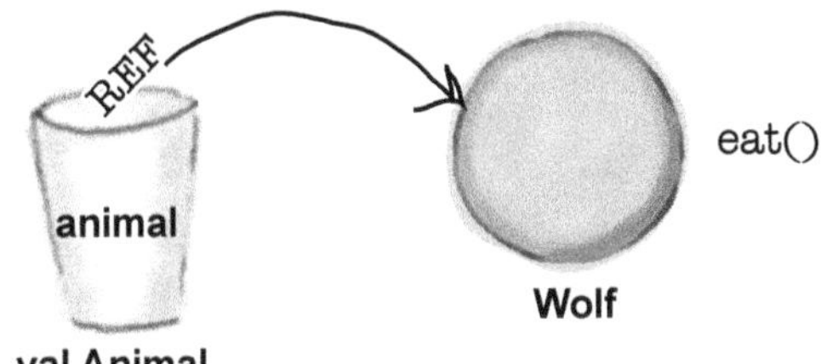

In the above code, the compiler knows that the underlying object is a `Wolf`, so it's safe to run any code that's `Wolf`-specific. This means that if we want to call the `eat` function for each `Animal` object in an array of `Roamables`, we can use the following:

```
val roamables = arrayOf(Hippo(), Wolf(), Vehicle())
for (item in roamables) {
    item.roam()
    if (item is Animal) {
        item.eat()
    }
}
```

If the item is an Animal, the compiler knows it can call the item's eat() function.

Use the is operator to check if the underlying object is the specified type (or one of its subtypes).

You can use the `is` operator in a variety of situations. Let's find out more.

Where to use the is operator

Here are some of the most common ways in which you might want to use the `is` operator:

As the condition for an if

As you've already seen, you can use the `is` operator as the condition for an `if`. The following code, for example, assigns a `String` of "Wolf" to variable `str` if the `animal` variable holds a reference to a `Wolf` object, and "not Wolf" if it doesn't:

```
val str = if (animal is Wolf) "Wolf" else "not Wolf"
```

Note that it must be possible for the underlying object to be the specified type or the code won't compile. You can't, say, test if an Animal variable holds a reference to an Int because Animal and Int are incompatible types.

In conditions using && and ||

You can build up more complex conditions using `&&` and `||`. The following code, for instance, tests whether a `Roamable` variable holds a reference to an `Animal` object, and if so, it further tests if the `Animal`'s `hunger` property is less than 5:

```
if (roamable is Animal && roamable.hunger < 5) {
    //Code to deal with a hungry Animal
}
```

The right side of the if condition only runs if roamable is an Animal, so we can access its hunger property.

You can also use `!is` to test if an object is *not* a particular type. The following code, for example, is like saying "if the roamable variable doesn't hold a reference to an Animal, or if the Animal's hunger property is greater than or equal to 5":

```
if (roamable !is Animal || x.hunger >= 5) {
    //Code to deal with a non-Animal, or with a non-hungry Animal
}
```

Remember, the right side of an || condition only runs if the left side is false. Therefore, the right side can only run if roamable is an Animal.

In a while loop

If you want to use the `is` operator as the condition for a `while` loop, you can do so using code like this:

```
while (animal is Wolf) {
    //Code that runs while the Animal is a Wolf
}
```

In the above example, the code continues to loop while the `animal` variable holds a reference to a `Wolf` object.

You can also use the `is` operator with a **`when`** statement. Let's find out what these are, and how to use them.

Use when to compare a variable against a bunch of options

A `when` statement is useful if you want to compare a variable against a set of different options. It's like using a chain of `if/else` expressions, but more compact and readable.

Here's an example of what a `when` statement looks like:

```
when (x) {
    0 -> println("x is zero")
    1, 2 -> println("x is 1 or 2")
    else -> {
        println("x is neither 0, 1 nor 2")
        println("x is some other value")
    }
}
```

Check the value of variable x.

When x is 0, run this code.

Run this code when x is 1 or 2.

when statements can have an else clause.

Run this block of code when x is some other value.

The above code takes the variable `x`, and checks its value against various options. It's like saying: "when *x* is 0, print "x is zero", when *x* is 1 or 2, print "x is 1 or 2", otherwise print some other text".

If you want to run different code depending on the underlying type of an object, you can use the `is` operator inside a `when` statement. The code below, for example, uses the `is` operator to check the type of the underlying object that's referenced by the `roamable` variable. When the type is `Wolf`, it runs code that's `Wolf`-specific, when the type is `Hippo`, it runs `Hippo`-specific code, and it runs other code if the type is some other `Animal` (not `Wolf` or `Hippo`):

```
when (roamable) {
    is Wolf -> {
    //Wolf-specific code
    }
    is Hippo -> {
        //Hippo-specific code
    }
    is Animal -> {
        //Code that runs if roamable is some other Animal
    }
}
```

Check the value of roamable.

This code will only run if roamable is a type of Animal that's not Wolf or Hippo.

Using when as an expression

You can also use `when` as an expression, which means that you can use it to return a value. The following code, for example, uses a `when` expression to assign a value to a variable:

```
var y = when (x) {
    0 -> true
    else -> false
}
```

When you use the `when` operator in this way, you *must* account for every value the variable you're checking can have, usually by including an `else` clause.

The is operator ^usually performs a smart cast

In most circumstances, the `is` operator performs a **smart cast**. *Casting* means that the compiler treats a variable as though its type is different to the one that it's declared as, and *smart casting* means that the compiler automatically performs the cast on your behalf. The code below, for example, uses the `is` operator to smart cast the variable named `item` to a `Wolf`, so that inside the body of the `if` condition, the compiler can treat the `item` variable as though it's a `Wolf`:

```
if (item is Wolf) {
    item.eat()
    item.makeNoise()
    //Other Wolf-specific code
}
```

item is smart cast to a Wolf for the duration of this code block.

The `is` operator performs a smart cast whenever the compiler can guarantee that the variable can't change between checking the object's type and when it's used. In the above code, for example, the compiler knows that the `item` variable can't be given a reference to a different type of variable in between the call to the `is` operator, and the `Wolf`-specific function calls.

But there are some situations in which smart casting doesn't happen. The `is` operator won't smart cast a `var` property in a class, for example, because the compiler can't guarantee that some other code won't sneak in and update the property. This means that the following code won't compile because the compiler can't smart cast the `r` variable to a `Wolf`:

```
class MyRoamable {
    var r: Roamable = Wolf()

    fun myFunction() {
        if (r is Wolf) {
            r.eat()
        }
    }
}
```

The compiler can't smart cast the Roamable property r to a Wolf. This is because the compiler can't guarantee that some other code won't update the property in between checking its type and its usage. The code therefore won't compile.

> **Relax**
>
> **You don't need to remember all the circumstances in which smart casting can't be used.**
>
> If you try and use smart casting inappropriately, the compiler will tell you.

So what can you do in this sort of situation?

Use as to perform an explicit cast

If you want to access the behavior of an underlying object but the compiler can't perform a smart cast, you can explicitly cast the object into the appropriate type.

Suppose you're sure that a `Roamable` variable named `r` holds a reference to a `Wolf` object, and you want to access the object's `Wolf`-specific behavior. In this situation, you can use the **as** operator to copy the reference that's held in the `Roamable` variable, and force it into a new `Wolf` variable. You can then use the `Wolf` variable to access the `Wolf` behavior. Here's the code to do this:

```
var wolf = r as Wolf
wolf.eat()
```

This code explicitly casts the object to a Wolf so that you can call its Wolf functions.

Note that the `wolf` and `r` variables **each hold a reference to the same `Wolf` object**. But whereas the `r` variable only knows that the object implements the `Roamable` interface, the `wolf` variable knows that the object is actually a `Wolf`, so it can treat the object like the `Wolf` it really is:

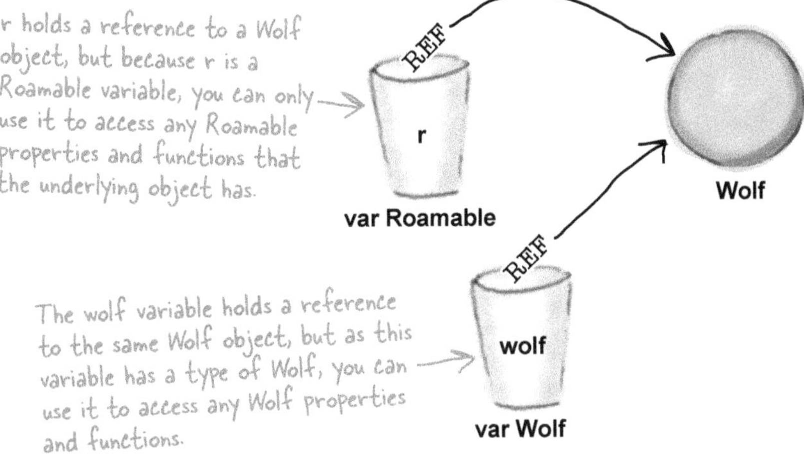

If you're not sure that the underlying object is a `Wolf`, you can use the `is` operator to check before you do the cast using code like this:

```
if (r is Wolf) {
    val wolf = r as Wolf
    wolf.eat()
}
```

If r is a Wolf, cast it as a Wolf and call its eat() function.

So now that you've seen how casting (and smart casting) works, let's update the code in our Animals project.

Update the Animals project

We've updated the code in our `main` function so that it includes an array of `Roamable` objects. Update your version of the function in file *Animals.kt* so that it matches ours below (our changes are in bold):

We're only changing the code in the main function.

```
...
fun main(args: Array<String>) {
    val animals = arrayOf(Hippo(), Wolf())
    for (item in animals) {
        item.roam()
        item.eat()
    }

    val vet = Vet()
    val wolf = Wolf()
    val hippo = Hippo()
    vet.giveShot(wolf)
    vet.giveShot(hippo)

    val roamables = arrayOf(Hippo(), Wolf(), Vehicle())
    for (item in roamables) {
        item.roam()
        if (item is Animal) {
            item.eat()
        }
    }
}
```

Create an an array of Roamables.

Call the eat() function for each Animal in the array.

Animals
src
Animals.kt

Vet: giveShot()
(interface) Roamable: roam()
Vehicle: roam()
Animal: image, food, habitat, hunger; makeNoise(), eat(), roam(), sleep()
Hippo: image, food, habitat; makeNoise(), eat()
Canine: roam()
Wolf: image, food, habitat; makeNoise(), eat()

Now that you've updated your code, let's take it for a test drive.

Test drive

Run your code. When the code loops through the `roamables` array, each item's roam function is called, but the `eat` function is only called if the underlying object is an `Animal`.

```
The Animal is roaming
The Hippo is eating grass
The Canine is roaming
The Wolf is eating meat
Hooooowl!
Grunt! Grunt!
The Animal is roaming
The Hippo is eating grass
The Canine is roaming
The Wolf is eating meat
The Vehicle is roaming
```

BE the Compiler

The code on the left represents a source file. Your job is to play like you're the compiler and say which of the code segments on the right would compile and produce the required output when inserted into the code on the left.

Output:

The code needs to produce this output.

Plane is flying
Superhero is flying

```
interface Flyable {
    val x: String

    fun fly() {
        println("$x is flying")
    }
}

class Bird : Flyable {
    override val x = "Bird"
}

class Plane : Flyable {
    override val x = "Plane"
}

class Superhero : Flyable {
    override val x = "Superhero"
}

fun main(args: Array<String>) {
    val f = arrayOf(Bird(), Plane(), Superhero())
    var x = 0
    while (x in 0..2) {
        [                    ]
        x++
    }
}
```

Each code segment goes here.

These are the code segments.

1
```
when (f[x]) {
    is Bird -> {
        x++
        f[x].fly()
    }
    is Plane, is Superhero ->
                    f[x].fly()
}
```

2
```
if (x is Plane || x is Superhero) {
    f[x].fly()
}
```

3
```
when (f[x]) {
    Plane, Superhero -> f[x].fly()
}
```

4
```
val y = when (f[x]) {
    is Bird -> false
    else -> true
}
if (y) {f[x].fly()}
```

BE the Compiler Solution

The code on the left represents a source file. Your job is to play like you're the compiler and say which of the code segments on the right would compile and produce the required output when inserted into the code on the left.

Output:

Plane is flying
Superhero is flying

```
interface Flyable {
    val x: String

    fun fly() {
        println("$x is flying")
    }
}

class Bird : Flyable {
    override val x = "Bird"
}

class Plane : Flyable {
    override val x = "Plane"
}

class Superhero : Flyable {
    override val x = "Superhero"
}

fun main(args: Array<String>) {
    val f = arrayOf(Bird(), Plane(), Superhero())
    var x = 0
    while (x in 0..2) {
        [                    ]
        x++
    }
}
```

1.

```
when (f[x]) {
    is Bird -> {
        x++
        f[x].fly()
    }
    is Plane, is Superhero ->
                    f[x].fly()
}
```

This code compiles and produces the correct output.

This won't compile as x is an Int, and can't be a Plane or Superhero.

2.

```
if (x is Plane || x is Superhero) {
    f[x].fly()
}
```

This won't compile because the is operator is required in order to check the type of f[x].

3.

```
when (f[x]) {
    Plane, Superhero -> f[x].fly()
}
```

4.

```
val y = when (f[x]) {
    is Bird -> false
    else -> true
}
if (y) {f[x].fly()}
```

This code compiles and produces the correct output.

Your Kotlin Toolbox

You've got Chapter 6 under your belt and now you've added abstract classes and interfaces to your toolbox.

You can download the full code for the chapter from https://tinyurl.com/HFKotlin.

CHAPTER 6

BULLET POINTS

- An abstract class can't be instantiated. It can contain both abstract and non-abstract properties and functions.
- Any class that contains an abstract property or function must be declared abstract.
- A class that's not abstract is called concrete.
- You implement abstract properties and functions by overriding them.
- All abstract properties and functions must be overridden in any concrete subclasses.
- An interface lets you define common behavior outside a superclass hierarchy so that independent classes can still benefit from polymorphism.
- Interfaces can have abstract or non-abstract functions.
- Interfaces properties can be abstract, or they can have getters and setters. They can't be initialized, and they don't have access to a backing field.
- A class can implement multiple interfaces.
- If a subclass inherits from a superclass (or implements an interface) named `A`, you can use the code:

  ```
  super<A>.myFunction
  ```

  to call the implementation of `myFunction` that's defined in `A`.
- If a variable holds a reference to an object, you can use the `is` operator to check the type of the underlying object.
- The `is` operator performs a smart cast when the compiler can guarantee that the underlying object can't have changed between the type check and its usage.
- The `as` operator lets you perform an explicit cast.
- A `when` expression lets you compare a variable against an exhaustive set of different options.

7 data classes

Dealing with Data

Nobody wants to spend their life reinventing the wheel.

Most applications include classes whose main purpose is to *store data*, so to make your coding life easier, the Kotlin developers came up with the concept of a **data class**. Here, you'll learn how data classes enable you to write code that's ***cleaner and more concise*** than you ever dreamed was possible. You'll explore the data class ***utility functions***, and discover how to ***destructure a data object into its component parts***. Along the way, you'll find out how ***default parameter values*** can make your code more flexible, and we'll introduce you to **Any**, the *mother of all superclasses*.

== calls a function named equals

As you already know, you can use the == operator to check for equality. Behind the scenes, each time you use the == operator, it calls a function named `equals`. Every object has an `equals` function, and the implementation of this function determines how the == operator will behave.

By default, the `equals` function checks for equality by checking whether two variables hold references to the same underlying object.

To see how this works, suppose that we have two `Wolf` variables named `w1` and `w2`. If `w1` and `w2` hold references to the same `Wolf` object, comparing them with the == operator will evaluate to `true`:

```
val w1 = Wolf()
val w2 = w1
//w1 == w2 is true
```

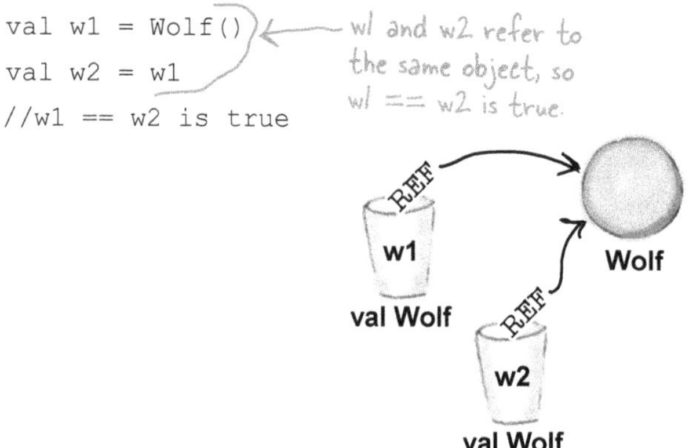

If, however, `w1` and `w2` hold references to separate `Wolf` objects, comparing them with the == operator will evaluate to `false`, *even if the objects hold identical property values.*

```
val w1 = Wolf()
val w2 = Wolf()
//w1 == w2 is false
```

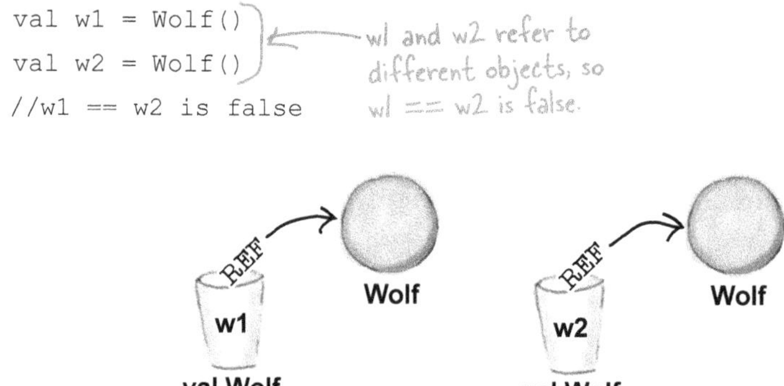

As we said earlier, every object that you create automatically includes an `equals` function. But where does this function come from?

equals is inherited from a superclass named Any

Each object has a function named `equals` because its class inherits the function from a class named **Any**. Class `Any` is the mother of all classes: the ultimate superclass of *everything*. Every class you define is a subclass of `Any` without you ever having to say it. So if you write the code for a class named `myClass` that looks like this:

```
class MyClass {
    ...
}
```

Every class is a subclass of the Any class, and inherits its behavior. Every class IS-A type of Any without you having to say so.

behind the scenes, the compiler automatically turns it into this:

```
class MyClass : Any() {
    ...
}
```

The compiler secretly makes each class a subclass of Any.

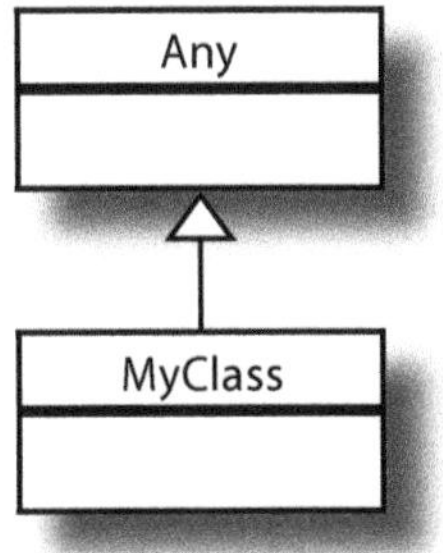

The importance of being Any

Having `Any` as the ultimate superclass has two key benefits:

It ensures that every class inherits common behavior.
The `Any` class defines important behavior that the system relies on, and as every class is a subclass of `Any`, this behavior is inherited by every object you create. The `Any` class defines a function named `equals`, for example, which means that every object automatically inherits this function.

It means you can use polymorphism with any object.
Every class is a subclass of `Any`, so every object you create has `Any` as its ultimate supertype. This means that you can create a function with `Any` parameters, or an `Any` return type, so that it will work with all types of object. It also means that you can create polymorphic arrays to hold objects of any type using code like this:

```
val myArray = arrayOf(Car(), Guitar(), Giraffe())
```

The compiler spots that each object in the array has a common supertype of Any, so it creates an array of type Array<Any>.

Let's take a closer look at the common behavior inherited from the `Any` class.

The common behavior defined by Any

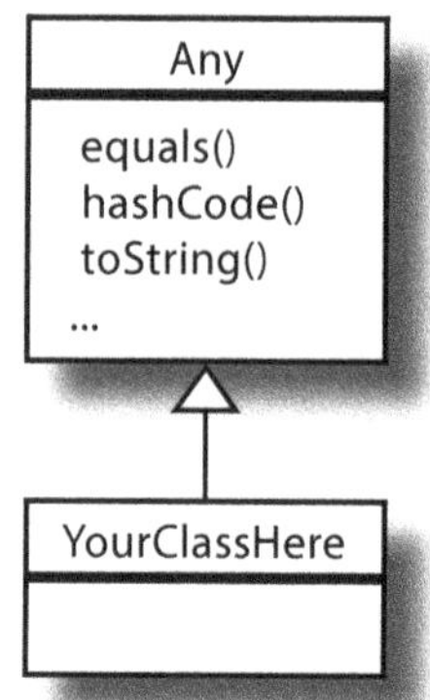

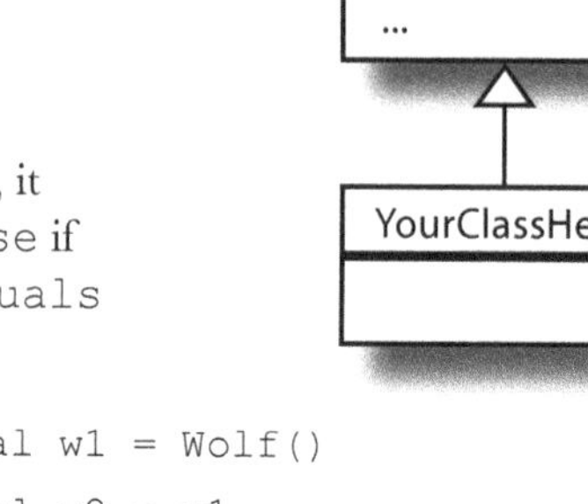

The Any class defines several functions that are inherited by every class. Here are the ones we care about most, along with an example of its default behavior:

equals(any: Any): Boolean

Tells you if two objects are considered "equal". By default, it returns `true` if it's used to test the same object, and `false` if it's used to test separate objects. Behind the scenes, the `equals` function gets called each time you use the == operator.

```
val w1 = Wolf()
val w2 = Wolf()
println(w1.equals(w2))
```

false

equals returns false because w1 and w2 hold references to different objects.

```
val w1 = Wolf()
val w2 = w1
println(w1.equals(w2))
```

true

equals returns true because w1 and w2 hold references to the same object. It's the same as testing if w1 == w2.

hashCode(): Int

Returns a hash code value for the object. They're often used by certain data structures to store and retrieve values more efficiently.

```
val w = Wolf()
println(w.hashCode())
```

523429237

This is the value of w's hash code.

toString(): String

Returns a `String` message that represents the object. By default, this is the name of the class and some other number that we rarely care about.

```
val w = Wolf()
println(w.toString())
```

Wolf@1f32e575

The Any class provides a default implementation for each of the above functions, and these implementations are inherited by every class. They can, however, be overridden if you want to change the default behavior of any of these functions.

By default, the equals function checks whether two objects are the same underlying object.

The equals function defines the behavior of the == operator.

We might want equals to check whether two objects are equivalent

There are some situations in which you might want to change the implementation of the `equals` function in order to change how the == operator behaves.

Suppose, for example, that you have a class named `Recipe` that lets you create objects that hold recipe data. In this situation, you might consider two `Recipe` objects to be equal (or equivalent) if they hold details of the same recipe. So if the `Recipe` class is defined as having two properties named `title` and `isVegetarian` using code like this:

```
class Recipe(val title: String, val isVegetarian: Boolean) {
}
```

Recipe
title isVegetarian

you might want the == operator to evaluate to `true` if it's used to compare two `Recipe` objects that have matching `title` and `isVegetarian` properties:

```
val r1 = Recipe("Chicken Bhuna", false)
val r2 = Recipe("Chicken Bhuna", false)
```

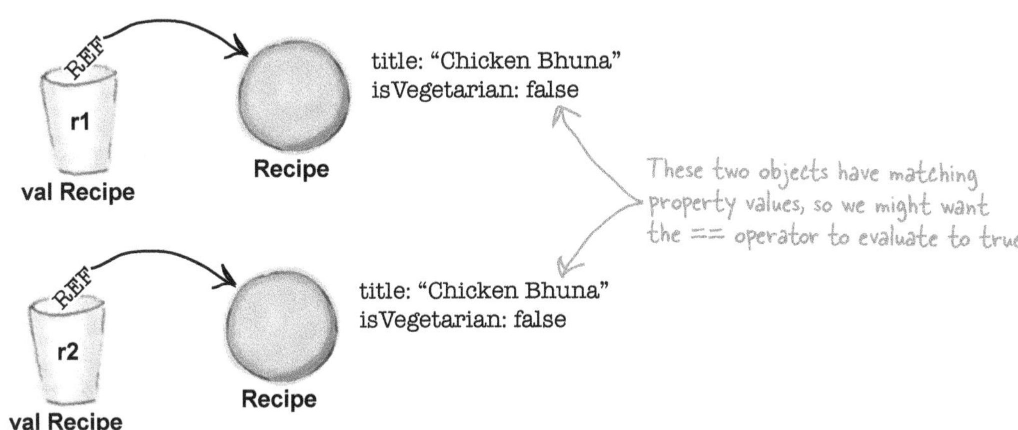

While you *could* change the behavior of the == operator by writing extra code to override the `equals` function, the Kotlin developers came up with a better approach: they came up with the concept of a **data class**. Let's find out what one of these is, and how to create one.

A data class lets you create data objects

A *data* class is one that lets you create objects whose main purpose is to store data. It includes features that are helpful when you're dealing with data, such as a new implementation of the `equals` function that checks whether two data objects hold the same property values. This is because if two objects store the same data, they can be considered equal.

You define a data class by prefixing a normal class definition with the **`data`** keyword. The following code, for example, changes the `Recipe` class we created earlier into a data class:

The data prefix turns a normal class into a data class.

```
data class Recipe(val title: String, val isVegetarian: Boolean) {
}
```

(Data) Recipe
title isVegetarian

How to create objects from a data class

You create objects from a data class in the same way that you create objects from a normal class: by calling its constructor. The following code, for example, creates a new `Recipe` data object, and assigns it to a new variable named `r1`:

```
val r1 = Recipe("Chicken Bhuna", false)
```

Data classes automatically override their `equals` function in order to change the behavior of the == operator so that it checks for object equality **based on the values of each object's properties**. If, for example, you create two `Recipe` objects that hold identical property values, comparing the two objects with the == operator will evaluate to *true*, because they hold the same data:

```
val r1 = Recipe("Chicken Bhuna", false)
val r2 = Recipe("Chicken Bhuna", false)
//r1 == r2 is true
```

r1 and r2 are considered "equal" as the two Recipe objects hold the same data.

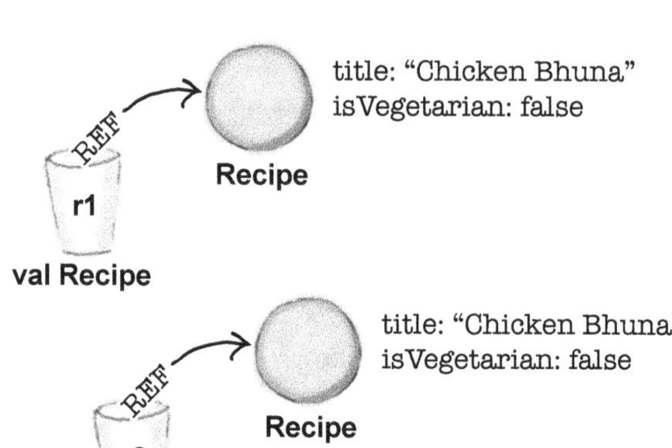

In addition to providing a new implementation of the `equals` function it inherits from the `Any` superclass, data classes also override the `hashCode` and `toString` functions. Let's take a look at how these are implemented.

Data classes override their inherited behavior

A data class needs its objects to play well with data, so it automatically provides the following implementations for the `equals`, `hashCode` and `toString` functions it inherits from the `Any` superclass:

Data objects are considered equal if their properties hold the same values.

The equals function compares property values

When you define a data class, its `equals` function (and therefore the == operator) continues to return `true` if it's used to test the same object. But it also returns `true` if the objects have identical values for the properties defined in its constructor:

```
val r1 = Recipe("Chicken Bhuna", false)
val r2 = Recipe("Chicken Bhuna", false)
println(r1.equals(r2))
```

```
true
```

Equal objects return the same hashCode value

If two data objects are considered equal (in other words, they have identical property values), the `hashCode` function returns the same value for each object:

```
val r1 = Recipe("Chicken Bhuna", false)
val r2 = Recipe("Chicken Bhuna", false)
println(r1.hashCode())
println(r2.hashCode())
```

```
241131113
241131113
```

You can think of a hash code as being like a label on a bucket. Objects that are considered equal are put in the same bucket, and the hash code tells the system where to look for them. Equal objects MUST have the same hash code value as the system depends on this. You'll find out more about this in Chapter 9.

toString returns the value of each property

Finally, the `toString` function no longer returns the name of the class followed by a number. Instead, it returns a useful `String` that contains the value of each property that's defined in the data class constructor:

```
val r1 = Recipe("Chicken Bhuna", false)
println(r1.toString())
```

```
Recipe(title=Chicken Bhuna, isVegetarian=false)
```

In addition to overriding the functions it inherits from the `Any` superclass, a data class also provides extra features that help you deal with data more effectively, such as the ability to copy a data object. Let's see how this works.

Copy data objects using the copy function

If you want to create a new copy of a data object, altering some of its properties but leaving the rest intact, you can do so using the **copy** function. To use, you call the function on the object you want to copy, passing in the names of any properties you wish to alter along with their new values.

The copy function lets you copy a data object, altering some of its properties. The original object remains intact.

Suppose that you have a `Recipe` object named `r1` that's defined using code like this:

```
val r1 = Recipe("Thai Curry", false)
```

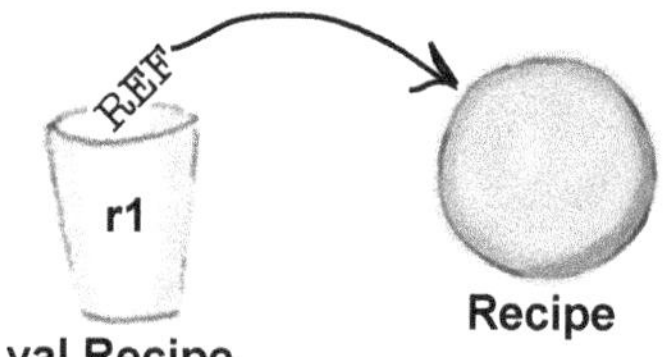

If you wanted to create a copy of the `Recipe` object, altering the value of its `isVegetarian` property to `true`, you could do so using the `copy` function like so:

```
val r1 = Recipe("Thai Curry", false)
val r2 = r1.copy(isVegetarian = true)
```

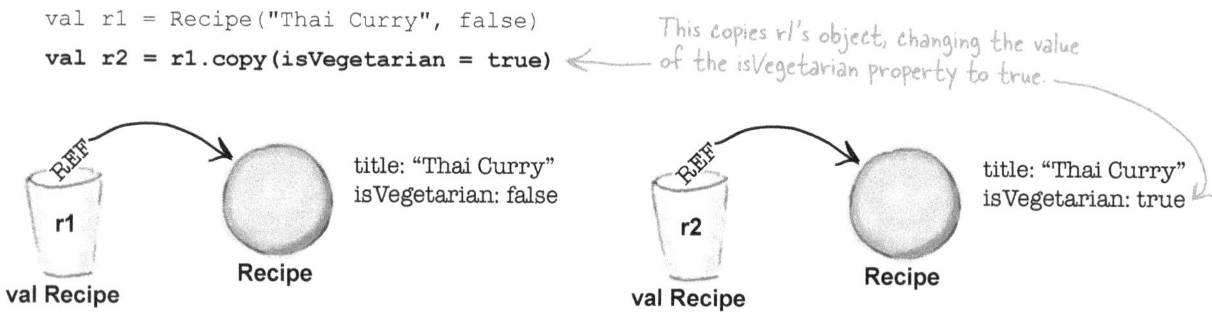

It's like saying "take a copy of *r1*'s object, change the value of its *isVegetarian* property to *true*, and assign the new object to a variable named *r2*". It creates a new copy of the object, and leaves the original object intact.

As well as the `copy` function, data classes also provide a set of functions that allow you to split a data object into its component property values in a process called **destructuring**. Let's see how.

Data classes define componentN functions...

When you define a data class, the compiler automatically adds a set of functions to the class that you can use as an alternate way of accessing its object's property values. These are known as `componentN` functions, where N represents the number of the property whose value you wish to retrieve (in order of declaration).

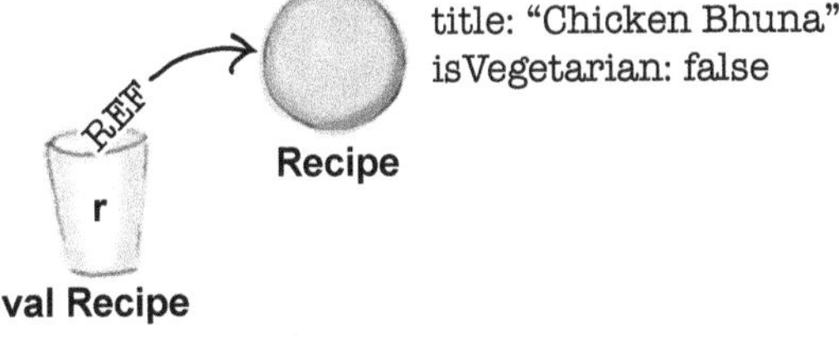

To see how `componentN` functions work, suppose that you have the following `Recipe` object:

```
val r = Recipe("Chicken Bhuna", false)
```

If you wanted to retrieve the value of the object's first property (its `title` property), you could do this by calling the object's `component1()` function like this:

```
val title = r.component1()
```

component1() returns the reference held by the first property defined in the data class constructor.

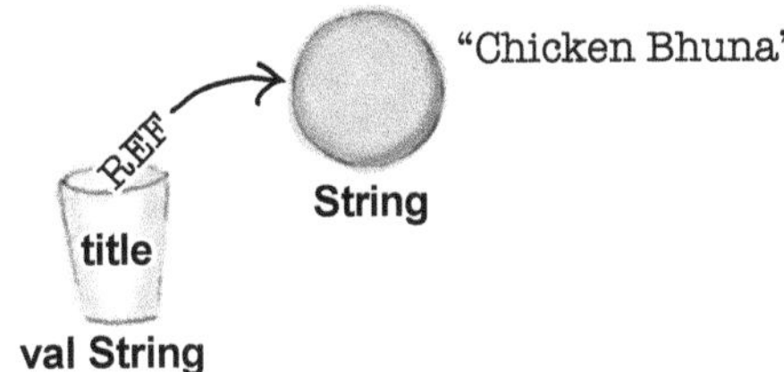

This does the same thing as the code:

```
val title = r.title
```

but it's more generic. So why is it so useful for a data class to have generic `ComponentN` functions?

...that let you destructure data objects

Having generic `componentN` functions is useful as it provides a quick way of splitting a data object into its component property values, or *destructuring* it.

Destructuring a data object splits it into its component parts.

Suppose, for example, that you wanted to take the property values of a `Recipe` object, and assign each property value to a separate variable. Instead of using the code:

```
val title = r.title
val vegetarian = r.isVegetarian
```

to explicitly process each property in turn, you can use the following code instead:

```
val (title, vegetarian) = r
```

Assigns the value of r's first property to title, and the value of its second property to vegetarian.

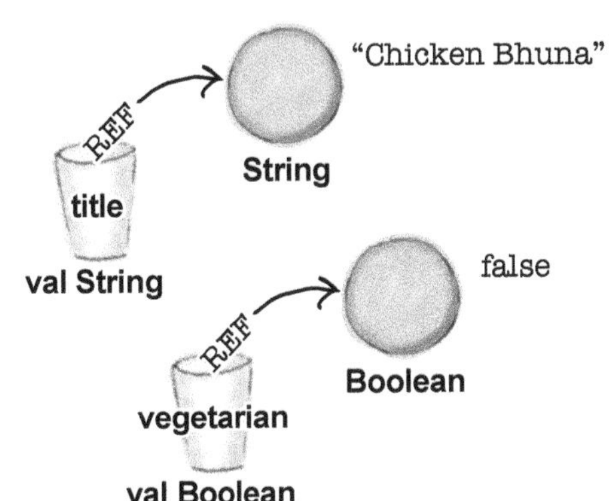

The above code is like saying "create two variables, *title* and *vegetarian*, and assign one of *r*'s property values to each one." It does the same thing as the code:

```
val title = r.component1()
val vegetarian = r.component2()
```

but it's more concise.

Data classes sound great, but I was wondering... Is there a definitive way of checking whether two variables refer to the same underlying object? It sounds like you can't rely on the == operator because its behavior depends on how the equals function has been implemented, and this may vary from class to class.

The === operator always lets you check whether two variables refer to the same underlying object.

If you want to check whether two variables refer to the same underlying object, irrespective of their type, you should use the === operator instead of ==. This is because the === operator always evaluates to `true` if (and *only* if) the two variables hold a reference to the same underlying object. This means that if, for example, you have two variables named `x` and `y`, and the code:

```
x === y
```

evaluates to `true`, then you know that the `x` and `y` variables must refer to the same underlying object:

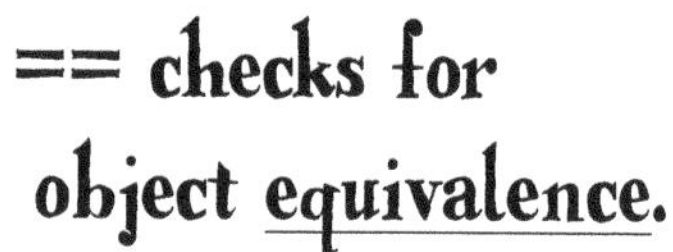

=== checks for object identity.

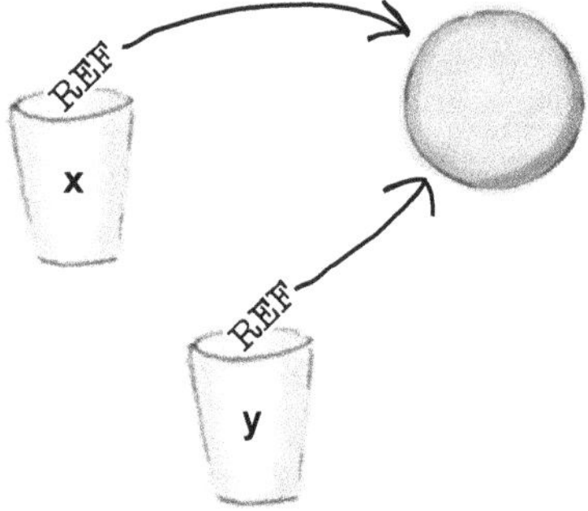

Unlike the == operator, the === operator doesn't rely on the `equals` function for its behavior. The === operator always behaves in this way irrespective of the type of class.

Now that you've seen how to create and use data classes, let's create a project for the `Recipe` code.

Create the Recipes project

Create a new Kotlin project that targets the JVM, and name the project "Recipes". Then create a new Kotlin file named *Recipes.kt* by highlighting the *src* folder, clicking on the File menu and choosing New → Kotlin File/Class. When prompted, name the file "Recipes", and choose File from the Kind option.

We'll add a new data class named `Recipe` to the project, and create some `Recipe` data objects. Here's the code—update your version of *Recipes.kt* to match ours:

We've omitted the {}'s as our data class has no body.

```
data class Recipe(val title: String, val isVegetarian: Boolean)

fun main(args: Array<String>) {
    val r1 = Recipe("Thai Curry", false)
    val r2 = Recipe("Thai Curry", false)
    val r3 = r1.copy(title = "Chicken Bhuna")
    println("r1 hash code: ${r1.hashCode()}")
    println("r2 hash code: ${r2.hashCode()}")
    println("r3 hash code: ${r3.hashCode()}")
    println("r1 toString: ${r1.toString()}")
    println("r1 == r2? ${r1 == r2}")
    println("r1 === r2? ${r1 === r2}")
    println("r1 == r3? ${r1 == r3}")
    val (title, vegetarian) = r1
    println("title is $title and vegetarian is $vegetarian")
}
```

Create a copy of r1, altering its title property.

Destructure r1.

(Data) Recipe

title
isVegetarian

Recipes
src
Recipes.kt

Test drive

When you run your code, the following text gets printed in the IDE's output window:

```
r1 hash code: -135497891
r2 hash code: -135497891
r3 hash code: 241131113
r1 toString: Recipe(title=Thai Curry, isVegetarian=false)
r1 == r2? true
r1 === r2? false
r1 == r3? false
title is Thai Curry and vegetarian is false
```

r1 == r2 is true because their objects have matching values. As they refer to separate objects, r1 === r2 is false.

there are no Dumb Questions

Q: You said that every class is a subclass of `Any`. I thought that each class could only have one direct superclass?

A: Behind the scenes, the `Any` class sits at the root of every superclass hierarchy, so every class you create is either a direct or indirect subclass of `Any`. This means that every class IS-A type of `Any`, and inherits the functions it defines: `equals`, `hashCode` and `toString`.

Q: I see. And you say that data classes automatically override these functions?

A: Yes. When you define a data class, the compiler secretly overrides the `equals`, `hashCode` and `toString` functions the class inherits so that they're more appropriate for objects whose main purpose is to hold data.

Q: Can I override these functions without creating a data class?

A: Yes, in exactly the same way that you override functions from any other class: by providing an implementation for the functions in the body of your class.

Q: Are there any rules I have to follow?

A: The main thing is that if you override the `equals` function, you should override the `hashCode` function as well.

If two objects are considered equal, they **must** have the same hash code value. Some collections use hash codes as an efficient way of storing objects, and the system assumes that if two objects are equal, they also have the same hash code. You'll find out more about this in Chapter 9.

Q: That sounds complicated.

A: It's certainly easier to create a data class, and using a data class means that you'll have cleaner code that's more concise. If you want to override the `equals`, `hashCode` and `toString` functions yourself, however, you can get the IDE to generate most of the code for you.

To get the IDE to generate implementations for the `equals`, `hashCode` or `toString` functions, start by writing the basic class definition, including any properties. Next, make sure that your text cursor is in the class, go to the Code menu, and select the Generate option. Finally, choose the function you want to generate code for.

Q: I've noticed that you've only defined data class properties in the constructor using `val`. Can I define them using `var` as well?

A: You can, but we'd strongly encourage you to make your data classes immutable by only creating `val` properties. Doing so means that once a data object has been created, it can't be updated, so you don't have to worry about some other code changing any of its properties. Only having `val` properties is also a requirement of certain data structures.

Q: Why do data classes include a `copy` function?

A: Data classes are usually defined using `val` properties so that they're immutable. Having a `copy` function is a good alternative to having data objects that can be modified as it lets you easily create another version of the object with modified property values.

Q: Can I declare that a data class is abstract? Or open?

A: No. Data classes can't be declared abstract or open, so you can't use a data class as a superclass. Data classes can implement interfaces, however, and from Kotlin 1.1, they can also inherit from other classes.

A short Kotlin program is listed below. One block of the program is missing. Your challenge is to match the candidate block of code (on the left), with the output that you'd see if the block were inserted. All the lines of output will be used, and some lines of output may be used more than once. Draw lines connecting the candidate blocks of code with their matching output.

```
data class Movie(val title: String, val year: String)

class Song(val title: String, val artist: String)

fun main(args: Array<String>) {
    var m1 = Movie("Black Panther", "2018")
    var m2 = Movie("Jurassic World", "2015")
    var m3 = Movie("Jurassic World", "2015")
    var s1 = Song("Love Cats", "The Cure")
    var s2 = Song("Wild Horses", "The Rolling Stones")
    var s3 = Song("Love Cats", "The Cure")

}
```

The candidate code goes here.

Candidates:

Match each candidate with one of the possible outputs.

```
println(m2 == m3)
```

```
println(s1 == s3)
```

```
var m4 = m1.copy()
println(m1 == m4)
```

```
var m5 = m1.copy()
println(m1 === m5)
```

```
var m6 = m2
m2 = m3
println(m3 == m6)
```

Possible output:

```
true
```

```
false
```

Mixed Messages Solution

A short Kotlin program is listed below. One block of the program is missing. Your challenge is to match the candidate block of code (on the left), with the output that you'd see if the block were inserted. All the lines of output will be used, and some lines of output may be used more than once. Draw lines connecting the candidate blocks of code with their matching output.

```
data class Movie(val title: String, val year: String)

class Song(val title: String, val artist: String)

fun main(args: Array<String>) {
    var m1 = Movie("Black Panther", "2018")
    var m2 = Movie("Jurassic World", "2015")
    var m3 = Movie("Jurassic World", "2015")
    var s1 = Song("Love Cats", "The Cure")
    var s2 = Song("Wild Horses", "The Rolling Stones")
    var s3 = Song("Love Cats", "The Cure")
    [                                        ]
}
```

The candidate code goes here.

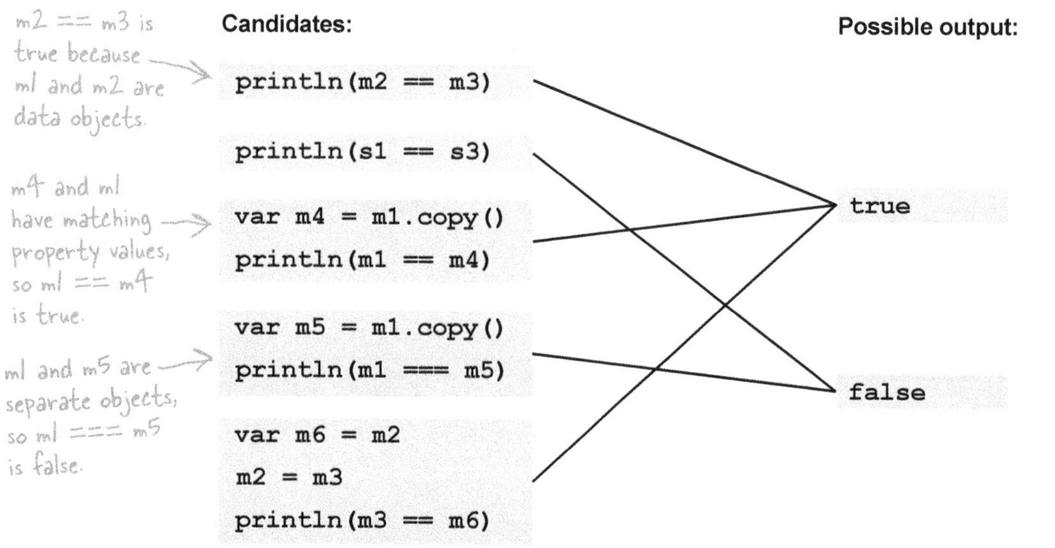

Generated functions only use properties defined in the constructor

So far, you've seen how to define a data class, and add properties to its constructor. The following code, for example, defines a data class named `Recipe` with properties named `title` and `isVegetarian`:

```
data class Recipe(val title: String, val isVegetarian: Boolean) {
}
```

(Data)
Recipe
title
isVegetarian

Just like any other sort of class, you can also add properties and functions to a data class by including them in the class body. But there's a Big Catch.

When the compiler generates implementations for data class functions, such as overriding the `equals` function and creating a `copy` function, **it only includes the properties defined in the primary constructor**. So if you add properties to a data class by defining them in the class body, *they won't be included in any of the generated functions.*

Suppose, for example, that you add a new `mainIngredient` property to the `Recipe` data class body like this:

```
data class Recipe(val title: String, val isVegetarian: Boolean) {
    var mainIngredient = ""
}
```

(Data)
Recipe
title
isVegetarian
mainIngredient

As the `mainIngredient` property has been defined in the main body of the class instead of the constructor, it's ignored by functions such as `equals`. This means that if you create two `Recipe` objects using code like this:

```
val r1 = Recipe("Thai curry", false)
r1.mainIngredient = "Chicken"
val r2 = Recipe("Thai curry", false)
r2.mainIngredient = "Duck"
println(r1 == r2)  // evaluates to true
```

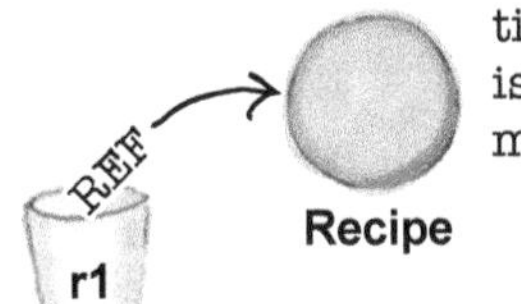

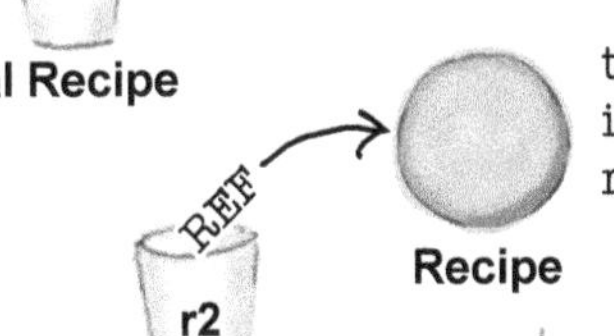

r1 == r2 is true because r1 and r2 have matching title and isVegetarian properties. The == operator ignores the mainIngredient property because it hasn't been defined in the constructor.

the == operator will only look at the `title` and `isVegetarian` properties to determine if the two objects are equal because only these properties have been defined in the data class constructor. If the two objects have different values for the `mainIngredient` property (as in the above example), the `equals` function won't look at this property when considering whether two objects are equal.

But what if your data class has many properties that you want to be included in the functions generated by the data class?

Initializing many properties can lead to cumbersome code

As you've just learned, any properties that you want to be included in the functions generated by a data class must be defined in its primary constructor. But if you have *many* such properties, your code can quickly become unwieldy. Each time you create a new object, you need to specify a value for each of its properties, so if you have a `Recipe` data class that looks like this:

```
data class Recipe(val title: String,
                  val mainIngredient: String,
                  val isVegetarian: Boolean,
                  val difficulty: String) {
}
```

(Data)
Recipe

title
mainIngredient
isVegetarian
difficulty

your code to create a `Recipe` object will look like this:

```
val r = Recipe("Thai curry", "Chicken",  false, "Easy")
```

This may not seem too bad if your data class has a small number of properties, but imagine if you needed to specify the values of 10, 20, or even *50* properties each time you needed to create a new object. Your code would quickly become much harder to manage.

So what can you do in this sort of situation?

Every data class must have a primary constructor, which must define at least one parameter. Each parameter must be prefixed with val or var.

Default parameter values to the rescue!

If your constructor defines many properties, you can simplify calls to it by assigning a default value or expression to one or more property definitions in the constructor. Here's how, for example, you would assign default values to the `isVegetarian` and `difficulty` properties in the `Recipe` class constructor:

```
data class Recipe(val title: String,
                  val mainIngredient: String,
                  val isVegetarian: Boolean = false,
                  val difficulty: String = "Easy") {
}
```

isVegetarian has a default value of false.

difficulty has a default value of "Easy".

(Data)
Recipe

title
mainIngredient
isVegetarian
difficulty

Let's see what difference this makes to the way in which we create new `Recipe` objects.

How to use a constructor's default values

When you have a constructor that uses default values, there are two main ways of calling it: by passing values in order of declaration, and by using named arguments. Let's see how both approaches work.

1. Passing values in order of declaration

This approach is the same as the one you've already been using, except that you don't need to provide values for any arguments that already have default values.

Suppose, for example, that we want to create a Spaghetti Bolognese `Recipe` object for a recipe that's not vegetarian and is easy to make. We can create this object by specifying the values of the first two properties in the constructor using the following code:

```
val r = Recipe("Spaghetti Bolognese", "Beef")
```

We've not specified values for the isVegetarian and difficulty property values, so the object uses their default values.

REF
r
val Recipe
Recipe

title: "Spaghetti Bolognese"
mainIngredient: "Beef"
isVegetarian: false
difficulty: "Easy"

The above code assigns values of "Spaghetti Bolognese" and "Beef" to the `title` and `mainIngredient` properties. It then uses the default values specified in the constructor for the remaining properties.

You can use this approach to override property values if you don't want to use the default values. If you wanted to create a `Recipe` object for a vegetarian version of Spaghetti Bolognese, for example, you could use the following:

```
val r = Recipe("Spaghetti Bolognese", "Tofu", true)
```

Assigns isVegetarian a value of true, and uses the default value for the difficulty property.

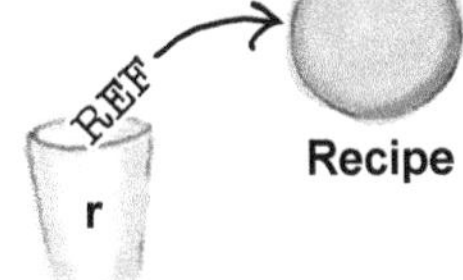

title: "Spaghetti Bolognese"
mainIngredient: "Tofu"
isVegetarian: true
difficulty: "Easy"

This assigns values of "Spaghetti Bolognese", "Tofu" and *true* to the first three properties defined in the `Recipe` constructor, and uses the default value of "Easy" for the final `difficulty` property.

Note that in order to use this approach, you must pass values in the order in which they are declared. You can't, say, omit the value of the `isVegetarian` property if you want to override the value of the `difficulty` property that comes after it. The following code, for example, is invalid:

```
val r = Recipe("Spaghetti Bolognese", "Beef", "Moderate")
```

This code won't compile, as the compiler expects the third argument to be a Boolean.

Now that you've seen how passing values in order of declaration works, let's look at how to use named arguments instead.

2. Using named arguments

Calling a constructor using named arguments lets you explicitly state which property should be assigned which value, without having to stick to the order in which properties are defined.

You must pass a value for every argument that doesn't have a default value assigned to it or your code won't compile.

Suppose, for example, that we want to create a Spaghetti Bolognese `Recipe` object that specifies the values of the `title` and `mainIngredient` properties, just as we did earlier. To do this using named arguments, you would use the following code:

```
val r = Recipe(title = "Spaghetti Bolognese",
               mainIngredient = "Beef")
```

This specifies the name of each property, and the value it should have.

The above code assigns values of "Spaghetti Bolognese" and "Beef" to the `title` and `mainIngredient` properties. It then uses the default values specified in the constructor for the remaining properties

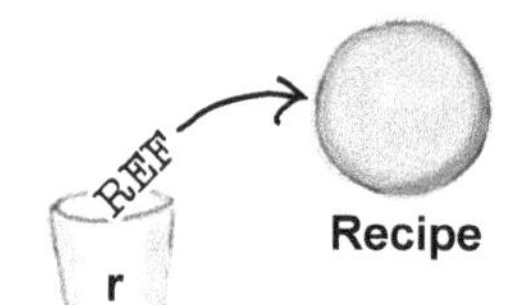

Note that because we're using named arguments, the order in which we specify the arguments doesn't matter. The following code, for example, does the same thing as the code above, and is equally valid:

```
val r = Recipe(mainIngredient = "Beef",
               title = "Spaghetti Bolognese")
```

With named arguments, the order in which you specify the value of each property doesn't matter.

The big advantage of using named arguments is that you only need to include arguments that have no default value, or whose default value you want to override. If you wanted to override the value of the `difficulty` property, for example, you could do so using code like this:

```
val r = Recipe(title = "Spaghetti Bolognese",
               mainIngredient = "Beef",
               difficulty = "Moderate")
```

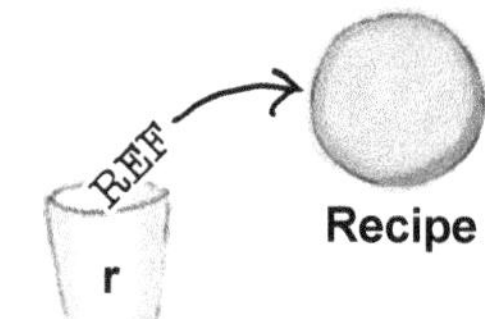

Using default parameter values and named arguments doesn't just apply to data class constructors; you can also use them with normal class constructors or functions. We'll show you how to use default values with functions after a small diversion.

Secondary Constructors

Even though secondary constructors aren't used all that much in Kotlinville, we thought we'd give you a quick overview so that you know what they look like.

Just as in other languages such as Java, classes in Kotlin let you define one or more **secondary constructors**. Secondary constructors are extra constructors that allow you to pass different parameter combinations to create objects. Most of the time, however, you don't need to use them as having default parameter values is so flexible.

Here's an example of a class named `Mushroom` that defines two constructors—a primary constructor defined in the class header, and a secondary constructor defined in the class body:

```
class Mushroom(val size: Int, val isMagic: Boolean) {
    constructor(isMagic_param: Boolean) : this(0, isMagic_param) {
        //Code that runs when the secondary constructor is called
    }
}
```

Primary constructor.

Secondary constructor.

Each secondary constructor starts with the `constructor` keyword, and is followed by the set of parameters used to call it. So in the above example, the code:

```
constructor(isMagic_param: Boolean)
```

creates a secondary constructor with a `Boolean` parameter.

If the class has a primary constructor, each secondary constructor must delegate to it. The following constructor, for example, calls the `Mushroom` class primary constructor (using the `this` keyword), passing it a value of 0 for the `size` property, and the value of the parameter `isMagic_param` for the `isMagic` parameter:

```
constructor(isMagic_param: Boolean) : this(0, isMagic_param)
```

This calls the primary constructor of the current class. It passes the primary constructor a value of 0 for the size, and the value of isMagic_param for the isMagic parameter.

You can define extra code that the secondary constructor should run when it's called in the secondary constructor's body:

```
constructor(isMagic_param: Boolean) : this(0, isMagic_param) {
    //Code that runs when the secondary constructor is called
}
```

Finally, once you've defined a secondary constructor, you can use it to create objects using code like this:

```
val m = Mushroom(true)
```

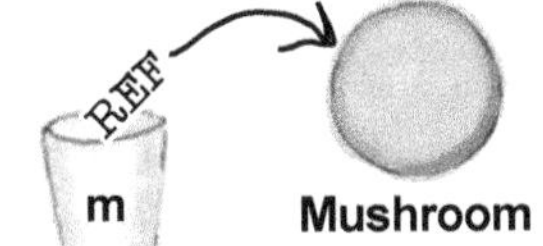

Functions can use default values too

Suppose we have a function named `findRecipes` that searches for recipes based on a set of criteria:

```
fun findRecipes(title: String,
                ingredient: String,
                isVegetarian: Boolean,
                difficulty: String) : Array<Recipe> {
    //Code to find recipes
}
```

Each time we call the function, we must pass it values for all four parameters in order for the code to compile like this:

```
val recipes = findRecipes("Thai curry", "", false, "")
```

We can make the function more flexible by assigning each parameter a default value. Doing so means that we no longer have to pass all four values to the function in order for it to compile, only the ones that we want to override:

This is the same function as the one above, but this time, we've given each parameter a default value.

```
fun findRecipes(title: String = "",
                ingredient: String = "",
                isVegetarian: Boolean = false,
                difficulty: String = "") : Array<Recipe> {
    //Code to find recipes
}
```

So if we wanted to pass the function a value of "Thai curry" for the `title` parameter and accept the default values for the rest, we could use the code:

```
val recipes = findRecipes("Thai curry")
```

Both of these call the findRecipes function, using a value of "Thai curry" for the title argument.

And if we wanted to pass the parameter value using named arguments, we could use the following instead:

```
val recipes = findRecipes(title = "Thai curry")
```

Using default values means that you can write functions that are much more flexible. But there are times when you might want to write a new version of the function instead by **overloading** it.

Overloading a function

Function overloading is when you have two or more functions with the same name but with different argument lists.

Suppose you have a function named addNumbers that looks like this:

```
fun addNumbers(a: Int, b: Int) : Int {
    return a + b
}
```

The function has two Int arguments, so you can only pass Int values to it. If you wanted to use it to add together two Doubles, you would have to convert these values to Ints before passing them to the function.

You can, however, make life much easier for the caller by overloading the function with a version that takes Doubles instead, like so:

```
fun addNumbers(a: Double, b: Double) : Double {
    return a + b
}
```

This is an overloaded version of the same function that uses Doubles instead of Ints.

This means that if you call the addNumbers function using the code:

```
addNumbers(2, 5)
```

then the system will spot that the parameters 2 and 5 are Ints, and call the Int version of the function. If, however, you call the addNumbers function using:

```
addNumbers(1.6, 7.3)
```

then the system will call the Double version of the function instead, as the parameters are both Doubles.

An overloaded function is just a different function that happens to have the same function name with different arguments. An overloaded function is NOT the same as an overridden function.

Dos and don'ts for function overloading:

- **The return types can be different.**
  You're free to change the return type of an overloaded function, so long as the argument lists are different.

- **You can't change ONLY the return type.**
  If only the return type is different, it's not a valid overload—the compiler will assume you're trying to override the function. And even that won't be legal unless the return type is a subtype of the return type declared in the superclass. To overload a function, you MUST change the argument list, although you can change the return type to anything.

Let's update the Recipes project

Now that you've learned how to use default parameter values and overload functions, let's update the code in the Recipes project.

Update your version of the code in file *Recipes.kt* so that it matches ours below (our changes are in bold):

```
data class Recipe(val title: String,
                  val mainIngredient: String,
                  val isVegetarian: Boolean = false,
                  val difficulty: String = "Easy") {
}

class Mushroom(val size: Int, val isMagic: Boolean) {
    constructor(isMagic_param: Boolean) : this(0, isMagic_param) {
        //Code that runs when the secondary constructor is called
    }
}

fun findRecipes(title: String = "",
                ingredient: String = "",
                isVegetarian: Boolean = false,
                difficulty: String = "") : Array<Recipe> {
    //Code to find recipes
    return arrayOf(Recipe(title, ingredient, isVegetarian, difficulty))
}

fun addNumbers(a: Int, b: Int) : Int {
    return a + b
}

fun addNumbers(a: Double, b: Double) : Double {
    return a + b
}
```

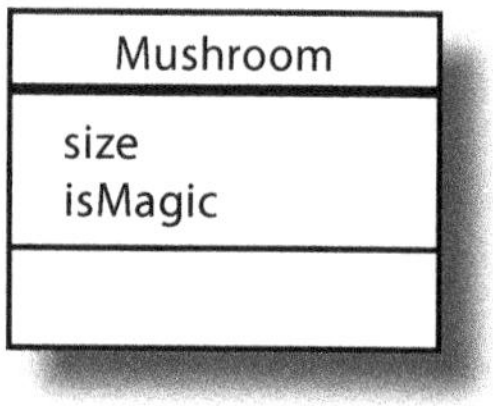

Add new mainIngredient and difficulty properties.

Assign default values to the isVegetarian and difficulty properties.

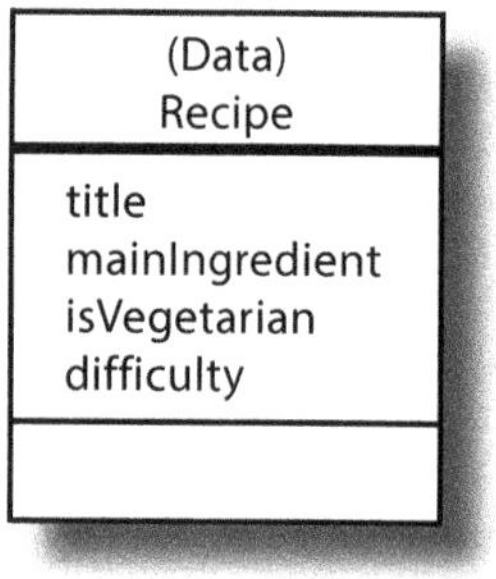

This is an example of a class with a secondary consructor, just so that you can see one in action.

This is an example of a function that uses default parameter values.

These are overloaded functions.

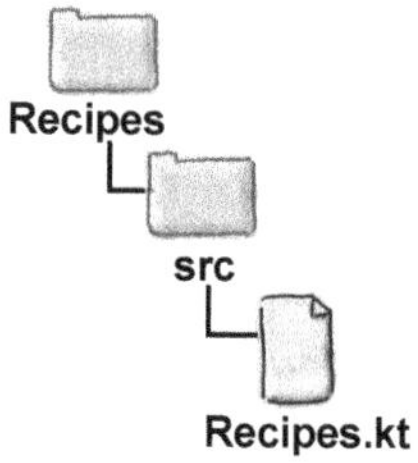

(Data) Recipe
title mainIngredient isVegetarian difficulty

Mushroom
size isMagic

Recipes
src
Recipes.kt

The code continued...

We've changed the Recipe primary constructor, so we need to change how it's called so that the code compiles.

```
fun main(args: Array<String>) {
    val r1 = Recipe("Thai Curry", "Chicken" false)
    val r2 = Recipe(title = "Thai Curry", mainIngredient = "Chicken" false)
    val r3 = r1.copy(title = "Chicken Bhuna")
    println("r1 hash code: ${r1.hashCode()}")
    println("r2 hash code: ${r2.hashCode()}")
    println("r3 hash code: ${r3.hashCode()}")
    println("r1 toString: ${r1.toString()}")
    println("r1 == r2? ${r1 == r2}")
    println("r1 === r2? ${r1 === r2}")
    println("r1 == r3? ${r1 == r3}")
    val (title, mainIngredient, vegetarian, difficulty) = r1
    println("title is $title and vegetarian is $vegetarian")

    val m1 = Mushroom(6, false)
    println("m1 size is ${m1.size} and isMagic is ${m1.isMagic}")
    val m2 = Mushroom(true)
    println("m2 size is ${m2.size} and isMagic is ${m2.isMagic}")

    println(addNumbers(2, 5))
    println(addNumbers(1.6, 7.3))
}
```

(In the code above, `false` is struck out in the r1 and r2 lines.)

Include Recipe's new properties when we destructure r1.

Create a Mushroom by calling its primary constructor.

Create a Mushroom by calling its secondary constructor.

Call the Int version of addNumbers.

Call the Double version of addNumbers.

Recipes
src
Recipes.kt

Test drive

When you run your code, the following text gets printed in the IDE's output window:

```
r1 hash code: 295805076
r2 hash code: 295805076
r3 hash code: 1459025056
r1 toString: Recipe(title=Thai Curry, mainIngredient=Chicken, isVegetarian=false, difficulty=Easy)
r1 == r2? true
r1 === r2? false
r1 == r3? false
title is Thai Curry and vegetarian is false
m1 size is 6 and isMagic is false
m2 size is 0 and isMagic is true
7
8.9
```

there are no Dumb Questions

Q: Can a data class include functions?

A: Yes. You define data class functions in exactly the same way that you define functions in a non-data class: by adding them to the class body.

Q: Default parameter values look really flexible.

A: They are! You can use them in class constructors (including data class constructors) and functions, and you can even have a default parameter value that's an expression. This means that you can write code that's flexible, but very concise.

Q: You said that using default parameter values mostly gets around the need for writing secondary constructors. Are there any situations where I may still need them?

A: The most common situation is if you need to extend a class in a framework (such as Android) that has multiple constructors.

You can find out more about using secondary constructors in Kotlin's online documentation:

https://kotlinlang.org/docs/reference/classes.html

Q: I want Java programmers to be able to use my Kotlin classes, but Java has no concept of default parameter values. Can I still use default parameter values in my Kotlin classes?

A: You can. When you call a Kotlin constructor or function from Java, just make sure that the Java code specifies a value for each parameter, even if it has a default parameter value.

If you plan on making a lot of Java calls to your Kotlin constructor or function, an alternative approach is to annotate each function or constructor that uses default parameter values with **`@JvmOverloads`**. This tells the compiler to automatically create overloaded versions that can more easily be called from Java.

Here's an example of how you use `@JvmOverloads` with a function:

```
@JvmOverloads fun myFun(str: String = ""){
    //Function code goes here
}
```

And here's an example of how you use it with a class that has a primary constructor:

```
class Foo @JvmOverloads constructor(i: Int = 0){
    //Class code coes here
}
```

Note that in order to annotate the primary constructor with `@JvmOverloads`, you must also prefix the constructor with the `constructor` keyword. Most of the time, this keyword is optional.

BE the Compiler

Here are two complete Kotlin files. Your job is to play like you're the compiler and determine whether each of these files will compile. If they won't compile, how would you fix them?

```
data class Student(val firstName: String, val lastName: String,
                   val house: String, val year: Int = 1)

fun main(args: Array<String>) {
    val s1 = Student("Ron", "Weasley", "Gryffindor")
    val s2 = Student("Draco", "Malfoy", house = "Slytherin")
    val s3 = s1.copy(firstName = "Fred", year = 3)
    val s4 = s3.copy(firstName = "George")

    val array = arrayOf(s1, s2, s3, s4)
    for ((firstName, lastName, house, year) in array) {
        println("$firstName $lastName is in $house year $year")
    }
}
```

```
data class Student(val firstName: String, val lastName: String,
                   val house: String, val year: Int = 1)

fun main(args: Array<String>) {
    val s1 = Student("Ron", "Weasley", "Gryffindor")
    val s2 = Student(lastName = "Malfoy", firstName = "Draco", year = 1)
    val s3 = s1.copy(firstName = "Fred")
    s3.year = 3
    val s4 = s3.copy(firstName = "George")

    val array = arrayOf(s1, s2, s3, s4)
    for (s in array) {
        println("${s.firstName} ${s.lastName} is in ${s.house} year ${s.year}")
    }
}
```

BE the Compiler Solution

Here are two complete Kotlin files. Your job is to play like you're the compiler and determine whether each of these files will compile. If they won't compile, how would you fix them?

```
data class Student(val firstName: String, val lastName: String,
                   val house: String, val year: Int = 1)

fun main(args: Array<String>) {
    val s1 = Student("Ron", "Weasley", "Gryffindor")
    val s2 = Student("Draco", "Malfoy", house = "Slytherin")
    val s3 = s1.copy(firstName = "Fred", year = 3)
    val s4 = s3.copy(firstName = "George")

    val array = arrayOf(s1, s2, s3, s4)
    for ((firstName, lastName, house, year) in array) {
        println("$firstName $lastName is in $house year $year")
    }
}
```

This will compile and run successfully. It prints out the firstName, lastName, house and year property values for each Student.

This line destructures each Student object in the array.

```
data class Student(val firstName: String, val lastName: String,
                   val house: String, val year: Int = 1)

fun main(args: Array<String>) {
    val s1 = Student("Ron", "Weasley", "Gryffindor")
    val s2 = Student(lastName = "Malfoy", firstName = "Draco", year = 1, house = "Slytherin")
    val s3 = s1.copy(firstName = "Fred", year = 3)
    s3.year = 3
    val s4 = s3.copy(firstName = "George")

    val array = arrayOf(s1, s2, s3, s4)
    for (s in array) {
        println("${s.firstName} ${s.lastName} is in ${s.house} year ${s.year}")
    }
}
```

(The line `s3.year = 3` is crossed out.)

This won't compile as a value is required for s2's house property, and as year is defined using val, its value can only be set when it's initialized.

Your Kotlin Toolbox

You've got Chapter 7 under your belt and now you've added data classes and default parameter values to your toolbox.

You can download the full code for the chapter from https://tinyurl.com/HFKotlin.

CHAPTER 7

BULLET POINTS

- The behavior of the == operator is determined by the implementation of the `equals` function.
- Every class inherits an `equals`, `hashCode` and `toString` function from the `Any` class because every class is a subclass of `Any`. These functions can be overridden.
- The `equals` function tells you if two objects are considered "equal". By default, it returns `true` if it's used to test the same underlying object, and `false` if it's used to test separate objects.
- The === operator lets you check whether two variables refer to the same underlying object irrespective of the object's type.
- A data class lets you create objects whose main purpose is to store data. It automatically overrides the `equals`, `hashCode` and `toString` functions, and includes `copy` and `componentN` functions.
- The data class `equals` function checks for equality by looking at each object's property values. If two data objects hold the same data, the `equals` function returns `true`.
- The `copy` function lets you create a new copy of a data object, altering some of its properties. The original object remains intact.
- `componentN` functions let you destructure data objects into their component property values.
- A data class generates its functions by considering the properties defined in its primary constructor.
- Constructors and functions can have default parameter values. You can call a constructor or function by passing parameter values in order of declaration or by using named arguments.
- Classes can have secondary constructors.
- An overloaded function is a different function that happens to have the same function name. An overloaded function must have different arguments, but may have a different return type.

Rules for data classes

* There must be a primary constructor.
* The primary constructor must define one or more parameters.
* Each parameter must be marked as val or var.
* Data classes must not be open or abstract.

8 nulls and exceptions

Everybody wants to write code that's safe.

And the great news is that Kotlin was designed with *code-safety at its heart*. We'll start by showing you how Kotlin's use of **nullable types** means that you'll *hardly ever experience a NullPointerException during your entire stay in Kotlinville*. You'll discover how to make *safe calls*, and how Kotlin's **Elvis** operator stops you being *all shook up*. And when we're done with nulls, you'll find out how to **throw and catch exceptions** like a pro.

How do you remove object references from variables?

As you already know, if you want to define a new `Wolf` variable and assign a `Wolf` object reference to it, you can do so using code like this:

```
var w = Wolf()
```

The compiler spots that you want to assign a `Wolf` object to the `w` variable, so it infers that the variable must have a type of `Wolf`:

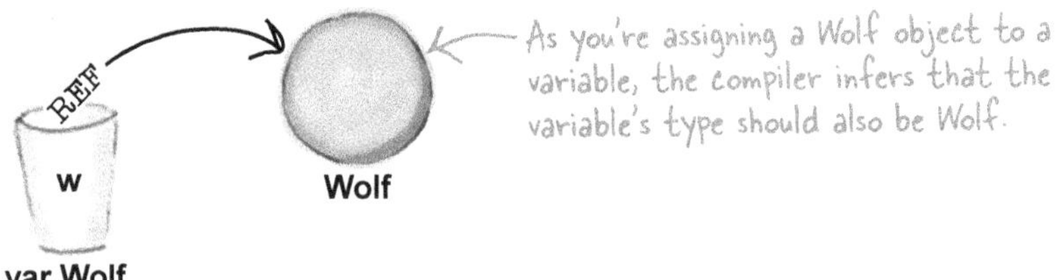

Once the compiler knows the variable's type, it ensures that it can *only* hold references to `Wolf` objects, including any `Wolf` subtypes. So if the variable is defined using `var`, you can update its value so that it holds a reference to an entirely different `Wolf` object using, for example:

```
w = Wolf()
```

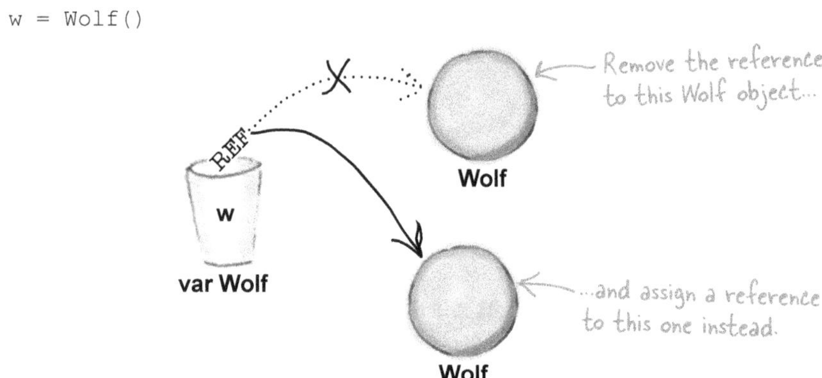

But what if you want to update the variable so that it holds a reference to *no object at all*? **How do you remove an object reference from a variable once one has been assigned?**

Remove an object reference using null

If you want to remove a reference to an object from a variable, you can do so by assigning it a value of **null**:

```
w = null
```

A null value means that the variable doesn't refer to an object: the variable still exists, but it doesn't point to anything

But there's a Big Catch. By default, *types in Kotlin won't accept null values*. **If you want a variable to hold null values, you must explicitly declare that its type is nullable.**

The Meaning of Null

When you set a variable to `null`, it's like deprogramming a remote control. You have a remote control (the variable), but no TV at the other end (the object).

A `null` reference has bits representing "null", but we don't know or care what those bits are. The system automatically handles this for us.

Why have nullable types?

A nullable type is one that allows null values. Unlike other programming languages, Kotlin tracks values that can be null to stop you from performing invalid actions on them. Performing invalid actions on null values is the most common cause of runtime problems in other languages such as Java, and can cause your application to crash in a heap when you least expect it. These problems, however, rarely happen in Kotlin because of its clever use of nullable types.

If you try to perform an invalid operation on a null value in Java, you'll be faced with a big fat NullPointerException. An exception is a warning that tells you something exceptionally bad has just happened. We'll look at exceptions in more detail later in the chapter.

You declare that a type is nullable by adding a question mark (?) to the end of the type. To create a nullable `Wolf` variable and assign a new `Wolf` object to it, for example, you would use the code:

```
var w: Wolf? = Wolf()
```

w is a Wolf?, which means it can hold references to Wolf objects, and null.

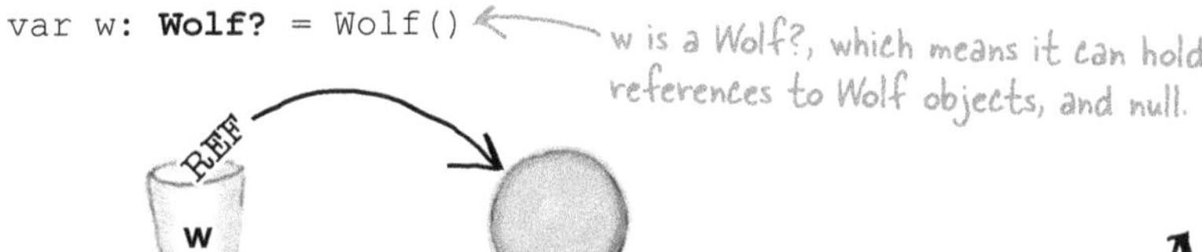

And if you wanted to remove the `Wolf` reference from the variable, you would use:

```
w = null
```

Setting w to null removes the reference to the Wolf object.

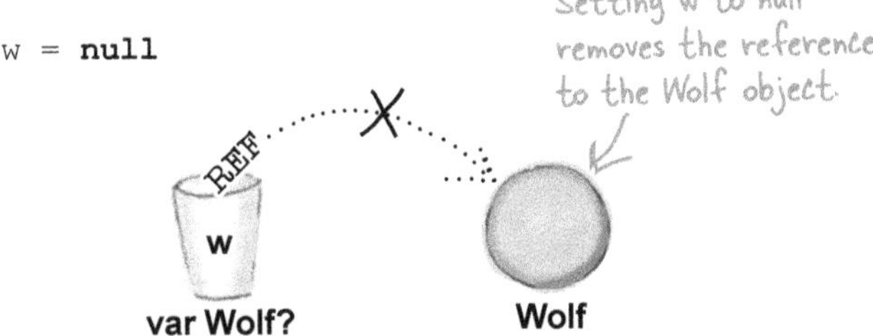

A nullable type is one that can hold null values in addition to its base type. A Duck? variable, for example, will accept Duck objects and null.

So where can you use nullable types?

You can use a nullable type everywhere you can use a non-nullable type

Every type you define can be turned into a nullable version of that type by simply adding a ? to the end of it. You can use nullable types in the same places that you would use plain old non-nullable types:

When defining variables and properties.
Any variable or property can be nullable, but you must explicitly define it as such by declaring its type, including the ?. The compiler is unable to infer when a type is nullable, and by default, it will always create a non-nullable type. So if you want to create a nullable `String` variable named `str` and instantiate it with a value of "Pizza", you must declare that it has a type of `String?` like this:

```
var str: String? = "Pizza"
```

Note that variables and properties can be instantiated with `null`. The following code, for example, compiles and prints the text "null":

```
var str: String? = null
println(str)
```

This is different to saying var str: String? = "" "" is a String object that contains no characters, whereas null is not a String object.

When defining parameters.
You can declare any function or constructor parameter type as nullable. The following code, for example, defines a function named `printInt` which takes a parameter of type `Int?` (a nullable `Int`):

```
fun printInt(x: Int?) {
    println(x)
}
```

When you define a function (or constructor) with a nullable parameter, you must still provide a value for that parameter when you call the function, even if that value is `null`. Just like with non-nullable parameter types, you can't omit a parameter unless it's been assigned a default value.

When defining function return types.
A function can have a nullable return type. The following function, for example, has a return type of `Long?`:

```
fun result() : Long? {
    //Code to calculate and return a Long?
}
```

The function must return a value that's a Long or null.

You can also create arrays of nullable types. Let's see how.

How to create an array of nullable types

An array of nullable types is one whose items are nullable. The following code, for example, creates an array named `myArray` that holds `String?`s (`String`s that are nullable):

```
var myArray: Array<String?> = arrayOf("Hi", "Hello")
```

An Array<String?> can hold Strings and nulls.

The compiler can, however, infer that the array should hold nullable types if the array is initialized with one or more `null` items. So when the compiler sees the following code:

```
var myArray = arrayOf("Hi", "Hello", null)
```

it spots that the array can hold a mixture of `String`s and `null`s, and infers that the array should have a type of `Array<String?>`:

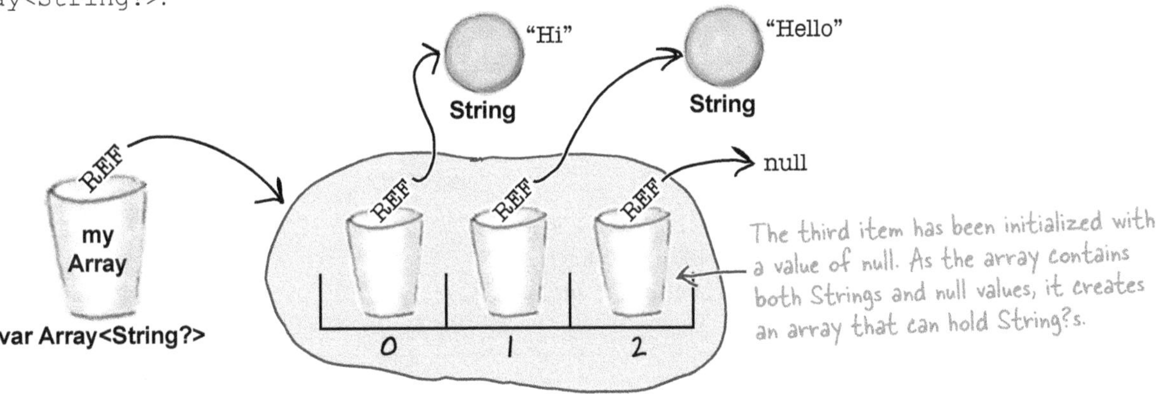

Now that you've learned how to define nullable types, let's see how to refer to its object's functions and properties.

Q: What happens if I initialize a variable with a null value, and let the compiler infer the variable's type? For example:

```
var x = null
```

A: The compiler sees that the variable needs to be able to hold null values, but as it has no information about any other kinds of object it might need to hold, it creates a variable that can only hold a value of `null`. This probably isn't what you want, so if you're going to initialize a variable with a null value, make sure you specify its type.

Q: You said in the previous chapter that every object is a subclass of `Any`. Can a variable whose type is `Any` hold null values?

A: No. If you want a variable to hold references to any type of object and null values, its type must be `Any?`. For example:

```
var z: Any?
```

How to access a nullable type's functions and properties

Suppose you have a variable whose type is nullable, and you want to access its object's properties and functions. You can't make function calls or refer to the properties of a null value as it doesn't have any. To stop you from performing any operations that are invalid, the compiler *insists* that you check that the variable is not null before giving you access to any functions or properties.

Imagine you have a `Wolf?` variable which has been assigned a reference to a new `Wolf` object like this:

```
var w: Wolf? = Wolf()
```

To access the underlying object's functions and properties, you first have to establish that the variable's value is not `null`. One way of achieving this is to check the value of the variable inside an `if`. The following code, for example, checks that `w`'s value is not `null`, and then calls the object's `eat()` function:

```
if (w != null) {
    w.eat()
}
```

The compiler knows that w is not null, so you can call the eat() function.

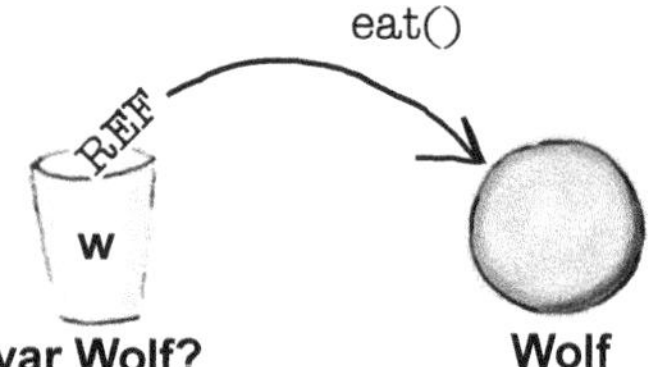

You can use this approach to build more complex conditions. The following code, for example, checks that the `w` variable's value is not `null`, and then calls its `eat()` function when its `hunger` property is less than 5:

```
if (w != null && w.hunger < 5) {
    w.eat()
}
```

The right side of the && is only executed if the left side is true, so here, the compiler knows that w can't be null, and it allows you to call w.hunger.

There are some situations, however, where this kind of code may still fail. If the `w` variable is used to define a `var` property in a class, for example, it's possible that a null value may have been assigned to it in between the null-check and its usage, so the following code won't compile:

```
class MyWolf {
    var w: Wolf? = Wolf()

    fun myFunction() {
        if (w != null){
            w.eat()
        }
    }
}
```

This won't compile because the compiler can't guarantee that some other code won't update the w property in between checking it's not null, and its usage.

Fortunately, there's a safer approach that avoids this kind of problem.

Keep things safe with safe calls

If you want to access a nullable type's properties and functions, an alternative approach is to use a **safe call**. A safe call lets you access functions and properties in a single operation without you having to perform a separate null-check.

To see how safe calls work, imagine you have a `Wolf?` property (as before) that holds a reference to a `Wolf` object like so:

```
var w: Wolf? = Wolf()
```

To make a safe call to the `Wolf`'s `eat` function, you would use the following code:

```
w?.eat()   <-- The ?. means that eat() is only called if w is not null.
```

This will only call the `Wolf`'s `eat` function when `w` is not `null`. It's like saying "if *w* is not null, call *eat*".

Similarly, the following code makes a safe call to w's `hunger` property:

```
w?.hunger
```

If `w` is not `null`, the expression returns a reference to the `hunger` property's value. If, however, `w` is `null`, the value of the entire expression evaluates to `null`. Here are the two scenarios:

?. is the safe call operator. It lets you safely access a nullable type's functions and properties.

Scenario A: w is not null.
The `w` variable holds a reference to a `Wolf` object, and the value of its `hunger` property is 10. The code `w?.hunger` evaluates to 10.

```
w?.hunger
//Returns 10
```

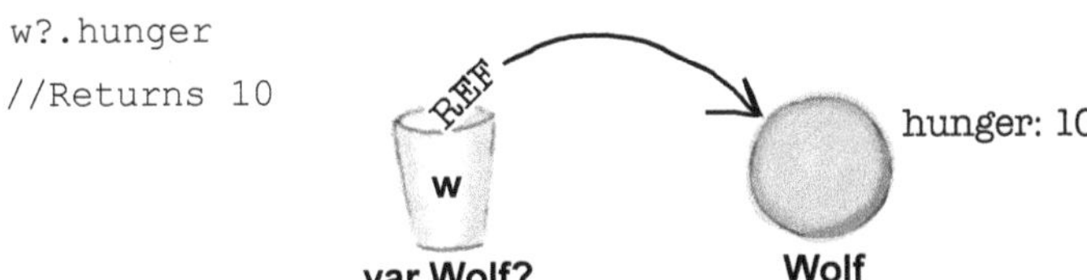

Scenario B: w is null.
The `w` variable holds a null value, not a `Wolf`, so the entire expression evaluates to `null`.

```
w?.hunger
//Returns null
```

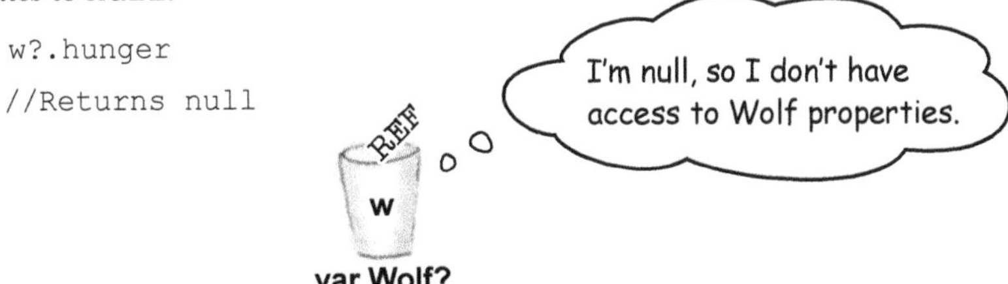

You can chain safe calls together

Another advantage of using safe calls is that you can chain them together to form expressions that are powerful yet concise.

Suppose you have a class named `MyWolf` that has a single `Wolf?` property named `w`. Here's the class definition:

```
class MyWolf {
    var w: Wolf? = Wolf()
}
```

Suppose also that you have a `MyWolf?` variable named `myWolf` like this:

```
var myWolf: MyWolf? = MyWolf()
```

If you wanted to get the value of the `hunger` property for the `myWolf` variable's `Wolf`, you could do so using code like this:

```
myWolf?.w?.hunger
```

If myWolf is not null, and w is not null, get hunger. Otherwise, use null.

It's like saying "If *myWolf* or *w* is null, return a null value. Otherwise, return the value of *w*'s *hunger* property". The expression returns the value of the `hunger` property if (and only if) `myWolf` and `w` are both not null. If either `myWolf` or `w` is `null`, the entire expression evaluates to `null`.

What happens when a safe call chain gets evaluated

Let's break down what happens when the system evaluates the safe call chain:

```
myWolf?.w?.hunger
```

The system first checks that myWolf is not null.
If `myWolf` is `null`, the entire expression evaluates to `null`. If `myWolf` is not `null` (as in this example), the system continues to the next part of the expression.

myWolf?.w?.hunger

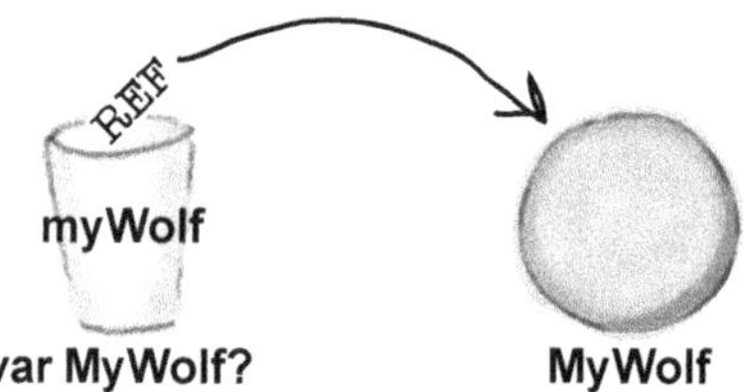

The story continues...

2 **The system then checks that myWolf's w property is not null.**
Provided `myWolf` is not `null`, the system moves on to the next part of the expression, the `w?` part.

If `w` is `null`, the entire expression evaluates to `null`. If `w` is not `null`, as in this example, the system moves onto the next part of the expression.

myWolf?.**w?**.hunger

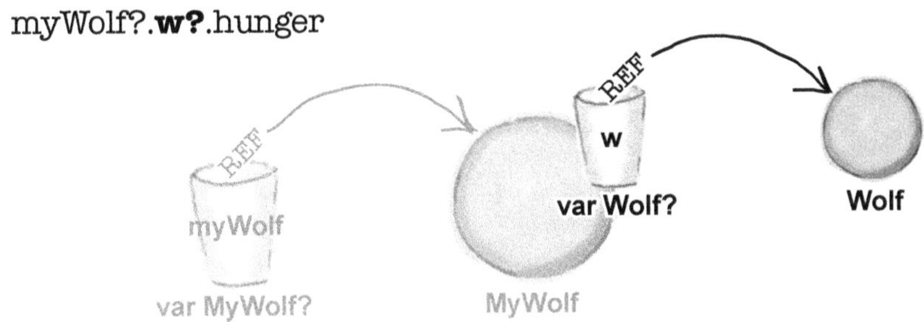

3 **If w is not null, it returns the value of w's hunger property.**
So long as neither the `myWolf` variable nor its `w` property are `null`, the expression returns the value of `w`'s `hunger` property. In this example, the expression evaluates to 10.

myWolf?.w?.**hunger**

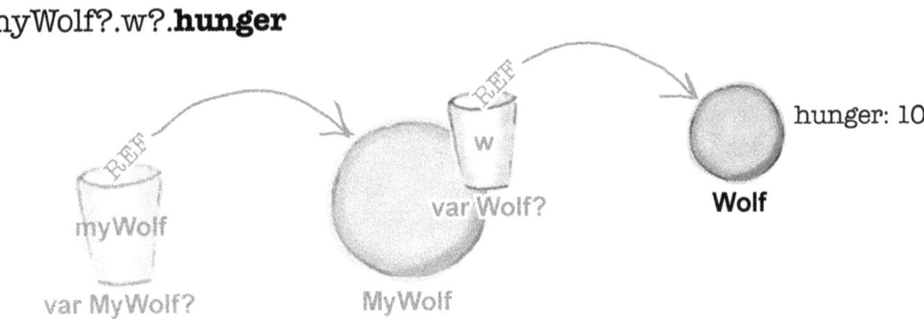

So as you can see, safe calls can be chained together to form concise expressions that are very powerful yet safe. But that's not the end of the story.

You can use safe calls to assign values...

As you might expect, you can use safe calls to assign a value to a variable or property. If you have a `Wolf?` variable named `w`, for example, you can assign the value of its `hunger` property to a new variable named `x` using code like this:

```
var x = w?.hunger
```

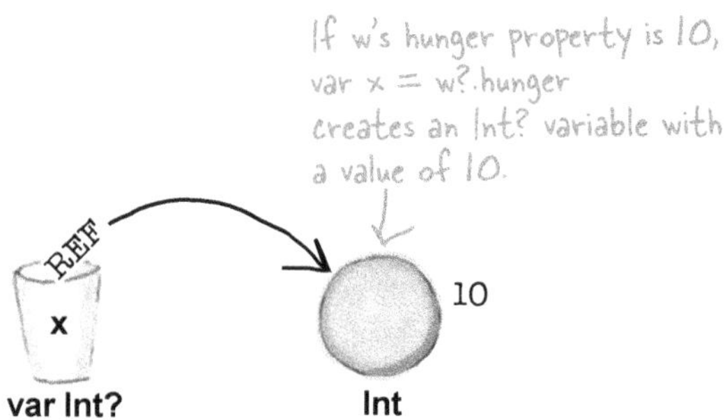

It's like saying "If *w* is null, set *x* to null, otherwise set *x* to the value of *w*'s *hunger* property". As the expression:

```
w?.hunger
```

can evaluate to an `Int` or `null` value, the compiler infers that `x` must have a type of `Int?`.

...and assign values to safe calls

You can also use a safe call on the left side of a variable or property assignment.

Suppose, for example, that you wanted to assign a value of 6 to w's `hunger` property, so long as `w` is not `null`. You can achieve this using the code:

```
w?.hunger = 6
```

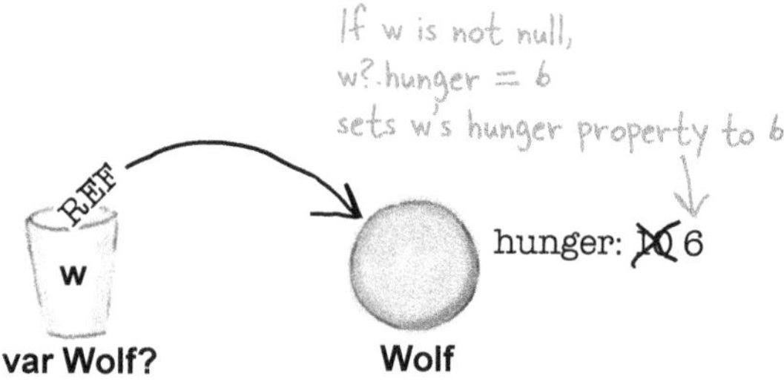

The code checks the value of `w`, and if it's not `null`, the code assigns a value of 6 to the `hunger` property. If `w` is `null`, however, the code does nothing.

You can use chains of safe calls in this situation too. The following code, for example, only assigns a value to the `hunger` property if both `myWolf` and `w` are not `null`:

```
myWolf?.w?.hunger = 2
```

It's like saying "if *myWolf* is not null, and *myWolf*'s *w* property value is not null, then assign a value of 2 to *w*'s *hunger* property":

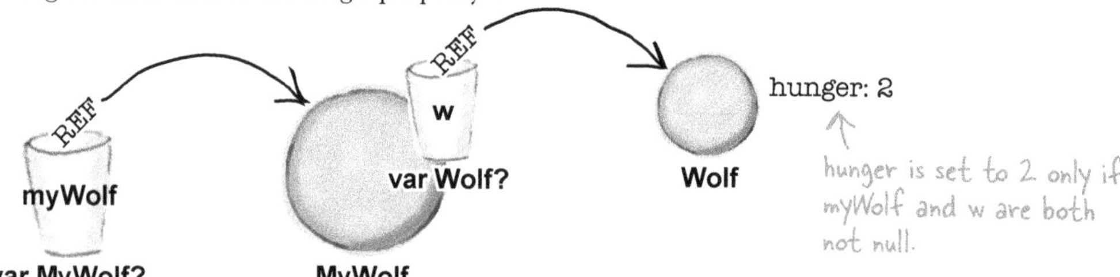

Now that you know how to make safe calls to nullable types, have a go at the following exercise.

BE the Compiler

Each of the Kotlin files on this page represents a complete source file. Your job is to play like you're the compiler, and determine whether each of these files will compile and produce the output on the right. If not, why not?

This is the required output.

```
Misty: Meow!
Socks: Meow!
```

A

```
class Cat(var name: String? = "") {
    fun Meow() { println("Meow!") }
}

fun main(args: Array<String>) {
    var myCats = arrayOf(Cat("Misty"),
                         null,
                         Cat("Socks"))
    for (cat in myCats) {
        if (cat != null) {
            print("${cat.name}: ")
            cat.Meow()
        }
    }
}
```

B

```
class Cat(var name: String? = null) {
    fun Meow() { println("Meow!") }
}

fun main(args: Array<String>) {
    var myCats = arrayOf(Cat("Misty"),
                         Cat(null),
                         Cat("Socks"))
    for (cat in myCats) {
        print("${cat.name}: ")
        cat.Meow()
    }
}
```

C

```
class Cat(var name: String? = null) {
    fun Meow() { println("Meow!") }
}

fun main(args: Array<String>) {
    var myCats = arrayOf(Cat("Misty"),
                         null,
                         Cat("Socks"))
    for (cat in myCats) {
        print("${cat?.name}: ")
        cat?.Meow()
    }
}
```

D

```
class Cat(var name: String = "") {
    fun Meow() { println("Meow!") }
}

fun main(args: Array<String>) {
    var myCats = arrayOf(Cat("Misty"),
                         Cat(null),
                         Cat("Socks"))
    for (cat in myCats) {
        if (cat != null) {
            print("${cat?.name}: ")
            cat?.Meow()
        }
    }
}
```

BE the Compiler Solution

Each of the Kotlin files on this page represents a complete source file. Your job is to play like you're the compiler, and determine whether each of these files will compile and produce the output on the right. If not, why not?

This is the required output.

```
Misty: Meow!
Socks: Meow!
```

A

```
class Cat(var name: String? = "") {
    fun Meow() { println("Meow!") }
}

fun main(args: Array<String>) {
    var myCats = arrayOf(Cat("Misty"),
                         null,
                         Cat("Socks"))
    for (cat in myCats) {
        if (cat != null) {
            print("${cat.name}: ")
            cat.Meow()
        }
    }
}
```

This compiles and produces the correct output.

B

```
class Cat(var name: String? = null) {
    fun Meow() { println("Meow!") }
}

fun main(args: Array<String>) {
    var myCats = arrayOf(Cat("Misty"),
                         Cat(null),
                         Cat("Socks"))
    for (cat in myCats) {
        print("${cat.name}: ")
        cat.Meow()
    }
}
```

This compiles, but the output is incorrect (the second Cat with a null name also Meows).

C

```
class Cat(var name: String? = null) {
    fun Meow() { println("Meow!") }
}

fun main(args: Array<String>) {
    var myCats = arrayOf(Cat("Misty"),
                         null,
                         Cat("Socks"))
    for (cat in myCats) {
        print("${cat?.name}: ")
        cat?.Meow()
    }
}
```

This compiles, but the output is incorrect (null gets printed for the second item in the myCats array).

D

```
class Cat(var name: String = "") {
    fun Meow() { println("Meow!") }
}

fun main(args: Array<String>) {
    var myCats = arrayOf(Cat("Misty"),
                         Cat(null),
                         Cat("Socks"))
    for (cat in myCats) {
        if (cat != null) {
            print("${cat?.name}: ")
            cat?.Meow()
        }
    }
}
```

This doesn't compile because a Cat can't have a null name.

Use let to run code if values are not null

When you use nullable types, you may want to execute code if (and only if) a particular value is not `null`. If you have a `Wolf?` variable named `w`, for example, you might want to print the value of `w`'s `hunger` property so long as `w` is not `null`.

One option for performing this kind of task is to use the code:

```
if (w != null ) {
    println(w.hunger)
}
```

But if the compiler can't guarantee that the `w` variable won't change in between the null-check and its usage, however, the code won't compile.

This can happen if, say, w defines a var property in a class, and you want to use its hunger property in a separate function. It's the same situation that you saw earlier in the chapter when we introduced the need for safe calls.

An alternative approach that will work in *all* situations is to use the code:

```
w?.let {
    println(it.hunger)
}
```

If w is not null, let's print its hunger.

It's like saying "if *w* is not *null*, let's print its *hunger*". Let's walk through this.

?.let allows you to run code for a value that's not null.

The **`let`** keyword used in conjunction with the safe call operator `?.` tells the compiler that you want to perform some action when the value it's operating on is not `null`. So the following code:

```
w?.let {
    // Code to do something
}
```

will only execute the code in its body if `w` is not `null`.

Once you've established that the value is not `null`, you can refer to it in the body of the `let` using **`it`**. So in the following code example, `it` refers to a non-nullable version of the `w` variable, allowing you to directly access its `hunger` property:

```
w?.let {
    println(it.hunger)
}
```

You can use "it" to directly access the Wolf's functions and properties.

Let's look at a couple more examples of when using `let` can be useful.

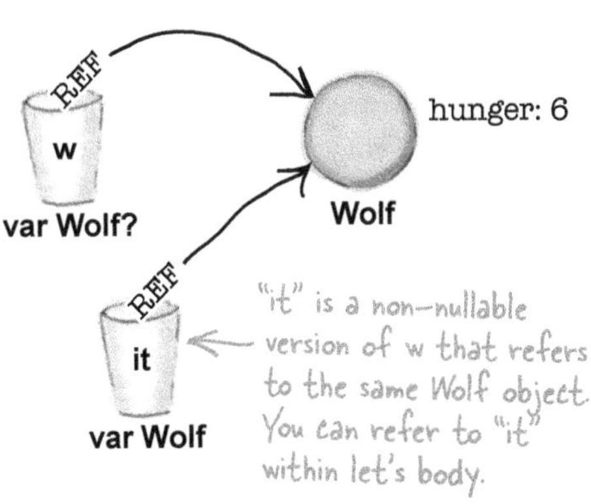

Using let with array items

`let` can also be used to perform actions using the non-null items of an array. You can use the following code, for example, to loop through an array of `String?`s, and print each item that is not `null`:

```
var array = arrayOf("Hi", "Hello", null)
for (item in array) {
    item?.let {
        println(it)   ← This line only runs for non-null items in the array
    }
}
```

Using let to streamline expressions

`let` is particularly useful in situations where you want to perform actions on the return value of a function which may be `null`.

Suppose you have a function named `getAlphaWolf` that has a return type of `Wolf?` like this:

```
fun getAlphaWolf() : Wolf? {
    return Wolf()
}
```

If you wanted to get a reference to the function's return value and call its `eat` function if it's not null, you could do so (in most situations) using the following code:

```
var alpha = getAlphaWolf()
if (alpha != null) {
    alpha.eat()
}
```

If you were to rewrite the code using `let`, however, you would no longer need to create a separate variable in which to hold the function's return value. Instead, you could use:

```
getAlphaWolf()?.let {   ← Using let is more concise. It's also safe,
    it.eat()              so you can use it in all situations.
}
```

It's like saying "get the alpha `Wolf`, and if it's not null, let it `eat`".

You must use curly braces to denote the `let` body.

If you omit the { }'s, your code won't compile.

Instead of using an if expression...

Another thing you may want to do when you have nullable types is use an `if` expression that specifies an alternate value for something that's `null`.

Suppose that you have a `Wolf?` variable named `w`, as before, and you want to use an expression that returns the value of `w`'s `hunger` property if `w` is not `null`, but defaults to -1 if `w` is `null`. In *most* situations, the following expression will work:

```
if (w != null) w.hunger else -1
```

But as before, if the compiler thinks there's a chance that the `w` variable may have been updated in between the null-check and its usage, the code won't compile because the compiler considers it to be unsafe.

Fortunately there's an alternative: the **Elvis operator**. ← [Note from editor: Elvis? Is this a joke? Return to sender.]

...you can use the safer Elvis operator

The Elvis operator `?:` is a safe alternative to an `if` expression. It's called the Elvis operator because when you tip it on its side, it looks a bit like Elvis.

This is the Elvis operator.

Here's an example of an expression that uses an Elvis operator:

```
w?.hunger ?: -1
```

The Elvis operator first checks the value on its left, in this case:

```
w?.hunger
```

If this value is not `null`, the Elvis operator returns it. If the value on the left is `null`, however, the Elvis operator returns the value on its right instead (in this case -1). So the code

```
w?.hunger ?: -1
```

is like saying "if *w* is not null and its `hunger` property is not null, return the value of the *hunger* property, otherwise return -1". It does the same thing as the code:

```
if (w?.hunger != null) w.hunger else -1
```

but because it's a safer alternative, you can use it anywhere.

Over the past few pages, you've seen how to access a nullable-type's properties and functions using safe calls, and how to use `let` and the Elvis operator in place of `if` statements and expressions. There's just one more option we want to mention that you can use to check for `null` values: the **not-null assertion operator**.

The Elvis operator ?: is a safe version of an if expression. It returns the value on its left if that is not null. Otherwise, it returns the value on its right.

The !! operator deliberately throws a NullPointerException

The not-null assertion operator, or `!!`, is different to the other methods for dealing with nulls that we've looked at over the past few pages. Instead of making sure that your code is safe by handling any null values, the not-null assertion operator deliberately throws a `NullPointerException` if something turns out to be `null`.

Suppose, as before, you have a `Wolf?` variable named `w`, and you want to assign the value of its `hunger` property to a new variable named `x` if `w` or `hunger` is not `null`. To do this using a not-null assertion, you would use the following code:

```
var x = w!!.hunger
```

Here, the !! makes the assertion that w is not null.

If `w` and `hunger` are is not `null`, as asserted, the value of the `hunger` property is assigned to `x`. But if `w` or `hunger` is `null`, a `NullPointerException` will get thrown, a message will be displayed in the IDE's output window, and the application will stop running.

The message that's displayed in the output window gives you information about the `NullPointerException` including a stack trace giving you the location of the not-null assertion that caused it. The following output, for example, tells you that the `NullPointerException` was thrown from the `main` function at line 45 in file *App.kt*:

Here's the NullPointerException, with a stack trace telling you where it occurred.

```
Exception in thread "main" kotlin.KotlinNullPointerException
        at AppKt.main(App.kt:45)
```

The exception happened at line 45.

The following output, on the other hand, tells you that the `NullPointerException` was thrown from a function named `myFunction` in class `MyWolf` at line 98 of file *App.kt*. This function was called from the `main` function at line 67 of the same file:

```
Exception in thread "main" kotlin.KotlinNullPointerException
        at MyWolf.myFunction(App.kt:98)
        at AppKt.main(App.kt:67)
```

So not-null assertions are useful if you want to test assumptions about your code, as they enable you to pinpoint problems.

As you've seen, the Kotlin compiler goes to great lengths to make sure that your code runs error-free, but there are still situations in which it's useful to know how to throw exceptions, and handle any that arise. We'll look at exceptions after we've shown you the full code for a new project that deals with `null` values.

Create the Null Values project

Create a new Kotlin project that targets the JVM, and name the project "Null Values". Then create a new Kotlin file named *App.kt* by highlighting the *src* folder, clicking on the File menu and choosing New → Kotlin File/Class. When prompted, name the file "App", and choose File from the Kind option.

We'll add various classes and functions to the project, and a `main` function that uses them, so that you can explore how null values work. Here's the code—update your version of *App.kt* to match ours:

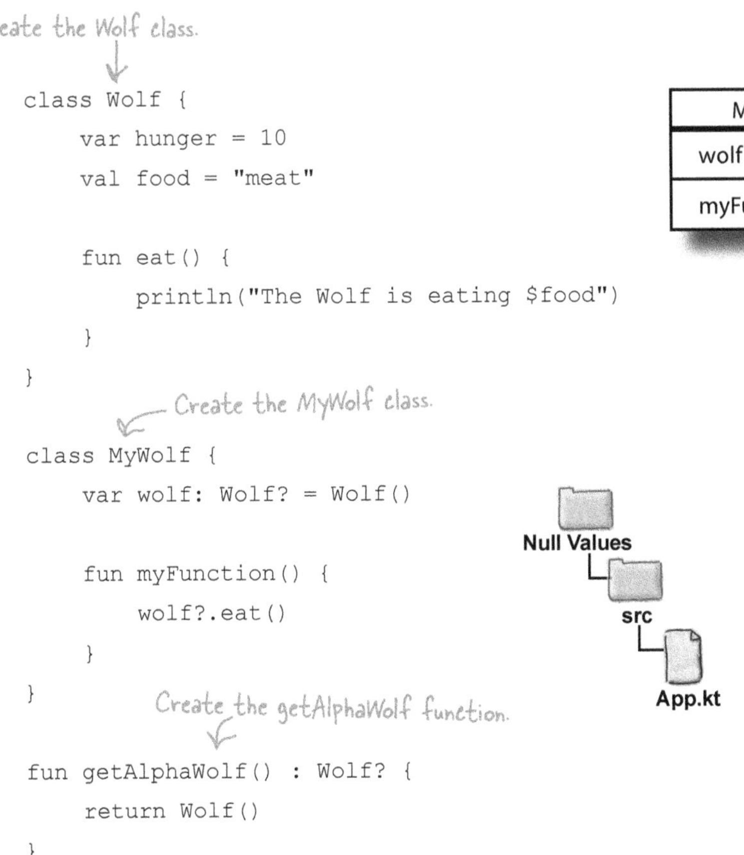


```
class Wolf {
    var hunger = 10
    val food = "meat"

    fun eat() {
        println("The Wolf is eating $food")
    }
}

class MyWolf {
    var wolf: Wolf? = Wolf()

    fun myFunction() {
        wolf?.eat()
    }
}

fun getAlphaWolf() : Wolf? {
    return Wolf()
}
```

We're using a cut-down version of the Wolf class we used in earlier chapters in order to keep the code simple.

MyWolf
wolf
myFunction()

Wolf
hunger food
eat()

The code continues on the next page.

The code continued...

```
fun main(args: Array<String>) {
    var w: Wolf? = Wolf()

    if (w != null) {
        w.eat()
    }

    var x = w?.hunger
    println("The value of x is $x")

    var y = w?.hunger ?: -1
    println("The value of y is $y")

    var myWolf = MyWolf()
    myWolf?.wolf?.hunger = 8
    println("The value of myWolf?.wolf?.hunger is ${myWolf?.wolf?.hunger}")

    var myArray = arrayOf("Hi", "Hello", null)
    for (item in myArray) {
        item?.let { println(it) }
    }

    getAlphaWolf()?.let { it.eat() }

    w = null
    var z = w!!.hunger
}
```

Use the Elvis operator to set y to the value of hunger if w is not null. If w is null, it sets y to -1.

This prints the non-null items in the array.

This will throw a NullPointerException as w is null.

MyWolf
wolf
myFunction()

Wolf
hunger food
eat()

Null Values
src
App.kt

Test drive

When we run the code, the following text gets printed in the IDE's output window:

```
The Wolf is eating meat
The value of x is 10
The value of y is 10
The value of myWolf?.wolf?.hunger is 8
Hi
Hello
The Wolf is eating meat
Exception in thread "main" kotlin.KotlinNullPointerException
        at AppKt.main(App.kt:55)
```

Pool Puzzle

Your **job** is to take code snippets from the pool and place them into the blank lines in the code. You may **not** use the same code snippet more than once, and you won't need to use all the code snippets. Your **goal** is to create two classes named Duck and MyDucks. MyDucks must contain an array of nullable Ducks, and include functions to make each Duck quack, and return the total height of all the Ducks.

```
class Duck(val height: ........ = null) {
    fun quack() {
        println("Quack! Quack!")
    }
}

class MyDucks(var myDucks: Array<..........>) {
    fun quack() {
        for (duck in myDucks) {
            .....................{
                ..........quack()
            }
        }
    }

    fun totalDuckHeight(): Int {
        var h:........... = ...........
        for (duck in myDucks) {
            h ......duck......height ........ 0
        }
        return h
    }
}
```

Note: each thing from the pool can only be used once!

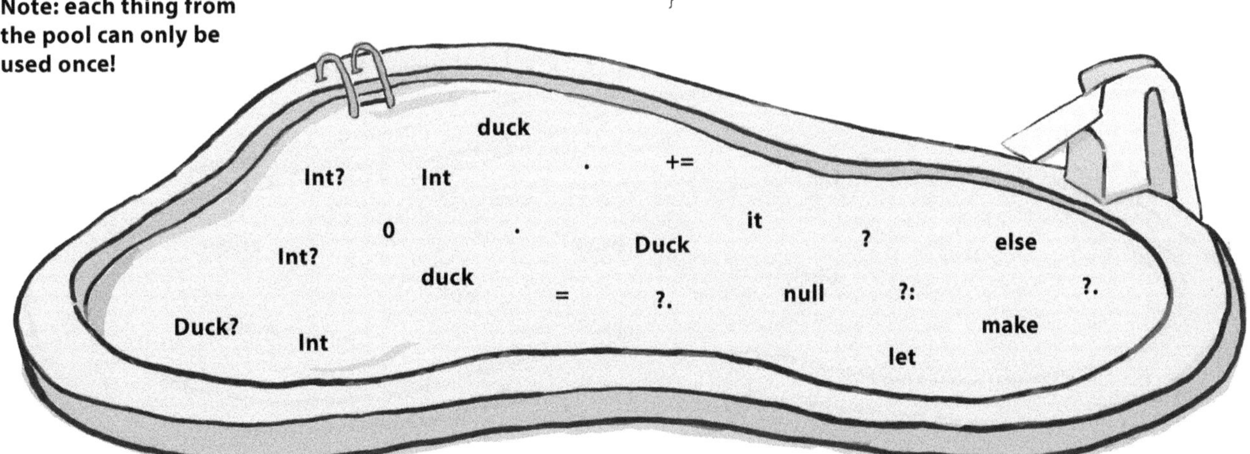

Pool Puzzle Solution

Your **job** is to take code snippets from the pool and place them into the blank lines in the code. You may **not** use the same code snippet more than once, and you won't need to use all the code snippets. Your **goal** is to create two classes named Duck and MyDucks. MyDucks must contain an array of nullable Ducks, and include functions to make each Duck quack, and return the total height of all the Ducks.

```
class Duck(val height: Int? = null) {
    fun quack() {
        println("Quack! Quack!")
    }
}

class MyDucks(var myDucks: Array<Duck?>) {
    fun quack() {
        for (duck in myDucks) {
            duck?.let {
                it.quack()
            }
        }
    }

    fun totalDuckHeight(): Int {
        var h: Int = 0
        for (duck in myDucks) {
            h += duck?.height ?: 0
        }
        return h
    }
}
```

This is Int?, not Int, as it must accept a null value.

myDucks is an array of nullable Ducks.

Here, we're using let to make each duck quack, but we could have used duck?.quack() instead.

totalDuckHeight() returns an Int, so h must be an Int, not an Int?.

If the duck and its height are not null, add the duck's height to h. Otherwise, add 0 to h instead.

You didn't need to use these snippets.

Int
.
.
Int?
Duck
?
else
duck
=
null
make

An exception is thrown in exceptional circumstances

As we said earlier, an exception is a type of warning about exceptional situations that pop up at runtime. It's a way for code to say "Something bad happened, I failed".

Suppose, for example, that you have a function named `myFunction` that converts a `String` parameter to an `Int`, and prints it:

```
fun myFunction(str: String) {
    val x = str.toInt()
    println(x)
    println("myFunction has ended")
}
```

If you pass a `String` such as "5" to `myFunction`, the code will successfully convert the `String` to an `Int`, and print the value 5, along with the text "myFunction has ended". If, however, you pass the function a `String` that can't be converted to an `Int`, like "I am a name, not a number", the code will stop running, and display an exception message like this:

Yikes.

```
Exception in thread "main" java.lang.NumberFormatException: For input string: "I am a name, not a number"
        at java.lang.NumberFormatException.forInputString(NumberFormatException.java:65)
        at java.lang.Integer.parseInt(Integer.java:580)
        at java.lang.Integer.parseInt(Integer.java:615)
        at AppKt.myFunction(App.kt:119)
        at AppKt.main(App.kt:3)
```

The exception stack trace mentions Java because we're running our code on the JVM.

You can catch exceptions that are thrown

When an exception gets thrown, you have two options for dealing with it:

- **You can leave the exception alone.**
  This will display a message in the output window, and stop your application (as above).

- **You can catch the exception and handle it.**
  If you know you might get an exception when you execute particular lines of code, you can prepare for it, and possibly recover from whatever caused it.

You've seen what happens when you leave exceptions alone, so let's look at how you catch them.

Catch exceptions using a try/catch

You catch exceptions by wrapping the risky code in a **try/catch** block. A try/catch block tells the compiler that you know an exceptional thing could happen in the code you want to execute, and that you're prepared to handle it. The compiler doesn't care how you handle it; it cares only that you say you're taking care of it.

Here's what a try/catch block looks like:

```
fun myFunction(str: String) {

    try {                                    ← Here's the try...
        val x = str.toInt()
        println(x)
    } catch (e: NumberFormatException) {     ← ...and here's the catch.
        println("Bummer")
    }

    println("myFunction has ended")
}
```

The **try** part of the try/catch block contains the risky code that might cause an exception. In the above example, this is the code:

```
try {
    val x = str.toInt()
    println(x)
}
```

The **catch** part of the block specifies the exception that you want to catch, and includes the code you want to run if it catches it. So if our risky code throws a NumberFormatException, we'll catch it and print a meaningful message like this:

```
catch (e: NumberFormatException) {
    println("Bummer")    ← This line will only run if an exception is caught.
}
```

Any code that follows the catch block then runs, in this case the code:

```
println("myFunction has ended")
```

Use finally for the things you want to do no matter what

If you have important cleanup code that you want to run regardless of an exception, you can put it in a **`finally`** block. The `finally` block is optional, but it's guaranteed to run no matter what.

To see how this works, suppose you want to bake something experimental that might go wrong.

You start by turning on the oven.

If the thing you try to cook succeeds, ***you have to turn off the oven***.

If the thing you try is a complete failure, ***you have to turn off the oven***.

You have to turn off the oven no matter what, so the code for turning the oven off belongs in a `finally` block:

```
try {
    turnOvenOn()
    x.bake()
} catch (e: BakingException) {
    println("Baking experiment failed")
} finally {
    turnOvenOff()
}
```

We always want to call turnOvenOff(), so it belongs in the finally block.

Without `finally`, you have to put the `turnOvenOff` function call in *both* the `try` and the `catch` because ***you have to turn off the oven no matter what***. A `finally` block lets you put all your important cleanup code in one place, instead of duplicating it like this:

```
try {
    turnOvenOn()
    x.bake()
    turnOvenOff()
} catch (e: BakingException) {
    println("Baking experiment failed")
    turnOvenOff()
}
```

try/catch/finally flow control

★ If the try block fails (an exception):
Flow control immediately moves to the `catch` block. When the `catch` block completes, the `finally` block runs. When the `finally` block completes, the rest of the code continues.

★ If the try block succeeds (no exception):
Flow control skips over the `catch` block and moves to the `finally` block. When the `finally` block completes, the rest of the code continues.

★ If the try or catch block has a return statement, finally will still run:
Flow jumps to the `finally` block, then back to the `return`.

An exception is an object of type Exception

Every exception is an object of type `Exception`. It's the superclass of all exceptions, so every type of exception inherits from it. On the JVM, for example, every exception has a function named `printStackTrace` that you can use to print the exception's stack trace using code like this:

I'm exceptional!

Exception

```
try {
    //Do risky thing
} catch (e: Exception) {
    e.printStackTrace()
    //Other code that runs when you get an exception
}
```

printStackTrace() is a function that's available to all exceptions running on the JVM. If you can't recover from an exception, use printStackTrace() to help you track down the cause of the problem.

There are many different types of exception, each one of which is a subtype of `Exception`. Some of the most common (or famous) are:

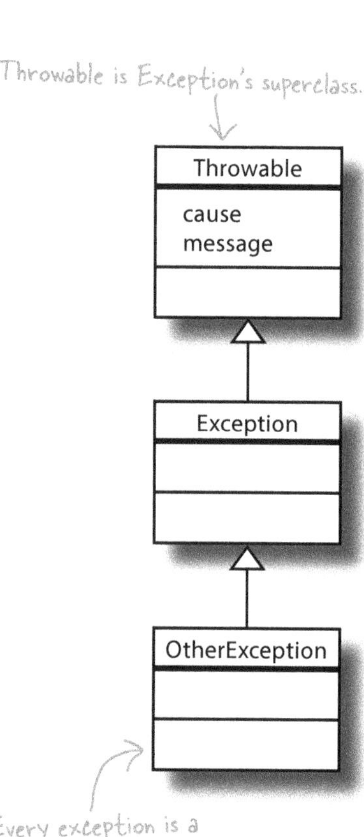

- **NullPointerException**
  Thrown when you try to perform operations on a null value. As you've seen, `NullPointerExceptions` are nearly extinct in Kotlinville.

- **ClassCastException**
  You'll get this if you try to cast an object to an incorrect type, like casting a `Wolf` into a `Tree`.

- **IllegalArgumentException**
  You can throw this if an illegal argument has been passed.

- **IllegalStateException**
  Use this if some object has state that's invalid.

You can also create your own types of exception by defining a new class with `Exception` as its superclass. The following code, for example, defines a new type of exception named `AnimalException`:

```
class AnimalException : Exception() { }
```

Defining your own types of exception can sometimes be useful if you want to deliberately throw exceptions in your own code. We'll look at how this is done after a small diversion.

Safe Casts Up Close

As you learned in Chapter 6, in most circumstances, the compiler will perform a smart cast each time you use the `is` operator. In the following code, for example, the compiler checks whether the `r` variable holds a `Wolf` object, so it can smart cast the variable from a `Roamable` to a `Wolf`:

```
val r: Roamable = Wolf()
if (r is Wolf) {
    r.eat()   <- Here, r has been smart cast to a Wolf.
}
```

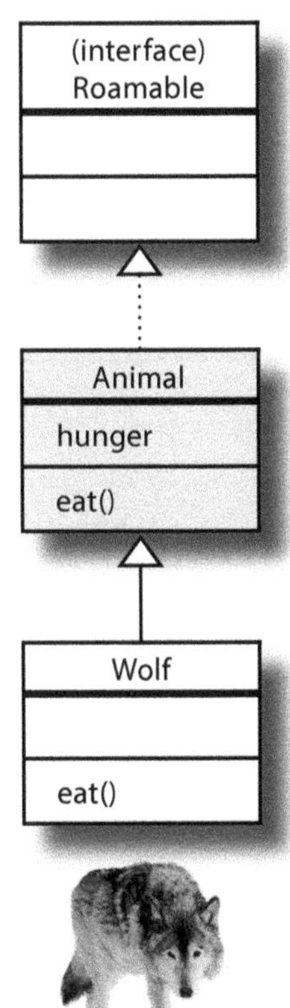

In some situations the compiler can't perform a smart cast as the variable may change in between you checking its type and its usage. The following code, for example, won't compile because the compiler can't be certain that the `r` property is still a `Wolf` after checking it:

```
class MyRoamable {
    var r: Roamable = Wolf()

    fun myFunction() {
        if (r is Wolf) {
            r.eat()   <- This won't compile, because the
        }                compiler can't guarantee that r still
    }                    holds a reference to a Wolf object.
}
```

You saw in Chapter 6 that you can deal with this by using the `as` keyword to explicitly cast `r` as a `Wolf` like this:

```
if (r is Wolf) {
    val wolf = r as Wolf   <- This will compile, but if r no longer
    wolf.eat()                holds a reference to a Wolf object,
}                             you'll get an exception at runtime.
```

But if `r` is assigned a value of some other type in between the type-check and the cast, the system will throw a `ClassCastException`.

The safe alternative is to perform a **safe cast** using the **as?** operator using code like this:

```
val wolf = r as? Wolf
```

This casts `r` as a `Wolf` if `r` holds an object of that type, and returns `null` if it doesn't. This saves you from getting a `ClassCastException` if your assumptions about the variable's type are incorrect.

as? lets you perform a safe explicit cast. If the cast fails, it returns null.

You can explicitly throw exceptions

It can sometimes be useful to deliberately throw exceptions in your own code. If you have a function named `setWorkRatePercentage`, for example, you might want to throw an `IllegalArgumentException` if someone tries to set a percentage that's less than 0 or greater than 100. Doing so forces the caller to address the problem, instead of relying on the function to decide what to do.

You throw an exception using the **throw** keyword. Here's how, for example, you'd get the `setWorkRatePercentage` function to throw an `IllegalArgumentException`:

```
fun setWorkRatePercentage(x: Int) {
    if (x !in 0..100) {
        throw IllegalArgumentException("Percentage not in range 0..100: $x")
    }
    //More code that runs if the argument is valid
}
```

This throws an IllegalArgumentException if x is not in the range 0..100

You could then catch the exception using code like this:

```
try {
    setWorkRatePercentage(110)
} catch(e: IllegalArgumentException) {
    //Code to handle the exception
}
```

The setWorkRatePercentage() function can't make anyone work at 110%, so the caller has to deal with the problem.

Exception Rules

- You can't have a `catch` or `finally` without a `try`.

```
callRiskyCode()
catch (e: BadException) { }
```

Not legal as there's no try.

- You can't put code between the `try` and the `catch`, or the `catch` and the `finally`.

```
try { callRiskyCode() }
x = 7
catch (e: BadException) { }
```

Not legal as you can't put code between the try and the catch.

- A `try` must be followed by either a `catch` or a `finally`.

```
try { callRiskyCode() }
finally { }
```

Legal because there's a finally, even though there's no catch.

- A `try` can have multiple `catch` blocks.

```
try { callRiskyCode() }
catch (e: BadException) { }
catch (e: ScaryException) { }
```

Legal because a try can have more than one catch.

try and throw are both expressions

Unlike in other languages such as Java, `try` and `throw` are *expressions*, so they can have return values.

How to use try as an expression

The return value of a `try` is either the last expression in the `try`, or the last expression in the `catch` (the `finally` block, if there, doesn't affect the return value). Consider the following code, for example:

```
val result = try { str.toInt() } catch (e: Exception) { null }
```

This is like saying "Try to assign str.toInt() to result, but if you can't, set result to null".

The code creates a variable named `result` of type `Int?`. The `try` block tries to convert the value of a `String` variable named `str` to an `Int`. If this is successful, it assigns the `Int` value to `result`. If the `try` block fails, however, it assigns `null` to `result` instead:

How to use throw as an expression

`throw` is also an expression, so you can, for example, use it with the Elvis operator using code like this:

```
val h = w?.hunger ?: throw AnimalException()
```

If `w` and `hunger` are not `null`, the above code assigns the value of `w`'s `hunger` property to a new variable named `h`. If, however, `w` or `hunger` are `null`, it throws an `AnimalException`.

there are no Dumb Questions

Q: You said that you can use `throw` in an expression. Does that mean `throw` has a type? What is it?

A: `throw` has a return type of **`Nothing`**. This is a special type that has no values, so a variable of type `Nothing?` can only hold a `null` value. The following code, for example, creates a variable named `x` of type `Nothing?` that can only be `null`:

```
var x = null
```

Q: I get it. `Nothing` is a type that has no values. Is there anything I might want to use that type for?

A: You can also use `Nothing` to denote code locations that can never be reached. You can, say, use it as the return type of a function that never returns:

```
fun fail(): Nothing {
    throw BadException()
}
```

The compiler knows that the code stops execution after `fail()` is called.

Q: In Java I have to declare when a method throws an exception.

A: That's correct, but you don't in Kotlin. Kotlin doesn't differentiate between checked and unchecked exceptions.

Sharpen your pencil

Look at the code on the left. What do you think the output will be when it's run? What do you think it would be if the code on line 2 were changed to the following?:

```
val test: String = "Yes"
```

Write your answers in the boxes on the right.

```
fun main(args: Array<String>) {
    val test: String = "No"

    try {
        println("Start try")
        riskyCode(test)
        println("End try")
    } catch (e: BadException) {
        println("Bad Exception")
    } finally {
        println("Finally")
    }

    println("End of main")
}

class BadException : Exception()

fun riskyCode(test: String) {
    println("Start risky code")

    if (test == "Yes") {
        throw BadException()
    }

    println("End risky code")
}
```

Output when test = "No"

Output when test = "Yes"

Answers on page 248.

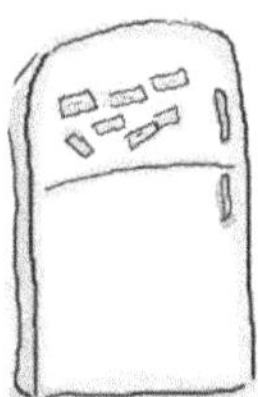

Code Magnets

Some Kotlin code is all scrambled up on the fridge. See if you can reconstruct the code so that if `myFunction` is passed a `String` of "Yes", it prints the text "thaws", and if `myFunction` is passed a `String` of "No", it prints the text "throws".

The magnets need to go in this space.

```
}

fun riskyCode(test:String) {
```

```
print("h")
```

```
} finally {
```

```
class BadException : Exception()

fun myFunction(test: String) {
```

```
if (test == "Yes") {
```

```
throw BadException()
```

```
print("w")
```

```
riskyCode(test)
```

```
print("t")
```

```
try {
```

```
print("a")
```

```
}
```

```
print("s")
```

```
print("o")
```

```
print("r")
```

```
}
```

```
} catch (e: BadException) {
```

```
}
```

Answers on page 249.

Sharpen your pencil Solution

Look at the code on the left. What do you think the output will be when it's run? What do you think it would be if the code on line 2 were changed to the following?:

```
val test: String = "Yes"
```

Write your answers in the boxes on the right.

```
fun main(args: Array<String>) {
    val test: String = "No"

    try {
        println("Start try")
        riskyCode(test)
        println("End try")
    } catch (e: BadException) {
        println("Bad Exception")
    } finally {
        println("Finally")
    }

    println("End of main")
}

class BadException : Exception()

fun riskyCode(test: String) {
    println("Start risky code")

    if (test == "Yes") {
        throw BadException()
    }

    println("End risky code")
}
```

Output when test = "No"

Start try
Start risky code
End risky code
End try
Finally
End of main

Output when test = "Yes"

Start try
Start risky code
Bad Exception
Finally
End of main

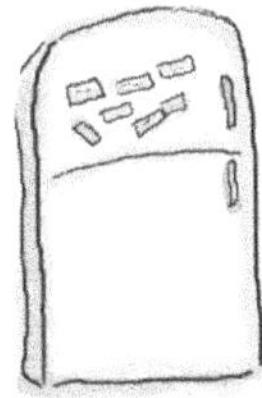

Code Magnets Solution

Some Kotlin code is all scrambled up on the fridge. See if you can reconstruct the code so that if `myFunction` is passed a `String` of "Yes", it prints the text "thaws", and if `myFunction` is passed a `String` of "No", it prints the text "throws".

```
class BadException : Exception()       <- Create a subclass of Exception.

fun myFunction(test: String) {        <- Create myFunction.
    try {
        print("t")
        riskyCode(test)                <- Try to run this code.
        print("o")
    } catch (e: BadException) {
        print("a")                     <- Run this code if a BadException is thrown.
    } finally {
        print("w")                     <- This code runs no matter what.
    }
    print("s")
}

fun riskyCode(test:String) {           <- Create riskyCode
    print("h")
    if (test == "Yes") {
        throw BadException()           <- Throw a BadException if test == "Yes"
    }
    print("r")
}
```

CHAPTER 8

Your Kotlin Toolbox

You've got Chapter 8 under your belt and now you've added nulls and exceptions to your toolbox.

You can download the full code for the chapter from https://tinyurl.com/HFKotlin.

BULLET POINTS

- `null` is a value that means a variable doesn't hold a reference to an object. The variable exists, but it doesn't refer to anything.
- A nullable type can hold null values in addition to its base type. You define a type as nullable by adding a `?` to the end of it.
- To access a nullable variable's properties and functions, you must first check that it's not `null`.
- If the compiler can't guarantee that a variable is not `null` in between a null-check and its usage, you must access properties and functions using the safe call operator (`?.`).
- You can chain safe calls together.
- To execute code if (and only if) a value is not `null`, use `?.let`.
- The Elvis operator (`?:`) is a safe alternative to an `if` expression.
- The not-null assertion operator (`!!`) throws a `NullPointerException` if the subject of your assertion is `null`.
- An exception is a warning that occurs in exceptional situations. It's an object of type `Exception`.
- Use `throw` to throw an exception.
- Catch an exception using `try/catch/finally`.
- `try` and `throw` are expressions.
- Use a safe cast (`as?`) to avoid getting a `ClassCastException`.

9 collections

Get Organized

Ever wanted something more flexible than an array?

Kotlin comes with a bunch of useful **collections** that give you more flexibility and greater control over how you ***store and manage groups of objects***. Want to keep a *resizeable list that you can keep adding to*? Want to *sort, shuffle or reverse its contents*? Want to *find something by name*? Or do you want something that will automatically *weed out duplicates* without you lifting a finger? If you want any of these things, or more, keep reading. It's all here...

Arrays can be useful...

So far, each time we've wanted to hold references to a bunch of objects in one place, we've used an array. Arrays are quick to create, and have many useful functions. Here are some of the things you can do with an array (depending on the type of its items):

- **Make an array:**

```
var array = arrayOf(1, 3, 2)
```

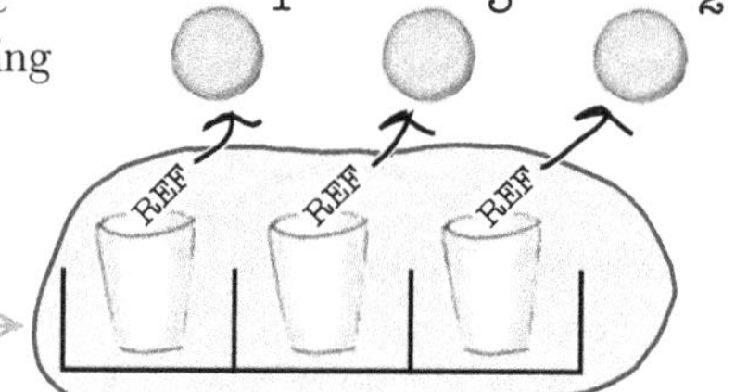

- **Make an array initialized with nulls:**

```
var nullArray: Array<String?> = arrayOfNulls(2)
```

Creates an array of size 2 initialized with null values. It's like saying: arrayOf(null, null)

- **Find out the size of the array:**

```
val size = array.size
```

array has space for three items, so its size is 3.

- **Reverse the order of the items in the array:**

```
array.reverse()
```

Flips the order of the items in the array.

- **Find out if it contains something:**

```
val isIn = array.contains(1)
```

array contains 1, so this returns true.

- **Calculate the sum of its items (if they're numeric):**

```
val sum = array.sum()
```

This returns 6 as 2 + 3 + 1 = 6.

- **Calculate the average of its items (if they're numeric):**

```
val average = array.average()
```

This returns a Double—in this case, (2 + 3 + 1)/3 = 2.0.

- **Find out the minimum or maximum item (works for numbers, Strings, Chars and Booleans):**

```
array.min()
array.max()
```

min() returns 1, as this is the lowest value in the array. max() returns 3 as this is the highest.

- **Sort the array in a natural order (works for numbers, Strings, Chars and Booleans):**

```
array.sort()
```

Changes the order of the items in array so they go from the lowest value to the highest, or from false to true.

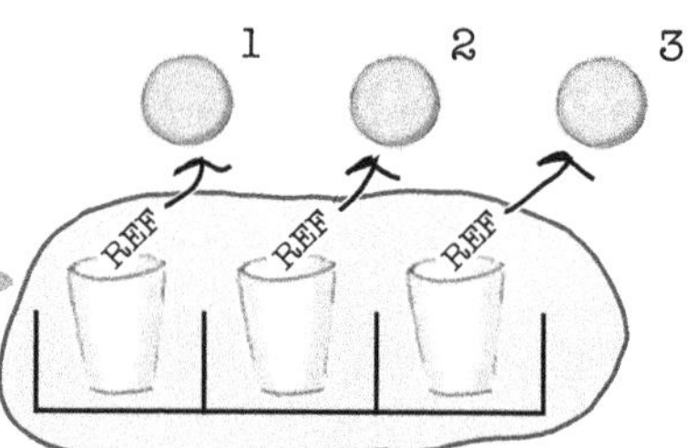

But arrays aren't perfect.

...but there are things an array can't handle

Even though an array lets you perform many useful actions, there are two important areas in which arrays fall short.

You can't change an array's size

When you create an array, the compiler infers its size from the number of items it's initialized with. Its size is then fixed forever. The array won't grow if you want to add a new item to it, and it won't shrink if you want to remove an item.

Arrays are mutable, so they can be updated

Another limitation is that once you create an array you can't stop it from being amended. If you create an array using code like this:

```
val myArray = arrayOf(1, 2, 3)
```

there's nothing to stop the array being updated like so:

```
myArray[0] = 6
```

If your code relies on the array not changing, this may be a source of bugs in your application.

So what's the alternative?

Q: Can't I remove an item from an array by setting it to `null`?

A: If you create an array that holds nullable types, you can set one or more of its items to `null` using code like this:

```
val a: Array<Int?> = arrayOf(1, 2, 3)
a[2] = null
```

This doesn't change the size of the array, however. In the above example, the array's size is still 3 even though one of its items has been set to `null`.

Q: Couldn't I create a copy of the array that has a different size?

A: You could, and arrays even have a function named `plus` that makes this easier; `plus` copies the array, and adds a new item to the end of it. But this doesn't change the size of the original array.

Q: Is that a problem?

A: Yes. You'll need to write extra code, and if other variables hold references to the old version of the array, this might lead to buggy code.

There are, however, good alternatives to using an array, which we'll look at next.

When in doubt, go to the Library

Kotlin ships with hundreds of pre-built classes and functions that you can use in your code. You've already met some of these, like `String` and `Any`. And the great news for us is that the **Kotlin Standard Library** includes classes that provide great alternatives to arrays.

In the Kotlin Standard Library, classes and functions are grouped into **packages**. Every class belongs to a package, and each package has a name. The *kotlin* package, for example, holds core functions and types, and the *kotlin.math* package holds mathematical functions and constants.

The package we're interested in here is the *kotlin.collections* package. This package includes a number of classes that let you group objects together in a **collection**. Let's look at the main collection types.

Standard Library

You can see what's in the Kotlin Standard Library by browsing to:

https://kotlinlang.org/api/latest/jvm/stdlib/index.html

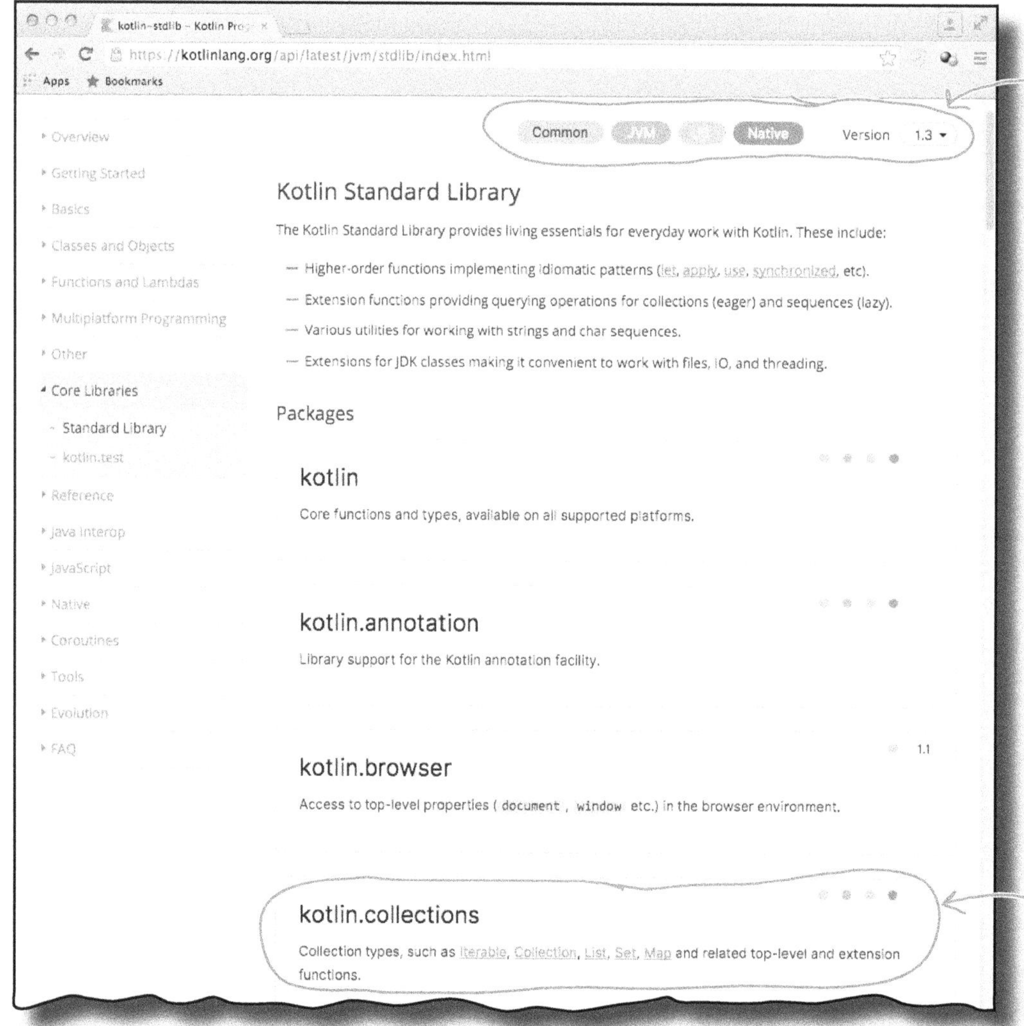

You can use these filters to display only those collections that are relevant to a particular platform or Kotlin version.

Here's the kotlin.collections package in the Kotlin Standard Library.

List, Set and Map

Kotlin has three main types of collection—**`List`**, **`Set`** and **`Map`**—and each one has its own distinct purpose:

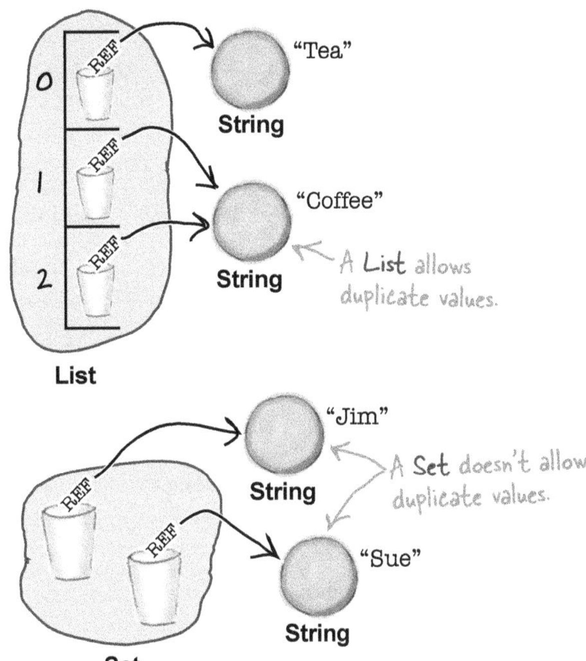

List - when sequence matters

A `List` knows and cares about index position. It knows where something is in the `List`, and you can have more than one element referencing the same object.

Set - when uniqueness matters

A `Set` doesn't allow duplicates, and doesn't care about the order in which values are held. You can never have more than one element referencing the same object, or more than one element referencing two objects that are considered equal.

Map - when finding something by key matters

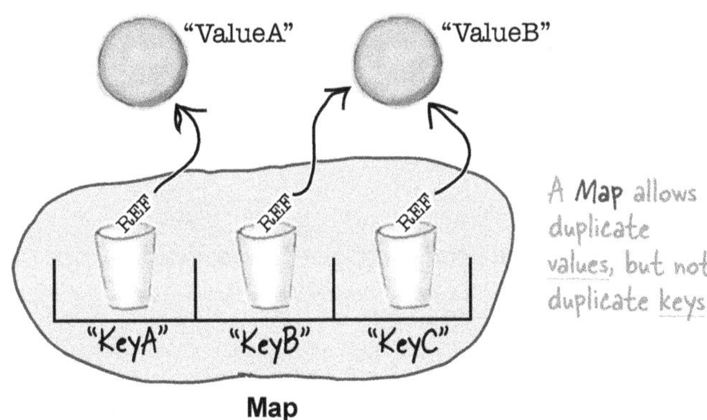

A `Map` uses key/value pairs. It knows the value associated with a given key. You can have two keys that reference the same object, but you can't have duplicate keys. Although keys are typically `String` names (so that you can make name/value property lists, for example), a key can be any object.

Simple `List`s, `Set`s and `Map`s are *immutable*, which means that you can't add or remove items after the collection has been initialized. If you want to be able to add or remove items, Kotlin has mutable subtypes that you can use instead: **`MutableList`**, **`MutableSet`** and **`MutableMap`**. So if you want all the benefits of using a `List` and you want to be able to update its contents, use a `MutableList`.

Now that you've seen the three main types of collection that Kotlin has to offer, let's find out how you use each one, starting with a `List`.

Fantastic Lists...

You create a **List** in a similar way to how you create an array: by calling a function named **listOf**, passing in the values you want the List to be initialized with. The following code, for example, creates a List, initializes it with three Strings, and assigns it to a new variable named shopping:

```
val shopping = listOf("Tea", "Eggs", "Milk")
```

The code creates a List containing String values of "Tea", "Eggs" and "Milk".

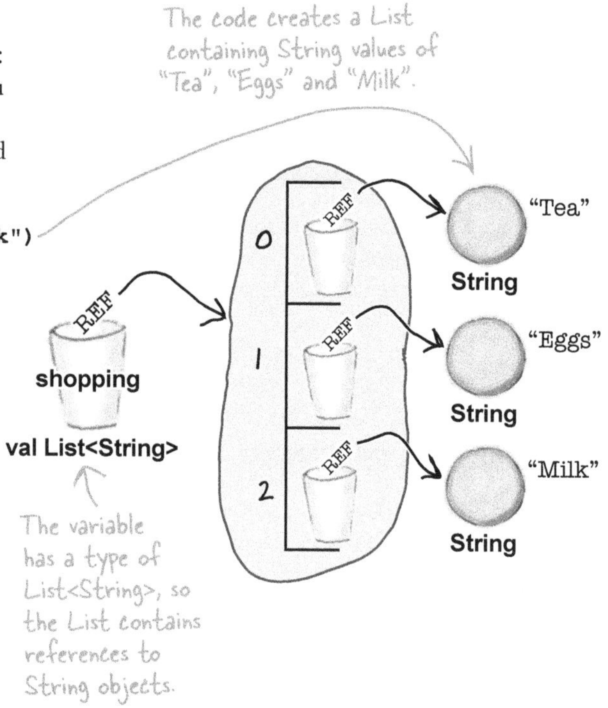

The compiler infers the type of object each List should contain by looking at the type of each value that's passed to it when it's created. The above List, for example, is initialized with three Strings, so the compiler creates a List of type List<String>. You can also explicitly define the List's type using code like this:

```
val shopping: List<String>
shopping = listOf("Tea", "Eggs", "Milk")
```

The variable has a type of List<String>, so the List contains references to String objects.

...and how to use them

Once you've created a List, you can access the items it contains using the **get** function. The following code, for example, checks that the size of the List is greater than 0, then prints the item at index 0:

```
if (shopping.size > 0) {
    println(shopping.get(0))
    //Prints "Tea"
}
```

It's a good idea to check the size of the List first because get() will throw an ArrayIndexOutOfBoundsException if it's passed an invalid index.

You can loop through all items in a List like so:

```
for (item in shopping) println (item)
```

And you can also check whether the List contains a reference to a particular object, and retrieve its index:

```
if (shopping.contains("Milk")) {
    println(shopping.indexOf("Milk"))
    //Prints 2
}
```

As you can see, using a List is a lot like using an array. The big difference, however, is that a List is immutable—you can't update any of the references it stores.

Lists and other collections can hold references to any type of object: Strings, Ints, Ducks, Pizzas and so on.

Create a MutableList...

If you want a `List` whose values you can update, you need to use a **`MutableList`**. You define a `MutableList` in a similar way to how you define a `List`, except this time, you use the **`mutableListOf`** function instead:

```
val mShopping = mutableListOf("Tea", "Eggs")
```

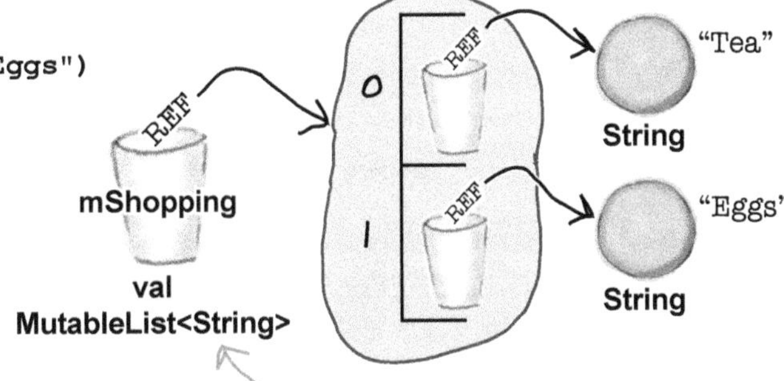

`MutableList` is a subtype of `List`, so you can call the same functions on a `MutableList` that you can on a `List`. The big difference, however, is that `MutableList`s have extra functions that you can use to add or remove values, or update or rearrange existing ones.

..and add values to it

You add new values to a `MutableList` using the **add** function. If you want to add a new value to the end of the `MutableList`, you pass the value to the `add` function as a single parameter. The following code, for example, adds "Milk" to the end of `mShopping`:

```
mShopping.add("Milk")
```

This increases the size of the `MutableList` so that it now holds three values instead of two.

If you want to insert a value at a specific index instead, you can do so by passing the index value to the `add` function in addition to the value. If you wanted to insert a value of "Milk" at index 1 instead of adding it to the end of the `MutableList`, you could do so using the following code:

```
mShopping.add(1, "Milk")
```

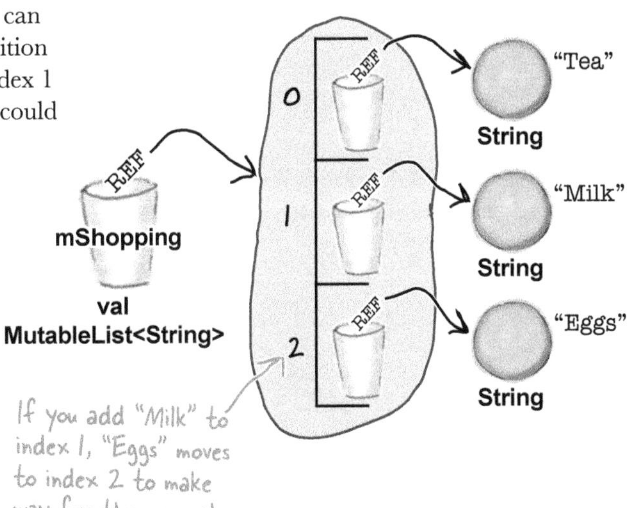

Inserting a value at a specific index in this way forces other values to move along to make space for it. In this example, the "Eggs" value moves from index 1 to index 2 so that "Milk" can be inserted at index 1.

As well as adding values to a `MutableList`, you can also remove or replace them. Let's see how.

You can remove a value...

There are two ways of removing a value from a `MutableList`.

The first way is to call the **`remove`** function, passing in the value you want to remove. The following code, for example, checks whether `mShopping` contains the `String` "Milk", then removes it:

```
if (mShopping.contains("Milk")) {
    mShopping.remove("Milk")
}
```

The second way is to use the **`removeAt`** function to remove the value at a given index. The following code, for example, makes sure that the size of `mShopping` is greater than 1, then removes the value at index 1:

```
if (mShopping.size > 1) {
    mShopping.removeAt(1)
}
```

Whichever approach you use, removing a value from the `MutableList` causes it to shrink.

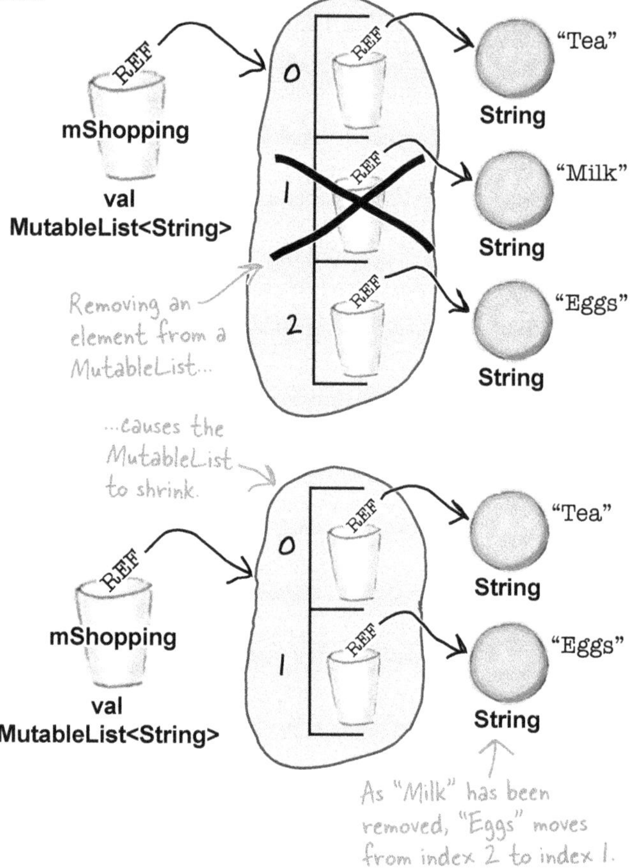

...and replace one value with another

If you want to update the `MutableList` so that the value at a particular index is replaced with another, you can do so using the **`set`** function. The following code, for instance, replaces the "Tea" value at index 0 with "Coffee":

```
if (mShopping.size > 0) {
    mShopping.set(0, "Coffee")
}
```

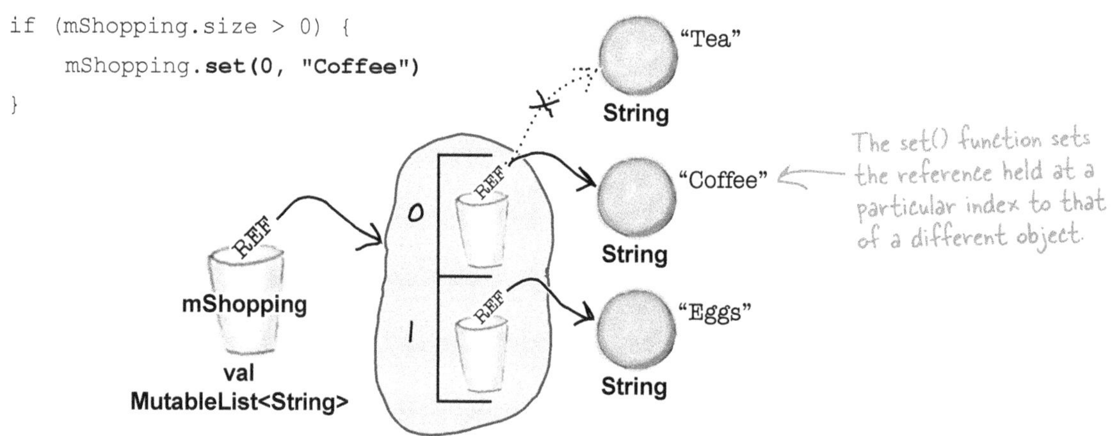

You can change the order and make bulk changes...

`MutableList` also includes functions to change the order in which items are held. You can, say, sort the `MutableList` in a natural order using the **`sort`** function, or reverse it using **`reverse`**:

```
mShopping.sort()
mShopping.reverse()
```

Together, these lines sort the MutableList in reverse order.

Or you can use the **`shuffle`** function to randomize it:

```
mShopping.shuffle()
```

And there are useful functions for making bulk changes to the `MutableList` too. You can, for example, use the **`addAll`** function to add all the items that are held in another collection. The following code, for instance, adds "Cookies" and "Sugar" to `mShopping`:

```
val toAdd = listOf("Cookies", "Sugar")
mShopping.addAll(toAdd)
```

The **`removeAll`** function removes items that are held in another collection:

```
val toRemove = listOf("Milk", "Sugar")
mShopping.removeAll(toRemove)
```

And the **`retainAll`** function retains all the items that are held in another collection and removes everything else:

```
val toRetain = listOf("Milk", "Sugar")
mShopping.retainAll(toRetain)
```

You can also use the **`clear`** function to remove every item like this:

```
mShopping.clear()
```

This empties mShopping so its size is 0.

...or take a copy of the entire MutableList

It can sometimes be useful to copy a `List`, or `MutableList`, so that you can save a snapshot of its state. You can do this using the **`toList`** function. The following code, for example, copies `mShopping`, and assigns the copy to a new variable named `shoppingCopy`:

```
val shoppingCopy = mShopping.toList()
```

The `toList` function returns a `List`, not a `MutableList`, so `shoppingCopy` can't be updated. Other useful functions you can use to copy the `MutableList` include **`sorted`** (which returns a sorted `List`), **`reversed`** (which returns a `List` with the values in reverse order), and **`shuffled`** (which returns a `List` and shuffles its values).

MutableList also has a toMutableList() function which returns a copy that's a new MutableList.

there are no Dumb Questions

Q: What's a package?

A: A package is a grouping of classes and functions. They're useful for a couple of reasons.

First, they help organize a project or library. Rather than just having one large pile of classes, they're all grouped into packages for specific kinds of functionality.

Second, they give you name-scoping, which means that multiple people can write classes with the same name, just so long as they're in different packages.

You'll find out more about structuring your code into packages in Appendix III.

Q: In Java I have to import any packages I want to use, including collections. Do I in Kotlin?

A: Kotlin automatically imports many packages from the Kotlin Standard Library, including *kotlin.collections*. There are still situations where you need to explicitly import packages, however, and you can find out more in Appendix III.

Create the Collections project

Now that you've learned about `Lists` and `MutableLists`, let's create a project that uses them.

Create a new Kotlin project that targets the JVM, and name the project "Collections". Then create a new Kotlin file named *Collections.kt* by highlighting the *src* folder, clicking on the File menu and choosing New → Kotlin File/Class. When prompted, name the file "Collections", and choose File from the Kind option.

Next, add the following code to *Collections.kt*:

```
fun main(args: Array<String>) {
    val mShoppingList = mutableListOf("Tea", "Eggs", "Milk")
    println("mShoppingList original: $mShoppingList")
    val extraShopping = listOf("Cookies", "Sugar", "Eggs")
    mShoppingList.addAll(extraShopping)
    println("mShoppingList items added: $mShoppingList")
    if (mShoppingList.contains("Tea")) {
        mShoppingList.set(mShoppingList.indexOf("Tea"), "Coffee")
    }
    mShoppingList.sort()
    println("mShoppingList sorted: $mShoppingList")
    mShoppingList.reverse()
    println("mShoppingList reversed: $mShoppingList")
}
```

Collections
src
Collections.kt

Test drive

When we run the code, the following text gets printed in the IDE's output window:

```
mShoppingList original: [Tea, Eggs, Milk]
mShoppingList items added: [Tea, Eggs, Milk, Cookies, Sugar, Eggs]
mShoppingList sorted: [Coffee, Cookies, Eggs, Eggs, Milk, Sugar]
mShoppingList reversed: [Sugar, Milk, Eggs, Eggs, Cookies, Coffee]
```

Printing a List or MutableList prints each item in index order inside square brackets.

Next, have a go at the following exercise.

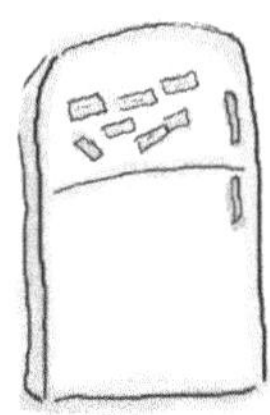

Code Magnets

Somebody used fridge magnets to create a working `main` function that produces the output shown on the right. Unfortunately a freak sharknado has dislodged the magnets. See if you can reconstruct the function.

The function needs to produce this output.

```
[Zero, Two, Four, Six]
[Two, Four, Six, Eight]
[Two, Four, Six, Eight, Ten]
[Two, Four, Six, Eight, Ten]
```

Your code needs to go here.

```
a.add(2, "Four")
```

```
a.add(0, "Zero")
a.add(1, "Two")
```

```
var a: MutableList<String> = mutableListOf()
```

```
println(a)
```

```
println(a)
```

```
fun main(args: Array<String>) {
```

```
if (a.indexOf("Four") != 4) a.add("Ten")
```

```
println(a)
```

```
a.add(3, "Six")
println(a)
```

```
if (a.contains("Zero")) a.add("Eight")
```

```
}
```

```
a.removeAt(0)
```

```
if (a.contains("Zero")) a.add("Twelve")
```

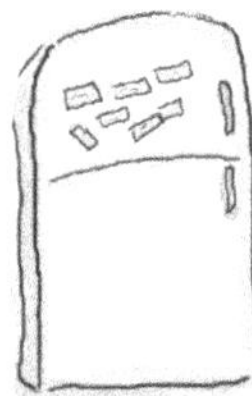

Code Magnets Solution

Somebody used fridge magnets to create a working `main` function that produces the output shown on the right. Unfortunately a freak sharknado has dislodged the magnets. See if you can reconstruct the function.

```
[Zero, Two, Four, Six]
[Two, Four, Six, Eight]
[Two, Four, Six, Eight, Ten]
[Two, Four, Six, Eight, Ten]
```

```
fun main(args: Array<String>) {
    var a: MutableList<String> = mutableListOf()
    a.add(0, "Zero")
    a.add(1, "Two")
    a.add(2, "Four")
    a.add(3, "Six")
    println(a)
    if (a.contains("Zero")) a.add("Eight")
    a.removeAt(0)
    println(a)
    if (a.indexOf("Four") != 4) a.add("Ten")
    println(a)
    if (a.contains("Zero")) a.add("Twelve")
    println(a)
}
```

Lists allow duplicate values

As you've already learned, using a `List`, or `MutableList`, gives you more flexibility than using an array. Unlike an array, you can explicitly choose whether the collection should be immutable, or whether your code can add, remove and update its values.

There are some situations, however, where using a `List` (or `MutableList`) doesn't quite work.

Imagine you're arranging a meal out with a group of friends, and you need to know how many people are going so that you can book a table. You could use a `List` for this, but there's a problem: **a `List` can hold duplicate values**. It's possible, for example, to create a `List` of friends where some of the friends are listed twice:

```
val friendList = listOf("Jim",
                        "Sue",
                        "Sue",
                        "Nick",
                        "Nick")
```

Here, there are three friends named Jim, Sue and Nick, but Sue and Nick are listed twice.

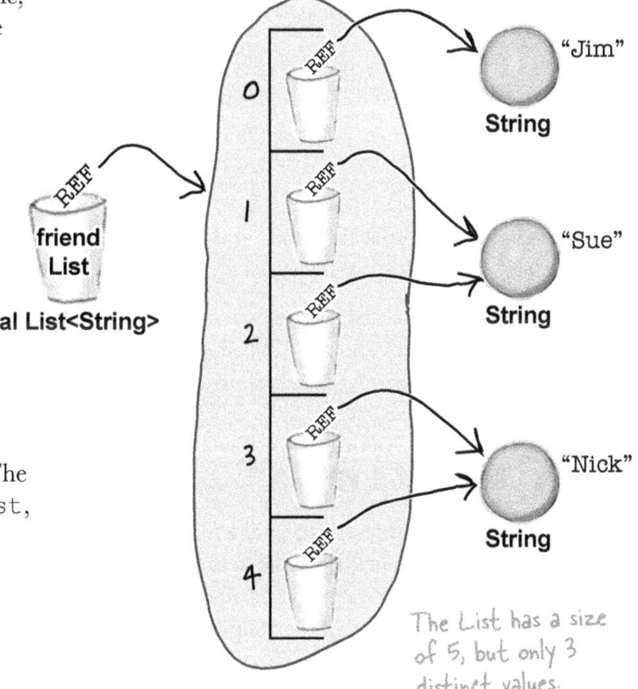

The List has a size of 5, but only 3 distinct values.

But if you want to know how many *distinct* friends are in the `List`, you can't simply use the code:

```
friendList.size
```

to find out how many people you should book a table for. The `size` property only sees that there are five items in the `List`, and it doesn't care that two of these items are duplicates.

In this kind of situation, we need to use a collection that doesn't allow duplicate values to be held. So what type of collection should we use?

Earlier in the chapter, we discussed the different types of collection that are available in Kotlin. Which type of collection do you think would be most appropriate for this situation?

....

How to create a Set

If you need a collection that doesn't allow duplicates, you can use a **`Set`**: an unordered collection with no duplicate values.

You create a `Set` by calling a function named **`setOf`**, passing in the values you want the `Set` to be initialized with. The following code, for example, creates a `Set`, initializes it with three `String`s, and assigns it to a new variable named `friendSet`:

```
val friendSet = setOf("Jim", "Sue", "Nick")
```

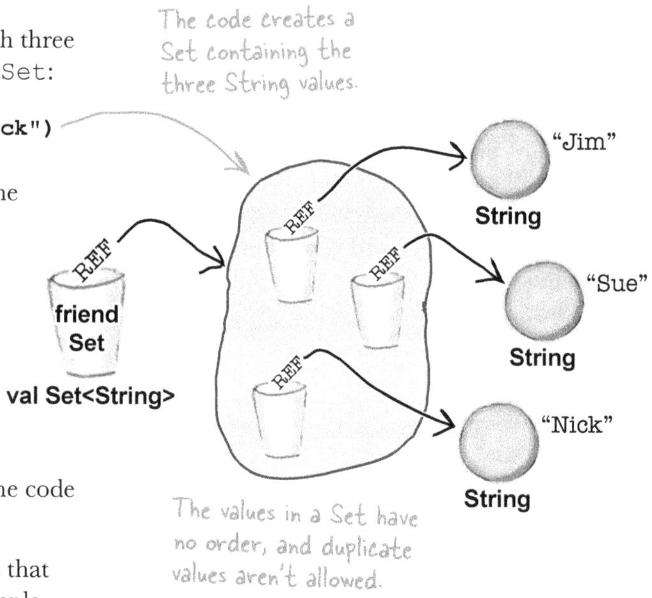

The code creates a Set containing the three String values.

A `Set` can't hold duplicate values, so if you try to define one using code like this:

```
val friendSet = setOf("Jim",
                      "Sue",
                      "Sue",
                      "Nick",
                      "Nick")
```


The values in a Set have no order, and duplicate values aren't allowed.

the `Set` ignores the duplicate "Sue" and "Nick" values. The code creates a `Set` that holds three distinct `String`s as before.

The compiler infers the `Set`'s type by looking at the values that are passed to it when it's created. The above code, for example, initializes a `Set` with `String` values, so the compiler creates a `Set` of type `Set<String>`.

How to use a Set's values

A `Set`'s values are unordered, so unlike a `List`, there's no `get` function you can use to get the value at a specified index. You can, however, still use the `contains` function to check whether a `Set` contains a particular value using code like this:

```
val isFredGoing = friendSet.contains("Fred")
```

This returns true if friendSet has a "Fred" value, and false if it doesn't.

And you can also loop through a `Set` like this:

```
for (item in friendSet) println(item)
```

A `Set` is immutable, so you can't add values to it, or remove existing ones. To do this kind of thing, you'd need to use a `MutableSet` instead. But before we show you how to create and use one of these, there's an Important Question we need to look at: **how does a `Set` decide whether a value is a duplicate?**

Unlike a List, a Set is unordered, and can't contain duplicate values.

How a Set checks for duplicates

To answer this question, let's go through the steps a Set takes when it decides whether or not a value is a duplicate.

The Set gets the object's hash code, and compares it with the hash codes of the objects already in the Set.

A Set uses hash codes to store its elements in a way that makes it much faster to access. It uses the hash code as a kind of label on a "bucket" where it stores elements, so all objects with a hash code of, say, 742, are stored in the bucket labeled 742.

If the Set has no matching hash codes for the new value, the Set assumes that it's not a duplicate, and adds the new value. If, however, the Set has matching hash codes, it needs to perform extra tests, and moves on to step 2.

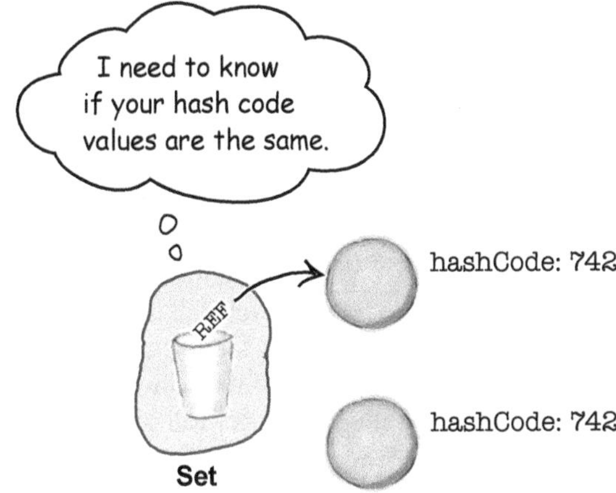

The Set uses the === operator to compare the new value against any objects it contains with the same hash code.

As you learned in Chapter 7, the === operator is used to check whether two references refer to the same object. So if the === operator returns `true` for any object with the same hash code, the Set knows that the new value is a duplicate, so it rejects it. If the === operator returns `false`, however, the Set moves on to step 3.

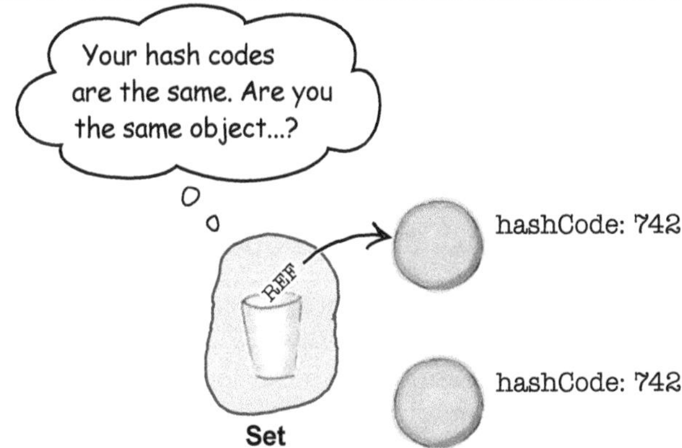

The Set uses the == operator to compare the new value against any objects it contains with matching hash codes.

The == operator calls the value's `equals` function. If this returns `true`, the Set treats the new value as a duplicate, and rejects it. If the == operator returns `false`, however, the Set assumes that the new value is not a duplicate, and adds it.

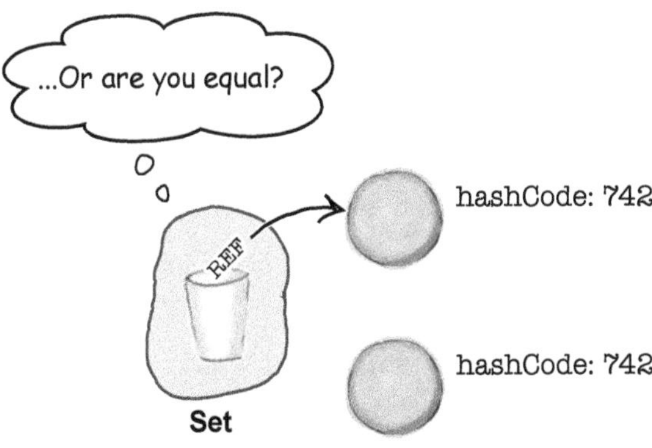

So there are two situations in which a Set views a value as a duplicate: if it's the *same* object, or *equal* to a value it already contains. Let's look at this in more detail.

Hash codes and equality

As you learned in Chapter 7, the === operator checks whether two references point to the same object, and the == operator checks whether the references point to objects that should be considered equal. A Set, however, *only uses these operators once it's established that the two objects have matching hash code values*. This means that in order for a Set to work properly, **equal objects must have matching hash codes**.

Let's see how this applies to the === and == operators.

Equality using the === operator

If you have two references that refer to the same object, you'll get the same result when you call the hashCode function on each reference. If you don't override the hashCode function, the default behavior (which it inherits from the Any superclass) is that each object will get a unique hash code.

When the following code runs, the Set spots that a and b have the same hash code and refer to the same object, so one value gets added to the Set:

```
val a = "Sue"
val b = a
val set = setOf(a, b)
```

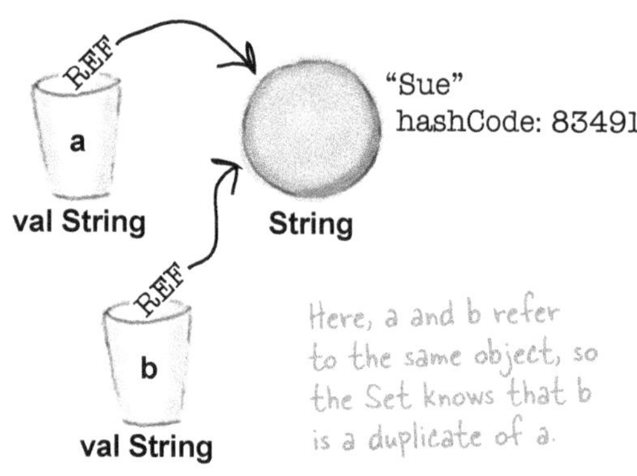

Equality using the == operator

If you want a Set to treat two different Recipe objects as equal, or equivalent, you have two options: make Recipe a data class, or override the hashCode and equals functions it inherits from Any. Making Recipe a data class is easiest as it automatically overrides the two functions.

As we said above, the default behavior (from Any) is to give each object a unique hash code value. So you *must* override hashCode to be sure that two equivalent objects return the same hash code. But you must also override equals so that the == operator returns true when it's used to compare objects with matching property values.

In the following example, one value will be added to the Set if Recipe is a data class:

```
val a = Recipe("Thai Curry")
val b = Recipe("Thai Curry")
val set = setOf(a, b)
```

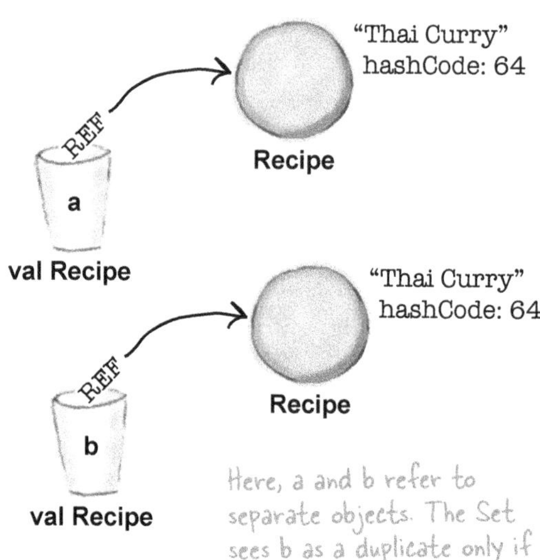

Rules for overriding hashCode and equals

If you decide to manually override the `hashCode` and `equals` functions in your class instead of using a data class, there are a number of laws you must abide by. Failure to do so will make the Kotlin universe collapse because things like `Sets` won't work properly, so make sure you follow them.

Here are the rules:

- If two objects are equal, they must have matching hash codes.
- If two objects are equal, calling `equals` on either object must return `true`. In other words, if `(a.equals(b))` then `(b.equals(a))`.
- If two objects have the same hash code value, they are not required to be equal. But if they're equal, they must have the same hash code value.
- So, if you override `equals`, you must override `hashCode`.
- The default behavior of the `hashCode` function is to generate a unique integer for each object. So if you don't override `hashCode` in a non-data class, no two objects of that type can ever be considered equal.
- The default behavior of the `equals` function is to do a === comparison, which tests whether the two references refer to a single object. So if you don't override `equals` in a non-data class, no two objects can ever be considered equal since references to two different objects will always contain a different bit pattern.

a.equals(b) must also mean that a.hashCode() == b.hashCode()

But a.hashCode() == b.hashCode() does not have to mean that a.equals(b)

there are no Dumb Questions

Q: How can hash codes be the same even if objects aren't equal?

A: As we said earlier, a `Set` uses hash codes to store its elements in a way that makes it much faster to access. If you want to find an object in a `Set`, it doesn't have to start searching from the beginning, looking at each element to see if it matches. Instead, it uses the hash code as a label on a "bucket" where it stored the element. So if you say "I want to find an object in the Set that looks like this one...", the `Set` gets the hash code value from the object you give it, then goes straight to the bucket for that hash code.

This isn't the whole story, but it's more than enough for you to use a `Set` effectively and understand what's going on.

The point is that hash codes can be the same without necessarily guaranteeing that the objects are equal, because the "hashing algorithm" used in the `hashCode` function might happen to return the same value for multiple objects. And yes, that means that multiple objects would all land in the same bucket in the `Set` (because each bucket represents a separate hash code value), but that's not the end of the world. It might mean that the `Set` is a little less efficient, or that it's filled with an extremely large number of elements, but if the `Set` finds more than one object in the same hash code bucket, the `Set` will simply use the === and == operators to look for a perfect match. In other words, hash code values are sometimes used to narrow down the search, but to find the one exact match, the `Set` still has to take all the objects in that one bucket (the bucket for all the objects with the same hash code) and see if there's a matching object in that bucket.

How to use a MutableSet

Now that you know about `Set`s, let's look at **`MutableSet`**s. A `MutableSet` is a subtype of `Set`, but with extra functions that you can use to add and remove values.

You define a `MutableSet` using the **`mutableSetOf`** function like this:

```
val mFriendSet = mutableSetOf("Jim", "Sue")
```

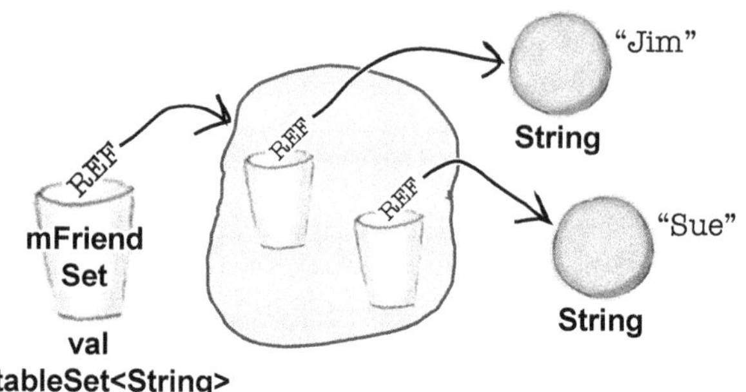

This initializes a `MutableSet` with two `String`s, so the compiler infers that you want a `MutableSet` of type `MutableSet<String>`.

You add new values to a `MutableSet` using the **`add`** function. The following code, for example, adds "Nick" to `mFriendSet`:

```
mFriendSet.add("Nick")
```

The `add` function checks whether the object it's passed already exists in the `MutableSet`. If it finds a duplicate value, it returns `false`. If it's not a duplicate, however, the value gets added to the `MutableSet` (increasing its size by one) and the function returns `true` to indicate that the operation was successful.

You remove values from a `MutableSet` using the `remove` function. The following code, for example, removes "Nick" from `mFriendSet`:

```
mFriendSet.remove("Nick")
```

If "Nick" exists in the `MutableSet`, the function removes it and returns `true`. If there's no matching object, however, the function simply returns `false`.

You can also use the **`addAll`**, **`removeAll`** and **`retainAll`** functions to make bulk changes to the `MutableSet`, just as you can for a `MutableList`. The `addAll` function, for example, adds all the items to the `MutableSet` that are held in another collection, so you can use the following code to add "Joe" and "Mia" to `mFriendSet`:

```
val toAdd = setOf("Joe", "Mia")
mFriendSet.addAll(toAdd)
```

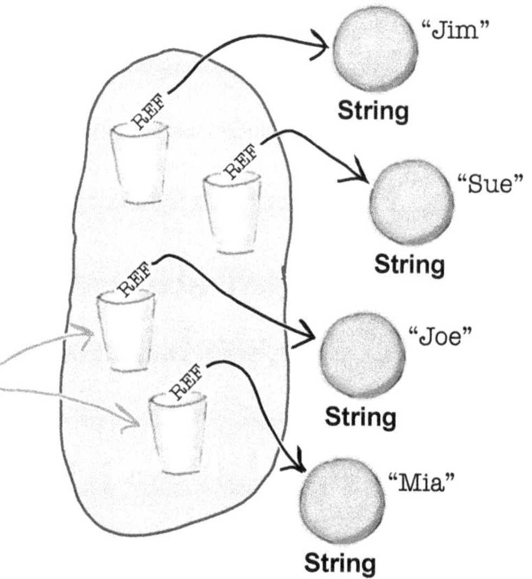

And just as you can with a `MutableList`, you can use the **`clear`** function to remove every item from the `MutableSet`:

```
mFriendSet.clear()
```

You can copy a MutableSet

If you want to take a snapshot of a `MutableSet` you can do so, just as you can with a `MutableList`. You can use the **`toSet`** function, for example, to take an immutable copy of `mFriendSet`, and assign the copy to a new variable named `friendSetCopy`:

```
val friendSetCopy = mFriendSet.toSet()
```

You can also copy a `Set` or `MutableSet` into a new `List` object using **`toList`**:

```
val friendList = mFriendSet.toList()
```

And if you have a `MutableList` or `List`, you can copy it into a `Set` using its **`toSet`** function:

MutableSet also has a toMutableSet() function (which copies it to a new MutableSet), and toMutableList() (which copies it to a new MutableList).

```
val shoppingSet = mShopping.toSet()
```

Copying a collection into another type can be particularly useful when you want to perform some action that would otherwise be inefficient. You can, for example, check whether a `List` contains duplicate values by copying the `List` into a `Set`, and checking the `size` of each collection. The following code uses this technique to check whether `mShopping` (a `MutableList`) contains duplicates:

This creates a Set version of mShopping, and gets its size.

```
if (mShopping.size > mShopping.toSet().size) {
    //mShopping has duplicate values
}
```

If `mShopping` contains duplicates, its size will be greater than when it's copied into a `Set`, because converting the `MutableList` to a `Set` will remove the duplicate values.

This is a List. It has three elements, so its size is 3.

0 REF
1 REF
2 REF

"Tea"
String
"Coffee"
String

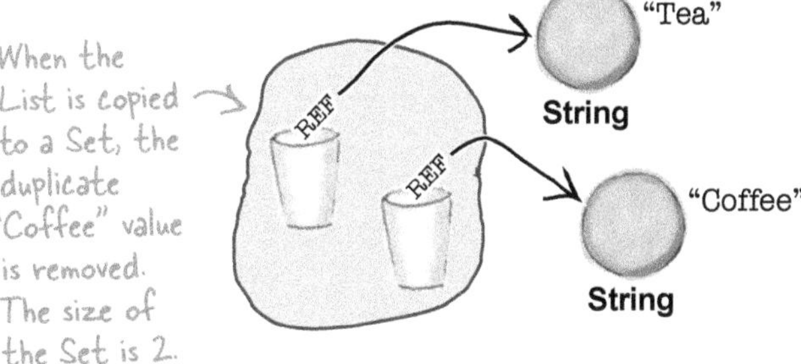

Update the Collections project

Now that you know about `Sets` and `MutableSets`, let's update the Collections project so that it uses them.

Update your version of *Collections.kt* to match ours below (our changes are in bold):

```
fun main(args: Array<String>) {
    val var mShoppingList = mutableListOf("Tea", "Eggs", "Milk")
    println("mShoppingList original: $mShoppingList")
    val extraShopping = listOf("Cookies", "Sugar", "Eggs")
    mShoppingList.addAll(extraShopping)
    println("mShoppingList items added: $mShoppingList")
    if (mShoppingList.contains("Tea")) {
        mShoppingList.set(mShoppingList.indexOf("Tea"), "Coffee")
    }
    mShoppingList.sort()
    println("mShoppingList sorted: $mShoppingList")
    mShoppingList.reverse()
    println("mShoppingList reversed: $mShoppingList")

    val mShoppingSet = mShoppingList.toMutableSet()
    println("mShoppingSet: $mShoppingSet")
    val moreShopping = setOf("Chives", "Spinach", "Milk")
    mShoppingSet.addAll(moreShopping)
    println("mShoppingSet items added: $mShoppingSet")
    mShoppingList = mShoppingSet.toMutableList()
    println("mShoppingList new version: $mShoppingList")
}
```

Update mShoppingList to a var so that we can replace it with another MutableList<String> later in the code.

Add this code.

Collections
src
Collections.kt

Let's take the code for a test drive.

Test drive

When we run the code, the following text gets printed in the IDE's output window:

```
mShoppingList original: [Tea, Eggs, Milk]
mShoppingList items added: [Tea, Eggs, Milk, Cookies, Sugar, Eggs]
mShoppingList sorted: [Coffee, Cookies, Eggs, Eggs, Milk, Sugar]
mShoppingList reversed: [Sugar, Milk, Eggs, Eggs, Cookies, Coffee]
mShoppingSet: [Sugar, Milk, Eggs, Cookies, Coffee]
mShoppingSet items added: [Sugar, Milk, Eggs, Cookies, Coffee, Chives, Spinach]
mShoppingList new version: [Sugar, Milk, Eggs, Cookies, Coffee, Chives, Spinach]
```

Printing a Set or MutableSet prints each item inside square brackets.

there are no Dumb Questions

Q: You said that I can create a `List` copy of a `Set`, and a `Set` copy of a `List`. Can I do something similar with an array?

A: Yes, you can. Arrays have a bunch of functions that you can use to copy the array to a new collection: `toList()`, `toMutableList()`, `toSet()` and `toMutableSet()`. So the following code creates an array of `Int`s, then copies it into a `Set<Int>`:

```
val a = arrayOf(1, 2, 3)
val s = a.toSet()
```

Similarly, `List` and `Set` (and therefore `MutableList` and `MutableSet`) have a function named `toTypedArray()` that copies the collection to a new array of the appropriate type. So the code:

```
val s = setOf(1, 2, 3)
val a = s.toTypedArray()
```

creates an array of type `Array<Int>`.

Q: Can I sort a `Set`?

A: No, a `Set` is an unordered collection so you can't sort it directly. You can, however, use its `toList()` function to copy the `Set` into a `List`, and you can then sort the `List`.

Q: Can I use the == operator to compare the contents of two `Set`s?

A: Yes, you can. Suppose you have two `Set`s, `a` and `b`. If `a` and `b` contain the same values, `a == b` will return `true`, as in the following example:

```
val a = setOf(1, 2, 3)
val b = setOf(3, 2, 1)
//a == b is true
```

If the two sets compare different values, however, the result will be `false`.

Q: That's clever. What if one of the `Set`s is a `MutableSet`? Do I first need to copy it to a `Set`?

A: You can use == without copying the `MutableSet` to a `Set`. In the following example, `a == b` returns `true`:

```
val a = setOf(1, 2, 3)
val b = mutableSetOf(3, 2, 1)
```

Q: I see. Does == work with `List`s too?

A: Yes, you can use == to compare the contents of two `List`s. It will return `true` if the `List`s hold the same values against the same indexes, and `false` if the `List`s hold different values, or hold the same values in a different order. So in the following example, `a == b` returns `true`:

```
val a = listOf(1, 2, 3)
val b = listOf(1, 2, 3)
```

BE the Set

Here are four Duck classes. Your job is to play like you're the Set, and say which classes will produce a Set containing precisely one item when used with the main function on the right. Do any Ducks break the hashCode() and equals() rules? If so, how?

This is the main function.

```
fun main(args: Array<String>) {
    val set = setOf(Duck(), Duck(17))
    println(set)
}
```

A

```
class Duck(val size: Int = 17) {
    override fun equals(other: Any?): Boolean {
        if (this === other) return true
        if (other is Duck && size == other.size) return true
        return false
    }

    override fun hashCode(): Int {
        return size
    }
}
```

B

```
class Duck(val size: Int = 17) {
    override fun equals(other: Any?): Boolean {
        return false
    }

    override fun hashCode(): Int {
        return 7
    }
}
```

C

```
data class Duck(val size: Int = 18)
```

D

```
class Duck(val size: Int = 17) {
    override fun equals(other: Any?): Boolean {
        return true
    }

    override fun hashCode(): Int {
        return (Math.random() * 100).toInt()
    }
}
```

Answers on page 274.

Sharpen your pencil

Four friends have each made a `List` of their pets. One item in the `List` represents one pet. Here are the four lists:

```
val petsLiam = listOf("Cat", "Dog", "Fish", "Fish")
val petsSophia = listOf("Cat", "Owl")
val petsNoah = listOf("Dog", "Dove", "Dog", "Dove")
val petsEmily = listOf("Hedgehog")
```

Write the code below to create a new collection named `pets` that contains each pet.

....

....

....

....

....

How would you use the `pets` collection to get the total number of pets?

....

Write the code to print how many types of pet there are.

....

....

How would you list the types of pet in alphabetical order?

....

....

....

Answers on page 275.

BE the Set Solution

Here are four Duck classes. Your job is to play like you're the Set, and say which classes will produce a Set containing precisely one item when used with the main function on the right. Do any Ducks break the hashCode() and equals() rules? If so, how?

This is the main function.

```
fun main(args: Array<String>) {
    val set = setOf(Duck(), Duck(17))
    println(set)
}
```

A

```
class Duck(val size: Int = 17) {
    override fun equals(other: Any?): Boolean {
        if (this === other) return true
        if (other is Duck && size == other.size) return true
        return false
    }

    override fun hashCode(): Int {
        return size
    }
}
```

This follows the hashCode() and equals() rules. The Set recognizes that the second Duck is a duplicate, so the main function creates a Set that contains one item.

B

```
class Duck(val size: Int = 17) {
    override fun equals(other: Any?): Boolean {
        return false
    }

    override fun hashCode(): Int {
        return 7
    }
}
```

This produces a Set with two items. The class breaks the hashCode() and equals() rules as equals() always returns false, even if it's used to compare an object with itself.

C

```
data class Duck(val size: Int = 18)
```

This follows the rules, but produces a Set with two items.

D

```
class Duck(val size: Int = 17) {
    override fun equals(other: Any?): Boolean {
        return true
    }

    override fun hashCode(): Int {
        return (Math.random() * 100).toInt()
    }
}
```

This produces a Set with two items. The class breaks the rules as hashCode() returns a random number. The rules say that equal objects should have the same hash code.

Sharpen your pencil Solution

Four friends have each made a `List` of their pets. One item in the `List` represents one pet. Here are the four lists:

```
val petsLiam = listOf("Cat", "Dog", "Fish", "Fish")
val petsSophia = listOf("Cat", "Owl")
val petsNoah = listOf("Dog", "Dove", "Dog", "Dove")
val petsEmily = listOf("Hedgehog")
```

Write the code below to create a new collection named `pets` that contains each pet.

```
var pets: MutableList<String> = mutableListOf()
pets.addAll(petsLiam)
pets.addAll(petsSophia)
pets.addAll(petsNoah)
pets.addAll(petsEmily)
```

Don't worry if your answers looks different to ours. There are different ways of getting the same result.

How would you use the `pets` collection to get the total number of pets?

```
pets.size
```

Write the code below to print how many types of pet there are.

```
val petSet = pets.toMutableSet()
println(petSet.size)
```

How would you list the types of pet in alphabetical order?

```
val petList = petSet.toMutableList()
petList.sort()
println(petList)
```

Time for a Map

These are the Map's values.

"Value1"

"Value2"

REF

"KeyA" "KeyB" "KeyC"

These are the Map's keys.

Lists and Sets are great, but there's one more type of collection we want to introduce you to: a **Map**. A Map is a collection that acts like a property list. You give it a key, and the Map gives you back the value associated with that key. Although keys are usually Strings, they can be any type of object.

Each entry in a Map is actually two objects—a ***key*** and a ***value***. Each key has a single value associated with it. You can have duplicate *values*, but you can't have duplicate *keys*.

How to create a Map

You create a Map by calling a function named **mapOf**, passing in the key/value pairs you want the Map to be initialized with. The following code, for example, creates a Map with three entries. The keys are the Strings ("Recipe1", "Recipe2" and "Recipe3"), and the values are the Recipe objects:

```
val r1 = Recipe("Chicken Soup")
val r2 = Recipe("Quinoa Salad")
val r3 = Recipe("Thai Curry")

val recipeMap = mapOf("Recipe1" to r1, "Recipe2" to r2, "Recipe3" to r3)
```

Each entry takes the form Key to Value. The keys are normally Strings, as in this example.

As you might expect, the compiler infers the type of the key/value pairs by looking at the entries it's initialized with. The above Map, for example, is initialized with String keys and Recipe values, so it creates a Map of type Map<String, Recipe>. You can also explicitly define the Map's type using code like this:

```
val recipeMap: Map<String, Recipe>
```

In general, the Map's type takes the form:

```
Map<key_type, value_type>
```

Now that you know how to create a Map, let's see how to use one.

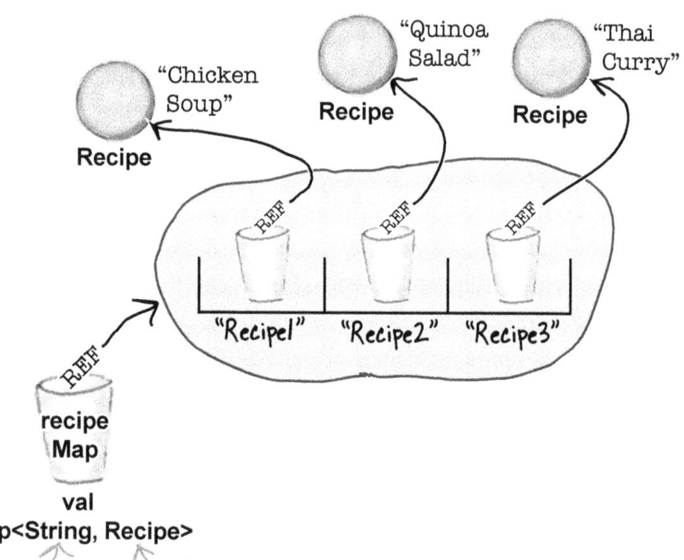

How to use a Map

There are three main things you might want to do with a Map: check whether it contains a specific key or value, retrieve a value for a specified key, or loop through the Map's entries.

You check whether a Map contains a particular key or value using its **containsKey** and **containsValue** functions. The following code, for example, checks whether the Map named recipeMap contains the key "Recipe1":

```
recipeMap.containsKey("Recipe1")
```

And you can find out whether recipeMap contains a Recipe for Chicken Soup using the containsValue function like this:

```
val recipeToCheck = Recipe("Chicken Soup")
if (recipeMap.containsValue(recipeToCheck)) {
    //Code that runs if the Map contains the value
}
```

Here, we're assuming that Recipe is a data class, so the Map can spot when two Recipe objects are equal.

You can get the value for a specified key using the **get** and **getValue** functions. get returns a null value if the specified key doesn't exist, whereas getValue throws an exception. Here's how, for example, you would use the getValue function to get the Recipe object associated with the "Recipe1" key:

```
if (recipeMap.containsKey("Recipe1")) {
    val recipe = recipeMap.getValue("Recipe1")
    //Code to use the Recipe object
}
```

If recipeMap doesn't contain a "Recipe1" key, this line will throw an exception.

You can also loop through a Map's entries. Here's how, for example, you would use a for loop to print each key/value pair in recipeMap:

```
for ((key, value) in recipeMap) {
    println("Key is $key, value is $value")
}
```

A Map is immutable, so you can't add or remove key/value pairs, or update the value held against a specific key. To perform this kind of action, you need to use a MutableMap instead. Let's see how these work.

Create a MutableMap

You define a **`MutableMap`** in a similar way to how you define a `Map`, except that you use the **`mutableMapOf`** function instead of `mapOf`. The following code, for example, creates a `MutableMap` with three entries, as before:

```
val r1 = Recipe("Chicken Soup")
val r2 = Recipe("Quinoa Salad")

val mRecipeMap = mutableMapOf("Recipe1" to r1, "Recipe2" to r2)
```

The `MutableMap` is initialized with `String` keys and `Recipe` values, so the compiler infers that it must be a `MutableMap` of type `MutableMap<String, Recipe>`.

`MutableMap` is a subtype of `Map`, so you can call the same functions on a `MutableMap` that you can on a `Map`. A `MutableMap`, however, has extra functions that you can use to add, remove and update key/value pairs.

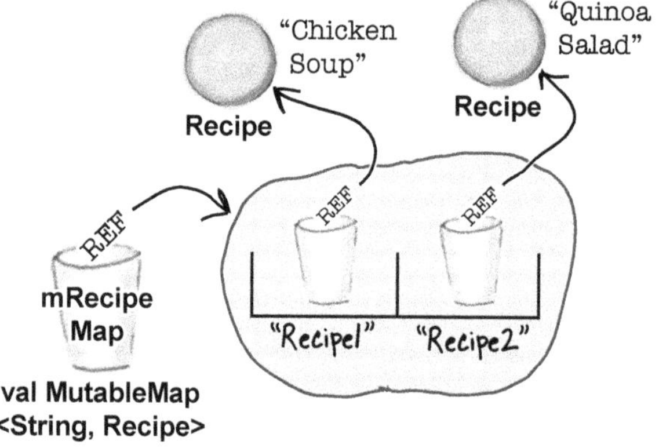

If you pass String keys and Recipe values to the mutableMapOf() function, the compiler infers that you want an object of type MutableMap<String, Recipe>.

Put entries in a MutableMap

You put entries into a `MutableMap` using the **`put`** function. The following code, for example, puts a key named "Recipe3" into `mRecipeMap`, and associates it with a `Recipe` object for Thai Curry:

```
val r3 = Recipe("Thai Curry")
mRecipeMap.put("Recipe3", r3)
```

Specify the key first, then the value.

If the `MutableMap` already contains the specified key, the `put` function replaces the value for that key, and returns the original value.

You can put many key/value pairs into the `MutableMap` at once using the **`putAll`** function. This takes one argument, a `Map` containing the entries you want to add. The following code, for example, adds Jambalaya and Sausage Rolls `Recipe` objects to a `Map` named `recipesToAdd`, and then puts these entries into `mRecipeMap`:

```
val r4 = Recipe("Jambalaya")
val r5 = Recipe("Sausage Rolls")
val recipesToAdd = mapOf("Recipe4" to r4, "Recipe5" to r5)
mRecipeMap.putAll(recipesToAdd)
```

Next, let's look at how you remove values.

You can remove entries from a MutableMap

You remove an entry from a `MutableMap` using the **`remove`** function. This function is overloaded so that there are two ways of calling it.

The first way is to pass to the `remove` function the key whose entry you want to remove. The following code, for example, removes the entry from `mRecipeMap` that has a key of "Recipe2":

```
mRecipeMap.remove("Recipe2")
```

Remove the entry with a key of "Recipe2"

The second way is to pass the `remove` function the key name and a value. In this case, the function will only remove the entry if it finds a match for both the key and the value. So the following code only removes the entry for "Recipe2" if it is associated with a Quinoa Salad `Recipe` object:

```
val recipeToRemove = Recipe("Quinoa Salad")
mRecipeMap.remove("Recipe2", recipeToRemove)
```

Remove the entry with a key of "Recipe2", but only if its value is a Quinoa Salad Recipe object.

Whichever approach you use, removing an entry from the `MutableMap` reduces its size.

Finally, you can use the **`clear`** function to remove every entry from the `MutableMap`, just as you can with `MutableLists` and `MutableSets`:

```
mRecipeMap.clear()
```

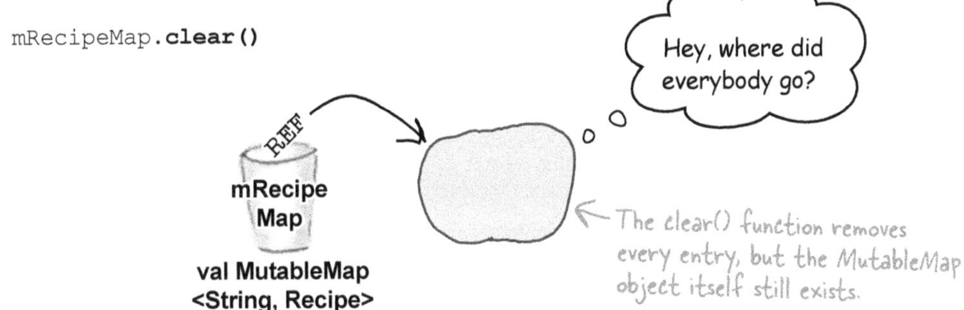

Now that you've seen how to update a `MutableMap`, let's look at how you can take copies of one.

You can copy Maps and MutableMaps

Just like the other types of collection you've seen, you can take a snapshot of a MutableMap. You can use the **toMap** function, for example, to take a read-only copy of mRecipeMap, and assign the copy to a new variable:

```
val recipeMapCopy = mRecipeMap.toMap()
```

You can copy a Map or MutableMap into a new List object containing all the key/value pairs using **toList** like this:

A MutableMap also has toMutableMap() and toMutableList() functions.

```
val RecipeList = mRecipeMap.toList()
```

And you can also get direct access to the key/value pairs using the Map's **entries** property. The entries property returns a Set if it's used with a Map, and returns a MutableSet if it's used with a MutableMap. The following code, for example, returns a MutableSet of mRecipeMap's key/value pairs:

```
val recipeEntries = mRecipeMap.entries
```

Other useful properties are **keys** (which returns a Set, or MutableSet, of the Map's keys), and **values** (which returns a generic collection of the Map's values). You can use these properties to, say, check whether a Map contains duplicate values using code like this:

Note that the entries, keys and values properties are the actual contents of the Map, or MutableMap. They're not copies. And if you're using a MutableMap, these properties are updatable.

```
if (mRecipeMap.size > mRecipeMap.values.toSet().size) {
    println("mRecipeMap contains duplicates values")
}
```

This is because the code:

```
mRecipeMap.values.toSet()
```

copies the Map's values into a Set, which removes any duplicate values.

Now that you've learned how to use Maps and MutableMaps, let's add some to our Collections project.

The full code for the Collections project

Update your version of *Collections.kt* to match ours below (our changes are in bold):

```
data class Recipe(var name: String)   <— Add the Recipe data class.

fun main(args: Array<String>) {
    var mShoppingList = mutableListOf("Tea", "Eggs", "Milk")
    println("mShoppingList original: $mShoppingList")
    val extraShopping = listOf("Cookies", "Sugar", "Eggs")
    mShoppingList.addAll(extraShopping)
    println("mShoppingList items added: $mShoppingList")
    if (mShoppingList.contains("Tea")) {
        mShoppingList.set(mShoppingList.indexOf("Tea"), "Coffee")
    }
    mShoppingList.sort()
    println("mShoppingList sorted: $mShoppingList")
    mShoppingList.reverse()
    println("mShoppingList reversed: $mShoppingList")

    val mShoppingSet = mShoppingList.toMutableSet()
    println("mShoppingSet: $mShoppingSet")
    val moreShopping = setOf("Chives", "Spinach", "Milk")
    mShoppingSet.addAll(moreShopping)
    println("mShoppingSet items added: $mShoppingSet")
    mShoppingList = mShoppingSet.toMutableList()
    println("mShoppingList new version: $mShoppingList")

    val r1 = Recipe("Chicken Soup")
    val r2 = Recipe("Quinoa Salad")
    val r3 = Recipe("Thai Curry")
    val r4 = Recipe("Jambalaya")
    val r5 = Recipe("Sausage Rolls")
    val mRecipeMap = mutableMapOf("Recipe1" to r1, "Recipe2" to r2, "Recipe3" to r3)
    println("mRecipeMap original: $mRecipeMap")
    val recipesToAdd = mapOf("Recipe4" to r4, "Recipe5" to r5)
    mRecipeMap.putAll(recipesToAdd)
    println("mRecipeMap updated: $mRecipeMap")
    if (mRecipeMap.containsKey("Recipe1")) {
        println("Recipe1 is: ${mRecipeMap.getValue("Recipe1")}")
    }
}
```

Add this code.

Collections
src
Collections.kt

Let's take the code for a test drive.

Test drive

When we run the code, the following text gets printed in the IDE's output window:

```
mShoppingList original: [Tea, Eggs, Milk]
mShoppingList items added: [Tea, Eggs, Milk, Cookies, Sugar, Eggs]
mShoppingList sorted: [Coffee, Cookies, Eggs, Eggs, Milk, Sugar]
mShoppingList reversed: [Sugar, Milk, Eggs, Eggs, Cookies, Coffee]
mShoppingSet: [Sugar, Milk, Eggs, Cookies, Coffee]
mShoppingSet items added: [Sugar, Milk, Eggs, Cookies, Coffee, Chives, Spinach]
mShoppingList new version: [Sugar, Milk, Eggs, Cookies, Coffee, Chives, Spinach]
mRecipeMap original: {Recipe1=Recipe(name=Chicken Soup), Recipe2=Recipe(name=Quinoa Salad),
    Recipe3=Recipe(name=Thai Curry)}
mRecipeMap updated: {Recipe1=Recipe(name=Chicken Soup), Recipe2=Recipe(name=Quinoa Salad),
    Recipe3=Recipe(name=Thai Curry), Recipe4=Recipe(name=Jambalaya),
    Recipe5=Recipe(name=Sausage Rolls)}
Recipe1 is: Recipe(name=Chicken Soup)
```

Printing a Map or MutableMap prints each key/value pair inside curly braces.

there are no Dumb Questions

Q: Why does Kotlin have mutable and immutable versions of the same type of collection? Why not just have mutable versions?

A: Because it forces you to explicitly choose whether your collection should be mutable or immutable. This means that you can prevent collections from being updated if you don't want them to be.

Q: Can't I do that using `val` and `var`?

A: No. `val` and `var` specify whether or not the reference held by the variable can be replaced with another one after it's been initialized. If a variable defined using `val` holds a reference to a mutable collection, the collection can still be updated. `val` just means that the variable can only ever refer to that collection.

Q: Is it possible to create a non-updateable view of a mutable collection?

A: Suppose you have a `MutableSet` of `Int`s that's assigned to a variable named `x`:

```
val x = mutableSetOf(1, 2)
```

You can assign `x` to a `Set` variable named `y` using the following code:

```
val y: Set<Int> = x
```

As `y` is a `Set` variable, it can't update the underlying object without you first casting it to a `MutableSet`.

Q: Is that different to using `toSet`?

A: Yes. `toSet` *copies* a collection, so if changes are made to the original collection, these won't be picked up.

Q: Can I explicitly create and use Java collections using Kotlin?

A: Yes. Kotlin includes various functions that let you explicitly create Java collections. You can, for example, create an `ArrayList` using the `arrayListOf` function, and a `HashMap` using the `hashMapOf` function. These functions, however, create mutable objects.

We recommend that you stick with using the Kotlin collections we've discussed in this chapter unless there's a good reason why you shouldn't.

Pool Puzzle

Your **job** is to take code snippets from the pool and place them into the blank lines in the code. You may **not** use the same code snippet more than once, and you won't need to use all the code snippets. Your **goal** is to print the entries of a `Map` named `glossary` that provides definitions of all the collection types you've learned about.

```
fun main(args: Array<String>) {
    val term1 = "Array"
    val term2 = "List"
    val term3 = "Map"
    val term4 = ................
    val term5 = "MutableMap"
    val term6 = "MutableSet"
    val term7 = "Set"

    val def1 = "Holds values in no particular order."
    val def2 = "Holds key/value pairs."
    val def3 = "Holds values in a sequence."
    val def4 = "Can be updated."
    val def5 = "Can't be updated."
    val def6 = "Can be resized."
    val def7 = "Can't be resized."

    val glossary = ........(...... to "$def3 $def4 $def6",
            ...... to "$def1 $def5 $def7",
            ...... to "$def3 $def4 $def7",
            ...... to "$def2 $def4 $def6",
            ...... to "$def3 $def5 $def7",
            ...... to "$def1 $def4 $def6",
            ...... to "$def2 $def5 $def7")
    for ((key, value) in glossary) println("$key: $value")
}
```

Note: each thing from the pool can only be used once!

Pool snippets:

- "MutableArray"
- "MutableList"
- mapOf
- Map
- term1
- term2
- term3
- term4
- term5
- term6
- term7

Pool Puzzle Solution

Your **job** is to take code snippets from the pool and place them into the blank lines in the code. You may **not** use the same code snippet more than once, and you won't need to use all the code snippets. Your **goal** is to print the entries of a `Map` named `glossary` that provides definitions of all the collection types you've learned about.

```
fun main(args: Array<String>) {
    val term1 = "Array"
    val term2 = "List"
    val term3 = "Map"
    val term4 = "MutableList"
    val term5 = "MutableMap"
    val term6 = "MutableSet"
    val term7 = "Set"

    val def1 = "Holds values in no particular order."
    val def2 = "Holds key/value pairs."
    val def3 = "Holds values in a sequence."
    val def4 = "Can be updated."
    val def5 = "Can't be updated."
    val def6 = "Can be resized."
    val def7 = "Can't be resized."

    val glossary = mapOf (term4 to "$def3 $def4 $def6",
            term7 to "$def1 $def5 $def7",
            term1 to "$def3 $def4 $def7",
            term5 to "$def2 $def4 $def6",
            term2 to "$def3 $def5 $def7",
            term6 to "$def1 $def4 $def6",
            term3 to "$def2 $def5 $def7")
    for ((key, value) in glossary) println("$key: $value")
}
```

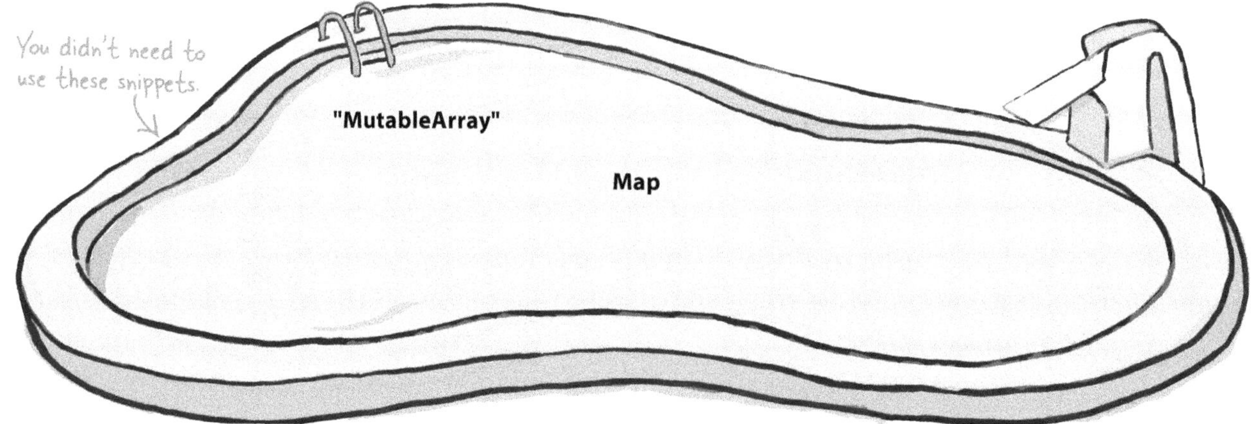

Mixed Messages

A short Kotlin program is listed below. One block of the program is missing. Your challenge is to match the candidate block of code (on the left), with the output that you'd see if the block were inserted. Not all the lines of output will be used, and some lines of output may be used more than once. Draw lines connecting the candidate blocks of code with their matching output.

```
fun main(args: Array<String>) {
    val mList = mutableListOf("Football", "Baseball", "Basketball")

}
```

The candidate code goes here.

Match each candidate with one of the possible outputs.

Candidates:

```
mList.sort()
println(mList)
```

```
val mMap = mutableMapOf("0" to "Netball")
var x = 0
for (item in mList) {
    mMap.put(x.toString(), item)
}
println(mMap.values)
```

```
mList.addAll(mList)
mList.reverse()
val set = mList.toSet()
println(set)
```

```
mList.sort()
mList.reverse()
println(mList)
```

Possible output:

```
[Netball]
```

```
[Baseball, Basketball, Football]
```

```
[Basketball]
```

```
[Football, Basketball, Baseball]
```

```
{Basketball}
```

```
[Basketball, Baseball, Football]
```

```
{Netball}
```

```
[Football]
```

```
{Basketball, Baseball, Football}
```

```
[Football, Baseball, Basketball]
```

Mixed Messages Solution

A short Kotlin program is listed below. One block of the program is missing. Your challenge is to match the candidate block of code (on the left), with the output that you'd see if the block were inserted. Not all the lines of output will be used, and some lines of output may be used more than once. Draw lines connecting the candidate blocks of code with their matching output.

```
fun main(args: Array<String>) {
    val mList = mutableListOf("Football", "Baseball", "Basketball")

}
```

The candidate code goes here.

Candidates:

```
mList.sort()
println(mList)
```

```
val mMap = mutableMapOf("0" to "Netball")
var x = 0
for (item in mList) {
    mMap.put(x.toString(), item)
}
println(mMap.values)
```

```
mList.addAll(mList)
mList.reverse()
val set = mList.toSet()
println(set)
```

```
mList.sort()
mList.reverse()
println(mList)
```

Possible output:

```
[Netball]
[Baseball, Basketball, Football]
[Basketball]
[Football, Basketball, Baseball]
{Basketball}
[Basketball, Baseball, Football]
{Netball}
[Football]
{Basketball, Baseball, Football}
[Football, Baseball, Basketball]
```

Your Kotlin Toolbox

You've got Chapter 9 under your belt and now you've added collections to your toolbox.

You can download the full code for the chapter from https://tinyurl.com/HFKotlin.

CHAPTER 9

BULLET POINTS

- Create an array initialized with `null` values using the `arrayOfNulls` function.
- Useful array functions include: `sort`, `reverse`, `contains`, `min`, `max`, `sum`, `average`.
- The Kotlin Standard Library contains pre-built classes and functions grouped into packages.
- A `List` is a collection that knows and cares about index position. It can contain duplicate values.
- A `Set` is an unordered collection that doesn't allow duplicate values.
- A `Map` is a collection that uses key/value pairs. It can contain duplicate values, but not duplicate keys.
- `List`, `Set` and `Map` are immutable. `MutableList`, `MutableSet` and `MutableMap` are mutable subtypes of these collections.
- Create a `List` using the `listOf` function.
- Create a `MutableList` using `mutableListOf`.
- Create a `Set` using the `setOf` function.
- Create a `MutableSet` using `mutableSetOf`.
- A `Set` checks for duplicates by first looking for matching hash code values. It then uses the === and == operators to check for referential or object equality.
- Create a `Map` using the `mapOf` function, passing in key/value pairs.
- Create a `MutableMap` using `mutableMapOf`.

10 generics

Know Your Ins from Your Outs

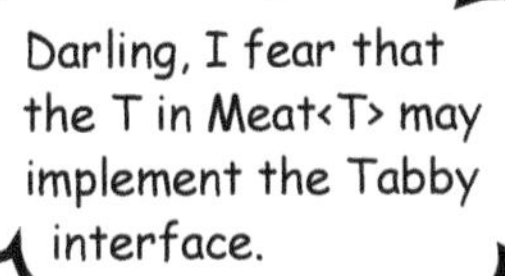

Everybody likes code that's consistent.

And one way of writing consistent code that's less prone to problems is to use ***generics***. In this chapter, we'll look at how **Kotlin's collection classes use generics** to stop you from putting a Cabbage into a List<Seagull>. You'll discover when and how to ***write your own generic classes, interfaces and functions***, and how to **restrict a generic type** to a specific supertype. Finally, you'll find out ***how to use covariance and contravariance,*** putting **YOU** in control of your generic type's behavior.

Collections use generics

As you learned in the previous chapter, each time you explicitly declare a collection's type, you must specify both the kind of collection you want to use, and the type of element it contains. The following code, for example, defines a variable that can hold a reference to a `MutableList` of `String`s:

```
val x: MutableList<String>
```

The element type is defined inside angle brackets <>, which means that it uses **generics**. Generics lets you write code that's type-safe. It's what makes the compiler stop you from putting a `Volkswagen` into a list of `Duck`s. The compiler knows that you can only put `Duck` objects into a `MutableList<Duck>`, which means that more problems are caught at compile-time.

WITHOUT generics, objects would go IN as a reference to Duck, Fish, Guitar and Car objects...

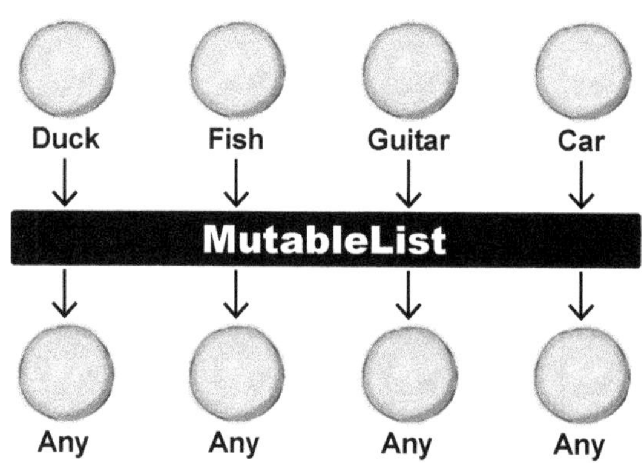

Without generics, there'd be no way to declare what type of objects the MutableList should contain.

...and come OUT as a reference of type Any.

WITH generics, objects go IN as a reference to only Duck objects...

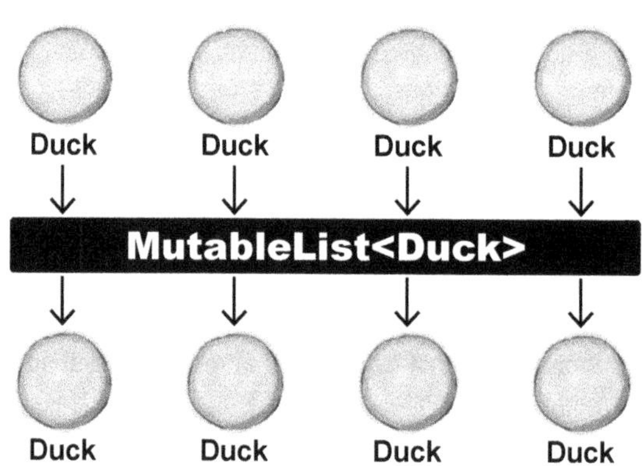

With generics, you can make sure that your collection only contains objects of the correct type. You don't have to worry about someone sticking a Pumpkin into a MutableList<Duck>, or that what you get out won't be a Duck.

...and come OUT as a reference of type Duck.

How a MutableList is defined

Let's look at the online documentation to see how MutableList is defined, and how it uses generics. There are two key areas we'll consider: the interface declaration, and how the add function is defined.

Understanding collection documentation (Or, what's the meaning of "E"?)

Here's a simplified version of the MutableList definition:

The "E" is a placeholder for the REAL type you use when you declare a MutableList.

MutableList inherits from the List and MutableCollection interfaces. Whatever type (the value of "E") you specify for the MutableList is automatically used for the type of the List and MutableCollection.

```
interface MutableList<E> : List<E>, MutableCollection<E> {

    fun add(index: Int, element: E): Unit

    //More code

}
```

Whatever "E" is determines what kind of things you're allowed to add to the MutableList.

MutableList uses "E" as a stand-in for the type of element you want the collection to hold and return. When you see an "E" in the documentation, you can do a mental find/replace to exchange it for whatever type you want it to hold.

MutableList<String>, for example, means that "E" becomes "String" in any function or variable declaration that uses "E". And MutableList<Duck> means that all instances of "E" become "Duck" instead.

Let's look at this in more detail.

there are no Dumb Questions

Q: So MutableList isn't a class?

A: No, it's an interface. When you create a MutableList using the mutableListOf function, the system creates an *implementation* of this interface. All you care about when you're using it, however, is that it has all the properties and functions defined in the MutableList interface.

Using type parameters with MutableList

When you write this code:

```
val x: MutableList<String>
```

It means that `MutableList`:

```
interface MutableList<E> : List<E>, MutableCollection<E> {

    fun add(index: Int, element: E): Unit

    //More code
}
```

is treated by the compiler as:

```
interface MutableList<String> : List<String>, MutableCollection<String> {

    fun add(index: Int, element: String): Unit

    //More code
}
```

In other words, the "E" is replaced by the *real* type (also called the *type parameter*) that you use when you define the `MutableList`. And that's why the `add` function won't let you add anything except objects with a type that's compatible with the type of "E". So if you make a `MutableList<String>`, the `add` function suddenly lets you add `Strings`. And if you make the `MutableList` of type `Duck`, suddenly the `add` function lets you add `Ducks`.

Things you can do with a generic class or interface

Here's a summary of some of the key things you can do when you're using a class or interface that has generic types:

- **Create an <u>instance</u> of a generified class.**
When you create a collection such as a `MutableList`, you have to tell it the type of objects you'll allow it to hold, or let the compiler infer it:

```
val duckList: MutableList<Duck>
duckList = mutableListOf(Duck("Donald"), Duck("Daisy"), Duck("Daffy"))

val list = mutableListOf("Fee", "Fi", "Fum")
```

- **Create a function that <u>takes</u> a generic type.**
You can create a function with a generic parameter by specifying its type, just as you would any other sort of parameter:

```
fun quack(ducks: MutableList<Duck>) {
    //Code to make the Ducks quack
}
```

- **Create a function that <u>returns</u> a generic type.**
A function can return a generic type too. The following code, for example, returns a `MutableList` of `Ducks`:

```
fun getDucks(breed: String): MutableList<Duck> {
    //Code to get Ducks for the specified breed
}
```

But there are still important questions that need answering about generics, such as how do you define your own generic classes and interfaces? And how does *polymorphism* work with generic types? If you have a `MutableList<Animal>`, what happens if you try to assign a `MutableList<Dog>` to it?

To answer these questions and more, we're going to create an application that uses generic types.

Here's what we're going to do

We're going to create an application that deals with pets. We'll create some pets, hold pet contests for them, and create pet retailers that can sell specific types of pet. And as we're using generics, we'll ensure that each contest and retailer we create can only deal with a specific type of pet.

Here are the steps that we'll follow:

1. **Create the Pet hierarchy.**
   We'll create a hierarchy of pets that will allow us to create three types of pet: cats, dogs and fish.

2. **Create the Contest class.**
   The `Contest` class will let us create contests for different types of pet. We'll use it to manage the contestant scores so that we can determine the winner. And as we want each contest to be limited to a specific type of pet, we'll define the `Contest` class using generics.

3. **Create the Retailer hierarchy.**
   We'll create a `Retailer` interface, and concrete implementations of this interface named `CatRetailer`, `DogRetailer` and `FishRetailer`. We'll use generics to ensure that each type of `Retailer` can only sell a specific type of pet, so that you can't buy a `Cat` from a `FishRetailer`.

4. **Create a Vet class.**
   Finally, we'll create a `Vet` class, so that we can assign a vet to each contest. We'll define the `Vet` class using generics to reflect the type of `Pet` each `Vet` specializes in treating.

We'll start by creating the pet class hierarchy.

Create the Pet class hierarchy

Our pet class hierarchy will comprise of four classes: a `Pet` class that we'll mark as abstract, and concrete subclasses named `Cat`, `Dog` and `Fish`. We'll add a `name` property to the `Pet` class, which its concrete subclasses will inherit.

We're marking `Pet` as abstract because we only want to be able to create objects that are a subtype of `Pet`, such as `Cat` or `Dog`, and as you learned in Chapter 6, marking a class as abstract prevents that class from being instantiated.

Here's the class hierarchy:

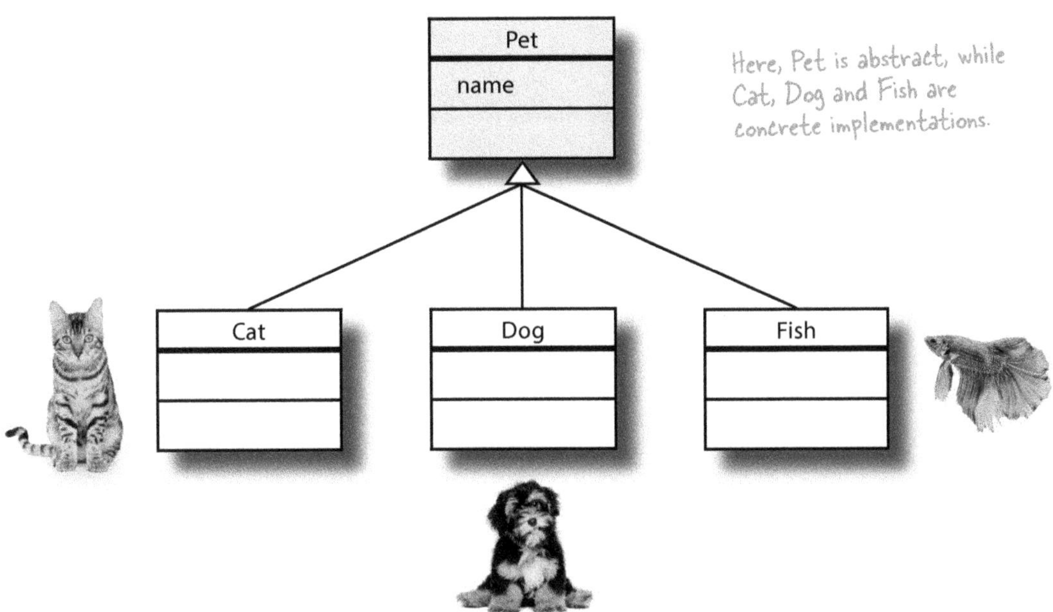

Here, Pet is abstract, while Cat, Dog and Fish are concrete implementations.

The code for the class hierarchy looks like this:

```
abstract class Pet(var name: String)

class Cat(name: String) : Pet(name)

class Dog(name: String) : Pet(name)

class Fish(name: String) : Pet(name)
```

Each subtype of Pet has a name (which it inherits from Pet), which gets set in the class constructor.

Next, let's create the `Contest` class so that we can hold contests for different kinds of pet.

Define the Contest class

We'll use the `Contest` class to help us manage the scores for a pet contest, and determine the winner. The class will have one property named `scores`, and two functions named `addScore` and `getWinners`.

We want each contest to be limited to a particular type of pet. A cat contest, for example, only has cat contestants, and only fish can take part in a fish contest. We'll enforce this rule using generics.

Declare that Contest uses a generic type

You specify that a class uses a generic type by putting the type name in angle brackets immediately after the class name. Here, we'll use "T" to denote the generic type. You can think of "T" as being a stand-in for the *real* type that each `Contest` object will deal with.

Here's the code:

```
class Contest<T> {
    //More code here
}
```

The <T> after the class name tells the compiler that T is a generic type.

Contest<T>

The generic type name can be anything that's a legal identifier, but the convention (which you should follow) is to use "T". The exception is if you're writing a collection class or interface, in which case the convention is to use "E" instead (for "Element"), or "K" and "V" (for "Key" and "Value") if it's a map.

You can restrict T to a specific supertype

In the above example, `T` can be replaced by any real type when the class is instantiated. You can, however, place restrictions on `T` by specifying that it has a *type*. The following code, for example, tells the compiler that `T` must be a type of `Pet`:

```
class Contest<T: Pet> {
    //More code here
}
```

T is a generic type that must be Pet, or one of its subtypes.

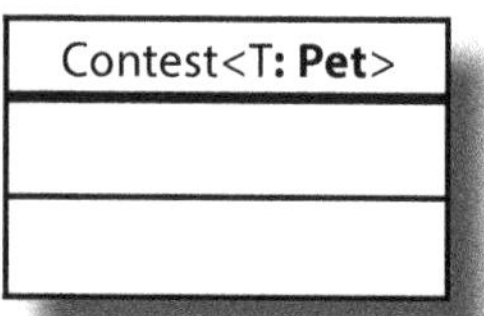

So the above code means that you can create `Contest` objects that deal with `Cats`, `Fish` or `Pets`, but not `Bicycles` or `Begonias`.

Next, let's add the `scores` property to the `Contest` class.

Add the scores property

The scores property needs to keep track of which contestant receives which score. We'll therefore use a MutableMap, with contestants as keys, and their scores as values. As each contestant is an object of type T and each score is an Int, the scores property will have a type of MutableMap<T, Int>. If we create a Contest<Cat> that deals with Cat contestants, the scores property's type will become MutableMap<Cat, Int>, but if we create a Contest<Pet> object, scores type will automatically become MutableMap<Pet, Int> instead.

Here's the updated code for the Contest class:

```
class Contest<T: Pet> {
    val scores: MutableMap<T, Int> = mutableMapOf()
    //More code here
}
```

This defines a MutableMap with T keys, and Int values, where T is the generic type of Pet that the Contest is dealing with.

Contest<T: Pet>
scores

Now that we've added the scores property, let's add the addScore and getWinners functions.

Create the addScore function

We want the addScore function to add a contestant's score to the scores MutableMap. We'll pass the contestant and score to the function as parameter values; so long as the score is 0 or above, the function will add them to the MutableMap as a key/value pair.

Here's the code for the function:

```
class Contest<T: Pet> {
    val scores: MutableMap<T, Int> = mutableMapOf()

    fun addScore(t: T, score: Int = 0) {
        if (score >= 0) scores.put(t, score)
    }

    //More code goes here
}
```

Put the contestant and its score in the MutableMap, so long as the score is greater than or equal to 0.

Contest<T: Pet>
scores
addScore

Finally, let's add the getWinners function.

Create the getWinners function

The `getWinners` function needs to return the contestants with the highest score. We'll get the value of the highest score from the `scores` property, and we'll return all contestants with this score in a `MutableSet`. As each contestant has a generic type of `T`, the function must have a return type of `MutableSet<T>`.

Here's the code for the `getWinners` function:

```
fun getWinners(): MutableSet<T> {
    val highScore = scores.values.max()
    val winners: MutableSet<T> = mutableSetOf()
    for ((t, score) in scores) {
        if (score == highScore) winners.add(t)
    }
    return winners
}
```

Get the highest value from scores.

Add any contestants with the highest score to a MutableSet.

Return the MutableSet of winners.

Contest<T: Pet>
scores
addScore **getWinners**

And here's the code for the complete `Contest` class:

```
class Contest<T: Pet> {
    val scores: MutableMap<T, Int> = mutableMapOf()

    fun addScore(t: T, score: Int = 0) {
        if (score >= 0) scores.put(t, score)
    }

    fun getWinners(): MutableSet<T> {
        val highScore = scores.values.max()
        val winners: MutableSet<T> = mutableSetOf()
        for ((t, score) in scores) {
            if (score == highScore) winners.add(t)
        }
        return winners
    }
}
```

We'll add this class to a new application a few pages ahead.

Now that we've written the `Contest` class, let's use it to create some objects.

Create some Contest objects

You create `Contest` objects by specifying what type of objects it should deal with, and calling its constructor. The following code, for example, creates a `Contest<Cat>` object named `catContest` that deals with `Cat` objects:

```
val catContest = Contest<Cat>()
```

This creates a Contest that will accept Cats.

This means that you can add `Cat` objects to its `scores` property, and use its `getWinners` function to return a `MutableSet` of `Cats`:

```
catContest.addScore(Cat("Fuzz Lightyear"), 50)
catContest.addScore(Cat("Katsu"), 45)
val topCat = catContest.getWinners().first()
```

getWinners() returns a MutableSet<Cat> because we've specified that catContest must deal with Cats.

And as `Contest` uses generics, the compiler prevents you from passing any non-`Cat` references to it. The following code, for example, won't compile:

```
catContest.addScore(Dog("Fido"), 23)
```

The compiler prevents you from adding non-Cats to a Contest<Cat>, so this line won't compile.

A `Contest<Pet>`, however, will accept any type of `Pet`, like this:

```
val petContest = Contest<Pet>()
petContest.addScore(Cat("Fuzz Lightyear"), 50)
petContest.addScore(Fish("Finny McGraw"), 56)
```

As a Contest<Pet> deals with Pets, contestants can be any subtype of Pet.

The compiler can infer the generic type

In some circumstances, the compiler can infer the generic type from the available information. If, say, you create a variable of type `Contest<Dog>`, the compiler will automatically infer that any `Contest` object you pass to it is a `Contest<Dog>` (unless you tell it otherwise). The following code, for example, creates a `Contest<Dog>` object and assigns it to `dogContest`:

```
val dogContest: Contest<Dog>
dogContest = Contest()
```

Here, you can use Contest() instead of Contest<Dog>() as the compiler can infer the object type from the variable type.

Where appropriate, the compiler can also infer the generic type from its constructor parameters. If, for example, we'd used a generic type parameter in the `Contest` class primary constructor like this:

```
class Contest<T: Pet>(t: T) {...}
```

The compiler would be able to infer that the following code creates a `Contest<Fish>`:

```
val contest = Contest(Fish("Finny McGraw"))
```

This is the same as creating a Contest using Contest<Fish>(Fish("Finny McGraw")). You can omit the <Fish> as the compiler infers it from the constructor argument.

Generic Functions Up Close

So far, you've seen how to define a function that uses a generic type inside a class definition. But what if you want to define a function with a generic type outside a class? Or what if you want a function inside a class to use a generic type that's not included in the class definition?

If you want to define a function with its own generic type, you can do so by declaring the generic type as part of the function definition. The following code, for example, defines a function named `listPet` with a generic type, `T`, that's limited to types of `Pet`. The function accepts a `T` parameter, and returns a reference to a `MutableList<T>` object:

For functions that declare their own generic type, the <T: Pet> goes **before** the function name.

```
fun <T: Pet> listPet(t: T): MutableList<T> {
    println("Create and return MutableList")
    return mutableListOf(t)
}
```

Notice that when you declare a generic function in this way, the type must be declared in angle brackets *before* the function name, like this:

```
fun <T: Pet> listPet...
```

To call the function, you must specify the type of object the function should deal with. The following code, for example, calls the `listPet` function, using angle brackets to specify that we're using it with `Cat` objects:

```
val catList = listPet<Cat>(Cat("Zazzles"))
```

The generic type, however, can be omitted if the compiler can infer it from the function's arguments. The following code, for example, is legal because the compiler can infer that the `listPet` function is being used with `Cats`:

```
val catList = listPet(Cat("Zazzles"))
```

These two function calls do the same thing, as the compiler can infer that you want the function to deal with Cats.

Create the Generics project

Now that you've seen how to create a class that uses generics, let's add it to a new application.

Create a new Kotlin project that targets the JVM, and name the project "Generics". Then create a new Kotlin file named *Pets.kt* by highlighting the *src* folder, clicking on the File menu and choosing New → Kotlin File/Class. When prompted, name the file "Pets", and choose File from the Kind option.

Next, update your version of *Pets.kt* to match ours below:

```
abstract class Pet(var name: String)

class Cat(name: String) : Pet(name)

class Dog(name: String) : Pet(name)

class Fish(name: String) : Pet(name)

class Contest<T: Pet> {
    val scores: MutableMap<T, Int> = mutableMapOf()

    fun addScore(t: T, score: Int = 0) {
        if (score >= 0) scores.put(t, score)
    }

    fun getWinners(): MutableSet<T> {
        val winners: MutableSet<T> = mutableSetOf()
        val highScore = scores.values.max()
        for ((t, score) in scores) {
            if (score == highScore) winners.add(t)
        }
        return winners
    }
}
```

Add the Pet hierarchy.

Add the Contest class.

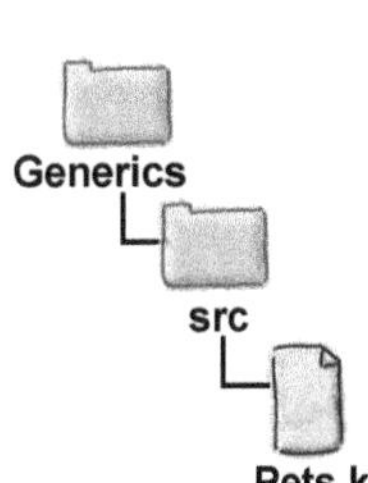

The code continues on the next page.

Pets
Contest
Retailers
Vet

The code continued...

```
fun main(args: Array<String>) {
    val catFuzz = Cat("Fuzz Lightyear")      ← Create two Cats and a Fish.
    val catKatsu = Cat("Katsu")
    val fishFinny = Fish("Finny McGraw")

    val catContest = Contest<Cat>()      ← Hold a Cat Contest (Cats-only).
    catContest.addScore(catFuzz, 50)
    catContest.addScore(catKatsu, 45)
    val topCat = catContest.getWinners().first()
    println("Cat contest winner is ${topCat.name}")

    val petContest = Contest<Pet>()      ← Hold a Pet Contest, that will
    petContest.addScore(catFuzz, 50)       accept all types of Pet.
    petContest.addScore(fishFinny, 56)
    val topPet = petContest.getWinners().first()
    println("Pet contest winner is ${topPet.name}")
}
```

Generics
src
Pets.kt

Test drive

When we run the code, the following text gets printed in the IDE's output window:

```
Cat contest winner is Fuzz Lightyear
Pet contest winner is Finny McGraw
```

After you've had a go at the following exercise, we'll look at the `Retailer` hierarchy.

there are no Dumb Questions

Q: Can a generic type be nullable?

A: Yes. If you have a function that returns a generic type, and you want this type to be nullable, simply add a `?` after the generic return type like this:

```
class MyClass<T> {
    fun myFun(): T?
}
```

Q: Can a class have more than one generic type?

A: Yes. You define multiple generic types by specifying them inside angle brackets, separated by a comma. If you wanted to define a class named `MyMap` with `K` and `V` generic types, you would define it using code like this:

```
class MyMap<K, V> {
    //Code goes here
}
```

Pool Puzzle

Your **job** is to take code snippets from the pool and place them into the blank lines in the code. You may **not** use the same code snippet more than once, and you won't need to use all the code snippets. Your **goal** is to create a class named `PetOwner` that accepts generic `Pet` types, which you must then use to create a new `PetOwner<Cat>` that holds references to two `Cat` objects.

pets holds a reference to each pet owned. It's initialized with a value that's passed to the PetOwner constructor.

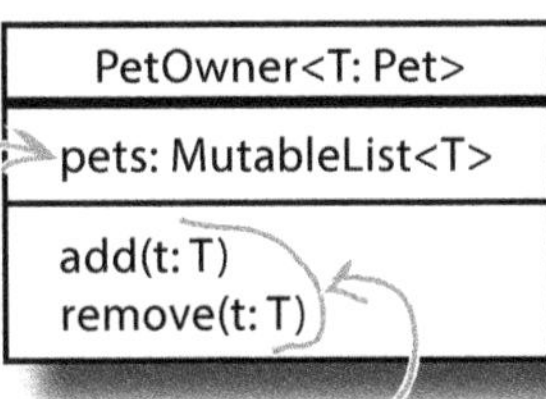

The add and remove functions are used to update the pets property. The add function adds a reference, and the remove function removes one.

```
class PetOwner ..................{
    val pets = mutableListOf(.....)

    fun add(.........) {
        pets.add(.....)
    }

    fun remove(.........) {
        pets.remove(.....)
    }
}

fun main(args: Array<String>) {
    val catFuzz = Cat("Fuzz Lightyear")
    val catKatsu = Cat("Katsu")
    val fishFinny = Fish("Finny McGraw")
    val catOwner = PetOwner ..................
    catOwner.add(catKatsu)
}
```

Note: each thing from the pool can only be used once!

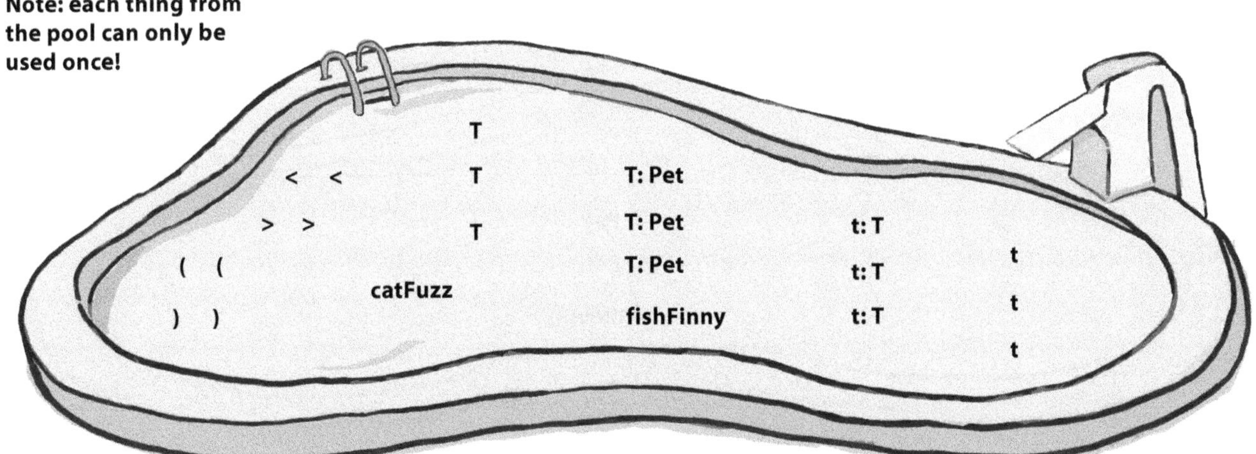

Pool Puzzle Solution

Your **job** is to take code snippets from the pool and place them into the blank lines in the code. You may **not** use the same code snippet more than once, and you won't need to use all the code snippets. Your **goal** is to create a class named PetOwner that accepts generic Pet types, which you must then use to create a new PetOwner<Cat> that holds references to two Cat objects.

PetOwner<T: Pet>
pets: MutableList<T>
add(t: T) remove(t: T)

Specify the generic type. The constructor.

```
class PetOwner <T: Pet>(t: T) {
    val pets = mutableListOf(t)

    fun add(t: T) {
        pets.add(t)
    }

    fun remove(t: T) {
        pets.remove(t)
    }
}

fun main(args: Array<String>) {
    val catFuzz = Cat("Fuzz Lightyear")
    val catKatsu = Cat("Katsu")
    val fishFinny = Fish("Finny McGraw")
    val catOwner = PetOwner(catFuzz)
    catOwner.add(catKatsu)
}
```

This creates a MutableList<T>.

Add/Remove T values.

Creates a PetOwner<Cat>, and initializes pets with a reference to catFuzz

You didn't need to use these snippets.

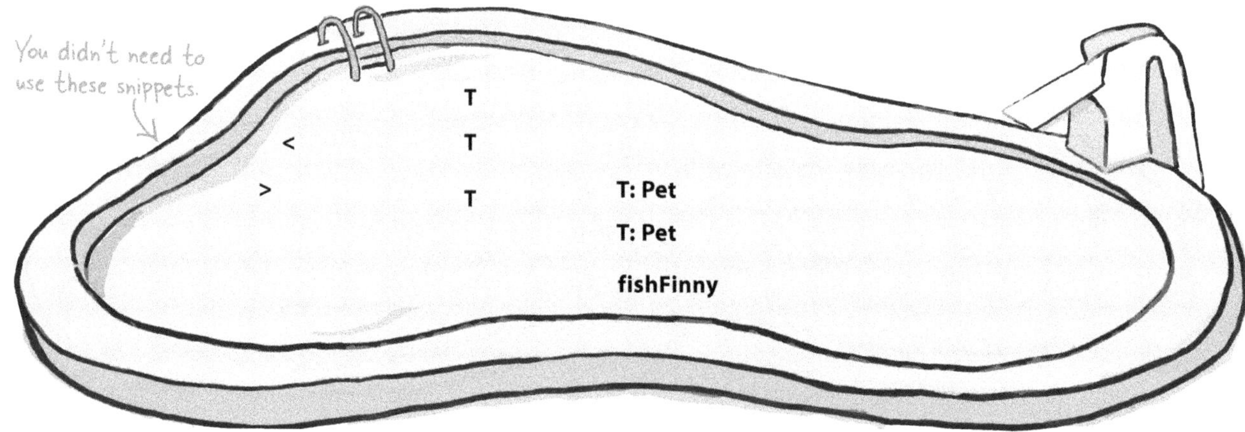

The Retailer hierarchy

We're going to use the Pet classes we created earlier to define a hierarchy of retailers that can sell different types of pet. To do this, we'll define a Retailer interface with a sell function, and three concrete classes named CatRetailer, DogRetailer and FishRetailer that implement the interface.

Each type of retailer should be able to sell a particular type of object. A CatRetailer, for example, can only sell Cats, and a DogRetailer can only sell Dogs. To enforce this, we'll use generics to specify the type of object that each class deals with. We'll add a generic type T to the Retailer interface, and specify that the sell function must return objects of this type. As the CatRetailer, DogRetailer and FishRetailer classes all implement this interface, each one will have to substitute the "real" type of object they deal with for the generic type T.

Here's the class hierarchy that we'll use:

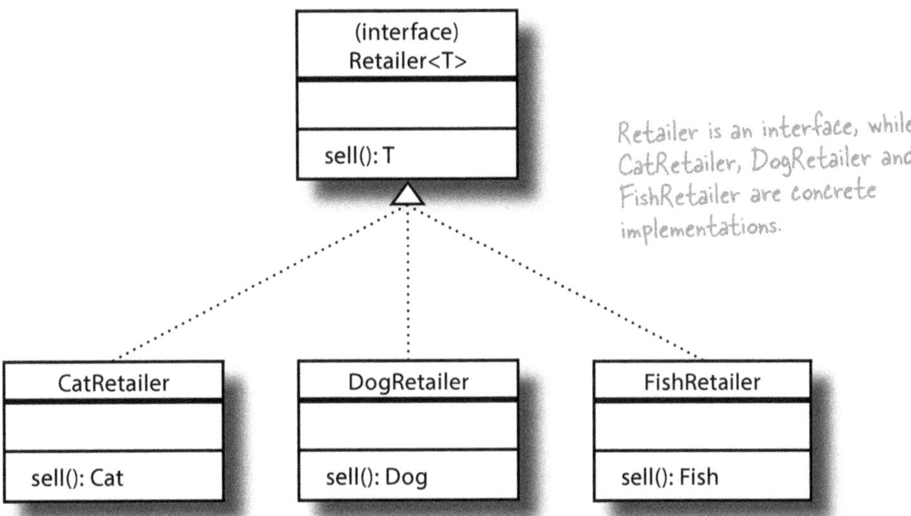

Now that you've seen the class hierarchy let's write the code for it, starting with the Retailer interface.

there are no Dumb Questions

Q: Why aren't you using a PetRetailer concrete class?

A: In the real world, it's quite likely that you'd want to include a PetRetailer which sells all types of Pet. Here, we're differentiating between the different types of Retailer so that we can teach you more important details about generics.

Define the Retailer interface

The `Retailer` interface needs to specify that it uses a generic type `T`, which is used as the return type for the `sell` function.

Here's the code for the interface:

```
interface Retailer<T> {
    fun sell(): T
}
```

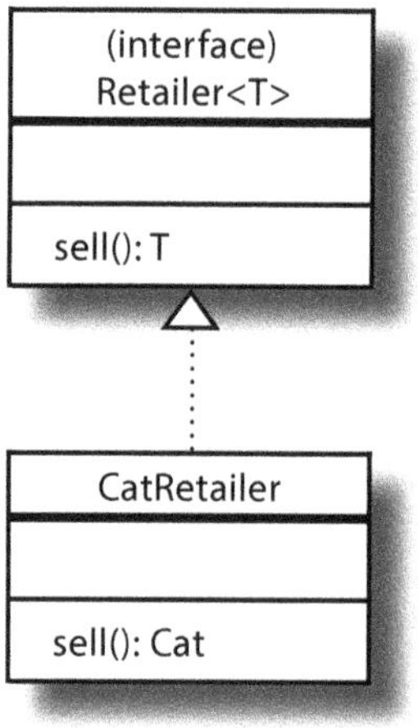

(interface)
Retailer<T>

sell(): T

The `CatRetailer`, `DogRetailer` and `FishRetailer` classes need to implement the `Retailer` interface, specifying the type of object each one deals with. The `CatRetailer` class, for example, only deals with `Cats`, so we'll define it using code like this:

```
class CatRetailer : Retailer<Cat> {
    override fun sell(): Cat {
        println("Sell Cat")
        return Cat("")
    }
}
```

The CatRetailer class implements the Retailer interface so that it deals with Cats. This means that the sell() function must return a Cat.

CatRetailer

sell(): Cat

Similarly, the `DogRetailer` class deals with `Dogs`, so we can define it like this:

```
class DogRetailer : Retailer<Dog> {
    override fun sell(): Dog {
        println("Sell Dog")
        return Dog("")
    }
}
```

DogRetailer replaces Retailer's generic type with Dog, so its sell() function must return a Dog.

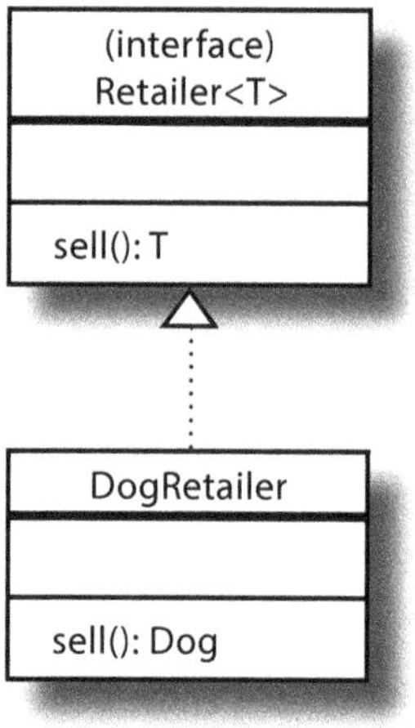

(interface)
Retailer<T>

sell(): T

DogRetailer

sell(): Dog

Each implementation of the `Retailer` interface must specify the type of object it deals with by replacing the "T" defined in the interface with the real type. The `CatRetailer` implementation, for example, replaces "T" with "Cat", so its `sell` function must return a `Cat`. If you try and use anything other than `Cat` (or a subtype of `Cat`) for `sell`'s return type, the code won't compile:

```
class CatRetailer : Retailer<Cat> {
    override fun sell(): Dog = Dog("")
}
```

This code won't compile because CatRetailer's sell() function must return a Cat, and a Dog is not a type of Cat.

So using generics means that you can place limits on how a class uses its types, making your code much more consistent and robust.

Now that we have the code for our retailers, let's create some objects.

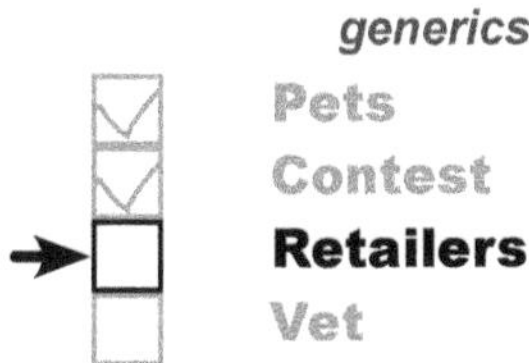

We can create CatRetailer, DogRetailer and FishRetailer objects...

As you might expect, you can create a `CatRetailer`, `DogRetailer` or `FishRetailer` object and assign it to a variable by explicitly declaring the variable's type, or letting the compiler infer it from the value that's assigned to it. The following code uses these techniques to create two `CatRetailer` variables and assign a `CatRetailer` object to each one:

```
val catRetailer1 = CatRetailer()
val catRetailer2: CatRetailer = CatRetailer()
```

...but what about polymorphism?

As `CatRetailer`, `DogRetailer` and `FishRetailer` implement the `Retailer` interface, we *should* be able to create a variable of type `Retailer` (with a compatible type parameter), and assign one of its subtypes to it. And this works if we assign a `CatRetailer` object to a `Retailer<Cat>` variable, or assign a `DogRetailer` to a `Retailer<Dog>`:

```
val dogRetailer: Retailer<Dog> = DogRetailer()
val catRetailer: Retailer<Cat> = CatRetailer()
```

These lines are legal because DogRetailer implements Retailer<Dog>, and CatRetailer implements Retailer<Cat>.

But if we try to assign one of these objects to a `Retailer<Pet>`, the code won't compile:

```
val petRetailer: Retailer<Pet> = CatRetailer()
```

This won't compile, even though CatRetailer is a Retailer<Cat>, and Cat is a subtype of Pet.

Even though `CatRetailer` is a type of `Retailer`, and `Cat` is a type of `Pet`, our current code won't let us assign a `Retailer<Cat>` object to a `Retailer<Pet>` variable. A `Retailer<Pet>` variable will only accept a `Retailer<Pet>` object. Not a `Retailer<Cat>`, nor a `Retailer<Dog>`, but only a `Retailer<Pet>`.

This behavior appears to violate the whole point of polymorphism. The great news, however, is that **we can adjust the generic type in the `Retailer` interface to control which types of objects a `Retailer<Pet>` variable can accept**.

Use out to make a generic type covariant

If you want to be able to use a generic subtype object in a place of a generic supertype, you can do so by prefixing the generic type with **out**. In our example, we want to be able to assign a Retailer<Cat> (a subtype) to a Retailer<Pet> (a supertype) so we'll prefix the generic type T in the Retailer interface with out like so:

```
interface Retailer<out T> {
    fun sell(): T
}
```

Here's the out prefix.

When we prefix a generic type with out, we say that the generic type is **covariant**. In other words, it means that a subtype can be used in place of a supertype.

If a generic type is covariant, it means that you can use a subtype in place of a supertype.

Making the above change means that a Retailer<Pet> variable can now be assigned Retailer objects that deal with Pet subtypes. The following code, for example, now compiles:

```
val petRetailer: Retailer<Pet> = CatRetailer()
```

The out prefix in the Retailer interface means that we can now assign a Retailer<Cat> to a Retailer<Pet> variable.

In general, a class or interface generic type may be prefixed with out if the class has functions that use it as a return type, or if the class has val properties of that type. You can't, however, use out if the class has function parameters or var properties of that generic type.

Another way of thinking about this is that a generic type that's prefixed with out can only be used in an "out" position, such as a function return type. It can't, however, be used in an "in" position, so a function can't receive a covariant type as a parameter value.

Collections are defined using covariant types

The out prefix isn't just used by generic classes and interfaces that you define yourself. They're also heavily used by Kotlin's built-in code, such as collections.

The List collection, for example, is defined using code like this:

```
public interface List<out E> ... { ... }
```

This means that you can, say, assign a List of Cats to a List of Pets, and the code will compile:

```
val catList: List<Cat> = listOf(Cat(""), Cat(""))
val petList: List<Pet> = catList
```

Now that you've seen how to make generic types covariant using out, let's add the code we've written to our project.

Pets
Contest
Retailers
Vet

Update the Generics project

Update your version of *Pets.kt* in the Generics project so that it matches ours below (our changes are in bold):

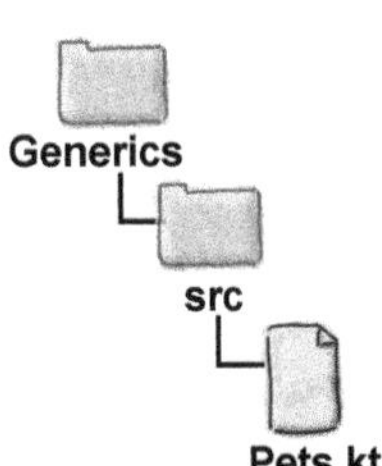


```
abstract class Pet(var name: String)
class Cat(name: String) : Pet(name)
class Dog(name: String) : Pet(name)
class Fish(name: String) : Pet(name)

class Contest<T: Pet> {
    val scores: MutableMap<T, Int> = mutableMapOf()

    fun addScore(t: T, score: Int = 0) {
        if (score >= 0) scores.put(t, score)
    }

    fun getWinners(): MutableSet<T> {
        val winners: MutableSet<T> = mutableSetOf()
        val highScore = scores.values.max()
        for ((t, score) in scores) {
            if (score == highScore) winners.add(t)
        }
        return winners
    }
}

interface Retailer<out T> {
    fun sell(): T
}

class CatRetailer : Retailer<Cat> {
    override fun sell(): Cat {
        println("Sell Cat")
        return Cat("")
    }
}

class DogRetailer : Retailer<Dog> {
    override fun sell(): Dog {
        println("Sell Dog")
        return Dog("")
    }
}
```

Add the Retailer interface.

Add the CatRetailer and DogRetailer classes.

The code continues on the next page.

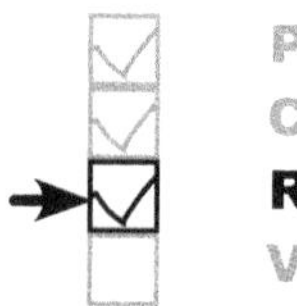

The code continued...

```
class FishRetailer : Retailer<Fish> {
    override fun sell(): Fish {
        println("Sell Fish")
        return Fish("")
    }
}

fun main(args: Array<String>) {
    val catFuzz = Cat("Fuzz Lightyear")
    val catKatsu = Cat("Katsu")
    val fishFinny = Fish("Finny McGraw")

    val catContest = Contest<Cat>()
    catContest.addScore(catFuzz, 50)
    catContest.addScore(catKatsu, 45)
    val topCat = catContest.getWinners().first()
    println("Cat contest winner is ${topCat.name}")

    val petContest = Contest<Pet>()
    petContest.addScore(catFuzz, 50)
    petContest.addScore(fishFinny, 56)
    val topPet = petContest.getWinners().first()
    println("Pet contest winner is ${topPet.name}")

    val dogRetailer: Retailer<Dog> = DogRetailer()
    val catRetailer: Retailer<Cat> = CatRetailer()
    val petRetailer: Retailer<Pet> = CatRetailer()
    petRetailer.sell()
}
```

Add the FishRetailer class.

Create some Retailer objects.

Generics
src
Pets.kt

Test drive

When we run the code, the following text gets printed in the IDE's output window:

Cat contest winner is Fuzz Lightyear

Pet contest winner is Finny McGraw

Sell Cat

Now that you've seen how to make generic types covariant using the `out` prefix, have a go at the following exercise.

BE the Compiler

Here are five classes and interfaces that use generics. Your job is to play like you're the Compiler, and determine whether each one will compile. If it won't compile, why not?

A

```
interface A<out T> {
    fun myFunction(t: T)
}
```

B

```
interface B<out T> {
    val x: T
    fun myFunction(): T
}
```

C

```
interface C<out T> {
    var y: T
    fun myFunction(): T
}
```

D

```
interface D<out T> {
    fun myFunction(str: String): T
}
```

E

```
abstract class E<out T>(t: T) {
    val x = t
}
```

BE the Compiler Solution

Here are five classes and interfaces that use generics. Your job is to play like you're the Compiler, and determine whether each one will compile. If it won't compile, why not?

A

```
interface A<out T> {
    fun myFunction(t: T)
}
```

This code won't compile because the covariant type T can't be used as a function parameter.

B

```
interface B<out T> {
    val x: T
    fun myFunction(): T
}
```

This code compiles successfully.

C

```
interface C<out T> {
    var y: T
    fun myFunction(): T
}
```

This code won't compile because the covariant type T can't be used as the type of a var property.

D

```
interface D<out T> {
    fun myFunction(str: String): T
}
```

This code compiles successfully.

E

```
abstract class E<out T>(t: T) {
    val x = t
}
```

This code compiles successfully.

Pets
Contest
Retailers
Vet

We need a Vet class

As we said earlier in the chapter, we want to be able to assign a vet to each contest in case there's a medical emergency with any of the contestants. As vets can specialize in treating different types of pet, we'll create a `Vet` class with a generic type `T`, and specify that it has a `treat` function that accepts an argument of this type. We'll also say that `T` must be a type of `Pet` so that you can't create a `Vet` that treats, say, `Planet` or `Broccoli` objects.

Here's the `Vet` class

```
class Vet<T: Pet> {
    fun treat(t: T) {
        println("Treat Pet ${t.name}")
    }
}
```

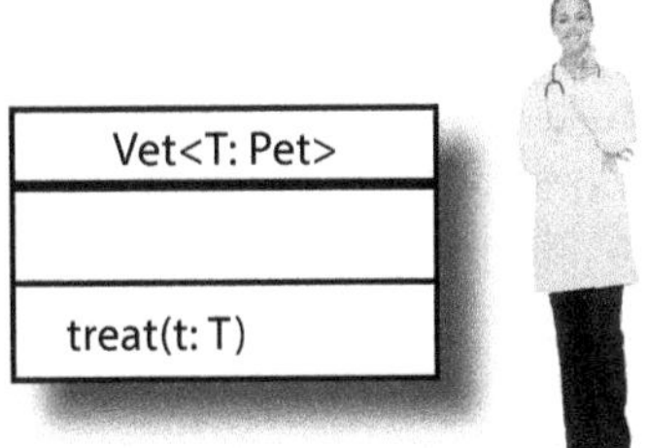

Next, let's change the `Contest` class so that it accepts a `Vet`.

Assign a Vet to a Contest

We want to make sure that each `Contest` has a `Vet`, so we'll add a `Vet` property to the `Contest` constructor. Here's the updated `Contest` code:

We're adding a Vet<T> to the Contest constructor so that you can't create a Contest without assigning a Vet to it.

```
class Contest<T: Pet>(var vet: Vet<T>) {
    val scores: MutableMap<T, Int> = mutableMapOf()

    fun addScore(t: T, score: Int = 0) {
        if (score >= 0) scores.put(t, score)
    }

    fun getWinners(): MutableSet<T> {
        val winners: MutableSet<T> = mutableSetOf()
        val highScore = scores.values.max()
        for ((t, score) in scores) {
            if (score == highScore) winners.add(t)
        }
        return winners
    }
}
```

Let's create some `Vet` objects, and assign them to `Contests`.

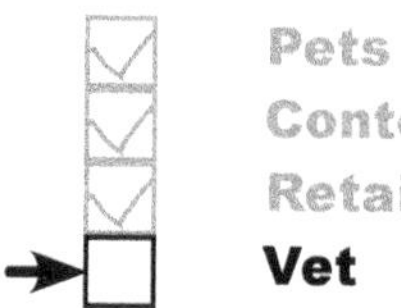

Create Vet objects

We can create `Vet` objects in the same way that we created `Contest` objects: by specifying the type of object each `Vet` object should deal with. The following code, for example, creates three objects—one each of type `Vet<Cat>`, `Vet<Fish>` and `Vet<Pet>`:

```
val catVet = Vet<Cat>()
val fishVet = Vet<Fish>()
val petVet = Vet<Pet>()
```

Each `Vet` can deal with a specific type of `Pet`. The `Vet<Cat>`, for example, can treat `Cats`, while a `Vet<Pet>` can treat any `Pet`, including both `Cats` and `Fish`. A `Vet<Cat>`, however, can't treat anything that's not a `Cat`, such as a `Fish`:

```
catVet.treat(Cat("Fuzz Lightyear"))
petVet.treat(Cat("Katsu"))
petVet.treat(Fish("Finny McGraw"))
catVet.treat(Fish("Finny McGraw"))
```

A Vet<Cat> and a Vet<Pet> can both treat Cats.

A Vet<Pet> can treat a Fish.

This line won't compile, as a Vet<Cat> can't treat a Fish.

Let's see what happens when we try passing `Vet` objects to `Contests`.

Pass a Vet to the Contest constructor

The `Contest` class has one parameter, a `Vet`, which must be able to treat the type of `Pet` that the `Contest` is for. This means that we can pass a `Vet<Cat>` to a `Contest<Cat>`, and a `Vet<Pet>` to a `Contest<Pet>` like this:

```
val catContest = Contest<Cat>(catVet)
val petContest = Contest<Pet>(petVet)
```

But there's a problem. A `Vet<Pet>` can treat all types of `Pet`, including `Cats`, but **we can't assign a `Vet<Pet>` to a `Contest<Cat>` as the code won't compile**:

```
val catContest = Contest<Cat>(petVet)
```

Even though a Vet<Pet> can treat Cats, a Contest<Cat> won't accept a Vet<Pet>, so this line won't compile.

So what should we do in this situation?

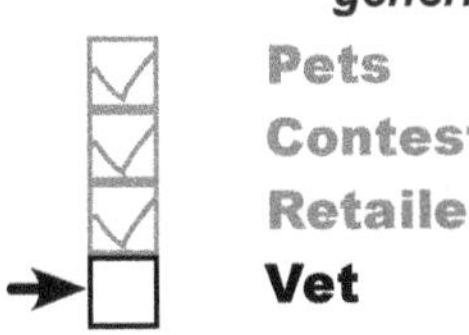

Use in to make a generic type contravariant

In our example, we want to be able to pass a `Pet<Vet>` to a `Contest<Cat>` in place of a `Pet<Cat>`. In other words, we want to be able to use a generic supertype in place of a generic subtype.

In this situation, we can solve the problem by prefixing the generic type used by the `Vet` class with **`in`**. `in` is the polar opposite of `out`. While `out` allows you to use a generic subtype in place of a supertype (like assigning a `Retailer<Cat>` to a `Retailer<Pet>`), `in` lets you use a generic supertype in place of a subtype. So prefixing the `Vet` class generic type with `in` like this:

Here's the in prefix.

```
class Vet<in T: Pet> {
    fun treat(t: T) {
        println("Treat Pet ${t.name}")
    }
}
```

means that we can use a `Vet<Pet>` in place of a `Vet<Cat>`. The following code now compiles:

```
val catContest = Contest<Cat>(Vet<Pet>())
```

The in prefix in the Vet class means that we can now use a Vet<Pet> in place of a Vet<Cat>, so this code now compiles.

If a generic type is contravariant, it means that you can use a supertype in place of a subtype. This is the opposite of covariance.

When we prefix a generic type with `in`, we say that the generic type is **contravariant**. In other words, it means that a supertype can be used in place of a subtype.

In general, a class or interface generic type may be prefixed with `in` if the class has functions that use it as a parameter type. You can't, however, use `in` if any of the class functions use it as a return type, or if that type is used by any properties, irrespective of whether they're defined using `val` or `var`.

In other words, a generic type that's prefixed with "in" can only be used in an "in" position, such as a function parameter value. It can't be used in "out" positions.

Should a Vet<Cat> ALWAYS accept a Vet<Pet>?

Before prefixing a class or interface generic type with `in`, you need to consider whether you want the generic subtype parameter to accept a supertype in every situation. `in` allows you, for example, to assign a `Vet<Pet>` object to `Vet<Cat>` variable, which may not be something that you always want to happen:

```
val catVet: Vet<Cat> = Vet<Pet>()
```

This line compiles as the Vet class uses an in prefix for T.

The great news is that in situations like this, you can tailor the circumstances in which a generic type is contravariant. Let's see how.

Pets
Contest
Retailers
→ **Vet**

A generic type can be locally contravariant

As you've seen, prefixing a generic type with `in` as part of the class or interface declaration makes the generic type globally contravariant. You can, however, restrict this behavior to specific properties or functions.

Suppose, for example, that we want to be able to use a `Vet<Pet>` reference in place of a `Vet<Cat>`, but *only* where it's being passed to a `Contest<Cat>` in its constructor. We can achieve this by removing the `in` prefix from the generic type in the `Vet` class, and adding it to the `vet` property in the `Contest` constructor instead.

Here's the code to do this:

Remove the in prefix from the Vet class...

```
class Vet<in T: Pet> {
    fun treat(t: T) {
        println("Treat Pet ${t.name}")
    }
}
class Contest<T: Pet>(var vet: Vet<in T>) {
    ...
}
```

...and add it to the Contest constructor instead. This means that T is contravariant, but **only** in the Contest constructor.

These changes mean that you can still pass a `Vet<Pet>` to a `Contest<Cat>` like this:

```
val catContest = Contest<Cat>(Vet<Pet>())
```

This line compiles, as you can use a Vet<Pet> in place of a Vet<Cat> in the Contest<Cat> constructor.

The compiler won't, however, let you assign a `Vet<Pet>` object to a `Vet<Cat>` variable as `Vet`'s generic type is not globally contravariant:

```
val catVet: Vet<Cat> = Vet<Pet>()
```

This line, however, won't compile as you can't globally use a Vet<Pet> in place of a Vet<Cat>.

Now that you've learned how to use contravariance, let's add the `Vet` code to our Generics project.

When a generic type has no in or out prefix, we say that the type is invariant. An invariant type can only accept references of that specific type.

Pets
Contest
Retailers
Vet

Update the Generics project

Update your version of *Pets.kt* in the Generics project so that it matches ours below (our changes are in bold):

Generics
src
Pets.kt

```
abstract class Pet(var name: String)
class Cat(name: String) : Pet(name)
class Dog(name: String) : Pet(name)
class Fish(name: String) : Pet(name)

class Vet<T: Pet> {
    fun treat(t: T) {
        println("Treat Pet ${t.name}")
    }
}

class Contest<T: Pet>(var vet: Vet<in T>) {
    val scores: MutableMap<T, Int> = mutableMapOf()

    fun addScore(t: T, score: Int = 0) {
        if (score >= 0) scores.put(t, score)
    }

    fun getWinners(): MutableSet<T> {
        val winners: MutableSet<T> = mutableSetOf()
        val highScore = scores.values.max()
        for ((t, score) in scores) {
            if (score == highScore) winners.add(t)
        }
        return winners
    }
}

interface Retailer<out T> {
    fun sell(): T
}

class CatRetailer : Retailer<Cat> {
    override fun sell(): Cat {
        println("Sell Cat")
        return Cat("")
    }
}
```

Add the Vet class.

Add a constructor to the Contest class.

The code continues on the next page.

The code continued...

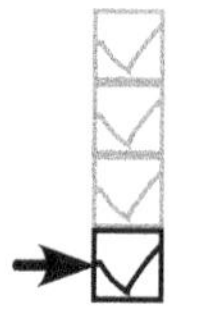


```
class DogRetailer : Retailer<Dog> {
    override fun sell(): Dog {
        println("Sell Dog")
        return Dog("")
    }
}

class FishRetailer : Retailer<Fish> {
    override fun sell(): Fish {
        println("Sell Fish")
        return Fish("")
    }
}

fun main(args: Array<String>) {
    val catFuzz = Cat("Fuzz Lightyear")
    val catKatsu = Cat("Katsu")
    val fishFinny = Fish("Finny McGraw")

    val catVet = Vet<Cat>()
    val fishVet = Vet<Fish>()
    val petVet = Vet<Pet>()

    catVet.treat(catFuzz)
    petVet.treat(catKatsu)
    petVet.treat(fishFinny)

    val catContest = Contest<Cat>(catVet)
    catContest.addScore(catFuzz, 50)
    catContest.addScore(catKatsu, 45)
    val topCat = catContest.getWinners().first()
    println("Cat contest winner is ${topCat.name}")
```

Generics
src
Pets.kt

Create some Vet objects.

Get the Vets to treat some Pets.

Assign a Vet<Cat> to the Contest<Cat>.

The code continues on the next page.

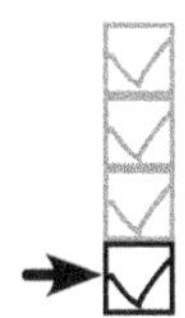

The code continued...

Assign a Vet<Pet> to the Contest<Pet>.

```
        val petContest = Contest<Pet>(petVet)
        petContest.addScore(catFuzz, 50)
        petContest.addScore(fishFinny, 56)
        val topPet = petContest.getWinners().first()
        println("Pet contest winner is ${topPet.name}")

        val fishContest = Contest<Fish>(petVet)

        val dogRetailer: Retailer<Dog> = DogRetailer()
        val catRetailer: Retailer<Cat> = CatRetailer()
        val petRetailer: Retailer<Pet> = CatRetailer()
        petRetailer.sell()
    }
```

Assign a Vet<Pet> to a Contest<Fish>.

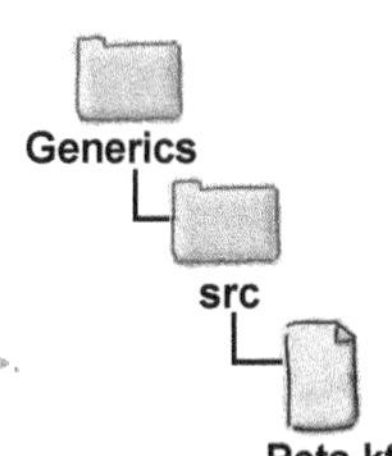

Test drive

When we run the code, the following text gets printed in the IDE's output window:

```
Treat Pet Fuzz Lightyear
Treat Pet Katsu
Treat Pet Finny McGraw
Cat contest winner is Fuzz Lightyear
Pet contest winner is Finny McGraw
Sell Cat
```

there are no Dumb Questions

Q: Couldn't I have just made `Contest`'s `vet` property a `Vet<Pet>`?

A: No. This would mean that the `vet` property could only accept a `Vet<Pet>`. And while you *could* make the `vet` property locally covariant using:

```
var vet: Vet<out Pet>
```

it would mean that you could assign a `Vet<Fish>` to a `Contest<Cat>`, which is unlikely to end well.

Q: Kotlin's approach to generics seems different to Java's. Is that right?

A: Yes, it is. With Java, generic types are always invariant, but you can use wildcards to get around some of the problems this creates. Kotlin, however, gives you far greater control as you can make generic types covariant, contravariant, or leave them as invariant.

BE the Compiler

Here are four classes and interfaces that use generics. Your job is to play like you're the Compiler, and determine whether each one will compile. If it won't compile, why not?

A

```
class A<in T>(t: T) {
    fun myFunction(t: T) { }
}
```

B

```
class B<in T>(t: T) {
    val x = t
    fun myFunction(t: T) { }
}
```

C

```
abstract class C<in T> {
    fun myFunction(): T { }
}
```

D

```
class E<in T>(t: T) {
    var y = t
    fun myFunction(t: T) { }
}
```

Answers on page 322.

Sharpen your pencil

Below is a complete Kotlin file listing. The code, however, won't compile. Which lines won't compile? What changes do you need to make to the class and interface definitions to make them compile?

Note: You may not amend the `main` function.

```
//Food types
open class Food

class VeganFood: Food()

//Sellers
interface Seller<T>

class FoodSeller: Seller<Food>

class VeganFoodSeller: Seller<VeganFood>

//Consumers
interface Consumer<T>

class Person: Consumer<Food>

class Vegan: Consumer<VeganFood>

fun main(args: Array<String>) {
    var foodSeller: Seller<Food>
    foodSeller = FoodSeller()
    foodSeller = VeganFoodSeller()

    var veganFoodConsumer: Consumer<VeganFood>
    veganFoodConsumer = Vegan()
    veganFoodConsumer = Person()
}
```

→ Answers on page 323.

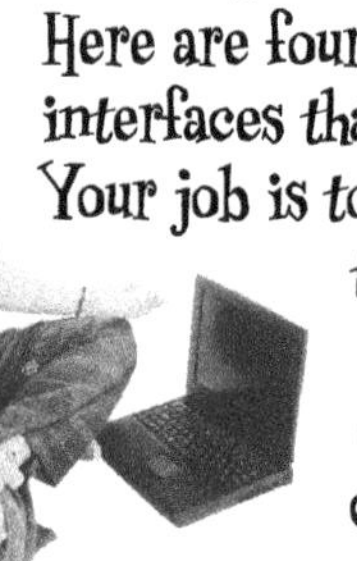

BE the Compiler Solution

Here are four classes and interfaces that use generics. Your job is to play like you're the Compiler, and determine whether each one will compile. If it won't compile, why not?

A

```
class A<in T>(t: T) {
    fun myFunction(t: T) { }
}
```

This code compiles successfully because the contravariant type T can be used as a constructor or function parameter type.

B

```
class B<in T>(t: T) {
    val x = t
    fun myFunction(t: T) { }
}
```

This code won't compile because T can't be used as the type of a val property.

C

```
abstract class C<in T> {
    fun myFunction(): T { }
}
```

This code won't compile because T can't be used as a function's return type.

D

```
class E<in T>(t: T) {
    var y = t
    fun myFunction(t: T) { }
}
```

This code won't compile because T can't be used as the type of a var property.

Sharpen your pencil Solution

Below is a complete Kotlin file listing. The code, however, won't compile. Which lines won't compile? What changes do you need to make to the class and interface definitions to make them compile?

Note: You may not amend the `main` function.

```
//Food types
open class Food

class VeganFood: Food()

//Sellers
interface Seller<out T>

class FoodSeller: Seller<Food>

class VeganFoodSeller: Seller<VeganFood>

//Consumers
interface Consumer<in T>

class Person: Consumer<Food>

class Vegan: Consumer<VeganFood>

fun main(args: Array<String>) {
    var foodSeller: Seller<Food>
    foodSeller = FoodSeller()
    foodSeller = VeganFoodSeller()

    var veganFoodConsumer: Consumer<VeganFood>
    veganFoodConsumer = Vegan()
    veganFoodConsumer = Person()
}
```

This line won't compile, as it's assigning a Seller<VeganFood> to a Seller<Food>. To make it compile, we must prefix T with out in the Seller interface.

This line won't compile, as it's assigning a Consumer<Food> to a Consumer<VeganFood>. To make it compile, we must prefix T with in in the Consumer interface.

CHAPTER 10

Your Kotlin Toolbox

You've got Chapter 10 under your belt and now you've added generics to your toolbox.

You can download the full code for the chapter from https://tinyurl.com/HFKotlin.

BULLET POINTS

- Generics let you write consistent code that's type-safe. Collections such as `MutableList` use generics.
- The generic type is defined inside angle brackets <>, for example:

```
class Contest<T>
```

- You can restrict the generic type to a specific supertype, for example:

```
class Contest<T: Pet>
```

- You create an instance of a class with a generic type by specifying the "real" type in angle brackets, for example:

```
Contest<Cat>
```

- Where possible, the compiler will infer the generic type.
- You can define a function that uses a generic type outside a class declaration, or one that uses a different generic type, for example:

```
fun <T> listPet(): List<T>{
    ...
}
```

- A generic type is invariant if it can only accept references of that specific type. Generic types are invariant by default.
- A generic type is covariant if you can use a subtype in place of a supertype. You specify that a type is covariant by prefixing it with `out`.
- A generic type is contravariant if you can use a supertype in place of a subtype. You specify that a type is contravariant by prefixing it with `in`.

11 lambdas and higher-order functions

Treating Code Like Data

Want to write code that's even more powerful and flexible?

If so, then you need **lambdas**. A *lambda*—or *lambda expression*—is a block of code that you can pass around just like an object. Here, you'll discover ***how to define a lambda***, ***assign it to a variable***, and then ***execute its code***. You'll learn about **function types**, and how these can help you write **higher-order functions** that use lambdas for their parameter or return values. And along the way, you'll find out how a little ***syntactic sugar can make your coding life sweeter***.

Introducing lambdas

Throughout this book, you've seen how to use Kotlin's built-in functions, and create your own. But even though we've covered a lot of ground, we're still just scratching the surface. Kotlin has a pile of functions that are *even more powerful* than the ones you've already encountered, but in order to use them, there's one more thing you need to learn: **how to create and use lambda expressions**.

A lambda expression, or **lambda**, is a type of object that holds a block of code. You can assign a lambda to a variable, just as you can any other sort of object, or pass a lambda to a function which can then execute the code it holds. This means that **you can use lambdas to pass specific behavior to a more generalized function**.

Using lambdas in this way is particularly useful when it comes to collections. The *collections* package has a built-in `sortBy` function, for example, that provides a generic implementation for sorting a `MutableList`; you specify *how* the function should sort the collection by passing it a lambda that describes the criteria:

What we're going to do

Before introducing you to the built-in functions that use lambdas, we want you to get to grips with how lambdas work, so in this chapter, you're going to learn how to do the following:

 **Define a lambda.**
You'll discover what a lambda looks like, how to assign it to a variable, what its type is, and how to invoke the code that it contains.

 **Create a higher-order function.**
You'll find out how to create a function that has a lambda parameter, and how to use a lambda as a function's return value.

Let's start by examining what a lambda looks like.

What lambda code looks like

We're going to write a simple lambda that adds 5 to an `Int` parameter value. Here's what the lambda for this looks like:

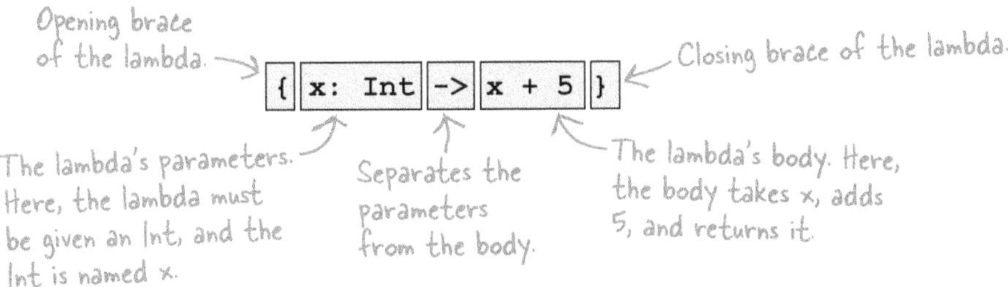

The lambda starts and ends with curly braces `{}`. All lambdas are defined within curly braces, so they can't be omitted.

Inside the curly braces, the lambda defines a single `Int` parameter named `x` using `x: Int`. Lambdas can have single parameters (as is the case here), multiple parameters, or none at all.

The parameter definition is followed by `->`. `->` is used to separate any parameters from the body. It's like saying "Hey, parameters, do this!"

Finally, the `->` is followed by the lambda body—in this case, `x + 5`. This is the code that you want to be executed when the lambda runs. The body can have multiple lines, and the last evaluated expression in the body is used as the lambda's return value.

In the example above, the lambda takes the value of `x`, and returns `x + 5`. It's like writing the function:

```
fun addFive(x: Int) = x + 5
```

except that lambdas have no name, so they're anonymous.

As we mentioned above, lambdas can have multiple parameters. The following lambda, for example, takes two `Int` parameters, `x` and `y`, and returns the result of `x + y`:

```
{ x: Int, y: Int -> x + y }
```

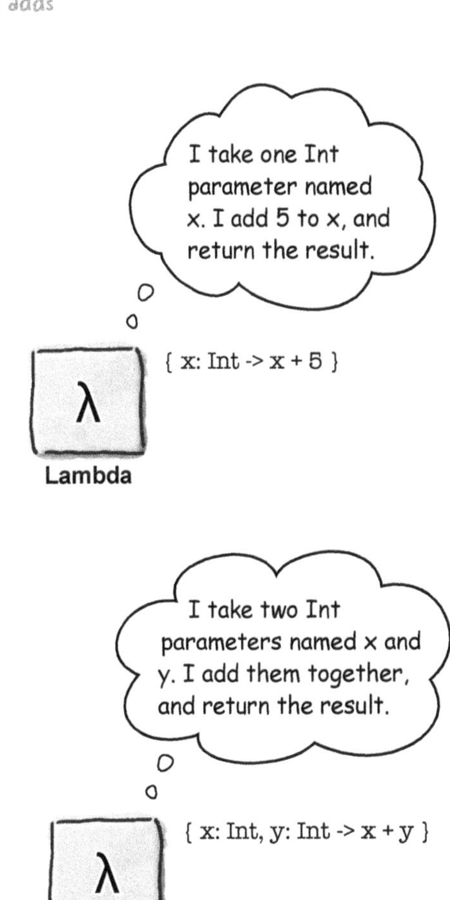

If the lambda has no parameters, you can omit the `->`. The following lambda, for example, has no parameters, and simply returns the `String` "Pow!":

```
{ "Pow!" }
```

This lambda has no parameters, so we can omit the ->.

Now that you know what a lambda looks like, let's see how you assign one to a variable.

You can assign a lambda to a variable

You assign a lambda to a variable in the same way that you assign any other sort of object to a variable: by defining the variable using `val` or `var`, then assigning the lambda to it. The following code, for example, assigns a lambda to a new variable named `addFive`:

```
val addFive = { x: Int -> x + 5 }
```

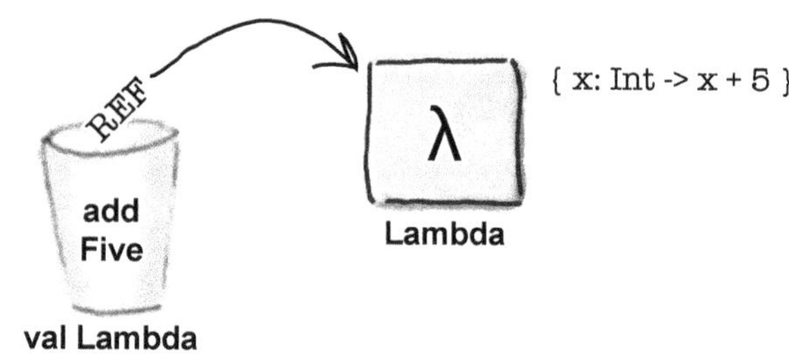

We've defined the `addFive` variable using `val`, so it can't be updated to hold a different lambda. To update the variable, it must be defined using `var` like this:

```
var addFive = { x: Int -> x + 5 }
addFive = { y: Int -> 5 + y }
```

Here, we can assign a new lambda to addFive because we've defined the variable using var.

When you assign a lambda to a variable, you're assigning a block of code to it, not the result of the code being run. To run the code in a lambda, you need to explicitly invoke it.

Execute a lambda's code by invoking it

Don't worry if lambda expressions seem a litle strange at first.

Take your time, and work through this chapter at a gentle pace, and you'll be fine.

You invoke a lambda by calling its `invoke` function, passing in the values for any parameters. The following code, for example, defines a variable named `addInts`, and assigns a lambda to it that adds together two `Int` parameters. The code then invokes the lambda, passing it parameter values of 6 and 7, and assigns the result to a new variable named `result`:

```
val addInts = { x: Int, y: Int -> x + y }
val result = addInts.invoke(6, 7)
```

You can also invoke the lambda using the following shortcut:

```
val result = addInts(6, 7)
```

This does the same thing as:

```
val result = addInts.invoke(6, 7)
```

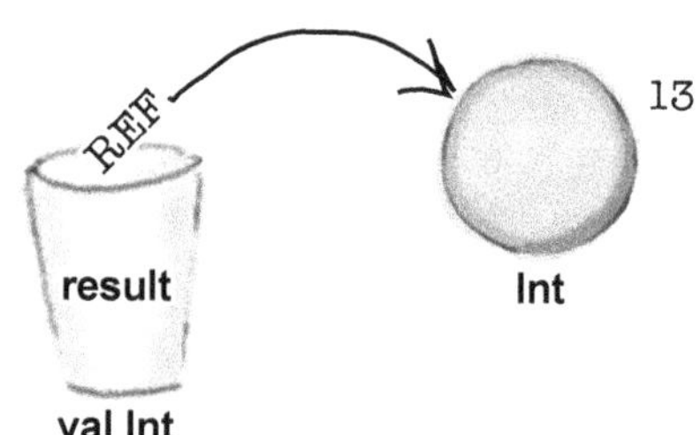

but with slightly less code. It's like saying "run the lambda expression held in variable *addInts* using parameter values of 6 and 7".

Let's go behind the scenes, and see what happens when you invoke a lambda.

What happens when you invoke a lambda

When you run the code:

```
val addInts = { x: Int, y: Int -> x + y }
val result = addInts(6, 7)
```

The following things happen:

val addInts = { x: Int, y: Int -> x + y }

This creates a lambda with a value of `{ x: Int, y: Int -> x + y }`. A reference to the lambda is assigned to a new variable named `addInts`.

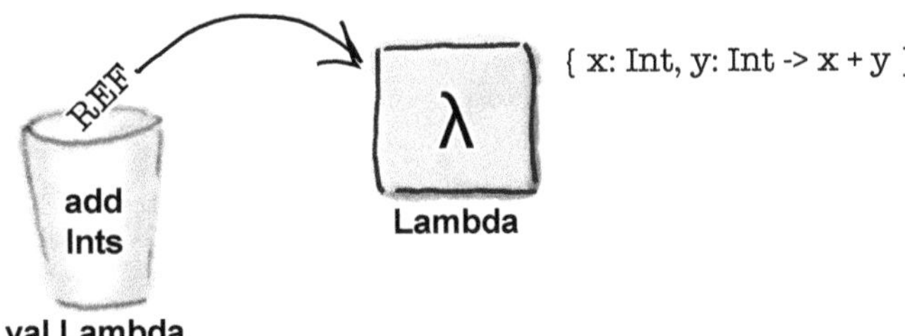

val result = **addInts(6, 7)**

This invokes the lambda referenced by `addInts`, passing it values of 6 and 7. The 6 lands in the lambda's `x` parameter, and the 7 lands in the lambda's `y` parameter.

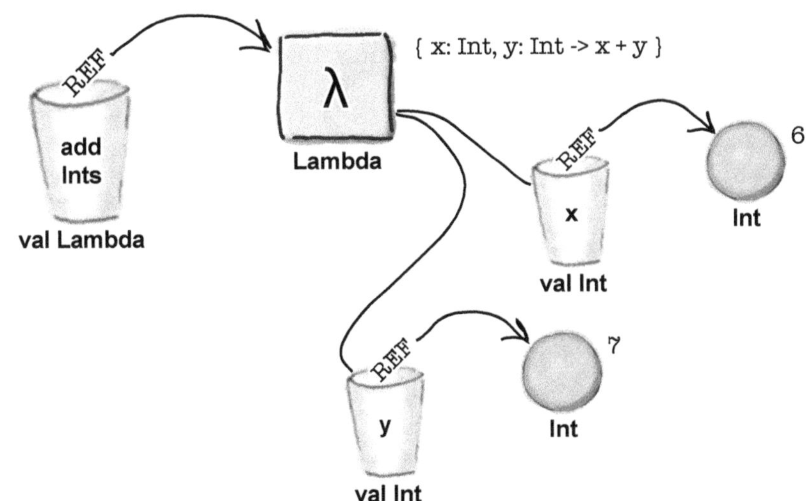

The story continues...

3 val addInts = { x: Int, y: Int -> **x + y** }

The lambda body executes, and calculates `x + y`. The lambda creates an `Int` object with a value of `13`, and returns a reference to it.

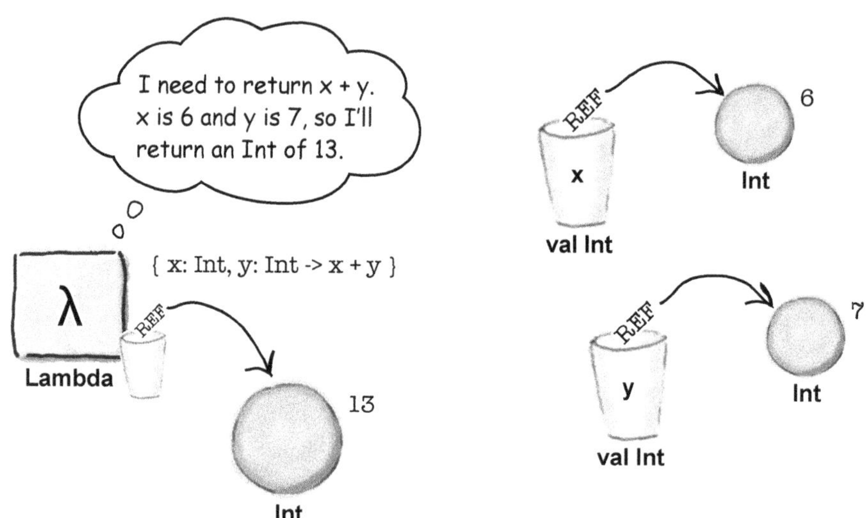

4 **val result =** addInts(6, 7)

The value returned by the lambda is assigned to a new `Int` variable named `result`.

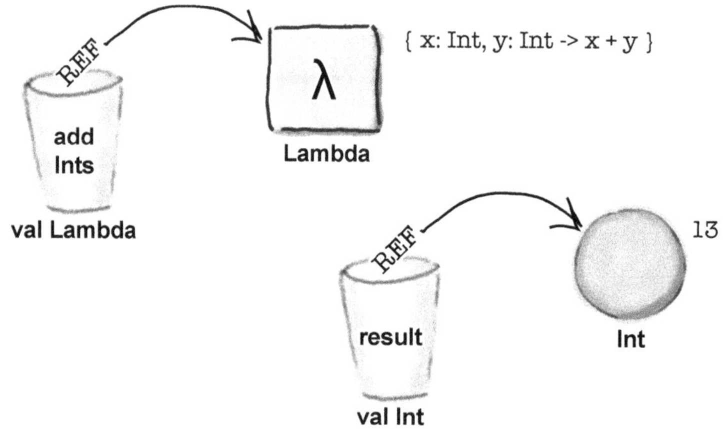

Now that you know what happens when you invoke a lambda, let's look at lambda types.

Lambda expressions have a type

Just like any other sort of object, a lambda has a type. The difference with a lambda's type, however, is that it doesn't specify a class name that the lambda implements. Instead, it specifies the type of the lambda's parameters and return value.

A lambda's type is also known as a <u>function type</u>.

A lambda's type takes the form:

```
(parameters) -> return_type
```

So if you have a lambda with a single `Int` parameter that returns a `String` like this:

```
val msg = { x: Int -> "The value is $x" }
```

its type is:

```
(Int) -> String
```

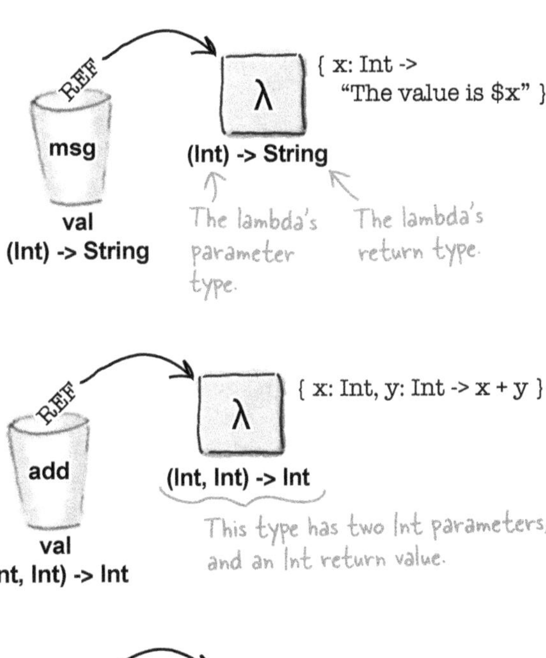

When you assign a lambda to a variable, the compiler infers the variable's type from the lambda that's assigned to it, as in the above example. Just like any other type of object, however, you can explicitly define the variable's type. The following code, for example, defines a variable named `add` that can hold a reference to a lambda which has two `Int` parameters, and returns an `Int`:

```
val add: (Int, Int) -> Int
add = { x: Int, y: Int -> x + y }
```

Similarly, the following code defines a variable named `greeting` that can hold a reference to a lambda with no parameters, and a `String` return value:

```
val greeting: () -> String
greeting = { "Hello!" }
```

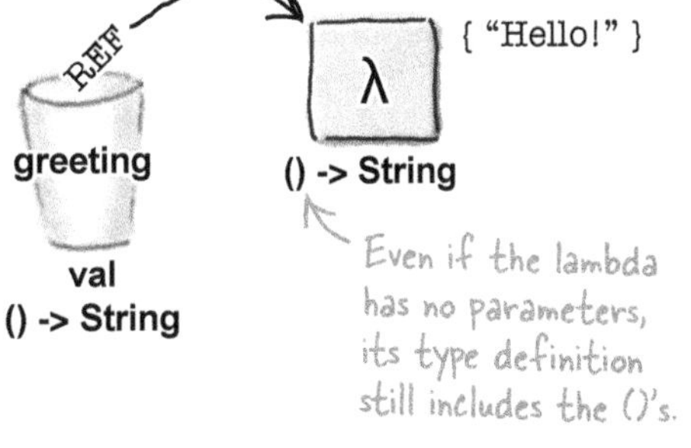

Just like with any other type of variable declaration, you can explicitly declare a variable's type and assign a value to it in a single line of code. This means that you can rewrite the above code as:

```
val greeting: () -> String = { "Hello!" }
```

Declare the variable. Specify its type. Assign a value to it.

The compiler can infer lambda parameter types

When you explicitly declare a variable's type, you can leave out any type declarations from the lambda that the compiler can infer.

Suppose that you have the following code, which assigns a lambda to a variable named `addFive`:

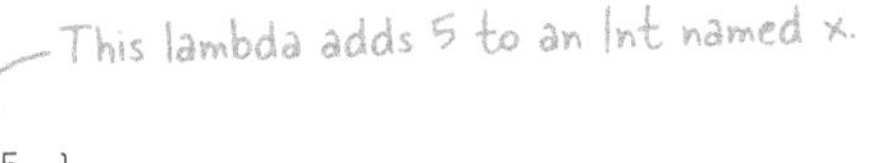


```
val addFive: (Int) -> Int = { x: Int -> x + 5 }
```

The compiler already knows from `addFive`'s type definition that any lambda that's assigned to the variable must have an `Int` parameter. This means that you can omit the `Int` type declaration from the lambda parameter definition because the compiler can infer its type:

```
val addFive: (Int) -> Int = { x -> x + 5 }
```

The compiler knows that x needs to be an Int, so we can omit its type.

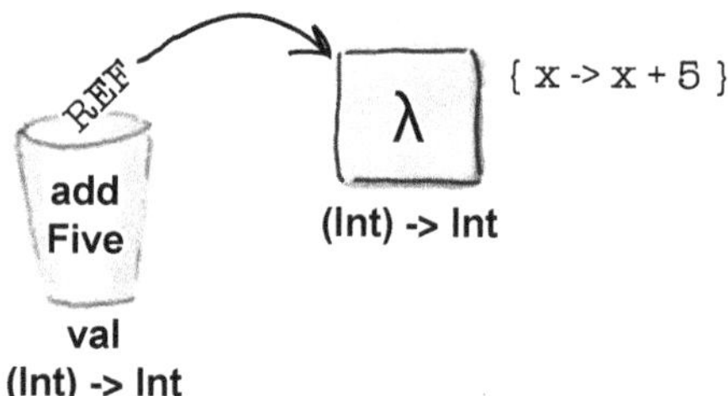

You can replace a single parameter with it

If you have a lambda which has a single parameter, and the compiler can infer its type, you can omit the parameter, and refer to it in the lambda body using the keyword `it`.

To see how this works, suppose, as above, that you have a lambda that's assigned to a variable using the code:

```
val addFive: (Int) -> Int = { x -> x + 5 }
```

As the lambda has a single parameter, `x`, and the compiler can infer that `x` is an `Int`, we can omit the `x` parameter from the lambda, and replace it with `it` in the lambda body like this:

```
val addFive: (Int) -> Int = { it + 5 }
```

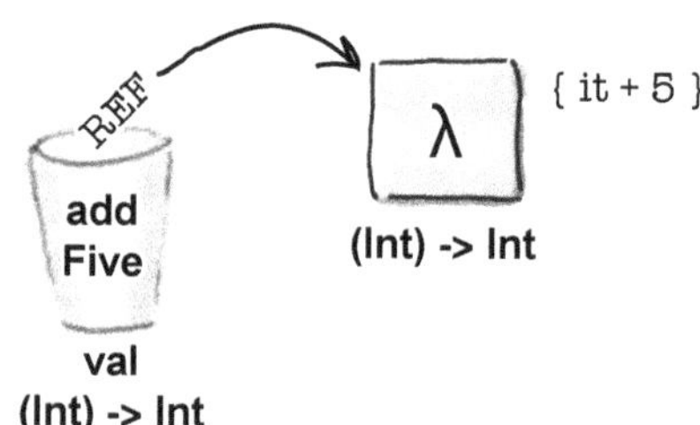

In the above code, `{ it + 5 }` is equivalent to `{ x -> x + 5 }`, but it's much more concise.

Note that you can only use the `it` syntax in situations where the compiler can infer the type of the parameter. The following code, for example, won't compile because the compiler can't tell what type `it` should be:

```
val addFive = { it + 5 }
```

This won't compile because the compiler can't infer its type.

Use the right lambda for the variable's type

As you already know, the compiler deeply cares about a variable's type. This applies to lambda types, as well as plain object types, which means that the compiler will only let you assign a lambda to a variable that is compatible with that variable's type.

Suppose you have a variable named `calculation` that can hold references to lambdas with two `Int` parameters and an `Int` return value like this:

```
val calculation: (Int, Int) -> Int
```

If you try to assign a lambda to `calculation` whose type doesn't match that of the variable, the compiler will get upset. The following code, for example, won't compile because the lambda explicitly uses `Doubles`:

```
calculation = { x: Double, y: Double -> x + y }
```

This won't compile, because the calculation variable will only accept a lambda with two Int parameters and an Int return type.

Use Unit to say a lambda has no return value

If you want to specify that a lambda has no return value, you can do so by declaring that its return type is `Unit`. The following lambda, for example, has no return value, and prints the text "Hi!" when it is invoked:

```
val myLambda: () -> Unit = { println("Hi!") }
```

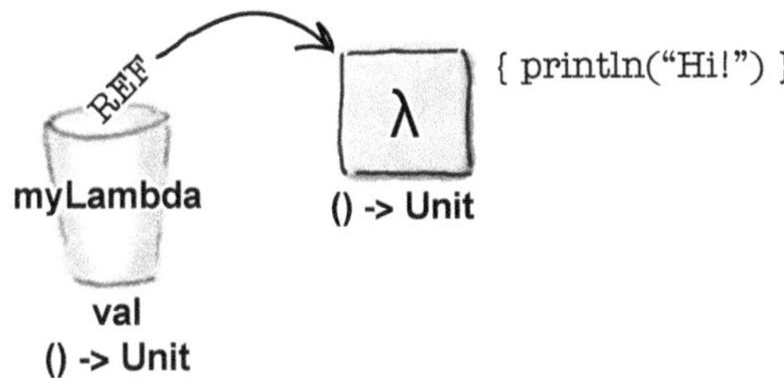

You can also use **`Unit`** to explicitly specify that you don't want to access the result of a lambda's calculation. The following code, for example, will compile, but you won't be able to access the result of `x + y`:

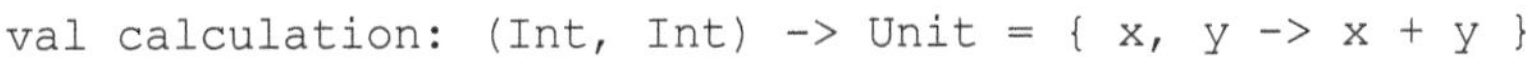

```
val calculation: (Int, Int) -> Unit = { x, y -> x + y }
```

there are no Dumb Questions

Q: Does the code

```
val x = { "Pow!" }
```

assign the text "Pow!" to x?

A: No. The above assigns a lambda to `x`, and not a `String`. The lambda, however, returns "Pow!" when it is executed.

Q: Can I assign a lambda to a variable of type `Any`?

A: Yes. An `Any` variable can accept a reference to any type of object, including lambdas.

Q: That `it` syntax looks familiar. Have I seen it before?

A: Yes! Back in Chapter 8 we used `it` with `let`. We didn't tell you at the time because we wanted you to focus on null values, but `let` is actually a function that accepts a lambda as a parameter.

Create the Lambdas project

Now that you've seen how to create lambdas, let's add some to a new application.

Create a new Kotlin project that targets the JVM, and name the project "Lambdas". Then create a new Kotlin file named *Lambdas.kt* by highlighting the *src* folder, clicking on the File menu and choosing New → Kotlin File/Class. When prompted, name the file "Lambdas", and choose File from the Kind option.

Next, update your version of *Lambdas.kt* to match ours below:

```
fun main(args: Array<String>) {
    var addFive = { x: Int -> x + 5 }
    println("Pass 6 to addFive: ${addFive(6)}")

    val addInts = { x: Int, y: Int -> x + y }
    val result = addInts.invoke(6, 7)
    println("Pass 6, 7 to addInts: $result")

    val intLambda: (Int, Int) -> Int = { x, y -> x * y }
    println("Pass 10, 11 to intLambda: ${intLambda(10, 11)}")

    val addSeven: (Int) -> Int = { it + 7 }
    println("Pass 12 to addSeven: ${addSeven(12)}")

    val myLambda: () -> Unit = { println("Hi!") }
    myLambda()
}
```

Lambdas
src
Lambdas.kt

Test drive

When we run the code, the following text gets printed in the IDE's output window:

```
Pass 6 to addFive: 11
Pass 6, 7 to addInts: 13
Pass 10, 11 to intLambda: 110
Pass 12 to addSeven: 19
Hi!
```

Mixed Messages

A short Kotlin program is listed below. One block of the program is missing. Your challenge is to match the candidate block of code (on the left), with the output that you'd see if the block were inserted. Not all the lines of output will be used, and some lines of output may be used more than once. Draw lines connecting the candidate blocks of code with their matching output.

```
fun main(args: Array<String>) {
    val x = 20
    val y = 2.3
    [                                  ]
}
```

The candidate code goes here.

Match each candidate with one of the possible outputs.

Candidates:

```
val lam1 = { x: Int -> x }
println(lam1(x + 6))
```

```
val lam2: (Double) -> Double
lam2 = { (it * 2) + 5}
println(lam2(y))
```

```
val lam3: (Double, Double) -> Unit
lam3 = { x, y -> println(x + y) }
lam3.invoke(y, y)
```

```
var lam4 = { y: Int -> (y/2).toDouble() }
print(lam4(x))
lam4 = { it + 6.3 }
print(lam4(7))
```

Possible output:

```
22.3
```

```
26
```

```
9.6
```

```
8.3
```

```
1.1513.3
```

```
9.3
```

```
10.013.3
```

```
4.6
```

Mixed Messages Solution

A short Kotlin program is listed below. One block of the program is missing. Your challenge is to match the candidate block of code (on the left), with the output that you'd see if the block were inserted. Not all the lines of output will be used, and some lines of output may be used more than once. Draw lines connecting the candidate blocks of code with their matching output.

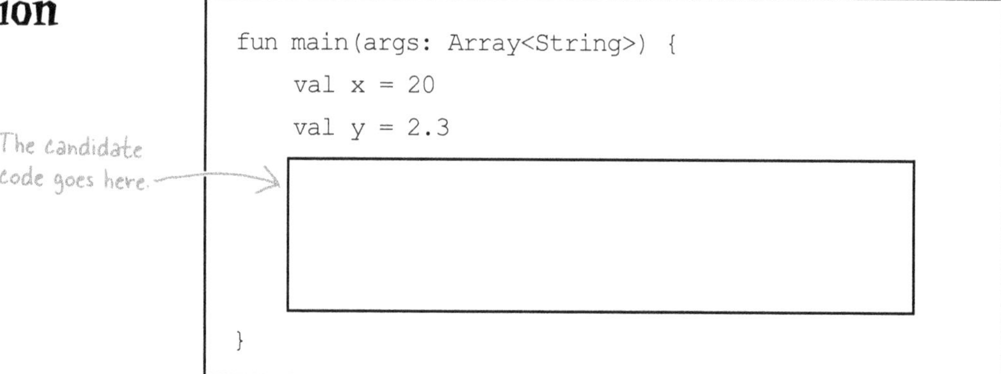

Candidates:

```
val lam1 = { x: Int -> x }
println(lam1(x + 6))
```

```
val lam2: (Double) -> Double
lam2 = { (it * 2) + 5}
println(lam2(y))
```

```
val lam3: (Double, Double) -> Unit
lam3 = { x, y -> println(x + y) }
lam3.invoke(y, y)
```

```
var lam4 = { y: Int -> (y/2).toDouble() }
print(lam4(x))
lam4 = { it + 6.3 }
print(lam4(7))
```

Possible output:

```
22.3
```

```
26
```

```
9.6
```

```
8.3
```

```
1.1513.3
```

```
9.3
```

```
10.013.3
```

```
4.6
```

Here is a list of variable definitions, and a list of lambdas. Which lambdas can be assigned to which variables? Draw lines connecting the lambdas with their matching variables.

Variable definitions:

```
var lambda1: (Double) -> Int

var lambda2: (Int) -> Double

var lambda3: (Int) -> Int

var lambda4: (Double) -> Unit

var lambda5
```

Lambdas:

```
{ it + 7.1 }

{ (it * 3) - 4 }

{ x: Int -> x + 56 }

{ println("Hello!") }

{ x: Double -> x + 75 }
```

Here is a list of variable definitions, and a list of lambdas. Which lambdas can be assigned to which variables? Draw lines connecting the lambdas with their matching variables.

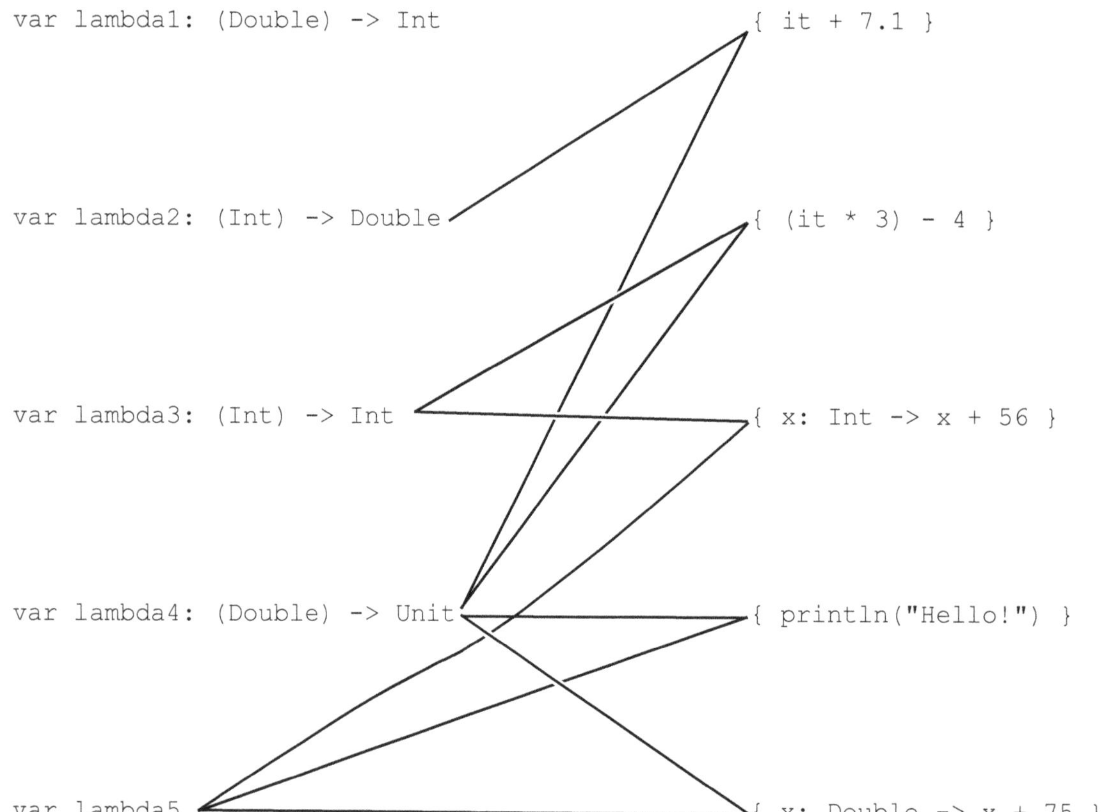

You can pass a lambda to a function

As well as assigning a lambda to a variable, you can also use one or more as function parameters. Doing so allows you to **pass specific behavior to a more generalized function**.

To see how this works, we're going to write a function named `convert` that converts a `Double` using some formula that's passed to it via a lambda, prints the result, and returns it. This will allow us to, say, convert a temperature from Centigrade to Fahrenheit, or convert a weight from kilograms to pounds, depending on the formula that we pass to it in the lambda argument.

We'll start by defining the function parameters.

A function that uses a lambda as a parameter or return value is known as a higher-order function.

Add a lambda parameter to a function by specifying its name and type

We need to tell the `convert` function two things in order for it to convert one `Double` to another: the `Double` we want to convert, and the lambda that specifies how it should be converted. We'll therefore use two parameters for the `convert` function: a `Double` and a lambda.

You define a lambda parameter in the same way that you define any other sort of function parameter: by specifying the parameter's type, and giving it a name. We'll name our lambda `converter`, and as we want the lambda to convert a `Double` to a `Double`, its type needs to be `(Double) -> Double` (a lambda that accepts a `Double` parameter, and returns a `Double`).

The function definition (excluding the function body) is below. As you can see, it specifies two parameters—a `Double` named `x`, and a lambda named `converter`—and returns a `Double`:

This is the x parameter, a Double.

```
fun convert(x: Double,
            converter: (Double) -> Double) : Double {
    //Code to convert the Double
}
```

This is a lambda parameter named converter. Its type is (Double) -> Double.

The function returns a Double.

Next, we'll write the code for the function body.

Invoke the lambda in the function body

We want the convert function to convert the value of the x parameter using the formula that's passed to it via the converter parameter (a lambda). We'll therefore invoke the converter lambda in the function body, passing it the value of x, and then print and return the result.

Here's the full code for the convert function:

```
fun convert(x: Double,
            converter: (Double) -> Double) : Double {
    val result = converter(x)
    println("$x is converted to $result")
    return result
}
```

Invokes the lambda named converter and assigns its return value to result.

Print the result.

Return the result.

Now that we've written the function, let's try calling it.

Call the function by passing it parameter values

You call a function with a lambda parameter in the same way that you call any other sort of function: by passing it a value for each argument—in this case, a Double and a lambda.

Let's use the convert function to convert 20.0 degrees Centigrade to Fahrenheit. To do this, we'll pass values of 20.0 and { c: Double -> c * 1.8 + 32 } to the function:

```
convert(20.0, { c: Double -> c * 1.8 + 32 })
```

This is the value we want to convert...

...and this is the lambda that we'll use to convert it. Note that we could use "it" in place of c because the lambda uses a single parameter whose type the compiler can infer.

When the above code runs, it returns a value of 68.0 (the value of 20.0 degrees Centigrade when it's converted to Fahrenheit).

Let's go behind the scenes, and break down what happens when the code runs.

What happens when you call the function

The following things happen when you call the `convert` function using the code:

```
val fahrenheit = convert(20.0, { c: Double -> c * 1.8 + 32 })
```

```
val fahrenheit = convert(20.0, { c: Double -> c * 1.8 + 32 })
```

This creates a `Double` object with a value of `20.0`, and a lambda with a value of `{ c: Double -> c * 1.8 + 32 }`.

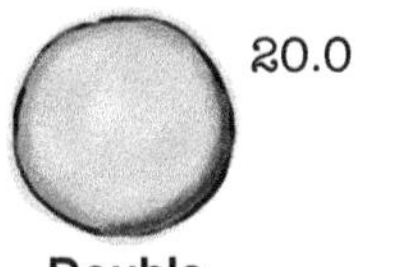

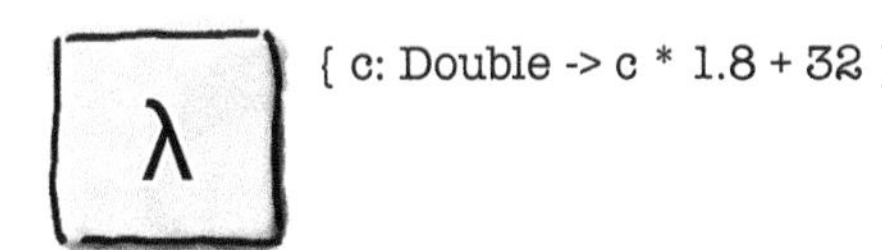

2

```
fun convert(x: Double, converter: (Double) -> Double) : Double {
    val result = converter(x)
    println("$x is converted to $result")
    return result
}
```

The code passes references to the objects it's created to the `convert` function. The `Double` lands in the `convert` function's `x` parameter, and the lambda lands in its `converter` parameter. The code then invokes the `converter` lambda, using `x` as the lambda's parameter.

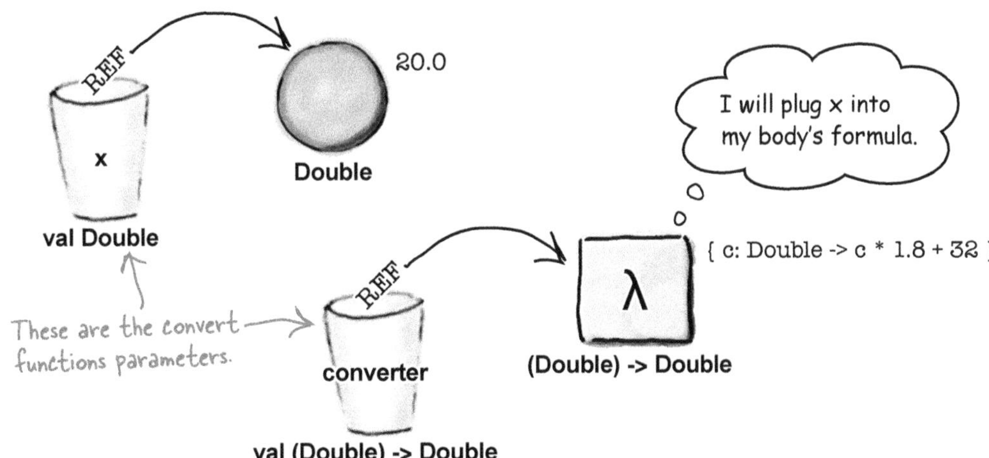

The story continues...

```
fun convert(x: Double, converter: (Double) -> Double) : Double {
    val result = converter(x)
    println("$x is converted to $result")
    return result
}
```

The lambda's body executes, and its result (a `Double` with a value of `68.0`) is assigned to a new variable named `result`. The function prints the values of the `x` and `result` variables, and returns a reference to the `result` object.

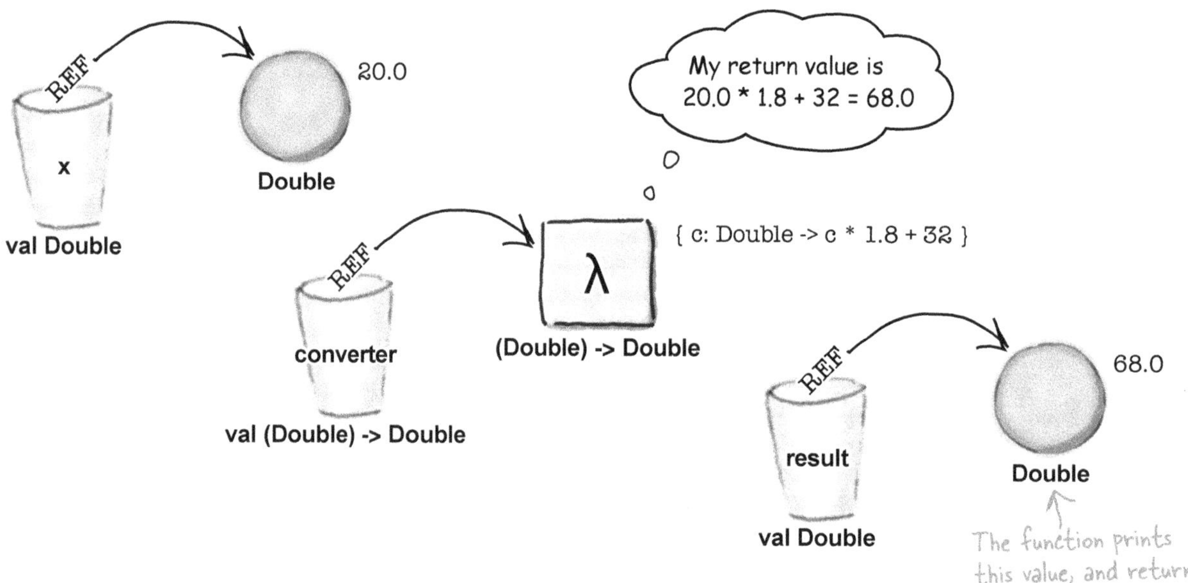

```
val fahrenheit = convert(20.0, { c: Double -> c * 1.8 + 32 })
```

A new `fahrenheit` variable gets created. It's assigned a reference to the object returned by the `convert` function.

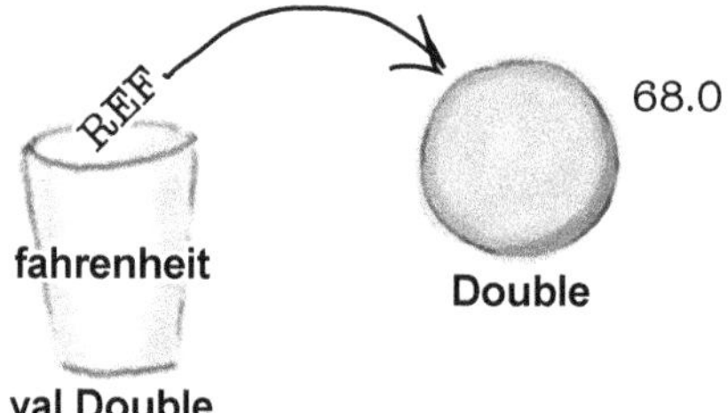

Now that you've seen what happens when you call a function with a lambda parameter, let's look at some shortcuts you can take when you call this kind of function.

You can move the lambda OUTSIDE the ()'s...

So far, you've seen how to call a function with a lambda parameter by passing arguments to the function inside the function's parentheses. We called the `convert` function, for example, using the following code:

```
convert(20.0, { c: Double -> c * 1.8 + 32 })
```

If the final parameter of a function you want to call is a lambda, as is the case with our `convert` function, you can move the lambda argument *outside* the function call's parentheses. The following code, for example, does the same thing as the code above, but we've moved the lambda outside the parentheses:

```
convert(20.0) { c: Double -> c * 1.8 + 32 }
```

The lambda is no longer enclosed by the function's closing parenthesis.

Here's the function's closing parenthesis.

...or remove the ()'s entirely

If you have a function that has just one parameter, and that parameter is a lambda, you can omit the parentheses entirely when you call the function.

To see how this works, suppose you have the following function named `convertFive` that converts the `Int` 5 to a `Double` using a conversion formula that's passed to it via a lambda. Here's the code for the function:

```
fun convertFive(converter: (Int) -> Double) : Double {
    val result = converter(5)
    println("5 is converted to $result")
    return result
}
```

As the `convertFive` function has a single parameter, a lambda, you can call the function like this:

```
convertFive { it * 1.8 + 32 }
```

Notice there are no parentheses in this function call. This is possible because the function has only one parameter, which is a lambda.

This does the same thing as:

```
convertFive() { it * 1.8 + 32 }
```

but we've removed the parentheses.

Now that you've learned how to write a function that uses a lambda parameter, let's update our project code.

Update the Lambdas project

We'll add the `convert` and `convertFive` functions to our Lambdas project. Update your version of *Lambdas.kt* in the project so that it matches ours below (our changes are in bold):

```
fun convert(x: Double,
            converter: (Double) -> Double) : Double {
    val result = converter(x)
    println("$x is converted to $result")
    return result
}

fun convertFive(converter: (Int) -> Double) : Double {
    val result = converter(5)
    println("5 is converted to $result")
    return result
}

fun main(args: Array<String>) {
    val addFive = { x: Int -> x + 5 }
    println("Pass 6 to addFive: ${addFive(6)}")

    val addInts = { x: Int, y: Int -> x + y }
    val result = addInts.invoke(6, 7)
    println("Pass 6, 7 to addInts: $result")

    val intLambda: (Int, Int) -> Int = { x, y -> x * y }
    println("Pass 10, 11 to intLambda: ${intLambda(10, 11)}")

    val addSeven: (Int) -> Int = { it + 7 }
    println("Pass 12 to addSeven: ${addSeven(12)}")

    val myLambda: () -> Unit = { println("Hi!") }
    myLambda()

    convert(20.0) { it * 1.8 + 32 }
    convertFive { it * 1.8 + 32 }
}
```

Add these two functions.

We no longer need these lines, so you can delete them.

Add these lines. Note we can use "it" because each lambda uses a single parameter whose type the compiler can infer.

Lambdas
src
Lambdas.kt

Let's take the code for a test drive.

Test drive

When we run the code, the following text gets printed in the IDE's output window:

```
20.0 is converted to 68.0
5 is converted to 41.0
```

Before we look at what else you can do with lambdas, have a go at the next exercise.

Lambda Formatting Up Close

As we said earlier in the chapter, a lambda body can include multiple lines of code. The following lambda, for example, prints the value of its parameter, and then uses it in a calculation:

```
{ c: Double -> println(c)
               c * 1.8 + 32 }
```

When you have a lambda whose body has multiple lines, the last evaluated expression is used as the lambda's return value. So in the above example, the return value is defined using the line:

```
c * 1.8 + 32
```

A lambda can also be formatted so that it looks like a code block, with its surrounding curly braces on different lines to the lambda's contents. The following code uses this technique to pass the lambda `{ it * 1.8 + 32 }` to the `convertFive` function:

```
convertFive {
    it * 1.8 + 32
}
```

there are no Dumb Questions

Q: It looks like there are quite a few shortcuts you can take when you use lambdas. Do I really need to know about them all?

A: It's useful to know about these shortcuts because once you get used to them, they can make your code more concise and readable. Alternative syntax that's designed to make your code easier to read is sometimes referred to as syntactic sugar, as it can make the language "sweeter" for humans. But even if you don't want to use the shortcuts we've discussed in your own code, they're still worth knowing about because you may encounter them in third-party code.

Q: Why are lambdas called lambdas?

A: It's because they come from an area of mathematics and computer science called Lambda Calculus, where small, anonymous functions are represented by the Greek letter λ (a lambda).

Q: Why aren't lambdas called functions?

A: A lambda is a type of function, but in most languages, functions always have names. As you've already seen, a lambda doesn't need to have a name.

Pool Puzzle

Your **job** is to take code snippets from the pool and place them into the blank lines in the code. You may **not** use the same code snippet more than once, and you won't need to use all the code snippets. Your **goal** is to create a function named `unless` that's called by the `main` function below. The `unless` function should have two parameters, a `Boolean` named `condition`, and a lambda named `code`. The function should invoke the `code` lambda when `condition` is `false`.

```
fun unless(..................., code:.............) {
    if (.............) {
        .........
    }
}

fun main(args: Array<String>) {
    val options = arrayOf("Red", "Amber", "Green")
    var crossWalk = options[(Math.random() * options.size).toInt()]
    if (crossWalk == "Green") {
        println("Walk!")
    }
    unless (crossWalk == "Green") { ← Print "Stop!" unless crossWalk == "Green".
        println("Stop!")
    }
}
```

Note: each thing from the pool can only be used once!

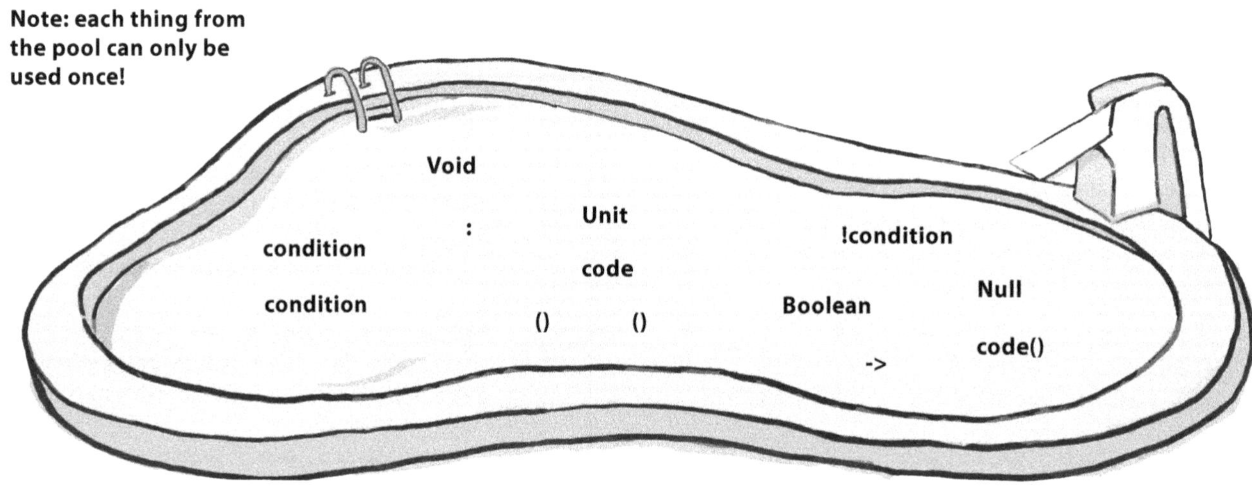

Answers on page 360.

A function can return a lambda

As well as using a lambda as a parameter, a function can also return one by specifying the lambda's type as its return type. The following code, for example, defines a function named `getConversionLambda` that returns a lambda of type `(Double) -> Double`. The exact lambda that's returned by the function depends on the value of the `String` that's passed to it.

The function has one parameter, a String.

It returns a lambda whose type is (Double) -> Double.

```
fun getConversionLambda(str: String): (Double) -> Double {
    if (str == "CentigradeToFahrenheit") {
        return { it * 1.8 + 32 }
    } else if (str == "KgsToPounds") {
        return { it * 2.204623 }
    } else if (str == "PoundsToUSTons") {
        return { it / 2000.0 }
    } else {
        return { it }
    }
}
```

λ

(Double) -> Double

The function returns one of these lambdas, depending on the value of the String that's passed to it.

You can invoke the lambda returned by a function, or use it as an argument for another function. The following code, for example, invokes `getConversionLambda`'s return value to get the value of 2.5 kilograms in pounds, and assigns it to a variable named pounds:

```
val pounds = getConversionLambda("KgsToPounds")(2.5)
```

This calls the getConversionLambda function...

...and this invokes the lambda returned by the function.

And the following example uses `getConversionLambda` to get a lambda that converts a temperature from Centigrade to Fahrenheit, and then passes it to the `convert` function:

Here, we're passing getConversionLambda's return value to the convert function.

```
convert(20.0, getConversionLambda("CentigradeToFahrenheit"))
```

You can even define a function that both receives and returns a lambda. We'll look at this next.

Write a function that receives AND returns lambdas

We're going to create a function named `combine` that takes two lambda parameters, combines them, and returns the result (another lambda). If the function is given lambdas for converting a value from kilograms to pounds, and converting a value from pounds to tons, it will return a lambda that converts a value from kilograms to US tons. We'll then be able to use this lambda elsewhere in our code.

λ Kgs to Pounds

λ Pounds to US Tons

combine()

λ Kgs to US Tons

We'll create a function that combines two lambdas into a single lambda.

We'll start by defining the function's parameters and return type.

Define the parameters and return type

All of the lambdas used by the `combine` function need to convert one `Double` value to another `Double` value, so each one has a type of `(Double) -> Double`. Our function definition therefore needs to look like this:

```
fun combine(lambda1: (Double) -> Double,
            lambda2: (Double) -> Double): (Double) -> Double {
    //Code to combine the two lambdas
}
```

The combine function has two lambda parameters of type (Double) -> Double.

The function also returns a lambda of this type.

Next, let's look at the function body.

Define the function body

The function body needs to return a lambda, and this lambda must have the following characteristics:

 It must take one parameter, a `Double`. We'll name this parameter `x`.

 The lambda's body should invoke `lambda1`, passing it the value of `x`. The result of this invocation should then be passed to `lambda2`.

We can achieve this using the following code:

```
fun combine(lambda1: (Double) -> Double,
            lambda2: (Double) -> Double): (Double) -> Double {
    return { x: Double -> lambda2(lambda1(x)) }
}
```

The lambda returned by combine takes a Double parameter named x.

x is passed to lambda1, which accepts and returns a Double. The result is then passed to lambda2, which also accepts and returns a Double.

Let's write some code that uses the function.

How to use the combine function

The combine function we've just created takes two lambdas, and combines them to form a third. This means that if we pass the function one lambda to convert a value from kilograms to pounds, and another to convert a value from pounds to US tons, the function will return a lambda that converts a value from kilograms to US tons.

Here's the code to do this:

```
//Define two conversion lambdas
val kgsToPounds = { x: Double -> x * 2.204623 }
val poundsToUSTons = { x: Double -> x / 2000.0 }

//Combine the two lambdas to create a new one
val kgsToUSTons = combine(kgsToPounds, poundsToUSTons)

//Invoke the kgsToUSTons lambda
val usTons = kgsToUSTons(1000.0)    //1.1023115
```

These lambdas convert a Double from kilograms to pounds, and from pounds to US Tons.

Pass the lambdas to the combine function. This produces a lambda that converts a Double from kilograms to US Tons.

Invoke the resulting lambda by passing it a value of 1000.0. This returns 1.1023115.

Let's go behind the scenes, and see what happens when the code runs.

What happens when the code runs

1. **val kgsToPounds = { x: Double -> x * 2.204623 }**
val poundsToUSTons = { x: Double -> x / 2000.0 }
val kgsToUSTons = **combine(kgsToPounds, poundsToUSTons)**

This creates two variables, and assigns a lambda to each one. A reference to each lambda is then passed to the combine function.

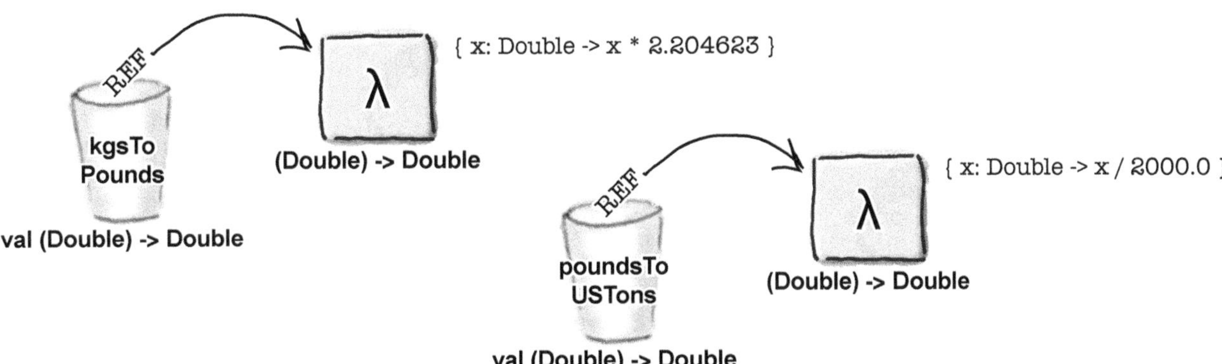

The story continues...

2

```
fun combine(lambda1: (Double) -> Double,
            lambda2: (Double) -> Double): (Double) -> Double {
    return { x: Double -> lambda2(lambda1(x)) }
}
```

The kgsToPounds lambda lands in the combine function's lambda1 parameter, and the poundsToUSTons lambda lands in its lambda2 parameter.

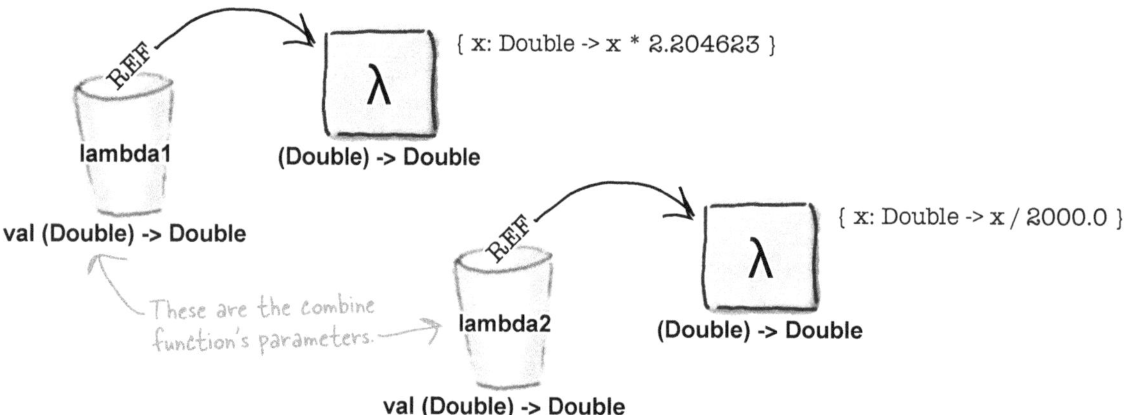

3

```
fun combine(lambda1: (Double) -> Double,
            lambda2: (Double) -> Double): (Double) -> Double {
    return { x: Double -> lambda2(lambda1(x)) }
}
```

lambda1(x) runs. As lambda1's body is x * 2.204623, where x is a Double, this creates a Double object with a value of x * 2.204623.

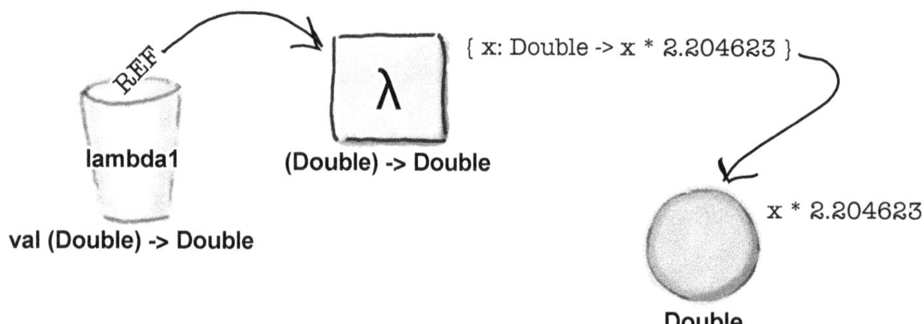

The story continues...

4

```
fun combine(lambda1: (Double) -> Double,
            lambda2: (Double) -> Double): (Double) -> Double {
    return { x: Double -> lambda2(lambda1(x)) }
}
```

The `Double` object with a value of `x * 2.204623` is then passed to `lambda2`. As `lambda2`'s body is `x / 2000.0`, this means that `x * 2.204623` is substituted for `x`. This creates a `Double` with a value of `(x * 2.204623) / 2000.0`, or `x * 0.0011023115`.

REF
lambda2
val (Double) -> Double
λ
(Double) -> Double
{ x: Double -> x / 2000.0 }
x * 0.0011023115
Double

5

```
fun combine(lambda1: (Double) -> Double,
            lambda2: (Double) -> Double): (Double) -> Double {
    return { x: Double -> lambda2(lambda1(x)) }
}
```

This creates the lambda `{ x: Double -> x * 0.0011023115 }`, and a reference to this lambda is returned by the function.

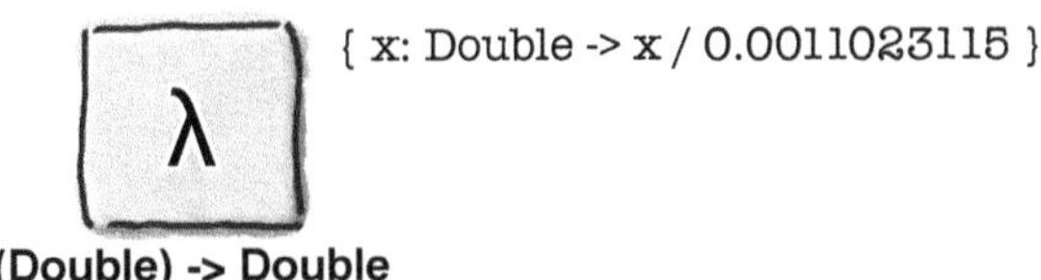

The story continues...

val kgsToUSTons = combine(kgsToPounds, poundsToUSTons)
val usTons = kgsToUSTons(1000.0)

The lambda returned by the `combine` function is assigned to a variable named `kgsToUSTons`. It's invoked using an argument of 1000.0, which returns a value of 1.1023115. This is assigned to a new variable named `usTons`.

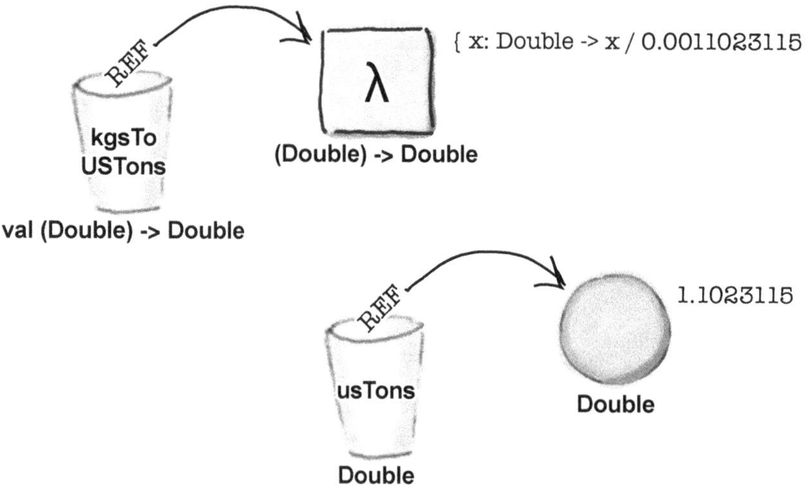

You can make lambda code more readable

We're nearly at the end of the chapter, but before we go, there's one more thing we want to show you: how to make your lambda code more readable.

When you use function types (the kind of type that's used to define a lambda), it can make your code cumbersome and less readable. The `combine` function, for instance, contains multiple references to the function type `(Double) -> Double`:

```
fun combine(lambda1: (Double) -> Double,
            lambda2: (Double) -> Double): (Double) -> Double {
    return { x: Double -> lambda2(lambda1(x)) }
}
```

The combine function has three instances of the function type (Double) -> Double.

You can, however, make your code more readable by replacing the function type with a **type alias**. Let's see what this is, and how to use one.

Use typealias to provide a different name for an existing type

A **type alias** lets you provide an alternative name for an existing type, which you can then use in your code. This means that if your code uses a function type such as `(Double) -> Double`, you can define a type alias that's used in its place, making your code more readable.

You define a type alias using the **`typealias`** keyword. Here's how, for example, you use it to define a type alias named `DoubleConversion` that we can use in place of the function type `(Double) -> Double`:

```
typealias DoubleConversion = (Double) -> Double
```

This type alias means that we can use DoubleConversion in place of (Double) -> Double.

(Double) -> Double

DoubleConversion

This means that our `convert` and `combine` functions can now become:

```
fun convert(x: Double,
            converter: DoubleConversion) : Double {
    val result = converter(x)
    println("$x is converted to $result")
    return result
}

fun combine(lambda1: DoubleConversion,
            lambda2: DoubleConversion): DoubleConversion {
    return { x: Double -> lambda2(lambda1(x)) }
}
```

We can use the DoubleConversion type alias in the convert and combine functions to make the code more readable.

Each time the compiler sees the type `DoubleConversion`, it knows that it's a placeholder for the type `(Double) -> Double`. The `convert` and `combine` functions above do the same things as before, but the code is more readable.

You can use `typealias` to provide an alternative name for any type, not just function types. You can, say, use:

```
typealias DuckArray = Array<Duck>
```

so that you can refer to the type `DuckArray` in place of `Array<Duck>`.

Let's update the code in our project.

Update the Lambdas project

We'll add the `DoubleConversion` type alias, and the `getConversionLambda` and `combine` functions, to our Lambdas project, along with some code that uses them. Update your version of *Lambdas.kt* in the project so that it matches ours below (our changes are in bold):

Add the typealias.

```
typealias DoubleConversion = (Double) -> Double
```

Replace the function type with the type alias.

```
fun convert(x: Double,
            converter: (Double) -> Double DoubleConversion) : Double {
    val result = converter(x)
    println("$x is converted to $result")
    return result
}
```

Remove this function as we no longer need it.

```
fun convertFive(converter: (Int) -> Double) : Double {
    val result = converter(5)
    println("5 is converted to $result")
    return result
}
```

Add the getConversionLambda function.

```
fun getConversionLambda(str: String): DoubleConversion {
    if (str == "CentigradeToFahrenheit") {
        return { it * 1.8 + 32 }
    } else if (str == "KgsToPounds") {
        return { it * 2.204623 }
    } else if (str == "PoundsToUSTons") {
        return { it / 2000.0 }
    } else {
        return { it }
    }
}
```

Lambdas
src
Lambdas.kt

Add the combine function.

```
fun combine(lambda1: DoubleConversion,
            lambda2: DoubleConversion): DoubleConversion {
    return { x: Double -> lambda2(lambda1(x)) }
}
```

The code continues on the next page.

The code continued...

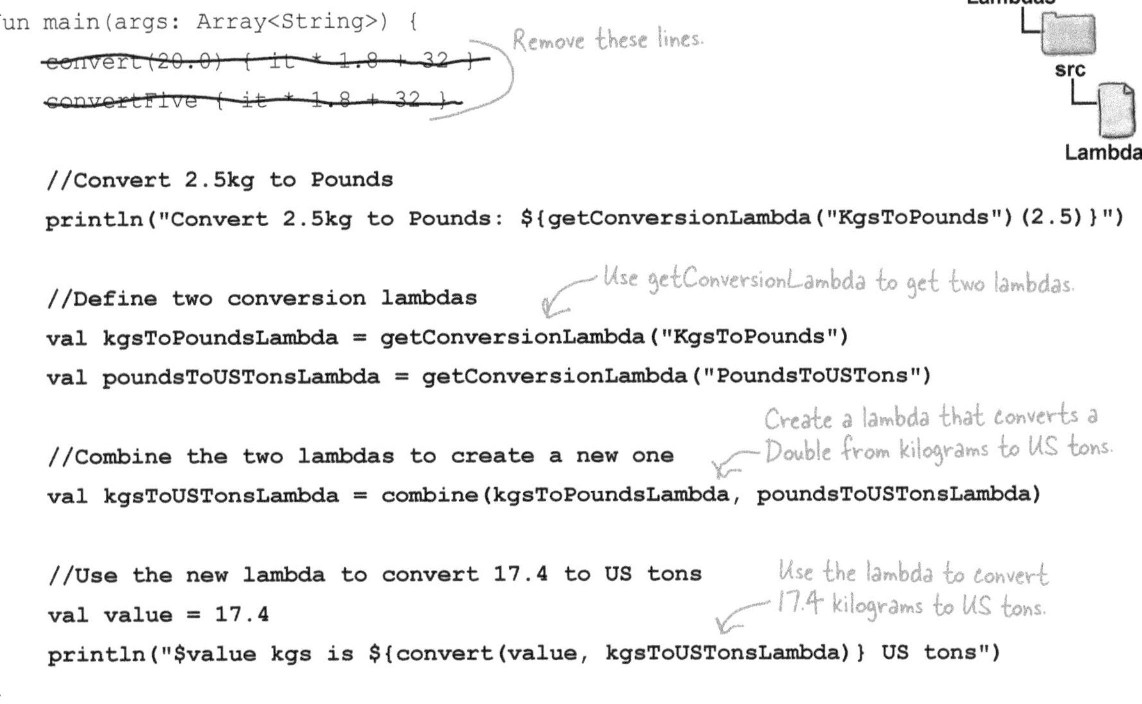

```
fun main(args: Array<String>) {
    convert(20.0) { it * 1.8 + 32 }
    convertFive { it * 1.8 + 32 }

    //Convert 2.5kg to Pounds
    println("Convert 2.5kg to Pounds: ${getConversionLambda("KgsToPounds")(2.5)}")

    //Define two conversion lambdas
    val kgsToPoundsLambda = getConversionLambda("KgsToPounds")
    val poundsToUSTonsLambda = getConversionLambda("PoundsToUSTons")

    //Combine the two lambdas to create a new one
    val kgsToUSTonsLambda = combine(kgsToPoundsLambda, poundsToUSTonsLambda)

    //Use the new lambda to convert 17.4 to US tons
    val value = 17.4
    println("$value kgs is ${convert(value, kgsToUSTonsLambda)} US tons")
}
```


Let's take the code for a test drive.

Test drive

When we run the code, the following text gets printed in the IDE's output window:

```
Convert 2.5kg to Pounds: 5.5115575
17.4 is converted to 0.0191802201
17.4 kgs is 0.0191802201 US tons
```

You've now learned how to use lambdas to create higher-order functions. Have a go at the following exercises, and in the next chapter, we'll introduce you to some of Kotlin's built-in higher-order functions, and show you how powerful and flexible they can be.

there are no Dumb Questions

Q: I've heard of functional programming. What's that?

A: Lambdas are an important part of functional programming. While non-functional programming reads *data input* and generates *data output*, functional programs can read *functions* as input, and generate *functions* as output. If your code includes higher-order functions, you are doing functional programming.

Q: Is functional programming very different from object-oriented programming?

A: They are both ways of factoring your code. In object-oriented programming you combine data with functions, and in functional programming you combine functions with functions. The two styles of programming are not incompatible; they are just different ways of looking at the world.

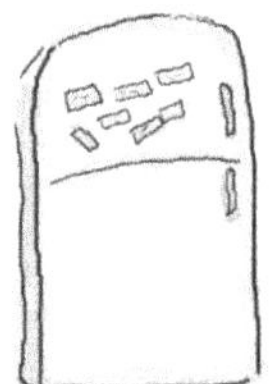

Code Magnets

Somebody used fridge magnets to create a `search` function that prints the names of items in a `List<Grocery>` that meet some criteria. Unfortunately, some of the magnets fell off. See if you can reconstruct the function.

The function goes here.

```
data class Grocery(val name: String, val category: String,
                   val unit: String, val unitPrice: Double)
```

This is the Grocery data class.

The main function uses the search function.

```
fun main(args: Array<String>) {
    val groceries = listOf(Grocery("Tomatoes", "Vegetable", "lb", 3.0),
            Grocery("Mushrooms", "Vegetable", "lb", 4.0),
            Grocery("Bagels", "Bakery", "Pack", 1.5),
            Grocery("Olive oil", "Pantry", "Bottle", 6.0),
            Grocery("Ice cream", "Frozen", "Pack", 3.0))
    println("Expensive ingredients:")
    search(groceries) {i: Grocery -> i.unitPrice > 5.0}
    println("All vegetables:")
    search(groceries) {i: Grocery -> i.category == "Vegetable"}
    println("All packs:")
    search(groceries) {i: Grocery -> i.unit == "Pack"}
}
```

Magnets:

```
println(l.name)    l in list    list:    ,    for (    (g: Grocery) -> Boolean    )
criteria(l)    }    search    fun    }    )    {    {    (
List<Grocery>    )    if (    criteria:    }    {
```

Answers on page 358.

BE the Compiler

Here are five functions. Your job is to play like you're the Compiler, and determine whether each one will compile. If it won't compile, why not?

A

```
fun myFun1(x: Int = 6, y: (Int) -> Int = 7): Int {
    return y(x)
}
```

B

```
fun myFun2(x: Int = 6, y: (Int) -> Int = { it }) {
    return y(x)
}
```

C

```
fun myFun3(x: Int = 6, y: (Int) -> Int = { x: Int -> x + 6 }): Int {
    return y(x)
}
```

D

```
fun myFun4(x: Int, y: Int,
           z: (Int, Int) -> Int = {
               x: Int, y: Int -> x + y
           }) {
    z(x, y)
}
```

E

```
fun myFun5(x: (Int) -> Int = {
    println(it)
    it + 7
}) {
    x(4)
}
```

Answers on page 359.

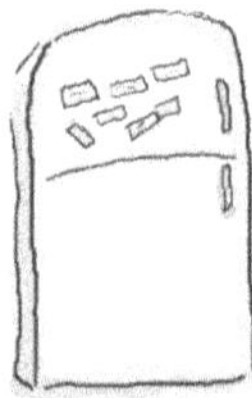

Code Magnets Solution

Somebody used fridge magnets to create a `search` function that prints the names of items in a `List<Grocery>` that meet some criteria. Unfortunately, some of the magnets fell off. See if you can reconstruct the function.

```
fun search ( list: List<Grocery> ,
             criteria: (g: Grocery) -> Boolean ) {
    for ( l in list ) {
        if ( criteria(l) ) { println(l.name) }
    }
}
```

```
data class Grocery(val name: String, val category: String,
                   val unit: String, val unitPrice: Double)

fun main(args: Array<String>) {
    val groceries = listOf(Grocery("Tomatoes", "Vegetable", "lb", 3.0),
            Grocery("Mushrooms", "Vegetable", "lb", 4.0),
            Grocery("Bagels", "Bakery", "Pack", 1.5),
            Grocery("Olive oil", "Pantry", "Bottle", 6.0),
            Grocery("Ice cream", "Frozen", "Pack", 3.0))
    println("Expensive ingredients:")
    search(groceries) {i: Grocery -> i.unitPrice > 5.0}
    println("All vegetables:")
    search(groceries) {i: Grocery -> i.category == "Vegetable"}
    println("All packs:")
    search(groceries) {i: Grocery -> i.unit == "Pack"}
}
```

BE the Compiler Solution

Here are five functions. Your job is to play like you're the Compiler, and determine whether each one will compile. If it won't compile, why not?

A

```
fun myFun1(x: Int = 6, y: (Int) -> Int = 7): Int {
    return y(x)
}
```

This won't compile, as it assigns a default Int value of 7 to a lambda.

B

```
fun myFun2(x: Int = 6, y: (Int) -> Int = { it }) {
    return y(x)
}
```

This line returns an Int.

This won't compile because the function returns an Int which isn't declared.

C

```
fun myFun3(x: Int = 6, y: (Int) -> Int = { x: Int -> x + 6 }): Int {
    return y(x)
}
```

This code compiles. Its parameters have default values of the correct type, and its return type is correctly declared.

D

```
fun myFun4(x: Int, y: Int,
           z: (Int, Int) -> Int = {
               x: Int, y: Int -> x + y
           }) {
    z(x, y)
}
```

This code compiles. The z variable is assigned a valid lambda as its default value.

E

```
fun myFun5(x: (Int) -> Int = {
    println(it)
    it + 7
}) {
    x(4)
}
```

This code compiles. The x variable is assigned a valid lambda as its default value, and this lambda spans multiple lines.

Pool Puzzle Solution

Your **job** is to take code snippets from the pool and place them into the blank lines in the code. You may **not** use the same code snippet more than once, and you won't need to use all the code snippets. Your **goal** is to create a function named `unless` that's called by the `main` function below. The `unless` function should have two parameters, a `Boolean` named `condition`, and a lambda named `code`. The function should invoke the `code` lambda when `condition` is `false`.

```
fun unless( condition: Boolean , code: () -> Unit ) {
    if ( !condition ) {
        code()
    }
}
```

If condition is false, invoke the code lambda.

```
fun main(args: Array<String>) {
    val options = arrayOf("Red", "Amber", "Green")
    var crossWalk = options[(Math.random() * options.size).toInt()]
    if (crossWalk == "Green") {
        println("Walk!")
    }
    unless (crossWalk == "Green") {
        println("Stop!")
    }
}
```

This is formatted like a code block, but it's actually a lambda. The lambda is passed to the unless function, and it runs if crossWalk is not "Green".

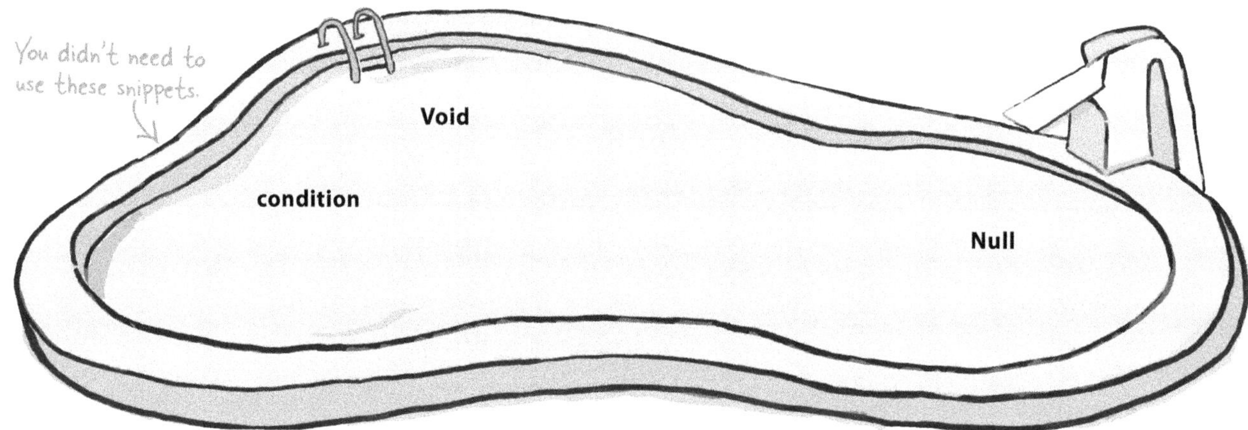

Your Kotlin Toolbox

You've got Chapter 11 under your belt and now you've added lambdas and higher-order functions to your toolbox.

You can download the full code for the chapter from https://tinyurl.com/HFKotlin.

BULLET POINTS

- A lambda expression, or lambda, takes the form:

```
{ x: Int -> x + 5 }
```

  The lambda is defined within curly braces, and can include parameters, and a body.

- A lambda can have multiple lines. The last evaluated expression in the body is used as the lambda's return value.
- You can assign a lambda to a variable. The variable's type must be compatible with the type of the lambda.
- A lambda's type has the format:

```
(parameters) -> return_type
```

- Where possible, the compiler can infer the lambda's parameter types.
- If the lambda has a single parameter, you can replace it with `it`.
- You execute a lambda by invoking it. You do this by passing the lambda any parameters in parentheses, or by calling its `invoke` function.
- You can pass a lambda to a function as a parameter, or use one as a function's return value. A function that uses a lambda in this way is known as a higher-order function.
- If the final parameter of a function is a lambda, you can move the lambda outside the function's parentheses when you call the function.
- If a function has a single parameter that's a lambda, you can omit the parentheses when you call the function.
- A type alias lets you provide an alternative name for an existing type. You define a type alias using `typealias`.

12 built-in higher-order functions

Power Up Your Code

Kotlin has an entire host of built-in higher-order functions. And in this chapter, we'll introduce you to some of the most useful ones. You'll meet the flexible ***filter family***, and discover how they can help you trim your collection down to size. You'll learn how to ***transform a collection using map***, ***loop through its items with forEach***, and how to ***group the items in your collection using groupBy***. You'll even use ***fold*** to perform complex calculations *using just one line of code*. By the end of the chapter, you'll be able to write code more **powerful than you ever thought possible**.

Kotlin has a bunch of built-in higher-order functions

As we said at the beginning of the previous chapter, Kotlin comes with a bunch of built-in higher-order functions that take a lambda parameter, many of which deal with collections. They enable you to filter a collection based on some criteria, for example, or group the items in a collection by a particular property value.

Each higher-order function has a generalized implementation, and its specific behavior is defined by the lambda that you pass to it. So if you want to filter a collection using the built-in `filter` function, you can specify the criteria that should be used by passing the function a lambda that defines it.

As many of Kotlin's higher-order functions are designed to work with collections, we're going to introduce you to some of the most useful higher-order functions defined in Kotlin's *collections* package. We'll explore these functions using a `Grocery` data class, and a `List` of `Grocery` items named `groceries`. Here's the code to define them:

```
data class Grocery(val name: String, val category: String,
                   val unit: String, val unitPrice: Double,
                   val quantity: Int)

fun main(args: Array<String>) {
    val groceries = listOf(Grocery("Tomatoes", "Vegetable", "lb", 3.0, 3),
                           Grocery("Mushrooms", "Vegetable", "lb", 4.0, 1),
                           Grocery("Bagels", "Bakery", "Pack", 1.5, 2),
                           Grocery("Olive oil", "Pantry", "Bottle", 6.0, 1),
                           Grocery("Ice cream", "Frozen", "Pack", 3.0, 2))
}
```

This is the Grocery data class.

The groceries List contains five Grocery items.

We'll start by looking at how to find the lowest or highest value in a collection of objects.

The min and max functions work with basic types

As you already know, if you have a collection of basic types, you can use the `min` and `max` functions to find the lowest or highest value. If you want to find the highest value in a `List<Int>`, for example, you can use the following code:

```
val ints = listOf(1, 2, 3, 4)
val maxInt = ints.max()     //maxInt == 4
```

The `min` and `max` functions work with Kotlin's basic types because they have a natural order. `Int`s can be arranged in numerical order, for example, which makes it easy to find out which `Int` has the highest value, and `String`s can be arranged in alphabetical order.

1, 2, 3, 4, 5...
"A", "B", "C"...

Numbers and Strings have a natural order, which means that you can use the min and max functions with them to determine the lowest or highest value.

The `min` and `max` functions, however, can't be used with types with no natural order. You can't use them, for example, with a `List<Grocery>` or a `Set<Duck>`, as the functions don't automatically know how `Grocery` items or `Duck` objects should be ordered. This means that for more complex types, you need a different approach.

The minBy and maxBy functions work with ALL types

If you want to find the lowest or highest value of a type that's more complex, you can use the **`minBy`** and **`maxBy`** functions. These functions work in a similar way to `min` and `max`, except that you can pass them criteria. You can use them, for example, to find the `Grocery` item with the lowest `unitPrice` or the `Duck` with the greatest `size`.

These items have no natural order. To find the highest or lowest value, we need to specify some criteria, such as unitPrice or quantity.

The `minBy` and `maxBy` functions each take one parameter: a lambda that tells the function which property it should use in order to determine which item has the lowest or highest value. If, for example, you wanted to find the item in a `List<Grocery>` with the highest `unitPrice`, you could do so using the `maxBy` function like this:

```
val highestUnitPrice = groceries.maxBy { it.unitPrice }
```

This code is like saying "Find the item in groceries with the highest unitPrice".

And if you wanted to find the item with the lowest `quantity` value, you would use `minBy`:

```
val lowestQuantity = groceries.minBy { it.quantity }
```

This line returns a reference to the item in groceries with the lowest quantity.

The lambda expression that you pass to the `minBy` or `maxBy` function must take a specific form in order for the code to compile and work correctly. We'll look at this next.

A closer look at minBy and maxBy's lambda parameter

When you call the minBy or maxBy function, you must provide it with a lambda which takes the following form:

```
{ i: item_type -> criteria }
```

The lambda must have one parameter, which we've denoted above using i: item_type. The parameter's type **must match the type of item that the collection deals with**, so if you want to use either function with a List<Grocery>, the lambda's parameter must have a type of Grocery:

```
{ i: Grocery -> criteria }
```

As each lambda has a single parameter of a known type, we can omit the parameter declaration entirely, and refer to the parameter in the lambda body using it.

The lambda body specifies the criteria that should be used to determine the lowest—or highest—value in the collection. This criteria is normally the name of a property—for example, { it.unitPrice }. It can be any type, just so long as the function can use it to determine which item has the lowest or highest property value.

minBy and maxBy work with collections that hold any type of object, making them much more flexible than min and max.

If you call minBy or maxBy on a collection that contains no items, the function will return a null value.

What about minBy and maxBy's return type?

When you call the minBy or maxBy function, its return type matches the type of the items held in the collection. If you use minBy with a List<Grocery>, for example, the function will return a Grocery. And if you use maxBy with a Set<Duck>, it will return a Duck.

Now that you know how to use minBy and maxBy, let's look at two of their close relatives: sumBy and sumByDouble.

there are no Dumb Questions

Q: Do the min and max functions only work with Kotlin's basic types, such as numbers and Strings?

A: min and max work with types where you can compare two values, and say whether one value is greater than another, which is the case for Kotlin's basic types. These types work in this way because behind the scenes, each one implements the Comparable interface, which defines how instances of that type should be ordered and compared.

In practice, min and max work with *any* type that implements Comparable. Instead of implementing Comparable in your own classes, however, we think that using the minBy and maxBy functions is a better approach as they give you more flexibility.

The sumBy and sumByDouble functions

As you may expect, the **sumBy** and **sumByDouble** functions return a sum of the items in a collection according to some criteria which you pass to it via a lambda. You can use these functions to, say, add together the quantity values for each item in a List<Grocery>, or return the sum of each unitPrice multiplied by the quantity.

The sumBy and sumByDouble functions are almost identical, except that sumBy works with Ints, and sumByDouble works with Doubles. To return the sum of a Grocery's quantity values, for example, you would use the sumBy function, as quantity is an Int:

sumBy adds Ints together, and returns an Int.

sumByDouble adds Doubles, and returns a Double.

```
val sumQuantity = groceries.sumBy { it.quantity }
```

This returns the sum of all quantity values in groceries.

And to return the sum of each unitPrice multiplied by the quantity value, you would use sumByDouble, as unitPrice * quantity is a Double:

```
val totalPrice = groceries.sumByDouble { it.quantity * it.unitPrice }
```

sumBy and sumByDouble's lambda parameter

Just like minBy and maxBy, you must provide sumBy and sumByDouble with a lambda that takes this form:

```
{ i: item_type -> criteria }
```

As before, item_type must match the type of item that the collection deals with. In the above examples, we're using the functions with a List<Grocery>, so the lambda's parameter must have a type of Grocery. As the compiler can infer this, we can omit the lambda parameter declaration, and refer to the parameter in the lambda body using it.

The lambda body tells the function what you want it to sum. As we said above, this must be an Int if you're using the sumBy function, and a Double if you're using sumByDouble. sumBy returns an Int value, and sumByDouble returns a Double.

Now that you know how to use minBy, maxBy, sumBy and sumByDouble, let's create a new project and add some code to it that uses these functions.

Watch it!

You can't use sumBy or sumByDouble directly on a Map.

You can, however, use them on a Map's keys, values or entries properties. The following code, for example, returns the sum of a Map's values:

```
myMap.values.sumBy { it }
```

Create the Groceries project

Create a new Kotlin project that targets the JVM, and name the project "Groceries". Then create a new Kotlin file named *Groceries.kt* by highlighting the *src* folder, clicking on the File menu and choosing New → Kotlin File/Class. When prompted, name the file "Groceries", and choose File from the Kind option.

Next, update your version of *Groceries.kt* to match ours below:

```
data class Grocery(val name: String, val category: String,
                   val unit: String, val unitPrice: Double,
                   val quantity: Int)

fun main(args: Array<String>) {
    val groceries = listOf(Grocery("Tomatoes", "Vegetable", "lb", 3.0, 3),
                           Grocery("Mushrooms", "Vegetable", "lb", 4.0, 1),
                           Grocery("Bagels", "Bakery", "Pack", 1.5, 2),
                           Grocery("Olive oil", "Pantry", "Bottle", 6.0, 1),
                           Grocery("Ice cream", "Frozen", "Pack", 3.0, 2))

    val highestUnitPrice = groceries.maxBy { it.unitPrice * 5 }
    println("highestUnitPrice: $highestUnitPrice")
    val lowestQuantity = groceries.minBy { it.quantity }
    println("lowestQuantity: $lowestQuantity")

    val sumQuantity = groceries.sumBy { it.quantity }
    println("sumQuantity: $sumQuantity")
    val totalPrice = groceries.sumByDouble { it.quantity * it.unitPrice }
    println("totalPrice: $totalPrice")
}
```

Groceries
src
Groceries.kt

Test drive

When we run the code, the following text gets printed in the IDE's output window:

```
highestUnitPrice: Grocery(name=Olive oil, category=Pantry, unit=Bottle, unitPrice=6.0, quantity=1)
lowestQuantity: Grocery(name=Mushrooms, category=Vegetable, unit=lb, unitPrice=4.0, quantity=1)
sumQuantity: 9
totalPrice: 28.0
```

BE the Compiler

Below is a complete Kotlin source file. Your job is to play like you're the Compiler, and determine whether the file will compile. If it won't compile, why not? How would you correct it?

```
data class Pizza(val name: String, val pricePerSlice: Double, val quantity: Int)

fun main(args: Array<String>) {
    val ints = listOf(1, 2, 3, 4, 5)

    val pizzas = listOf(Pizza("Sunny Chicken", 4.5, 4),
            Pizza("Goat and Nut", 4.0, 1),
            Pizza("Tropical", 3.0, 2),
            Pizza("The Garden", 3.5, 3))

    val minInt = ints.minBy({ it.value })
    val minInt2 = ints.minBy({ int: Int -> int })
    val sumInts = ints.sum()
    val sumInts2 = ints.sumBy { it }
    val sumInts3 = ints.sumByDouble({ number: Double -> number })
    val sumInts4 = ints.sumByDouble { int: Int -> int.toDouble() }

    val lowPrice = pizzas.min()
    val lowPrice2 = pizzas.minBy({ it.pricePerSlice })
    val highQuantity = pizzas.maxBy { p: Pizza -> p.quantity }
    val highQuantity3 = pizzas.maxBy { it.quantity }
    val totalPrice = pizzas.sumBy { it.pricePerSlice * it.quantity }
    val totalPrice2 = pizzas.sumByDouble { it.pricePerSlice * it.quantity }
}
```

BE the Compiler Solution

Below is a complete Kotlin source file. Your job is to play like you're the Compiler, and determine whether the file will compile. If it won't compile, why not? How would you correct it?

```
data class Pizza(val name: String, val pricePerSlice: Double, val quantity: Int)

fun main(args: Array<String>) {
    val ints = listOf(1, 2, 3, 4, 5)

    val pizzas = listOf(Pizza("Sunny Chicken", 4.5, 4),
            Pizza("Goat and Nut", 4.0, 1),
            Pizza("Tropical", 3.0, 2),
            Pizza("The Garden", 3.5, 3))

    val minInt = ints.minBy({ it~~.value~~ })
    val minInt2 = ints.minBy({ int: Int -> int })
    val sumInts = ints.sum()
    val sumInts2 = ints.sumBy { it }
    val sumInts3 = ints.sumByDouble({ ~~number: Double -> number~~ it.toDouble() })
    val sumInts4 = ints.sumByDouble { int: Int -> int.toDouble() }

    ~~val lowPrice = pizzas.min()~~
    val lowPrice2 = pizzas.minBy({ it.pricePerSlice })
    val highQuantity = pizzas.maxBy { p: Pizza -> p.quantity }
    val highQuantity3 = pizzas.maxBy { it.quantity }
    val totalPrice = pizzas.sumByDouble { it.pricePerSlice * it.quantity }
    val totalPrice2 = pizzas.sumByDouble { it.pricePerSlice * it.quantity }
}
```

As ints is a List<Int>, 'it' is an Int and has no value property.

This line won't compile, as the lambda's parameter needs to be an Int. We can replace the lambda with { it.toDouble() }.

The min function won't work with a List<Pizza>.

*{ it.pricePerSlice * it.quantity } returns a Double, so the sumBy function won't work. We need to use sumByDouble instead.*

Meet the filter function

The next stop on our tour of Kotlin's higher-order functions is **filter**. This function lets you search, or *filter*, a collection according to some criteria that you pass to it using a lambda.

For most collections, `filter` returns a `List` that includes all the items that match your criteria, which you can then use elsewhere in your code. If it's being used with a `Map`, however, it returns a `Map`. The following code, for example, uses the `filter` function to get a `List` of all the items in `groceries` whose `category` value is "Vegetable":

```
val vegetables = groceries.filter { it.category == "Vegetable" }
```

This returns a List containing those items from groceries whose category value is "Vegetable".

Just like the other functions you've seen in this chapter, the lambda that you pass to the `filter` function takes one parameter, whose type must match that of the items in the collection. As the lambda's parameter has a known type, you can omit the parameter declaration, and refer to it in the lambda body using `it`.

The lambda's body must return a `Boolean`, which is used for the `filter` function's criteria. The function returns a reference to all items from the original collection where the lambda body evaluates to `true`. The following code, for example, returns a `List` of `Grocery` items whose `unitPrice` is greater than 3.0:

```
val unitPriceOver3 = groceries.filter { it.unitPrice > 3.0 }
```

There's a whole FAMILY of filter functions

Kotlin has several variations of the `filter` function that can sometimes be useful. The `filterTo` function, for example, works like the `filter` function, except that it appends the items that match the specified criteria to another collection. The `filterIsInstance` function returns a `List` of all the items which are instances of a given class. And the `filterNot` function returns those items in a collection which *don't* match the criteria you pass to it. Here's how, for example, you would use the `filterNot` function to return a `List` of all `Grocery` items whose `category` value is not "Frozen":

You can find out more about Kotlin's filter family in the online documentation:

https://kotlinlang.org/api/latest/jvm/stdlib/kotlin.collections/index.html

```
val notFrozen = groceries.filterNot { it.category == "Frozen" }
```

filterNot returns those items where the lambda body evaluates to false.

Now that you've seen how the `filter` function works, let's look at another of Kotlin's higher-order functions: the `map` function.

Use map to apply a transform to your collection

The map function takes the items in a collection, and transforms each one according to some formula that you specify. It returns the results of this transformation as a new List.

Yes! The map function returns a List, and not a Map.

To see how this works, suppose you have a List<Int> that looks like this:

```
val ints = listOf(1, 2, 3, 4)
```

If you wanted to create a new List<Int> that contains the same items multiplied by two, you could do so using the map function like this:

```
val doubleInts = ints.map { it * 2 }
```

This returns a List containing the items 2, 4, 6 and 8.

And you can also use map to create a new List containing the name of each Grocery item in groceries:

```
val groceryNames = groceries.map { it.name }
```

This creates a new List, and populates it with the name of each Grocery item in groceries.

In each case, the map function returns a new List, and leaves the original collection intact. If, say, you use map to create a List of each unitPrice multiplied by 0.5 using the following code, the unitPrice of each Grocery item in the original collection stays the same:

```
val halfUnitPrice = groceries.map { it.unitPrice * 0.5 }
```

This returns a List containing each unitPrice multiplied by 0.5.

Just as before, the lambda that you pass to the map function has a single parameter whose type matches that of the items in the collection. You can use this parameter (usually referred to using it) to specify how you want each item in the collection to be transformed.

You can chain function calls together

As the filter and map functions each return a collection, you can chain higher-order function calls together to concisely perform more complex operations. If you wanted to create a List of each unitPrice multiplied by two, where the original unitPrice is greater than 3.0, you can do so by first calling the filter function on the original collection, and then using map to transform the result:

```
val newPrices = groceries.filter { it.unitPrice > 3.0 }
                         .map { it.unitPrice * 2 }
```

This calls the filter function, and then calls map on the resulting List.

Let's go behind the scenes and see what happens when this code runs.

What happens when the code runs

1 val newPrices = **groceries.filter { it.unitPrice > 3.0 }**
.map { it.unitPrice * 2 }

The `filter` function is called on `groceries`, a `List<Grocery>`. It creates a new `List` that holds references to those `Grocery` items whose `unitPrice` is greater than 3.0.

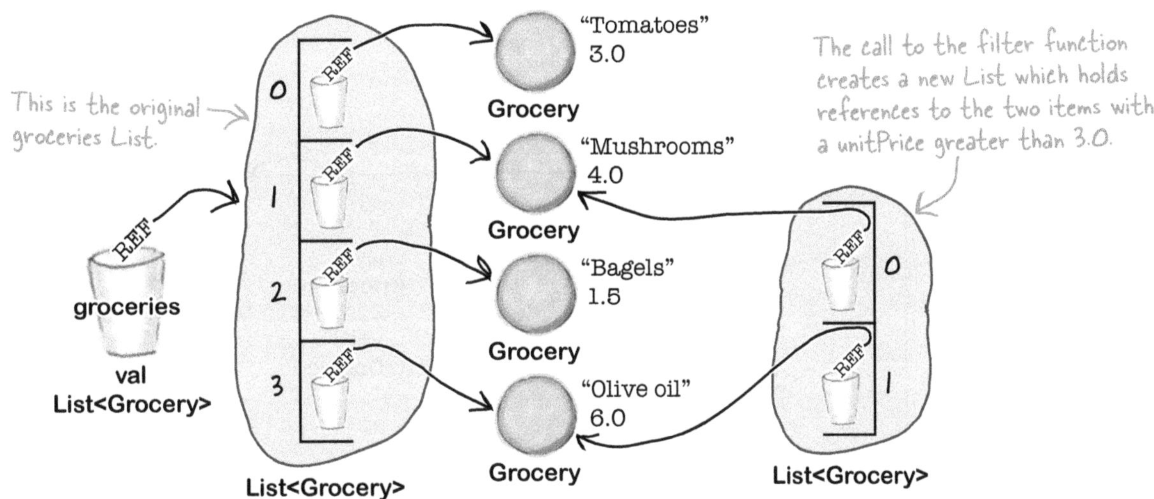

2 val newPrices = groceries.filter { it.unitPrice > 3.0 }
.map { it.unitPrice * 2 }

The `map` function is called on the new `List`. As the lambda `{ it.unitPrice * 2 }` returns a `Double`, the function creates a `List<Double>` containing a reference to each `unitPrice` multiplied by 2.

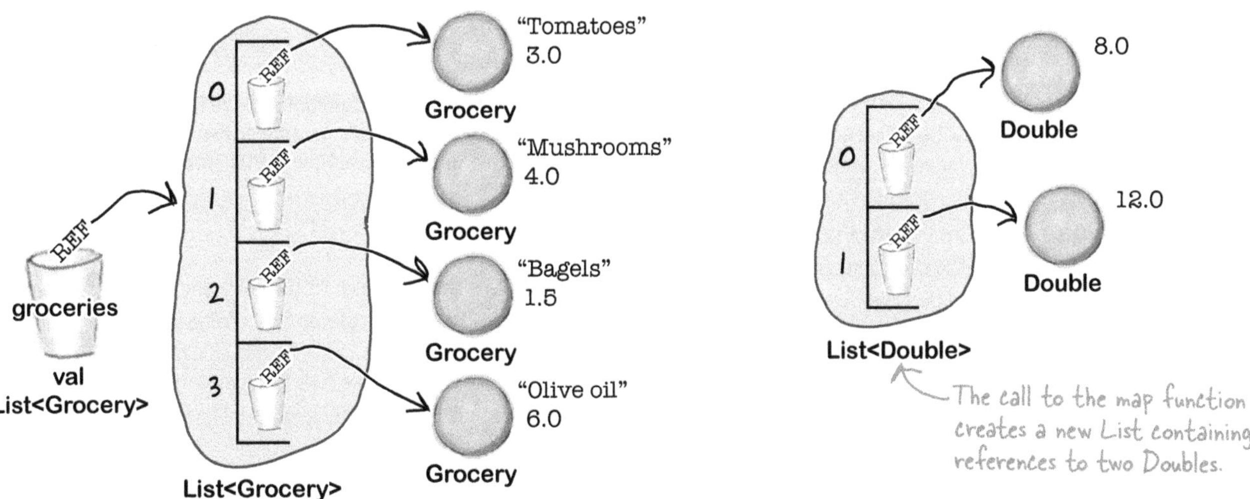

The story continues...

```
val newPrices = groceries.filter { it.unitPrice > 3.0 }
                         .map { it.unitPrice * 2 }
```

A new variable, `newPrices`, gets created, and the reference to the `List<Double>` returned by the `map` function is assigned to it.

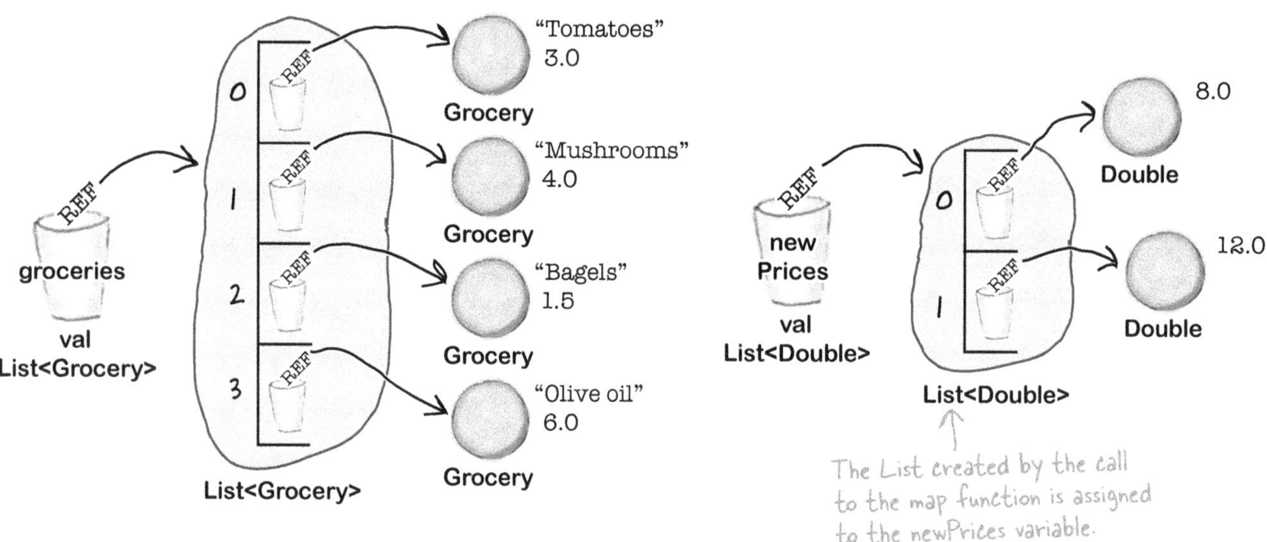

Now that you've seen what happens when higher-order functions are chained together, let's have a look at our next function: `forEach`.

Q: You said earlier that the `filter` function has a number of variations, like `filterTo` and `filterNot`. What about `map`? Are there variations of that function too?

A: Yes! Variations include `mapTo` (which appends the results of the transformation to an existing collection), `mapNotNull` (which omits any null values) and `mapValues` (which works with and returns a `Map`). You can find more details here:

https://kotlinlang.org/api/latest/jvm/stdlib/kotlin.collections/index.html

Q: For the higher-order functions we've looked at so far, you've said that the lambda's parameter type must match that of the items in the collection. How is that enforced?

A: Using generics.

As you may recall from Chapter 10, generics let you write code that uses types consistently. It stops you from adding a `Cabbage` reference to a `List<Duck>`. Kotlin's built-in higher-order functions use generics to make sure that they only accept and return values whose type is appropriate for the collection they're being used with.

forEach works like a for loop

The **forEach** function works in a similar way to a `for` loop, as it allows you to perform one or more actions against each item in a collection. You specify these actions using a lambda.

You can use forEach with arrays, Lists, Sets, and on a Map's entries, keys and values properties.

To see how `forEach` works, suppose you wanted to loop through each item in the `groceries List`, and print the `name` of each one. Here's how you could do this using a `for` loop:

```
for (item in groceries) {
    println(item.name)
}
```

And here's the equivalent code using the `forEach` function:

```
groceries.forEach { println(it.name) }
```

Note that { println(it.name) } is a lambda which we're passing to the forEach function. The lambda body can have multiple lines.

Both code examples do the same thing, but using `forEach` is slightly more concise.

But if forEach does the same thing as a for loop, isn't that just giving me **one more thing to remember**? What's the point in having **yet another function**?

As `forEach` is a function, you can use it in function call chains.

Imagine that you want to print the name of each item in groceries whose `unitPrice` is greater than 3.0. To do this using a `for` loop, you could use the code:

```
for (item in groceries) {
    if (item.unitPrice > 3.0) println(item.name)
}
```

But you can do this more concisely using:

```
groceries.filter { it.unitPrice > 3.0 }
         .forEach { println(it.name) }
```

So `forEach` lets you chain function calls together to perform powerful tasks in a way that's concise.

Let's take a closer look at `forEach`.

forEach has no return value

Just like the other functions that you've seen in this chapter, the lambda that you pass to the `forEach` function has a single parameter whose type matches that of the items in the collection. And as this parameter has a known type, you can omit the parameter declaration, and refer to the parameter in the lambda body using `it`.

Unlike other functions, however, the lambda's body has a `Unit` return value. This means that you can't use `forEach` to return the result of some calculation as you won't be able to access it. There is, however, a workaround.

Lambdas have access to variables

As you already know, a `for` loop's body has access to variables that have been defined outside the loop. The following code, for example, defines a `String` variable named `itemNames`, which is then updated in a `for` loop's body:

```
var itemNames = ""
for (item in groceries) {
    itemNames += "${item.name} "
}
println("itemNames: $itemNames")
```

You can update the itemNames variable inside the body of a for loop.

When you pass a lambda to a higher-order function such as `forEach`, the lambda has access to these same variables, *even though they've been defined outside the lambda.* This means that instead of using the `forEach` function's return value to get the result of some calculation, you can update a variable from inside the lambda body. The following code, for example, is valid:

```
var itemNames = ""
groceries.forEach({ itemNames += "${it.name} " })
println("itemNames: $itemNames")
```

You can also update the itemNames variable inside the body of the lambda that's passed to forEach.

The variables defined outside the lambda which the lambda can access are sometimes referred to as the lambda's **closure**. In clever words, we say that *the lambda can access its closure.* And as the lambda uses the `itemNames` variable in its body, we say that *the lambda's closure has* ***captured*** *the variable.*

Closure means that a lambda can access any local variables that it captures.

Now that you've learned how to use the `forEach` function, let's update our project code.

Update the Groceries project

We'll add some code to our Groceries project that uses the `filter`, `map` and `forEach` functions. Update your version of *Groceries.kt* in the project so that it matches ours below (our changes are in bold):

```
data class Grocery(val name: String, val category: String,
                   val unit: String, val unitPrice: Double,
                   val quantity: Int)

fun main(args: Array<String>) {
    val groceries = listOf(Grocery("Tomatoes", "Vegetable", "lb", 3.0, 3),
                           Grocery("Mushrooms", "Vegetable", "lb", 4.0, 1),
                           Grocery("Bagels", "Bakery", "Pack", 1.5, 2),
                           Grocery("Olive oil", "Pantry", "Bottle", 6.0, 1),
                           Grocery("Ice cream", "Frozen", "Pack", 3.0, 2))

    val highestUnitPrice = groceries.maxBy { it.unitPrice * 5 }
    println("highestUnitPrice: $highestUnitPrice")
    val lowestQuantity = groceries.minBy { it.quantity }
    println("lowestQuantity: $lowestQuantity")

    val sumQuantity = groceries.sumBy { it.quantity }
    println("sumQuantity: $sumQuantity")
    val totalPrice = groceries.sumByDouble { it.quantity * it.unitPrice }
    println("totalPrice: $totalPrice")

    val vegetables = groceries.filter { it.category == "Vegetable" }
    println("vegetables: $vegetables")
    val notFrozen = groceries.filterNot { it.category == "Frozen" }
    println("notFrozen: $notFrozen")

    val groceryNames = groceries.map { it.name }
    println("groceryNames: $groceryNames")
    val halfUnitPrice = groceries.map { it.unitPrice * 0.5 }
    println("halfUnitPrice: $halfUnitPrice")

    val newPrices = groceries.filter { it.unitPrice > 3.0 }
            .map { it.unitPrice * 2 }
    println("newPrices: $newPrices")
```

Delete these lines.

Add all these lines.

Groceries
src
Groceries.kt

The code continues on the next page.

The code continued...

Add these lines to the main function.

```
        println("Grocery names: ")
        groceries.forEach { println(it.name) }

        println("Groceries with unitPrice > 3.0: ")
        groceries.filter { it.unitPrice > 3.0 }
                .forEach { println(it.name) }

        var itemNames = ""
        groceries.forEach({ itemNames += "${it.name} " })
        println("itemNames: $itemNames")
    }
```

Groceries
src
Groceries.kt

Let's take the code for a test drive.

Test drive

When we run the code, the following text gets printed in the IDE's output window:

```
vegetables: [Grocery(name=Tomatoes, category=Vegetable, unit=lb, unitPrice=3.0, quantity=3),
Grocery(name=Mushrooms, category=Vegetable, unit=lb, unitPrice=4.0, quantity=1)]
notFrozen: [Grocery(name=Tomatoes, category=Vegetable, unit=lb, unitPrice=3.0, quantity=3),
Grocery(name=Mushrooms, category=Vegetable, unit=lb, unitPrice=4.0, quantity=1),
Grocery(name=Bagels, category=Bakery, unit=Pack, unitPrice=1.5, quantity=2),
Grocery(name=Olive oil, category=Pantry, unit=Bottle, unitPrice=6.0, quantity=1)]
groceryNames: [Tomatoes, Mushrooms, Bagels, Olive oil, Ice cream]
halfUnitPrice: [1.5, 2.0, 0.75, 3.0, 1.5]
newPrices: [8.0, 12.0]
Grocery names:
Tomatoes
Mushrooms
Bagels
Olive oil
Ice cream
Groceries with unitPrice > 3.0:
Mushrooms
Olive oil
itemNames: Tomatoes Mushrooms Bagels Olive oil Ice cream
```

Now that you've updated your project code, have a go at the following exercise, and then we'll look at our next higher-order function.

Pool Puzzle

Your **job** is to take code snippets from the pool and place them into the blank lines in the code. You may **not** use the same code snippet more than once, and you won't need to use all the code snippets. Your **goal** is to complete the `getWinners` function in the `Contest` class so that it returns a `Set<T>` of contestants with the highest score, and prints the name of each winner.

```
abstract class Pet(var name: String)

class Cat(name: String) : Pet(name)

class Dog(name: String) : Pet(name)

class Fish(name: String) : Pet(name)

class Contest<T: Pet>() {
    var scores: MutableMap<T, Int> = mutableMapOf()

    fun addScore(t: T, score: Int = 0) {
        if (score >= 0) scores.put(t, score)
    }

    fun getWinners(): Set<T> {
        val highScore = ..................
        val winners = scores........ { .......... == highScore } ........
        winners........ { println("Winner: ${........}") }
        return winners
    }
}
```

If this code looks familiar, it's because we wrote a different version of it in Chapter 10.

Note: each thing from the pool can only be used once!

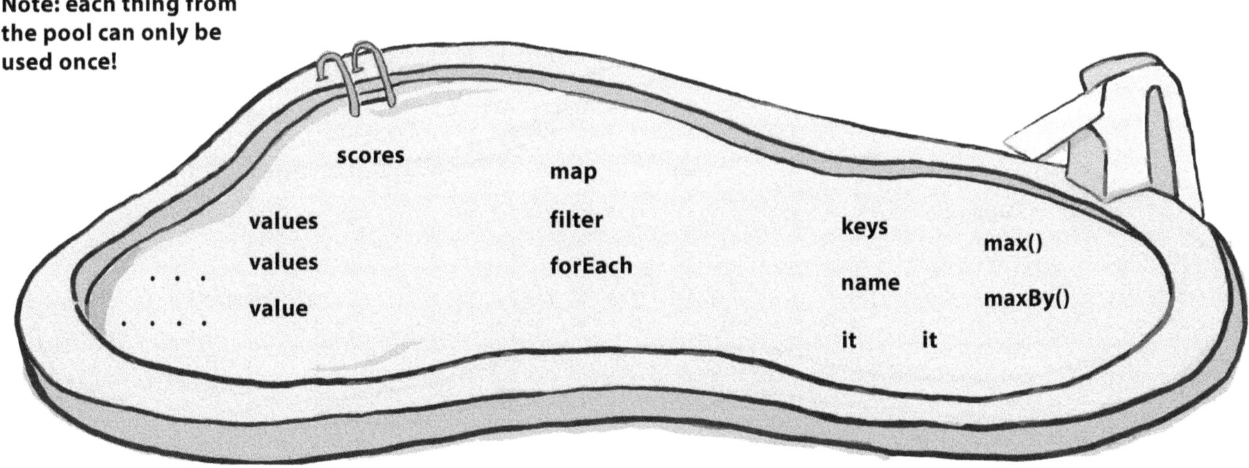

Pool Puzzle Solution

Your **job** is to take code snippets from the pool and place them into the blank lines in the code. You may **not** use the same code snippet more than once, and you won't need to use all the code snippets. Your **goal** is to complete the `getWinners` function in the `Contest` class so that it returns a `Set<T>` of contestants with the highest score, and prints the name of each winner.

```
abstract class Pet(var name: String)

class Cat(name: String) : Pet(name)

class Dog(name: String) : Pet(name)

class Fish(name: String) : Pet(name)

class Contest<T: Pet>() {
    var scores: MutableMap<T, Int> = mutableMapOf()

    fun addScore(t: T, score: Int = 0) {
        if (score >= 0) scores.put(t, score)
    }

    fun getWinners(): Set<T> {
        val highScore = scores.values.max()
        val winners = scores.filter { it.value == highScore }.keys
        winners.forEach { println("Winner: ${it.name}") }
        return winners
    }
}
```

The scores are held as Int values in a MutableMap named scores, so this gets the highest score value.

Filter scores to get the entries whose value is highScore. Then use its keys property to get the winners.

Use the forEach function to print the name of each winner.

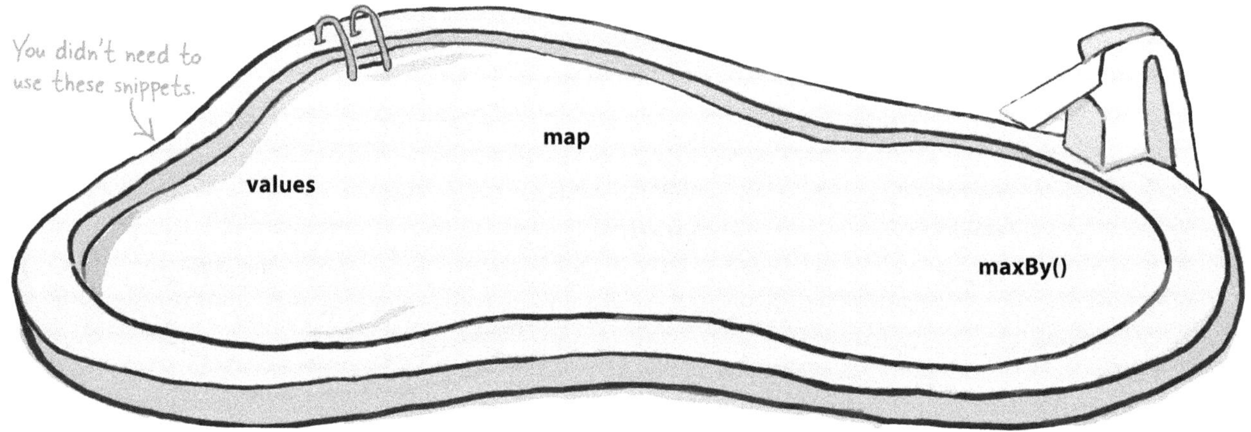

Use groupBy to split your collection into groups

The next function that we'll look at is **groupBy**. This function lets you group the items in your collection according to some criteria, such as the value of one of its properties. You can use it (in conjunction with other function calls) to, say, print the name of `Grocery` items grouped by `category` value:

Note that you can't use groupBy on a Map directly, but you can call it on its keys, values or entries properties.

The `groupBy` function accepts one parameter, a lambda, which you use to specify how the function should group the items in the collection. The following code, for example, groups the items in `groceries` (a `List<Grocery>`) by the `category` value:

```
val groupByCategory = groceries.groupBy { it.category }
```

This is like saying "group each item in groceries by its category value".

`groupBy` returns a `Map`. It uses the criteria passed via the lambda body for the keys, and each associated value is a `List` of items from the original collection. The above code, for example, creates a `Map` whose keys are the `Grocery` item `category` values, and each value is a `List<Grocery>`:

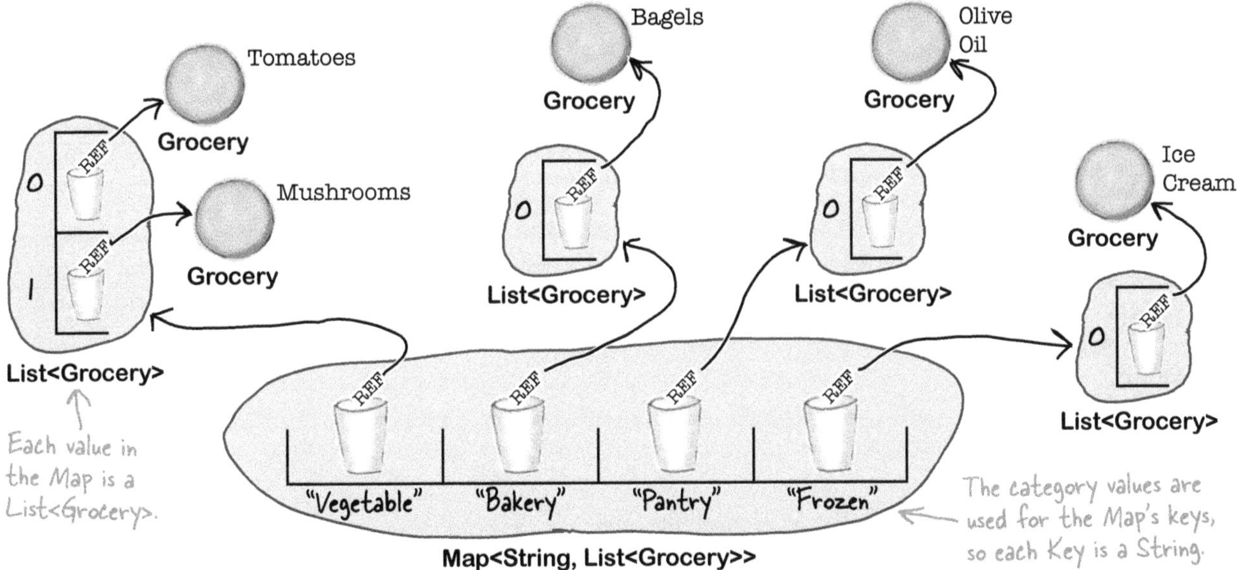

You can use groupBy in function call chains

As the groupBy function returns a Map with List values, you can make further higher-order function calls on its return value, just as you can with the filter and map functions.

Imagine that you want to print the value of each category for a List<Grocery>, along with the name of each Grocery item whose category property has that value. To do this, you can use the groupBy function to group the Grocery items by each category value, and then use the forEach function to loop through the resulting Map:

```
groceries.groupBy { it.category }.forEach {
    //More code goes here
}
```

groupBy returns a Map, which means that we can call the forEach function on its return value.

As the groupBy function uses the Grocery category values for its keys, we can print them by passing the code println(it.key) to the forEach function in its lambda:

```
groceries.groupBy { it.category }.forEach {
    println(it.key)
    //More code goes here
}
```

This prints the Map keys (the Grocery category values).

And as each of the Map's values is a List<Grocery>, we can make a further call to forEach in order to print the name of each grocery item:

```
groceries.groupBy { it.category }.forEach {
    println(it.key)
    it.value.forEach { println("    ${it.name}") }
}
```

This line gets the corresponding value for the Map's key. As this is a List<Grocery>, we can call forEach on it to print the name of the Grocery item.

So when you run the above code, it produces the following output:

```
Vegetable
    Tomatoes
    Mushrooms
Bakery
    Bagels
Pantry
    Olive oil
Frozen
    Ice cream
```

Now that you know how to use groupBy, let's look at the final function on our road trip: the fold function.

How to use the fold function

The **fold** function is arguably Kotlin's most flexible higher-order function. With fold, you can specify an initial value, and perform some operation on it for each item in a collection. You can use it to, say, multiply together each item in a List<Int> and return the result, or concatenate together the name of each item in a List<Grocery>, all in a single line of code.

fold can be called on a Map's keys, values and entries properties, but not on a Map directly.

Unlike the other functions we've seen in this chapter, fold takes two parameters: the initial value, and the operation that you want to perform on it, specified by a lambda. So if you have the following List<Int>:

```
val ints = listOf(1, 2, 3)
```

you can use fold to add each of its items to an initial value of 0 using the following code:

```
val sumOfInts = ints.fold(0) { runningSum, item -> runningSum + item }
```

This is the initial value.

This tells the function that you want to add the value of each item in the collection to the initial value.

The fold function's first parameter is the initial value—in this case, 0. This parameter can be any type, but it's usually one of Kotlin's basic types such as a number or String.

The second parameter is a lambda which describes the operation that you want to perform on the initial value for each item in the collection. In the above example, we want to add each item to the initial value, so we're using the lambda:

```
{ runningSum, item -> runningSum + item }
```

Here, we've decided to name the lambda parameters runningSum and item as we're adding the value of each item to a running sum. You can, however, give the parameters any valid variable name.

The lambda that you pass to fold has two parameters, which in this example we've named runningSum and item.

The first lambda parameter, runningSum, gets its type from the initial value that you specify. It's initialized with this initial value, so in the above example, runningSum is an Int that's initialized with 0.

The second lambda parameter, item, has the same type as the items in the collection. In the example above, we're calling fold on a List<Int>, so item's type is Int.

The lambda body specifies the operation you want to perform for each item in the collection, the result of which is then assigned to the lambda's first parameter variable. In the above example, the function takes the value of runningSum, adds it to the value of the current item, and assigns this new value to runningSum. When the function has looped through all items in the collection, fold returns the final value of this variable.

Let's break down what happens when we call the fold function.

Behind the scenes: the fold function

Here's what happens when we run the code:

```
val sumOfInts = ints.fold(0) { runningSum, item -> runningSum + item }
```

where `ints` is defined as:

```
val ints = listOf(1, 2, 3)
```

val sumOfInts = ints.fold(**0**) { **runningSum**, item -> runningSum + item }

This creates an `Int` variable named `runningSum` which is initialized with 0. This variable is local to the `fold` function.

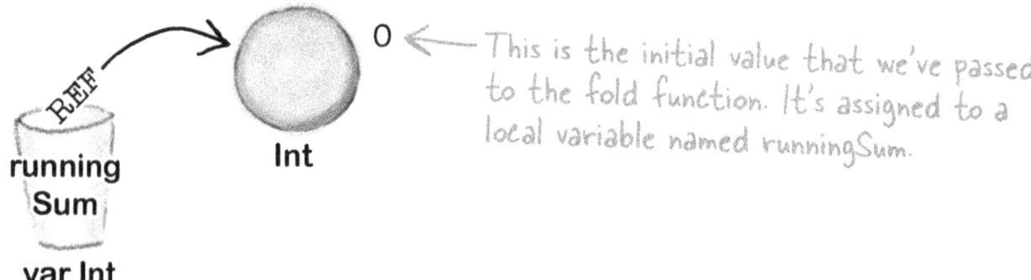

val sumOfInts = ints.fold(0) { runningSum, item -> **runningSum + item** }

The function takes the value of the first item in the collection (an `Int` with a value of 1) and adds it to the value of `runningSum`. This new value, 1, is assigned to `runningSum`.

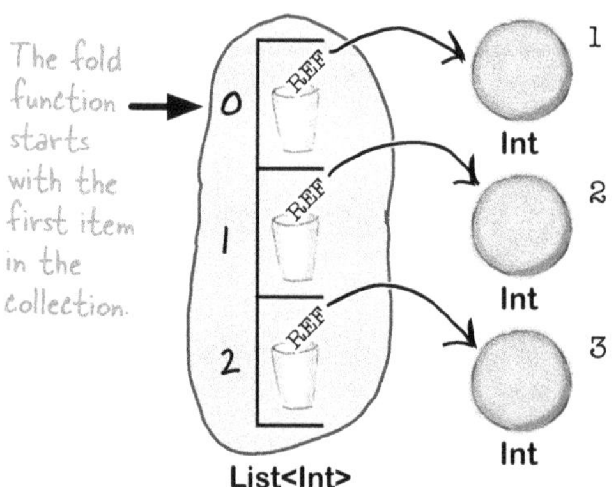

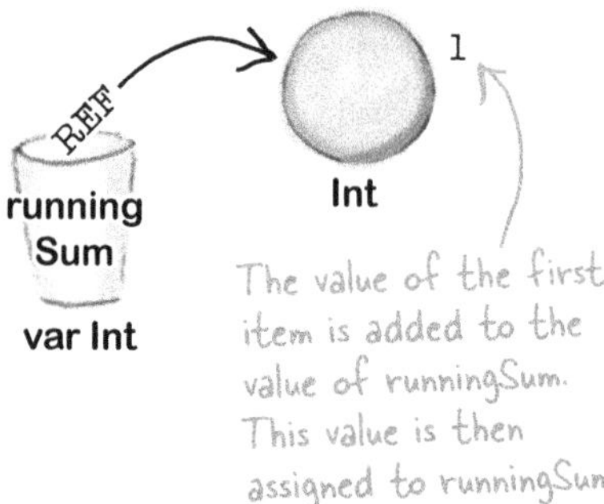

The story continues...

3 val sumOfInts = ints.fold(0) { runningSum, item -> **runningSum + item** }

The function moves to the second item in the collection, which is an `Int` with a value of 2. It adds this to `runningSum`, so that `runningSum`'s value becomes 3.

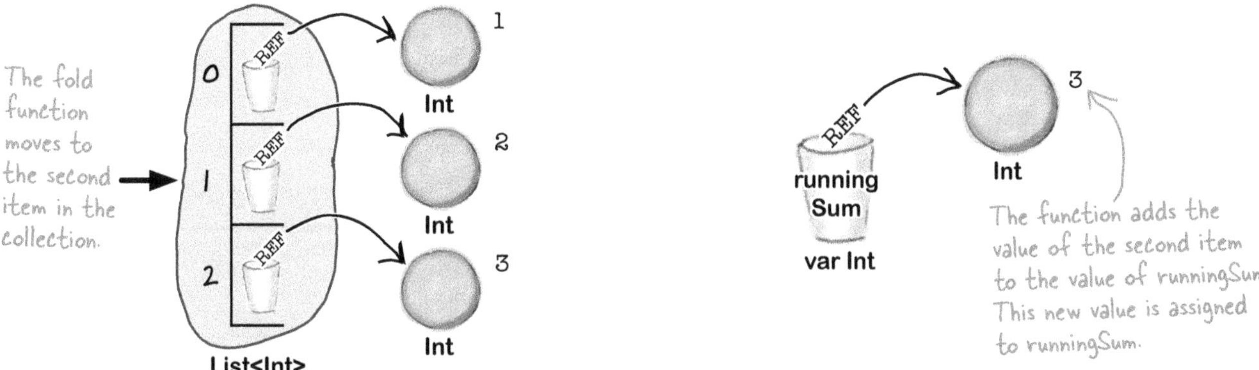

4 val sumOfInts = ints.fold(0) { runningSum, item -> **runningSum + item** }

The function moves to the third and final item in the collection: an `Int` with a value of 3. This value is added to `runningSum`, so that `runningSum`'s value becomes 6.

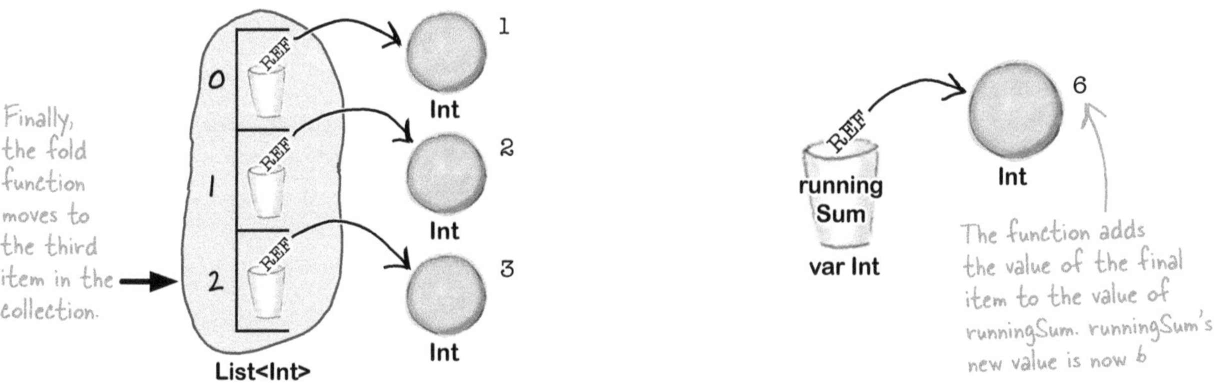

5 **val sumOfInts** = ints.fold(0) { runningSum, item -> runningSum + item }

As there are no more items in the collection, the function returns the final value of `runningSum`. This value is assigned to a new variable named `sumOfInts`.

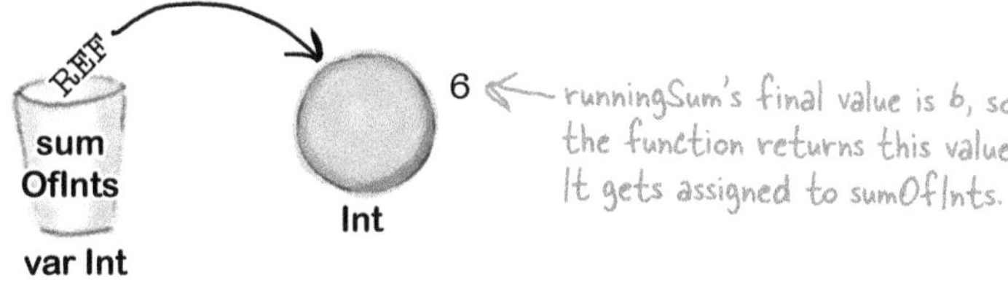

Some more examples of fold

Now that you've seen how to use the `fold` function to add together the values in a `List<Int>`, let's look at a few more examples.

Find the product of a List<Int>

If you want to multiply together all the numbers in a `List<Int>` and return the result, you can do so by passing the `fold` function an initial value of 1, and a lambda whose body performs the multiplication:

```
ints.fold(1) { runningProduct, item -> runningProduct * item }
```

Initialize runningProduct with 1.

Multiply runningSum with the value of each item.

Concatenate together the name of each item in a List<Grocery>

To return a `String` that contains the name of each `Grocery` item in a `List<Grocery>`, you can pass the `fold` function an initial value of `""`, and a lambda whose body performs the concatenation:

There's also a joinToString function which you can use to perform this kind of task.

```
groceries.fold("") { string, item -> string + " ${item.name}" }
```

Initialize string with "".

This is like saying:
string = string + " ${item.name}"
for each item in groceries.

Subtract the total price of items from an initial value

You can also use `fold` to work out how much change you'd have left if you were to buy all the items in a `List<Grocery>`. To do this, you'd set the initial value as the amount of money you have available, and use the lambda body to subtract the `unitPrice` of each item multiplied by the `quantity`:

```
groceries.fold(50.0) { change, item
                       -> change - item.unitPrice * item.quantity }
```

Initialize change with 50.0.

This subtracts the total price (unitPrice * quantity) from change for each item in groceries.

Now that you know how to use the `groupBy` and `fold` functions, let's update our project code.

Update the Groceries project

We'll add some code to our Groceries project that uses the `groupBy` and `fold` functions. Update your version of *Groceries.kt* in the project so that it matches ours below (our changes are in bold):

```
data class Grocery(val name: String, val category: String,
                   val unit: String, val unitPrice: Double,
                   val quantity: Int)

fun main(args: Array<String>) {
    val groceries = listOf(Grocery("Tomatoes", "Vegetable", "lb", 3.0, 3),
                           Grocery("Mushrooms", "Vegetable", "lb", 4.0, 1),
                           Grocery("Bagels", "Bakery", "Pack", 1.5, 2),
                           Grocery("Olive oil", "Pantry", "Bottle", 6.0, 1),
                           Grocery("Ice cream", "Frozen", "Pack", 3.0, 2))

    val vegetables = groceries.filter { it.category == "Vegetable" }
    println("vegetables: $vegetables")
    val notFrozen = groceries.filterNot { it.category == "Frozen" }
    println("notFrozen: $notFrozen")

    val groceryNames = groceries.map { it.name }
    println("groceryNames: $groceryNames")
    val halfUnitPrice = groceries.map { it.unitPrice * 0.5 }
    println("halfUnitPrice: $halfUnitPrice")

    val newPrices = groceries.filter { it.unitPrice > 3.0 }
            .map { it.unitPrice * 2 }
    println("newPrices: $newPrices")

    println("Grocery names: ")
    groceries.forEach { println(it.name) }

    println("Groceries with unitPrice > 3.0: ")
    groceries.filter { it.unitPrice > 3.0 }
            .forEach { println(it.name) }

    var itemNames = ""
    groceries.forEach({ itemNames += "${it.name} " })
    println("itemNames: $itemNames")
```

We no longer need these lines, so you can delete them.

Groceries
src
Groceries.kt

The code continues on the next page.

The code continued...

Groceries
src
Groceries.kt

Add these lines to the main function.

```
    groceries.groupBy { it.category }.forEach {
        println(it.key)
        it.value.forEach { println("    ${it.name}") }
    }

    val ints = listOf(1, 2, 3)
    val sumOfInts = ints.fold(0) { runningSum, item -> runningSum + item }
    println("sumOfInts: $sumOfInts")

    val productOfInts = ints.fold(1) { runningProduct, item -> runningProduct * item }
    println("productOfInts: $productOfInts")

    val names = groceries.fold("") { string, item -> string + " ${item.name}" }
    println("names: $names")

    val changeFrom50 = groceries.fold(50.0) { change, item
                                 -> change - item.unitPrice * item.quantity }
    println("changeFrom50: $changeFrom50")
}
```

Let's take the code for a test drive.

Test drive

When we run the code, the following text gets printed in the IDE's output window:

```
Vegetable
  Tomatoes
  Mushrooms
Bakery
  Bagels
Pantry
  Olive oil
Frozen
  Ice cream
sumOfInts: 6
productOfInts: 6
names:  Tomatoes Mushrooms Bagels Olive oil Ice cream
changeFrom50: 22.0
```

there are no Dumb Questions

Q: You said that some of the higher-order functions in this chapter can't be used directly with a `Map`. Why is that?

A: It's because `Map` is defined a little differently to `List` and `Set`, and this affects which functions will work with it.

Behind the scenes, `List` and `Set` inherit behavior from an interface named `Collection`, which in turn inherits behavior defined in the `Iterable` interface. `Map`, however, does not inherit from either of these interfaces. This means that `List` and `Set` are both types of `Iterable`, while `Map` isn't.

This distinction is important because functions such as `fold`, `forEach` and `groupBy` are designed to work with `Iterable`s. And because `Map` isn't an `Iterable`, you'll get a compiler error if you try to directly use any of these functions with a `Map`.

The great news, however, is that `Map`'s `entries`, `keys` and `values` properties are all types of `Iterable`: `entries` and `keys` are both `Set`s, and `values` inherits from the `Collection` interface. This means that while you can't call functions such as `groupBy` and `fold` on a `Map` directly, you can still use them with the `Map`'s properties.

Q: Do I always need to provide the `fold` function with an initial value? Can't I just use the first item in the collection as the initial value?

A: When you use the `fold` function, you *must* specify the initial value. This parameter is mandatory, and can't be omitted.

If you want to use the first item in the collection as the initial value, however, an alternative approach is to use the **`reduce`** function. This function works in a similar way to `fold`, except that you don't have to specify the initial value. It automatically uses the first item in the collection as the initial value.

Q: Does `fold` iterate through the collection in a specific order? Can I reverse this order?

A: The `fold` and `reduce` functions work through items in a collection from left to right, starting with the first item in the collection.

If you want to reverse this order, you can use the **`foldRight`** and **`reduceRight`** functions. These functions works on arrays and `List`s, but not on `Set`s or `Map`s.

Q: Can I update the variables in a lambda's closure?

A: Yes.

As you may recall, a lambda's closure refers to those variables defined outside the lambda body which the lambda has access to. Unlike some languages such as Java, you can update these variables in the lambda's body so long as they have been defined using `var`.

Q: Does Kotlin have many more higher-order functions?

A: Yes. Kotlin has far too many higher-order functions for us to cover in one chapter, so we decided to focus on just some of them: the ones which we think are the most useful or important. Now that you know how to use these functions, however, we're confident that you'll be able to take your knowledge, and apply it elsewhere.

You can find a full list of Kotlin's functions (including its higher-order functions) in the online documentation:

https://kotlinlang.org/api/latest/jvm/stdlib/index.html

Sharpen your pencil

The following code defines the `Grocery` data class, and a `List<Grocery>` named `groceries`:

```
data class Grocery(val name: String, val category: String,
                   val unit: String, val unitPrice: Double,
                   val quantity: Int)

val groceries = listOf(Grocery("Tomatoes", "Vegetable", "lb", 3.0, 3),
                       Grocery("Mushrooms", "Vegetable", "lb", 4.0, 1),
                       Grocery("Bagels", "Bakery", "Pack", 1.5, 2),
                       Grocery("Olive oil", "Pantry", "Bottle", 6.0, 1),
                       Grocery("Ice cream", "Frozen", "Pack", 3.0, 2))
```

Write the code below to find out how much will be spent on vegetables.

....

Create a `List` containing the name of each item whose total price is less than 5.0

....

Print the total cost of each category.

....

....

....

Print the name of each item that doesn't come in a bottle, grouped by unit.

....

....

....

....

Answers on page 392.

A short Kotlin program is listed below. One block of the program is missing. Your challenge is to match the candidate block of code (on the left), with the output that you'd see if the block were inserted. Not all the lines of output will be used, and some lines of output may be used more than once. Draw lines connecting the candidate blocks of code with their matching output.

```
fun main(args: Array<String>) {
    val myMap = mapOf("A" to 4, "B" to 3, "C" to 2, "D" to 1, "E" to 2)
    var x1 = ""
    var x2 = 0
    [                                              ]
    println("$x1$x2")
}
```

The candidate code goes here.

Match each candidate with one of the possible outputs.

Candidates:

```
x1 = myMap.keys.fold("") { x, y -> x + y}
x2 = myMap.entries.fold(0) { x, y -> x * y.value }
```

```
x2 = myMap.values.groupBy { it }.keys.sumBy { it }
```

```
x1 = "ABCDE"
x2 = myMap.values.fold(12) { x, y -> x - y }
```

```
x2 = myMap.entries.fold(1) { x, y -> x * y.value }
```

```
x1 = myMap.values.fold("") { x, y -> x + y }
```

```
x1 = myMap.values.fold(0) { x, y -> x + y }
                .toString()
x2 = myMap.keys.groupBy { it }.size
```

Possible output:

```
10
```

```
ABCDE0
```

```
ABCDE48
```

```
43210
```

```
432120
```

```
48
```

```
125
```

Answers on page 393.

Sharpen your pencil Solution

The following code defines the `Grocery` data class, and a `List<Grocery>` named `groceries`:

```
data class Grocery(val name: String, val category: String,
                   val unit: String, val unitPrice: Double,
                   val quantity: Int)

val groceries = listOf(Grocery("Tomatoes", "Vegetable", "lb", 3.0, 3),
                       Grocery("Mushrooms", "Vegetable", "lb", 4.0, 1),
                       Grocery("Bagels", "Bakery", "Pack", 1.5, 2),
                       Grocery("Olive oil", "Pantry", "Bottle", 6.0, 1),
                       Grocery("Ice cream", "Frozen", "Pack", 3.0, 2))
```

Write the code below to find out how much will be spent on vegetables.

```
groceries.filter { it.category == "Vegetable" }.sumByDouble { it.unitPrice * it.quantity }
```

Filter by category, then sum the total price.

Create a `List` containing the name of each item whose total price is less than 5.0

```
groceries.filter { it.unitPrice * it.quantity < 5.0 }.map { it.name }
```

Filter by unitPrice * quantity, then use map to transform the result.

Print the total cost of each category.

```
groceries.groupBy { it.category }.forEach {
    println("${it.key}: ${it.value.sumByDouble { it.unitPrice * it.quantity }}")
}
```

For each category...

print the key, followed by the result of sumByDouble for each value.

Print the name of each item that doesn't come in a bottle, grouped by unit.

```
groceries.filterNot { it.unit == "Bottle"}.groupBy { it.unit }.forEach {
                        println(it.key)
                        it.value.forEach { println("    ${it.name}") }
}
```

Group the results by unit.

Get the entries where the value of unit is not "Bottle"

Print each key in the resulting Map.

Each value in the Map is a List<Grocery>, so we can use forEach to loop through each List, and print the name of each item.

Mixed Messages Solution

A short Kotlin program is listed below. One block of the program is missing. Your challenge is to match the candidate block of code (on the left), with the output that you'd see if the block were inserted. Not all the lines of output will be used, and some lines of output may be used more than once. Draw lines connecting the candidate blocks of code with their matching output.

```
fun main(args: Array<String>) {
    val myMap = mapOf("A" to 4, "B" to 3, "C" to 2, "D" to 1, "E" to 2)
    var x1 = ""
    var x2 = 0
    [                                                  ]
    println("$x1$x2")
}
```

The candidate code goes here.

Candidates:

```
x1 = myMap.keys.fold("") { x, y -> x + y}
x2 = myMap.entries.fold(0) { x, y -> x * y.value }
```

```
x2 = myMap.values.groupBy { it }.keys.sumBy { it }
```

```
x1 = "ABCDE"
x2 = myMap.values.fold(12) { x, y -> x - y }
```

```
x2 = myMap.entries.fold(1) { x, y -> x * y.value }
```

```
x1 = myMap.values.fold("") { x, y -> x + y }
```

```
x1 = myMap.values.fold(0) { x, y -> x + y }
              .toString()
x2 = myMap.keys.groupBy { it }.size
```

Possible output:

```
10
ABCDE0
ABCDE48
43210
432120
48
125
```

CHAPTER 12

Your Kotlin Toolbox

You've got Chapter 12 under your belt and now you've added built-in higher-order functions to your toolbox.

You can download the full code for the chapter from https://tinyurl.com/HFKotlin.

BULLET POINTS

- Use `minBy` and `maxBy` to find the lowest or highest value in a collection. These functions take one parameter, a lambda whose body specifies the function criteria. The return type matches the type of items in the collection.
- Use `sumBy` or `sumByDouble` to return the sum of items in a collection. Its parameter, a lambda, specifies the thing you want to sum. If this is an `Int`, use `sumBy`, and if it's a `Double`, use `sumByDouble`.
- The `filter` function lets you search, or filter, a collection according to some criteria. You specify this criteria using a lambda, whose lambda body must return a `Boolean`. `filter` usually returns a `List` . If the function is being used with a `Map`, however, it returns a `Map` instead.
- The `map` function transforms the items in a collection according to some criteria that you specify using a lambda. It returns a `List`.
- `forEach` works like a `for` loop. It allows you to perform one or more actions for each item in a collection.
- Use `groupBy` to divide a collection into groups. It takes one parameter, a lambda, which defines how the function should group the items. The function returns a `Map`, which uses the lambda criteria for the keys, and a `List` for each value.
- The `fold` function lets you specify an initial value, and perform some operation for each item in a collection. It takes two parameters: the initial value and a lambda that specifies the operation you want to perform.

Leaving town...

It's been great having you here in Kotlinville

We're sad to see you leave, but there's nothing like taking what you've learned and putting it to use. There are still a few more gems for you in the back of the book and a handy index, and then it's time to take all these new ideas and put them into practice. Bon voyage!

appendix i: coroutines

Running Code in Parallel

Some tasks are best performed in the background.

If you want to read data from a slow external server, you probably don't want the rest of your code to hang around, waiting for the job to complete. In situations such as these, **coroutines are your new BFF**. Coroutines let you write code that's ***run asynchronously***. This means *less time hanging around*, a *better user experience*, and it can also *make your application more scalable*. Keep reading, and you'll learn the secret of how to talk to Bob, while simultaneously listening to Suzy.

Let's build a drum machine

Coroutines allow you to create multiple pieces of code that can run **asynchronously**. Instead of running pieces of code in sequence, one after the other, coroutines let you run them side-by-side.

Using coroutines means that you can launch a background job, such as reading data from an external server, without the rest of your code having to wait for the job to complete before doing anything else. This gives your user a more fluid experience, and it also makes your application more scalable.

To see the difference that using coroutines can make to your code, suppose you want to build a drum machine based on some code that plays a drum beat sequence. Let's start by creating the Drum Machine project by going through the following steps.

The code in this appendix applies to Kotlin 1.3 and above. In earlier versions, coroutines were marked as experimental.

1. Create a new GRADLE project

To write code that uses coroutines, we need to create a new **Gradle** project so that we can configure it to use coroutines. To do this, create a new project, select the Gradle option, check the Kotlin (Java) option, and make sure all the other options for additional libraries and frameworks are unchecked. Then click on the Next button.

Gradle is a build tool that lets you compile and deploy code, and include any third-party libraries that your code needs. We're using Gradle here so that we can add coroutines to our project a few pages ahead.

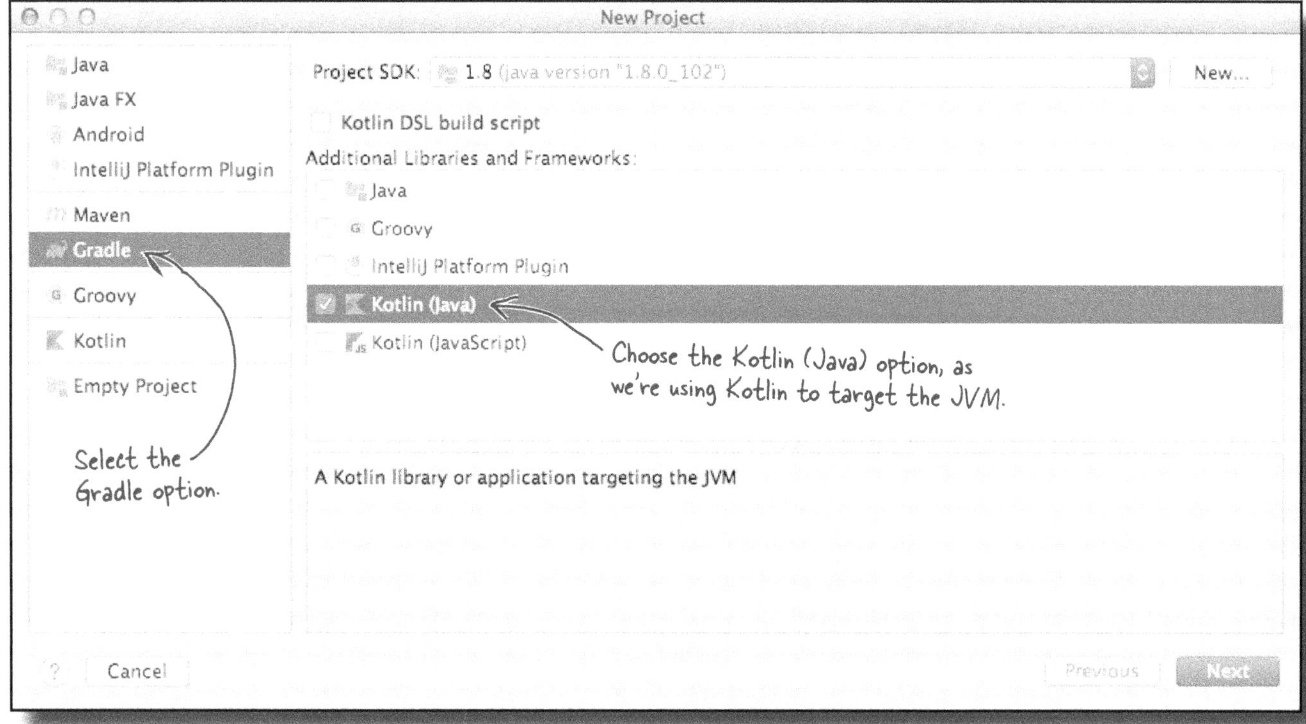

2. Enter an artifact ID

When you create a Gradle project, you need to specify an artifact ID. This is the basically the name of the project, except that, by convention, it should be lowercase. Enter an artifact ID of "drummachine", then click on the Next button.

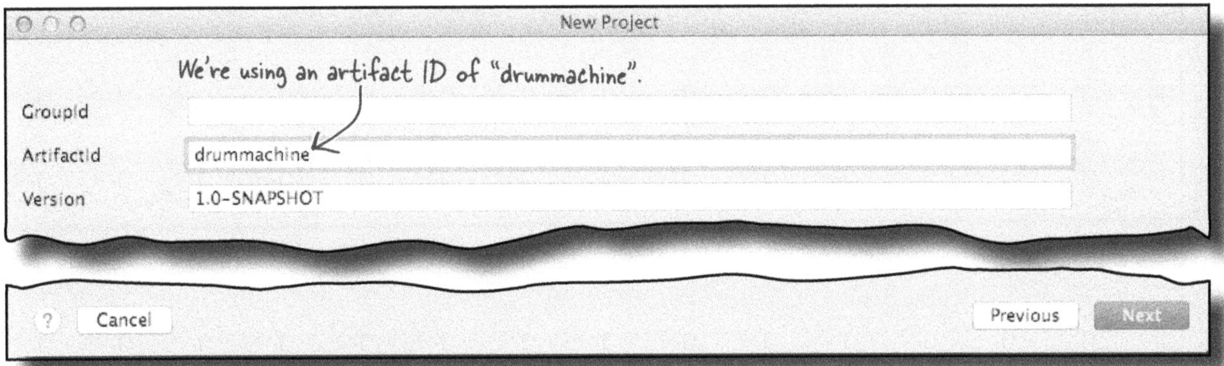

3. Specify configuration details

Next, you need to specify any changes to the default project configuration. Click on the Next button to accept the default values.

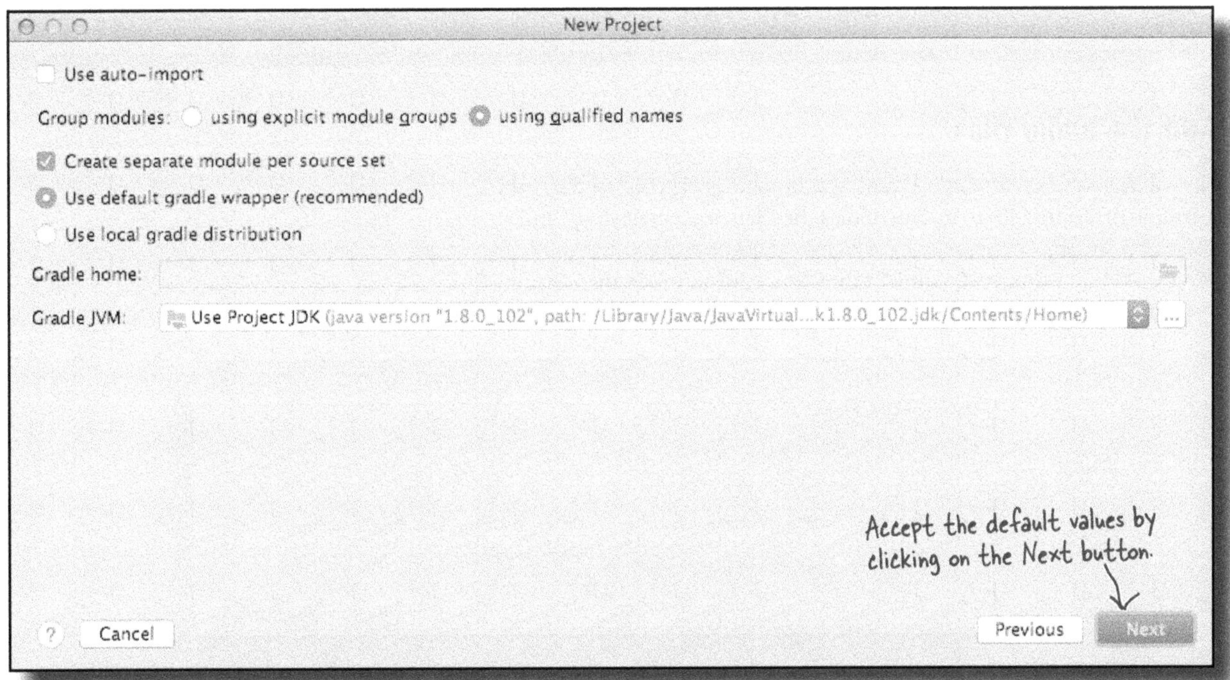

4. Specify the project name

Finally, we need to specify a project name. Name the project "Drum Machine", then click on the Finish button. IntelliJ IDEA will create your project.

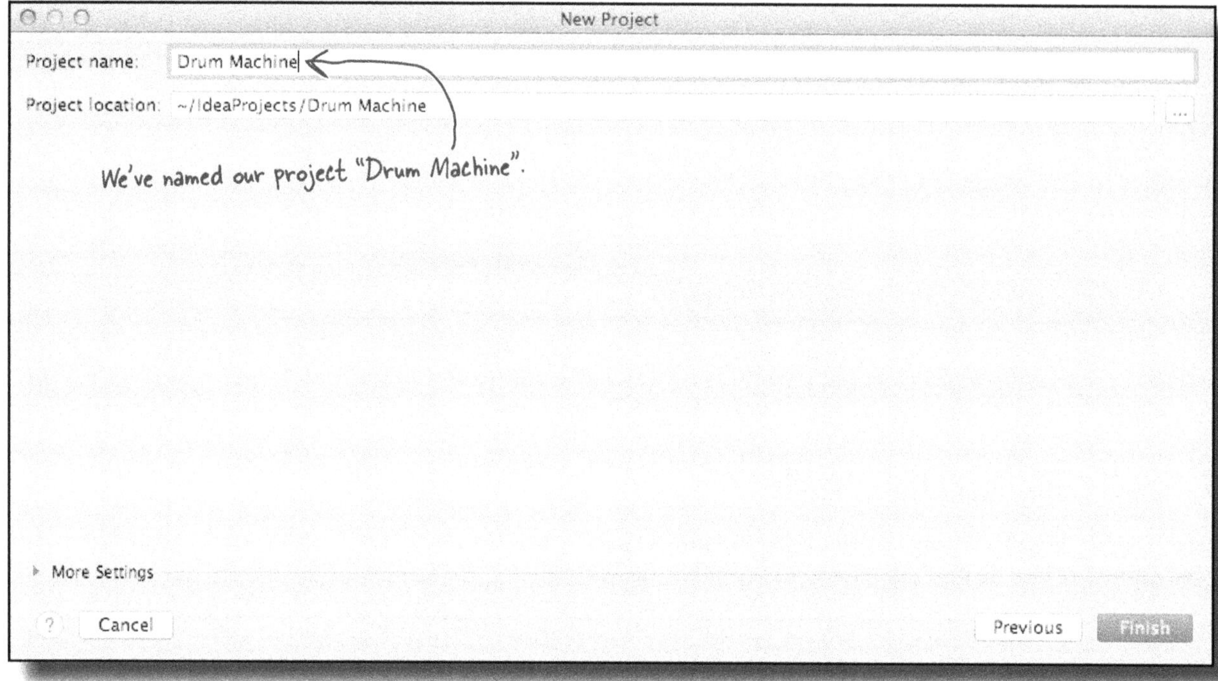

Add the audio files

Now that you've created the Drum Machine project, you need to add a couple of audio files to it. Download the files *crash_cymbal.aiff* and *toms.aiff* from *https://tinyurl.com/HFKotlin*, then drag them to your project. When prompted, confirm that you want to move them to the *Drum Machine* folder.

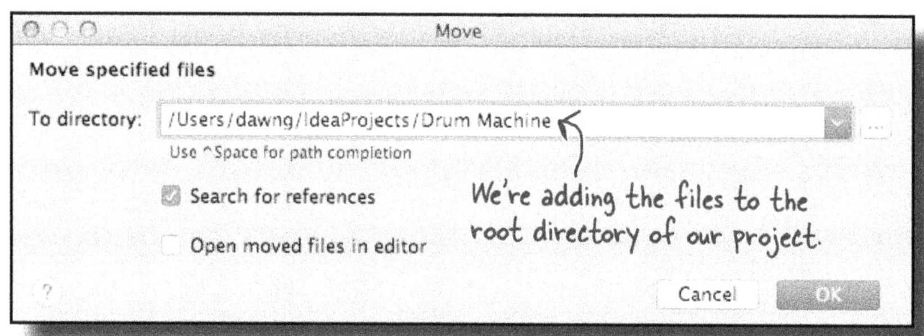

Add the code to the project

We've been given some code that plays a drum sequence, which we need to add to the project. Create a new Kotlin file named *Beats.kt* by highlighting the *src/main/kotlin* folder, clicking on the File menu and choosing New → Kotlin File/Class. When prompted, name the file "Beats", and choose File from the Kind option. Then update your version of *Beats.kt* to match ours below:

```
import java.io.File
import javax.sound.sampled.AudioSystem

fun playBeats(beats: String, file: String) {
    val parts = beats.split("x")
    var count = 0
    for (part in parts) {
        count += part.length + 1
        if (part == "") {
            playSound(file)
        } else {
            Thread.sleep(100 * (part.length + 1L))
            if (count < beats.length) {
                playSound(file)
            }
        }
    }
}

fun playSound(file: String) {
    val clip = AudioSystem.getClip()
    val audioInputStream = AudioSystem.getAudioInputStream(
        File(
            file
        )
    )
    clip.open(audioInputStream)
    clip.start()
}

fun main() {
    playBeats("x-x-x-x-x-x-", "toms.aiff")
    playBeats("x-----x-----", "crash_cymbal.aiff")
}
```

We're using two Java libraries, so we need to import them. You can find out more about import statements in Appendix III.

The beats parameter specifies the pattern of beats. The file parameter specifies the sound file to play.

Call playSound once for each "x" in the beats parameter.

Pauses the current thread of execution so that the sound file has time to run.

Plays the specified audio file.

Play the toms and cymbals sound files.

Drum Machine
src/main/kotlin
Beats.kt

Let's see what happens when the code runs.

Test drive

When we run the code, it plays the toms first (*toms.aiff*), followed by the cymbals (*crash_cymbal.aiff*). It does this in sequence, so once the toms have finished, the cymbals start playing:

Bam! Bam! Bam! Bam! Bam! Bam! Tish! Tish!

The code plays the toms sound file six times.

It then plays the cymbals sound file twice.

But what if we want to play the toms and cymbals in parallel?

Use coroutines to make beats play in parallel

As we said earlier, coroutines allow you to run multiple pieces of code asynchronously. In our example, this means that we can add our tom drum code to a coroutine so that it plays at the same time as the cymbals.

There are two things we need to do to achieve this:

1. **Add coroutines to the project as a dependency.**
   Coroutines are in a separate Kotlin library, which we need to add to our project before we can use them.

2. **Launch a coroutine.**
   The coroutine will include the code that plays the toms.

Let's do this now.

1. Add a coroutines dependency

If you want to use coroutines in your project, you first need to add it to your project as a dependency. To do this, open *build.gradle* with a double-click on the file name, and update the `dependencies` section like so:

Drum Machine
build.gradle

```
dependencies {
    compile "org.jetbrains.kotlin:kotlin-stdlib-jdk8"
    implementation 'org.jetbrains.kotlinx:kotlinx-coroutines-core:1.0.1'
}
```

Add this line to build.gradle to add the coroutines library to your project.

Then click on the Import Changes prompt to make the change take effect:

Click on Import Changes if prompted to do so.

Gradle projects need to be imported
Import Changes Enable Auto-Import

Next, we'll update our `main` function so that it uses a coroutine.

2. Launch a coroutine

We'll make our code play the toms sound file in a separate coroutine in the background by enclosing the code that plays it in a call to **`GlobalScope.launch`** from the `kotlinx.coroutines` library. Behind the scenes, this makes the code that plays the toms sound file run in the background so that the two sounds play in parallel.

Here's the new version of our `main` function—update your code with our changes (in bold):

```
...
import kotlinx.coroutines.*
...

fun main() {
    GlobalScope.launch { playBeats("x-x-x-x-x-x-", "toms.aiff") }
    playBeats("x-----x-----", "crash_cymbal.aiff")
}
```

Add this line so that we can use functions from the coroutines library in our code.

Launch a coroutine in the background.

Drum Machine
src/main/kotlin
Beats.kt

Let's see this in action by taking the code for a test drive.

Test drive

When we run the code, it plays the toms and cymbals in parallel. The toms sound plays in a separate coroutine in the background.

Now that you've seen how to launch a coroutine in the background, and the effect that this has, let's dive into coroutines a little deeper.

A coroutine is like a lightweight thread

Behind the scenes, launching a coroutine is like starting a separate thread of execution, or **thread**. Threads are really common in other languages such as Java, and both coroutines and threads can run in parallel and communicate with each other. The key difference, however, is that **it's more efficient to use coroutines in your code than it is to use threads**.

Starting a thread and keeping it running is quite expensive in terms of performance. The processor can usually only run a limited number of threads at the same time, and its more efficient to run as few threads as possible. Coroutines, on the other hand, run on a shared pool of threads by default, and the same thread can run many coroutines. As fewer threads are used, this makes it more efficient to use coroutines when you want to run tasks asynchronously.

In our code, we're using `GlobalScope.launch` to run a new coroutine in the background. Behind the scenes, this creates a new thread which the coroutine runs in, so that *toms.aiff* and *crash_cymbal.aiff* are played in separate threads. As it's more efficient to use as few threads as possible, let's find how we can use play the sound files in separate coroutines, but in the same thread.

Use runBlocking to run coroutines in the same scope

If you want your code to run in the same thread but in separate coroutines, you can use the **runBlocking** function. This is a higher-order function which blocks the current thread until the code that's passed to it finishes running. The runBlocking function defines a scope which is inherited by the code that's passed to it; in our example, we can use this scope to run separate coroutines in the same thread.

Here's a new version of our main function that does this—update your version of the code to include our changes (in bold):

```
fun main() {
    runBlocking {
        GlobalScope.launch { playBeats("x-x-x-x-x-x-", "toms.aiff") }
        playBeats("x-----x-----", "crash_cymbal.aiff")
    }
}
```

Wrap the code we want to run in a call to runBlocking.

Remove the reference to GlobalScope.

Drum Machine
src/main/kotlin
Beats.kt

Notice that we're now starting a new coroutine using launch instead of GlobalScope.launch. This is because we want to launch a coroutine that runs in the same thread, instead of in a separate background thread, and omitting the reference to GlobalScope allows the coroutine to use the same scope as runBlocking.

Let's see what happens when we run the code.

Test drive

When we run the code, the sound files play, but in sequence, not in parallel.

So what went wrong?

Thread.sleep pauses the current THREAD

As you may have noticed, when we added the `playBeats` function to our project, we included the following line:

```
Thread.sleep(100 * (part.length + 1L))
```

This uses a Java library to pause the current thread so that the sound file it's playing has time to run, and blocks the thread from doing anything else. As we're now playing the sound files in the same thread, they can no longer be played in parallel, even though they're in separate coroutines.

The delay function pauses the current COROUTINE

A better approach in this situation is to use the coroutines **`delay`** function instead. This has a similar effect to `Thread.sleep`, except that instead of pausing the current *thread*, it pauses the current *coroutine*. It suspends the coroutine for a specified length of time and this allows other code on the same thread to run instead. The following code, for example, delays the coroutine for 1 second:

```
delay(1000)
```

The delay function adds a pause, but it's more efficient than using Thread.sleep.

The `delay` function may be used in these two situations:

From inside a coroutine.

The following code, for example, calls the `delay` function inside a coroutine:

```
GlobalScope.launch {
    delay(1000)
    //code that runs after 1 second
}
```

Here, we're launching the coroutine then delaying its code for 1 second.

From inside a function that the compiler knows may pause, or suspend.

In our example, we want to use the `delay` function inside the `playBeats` function, which means that we need to tell the compiler that `playBeats`—and the `main` function which calls it—may suspend. To do this, we'll prefix both functions with the `suspend` prefix using code like this:

```
suspend fun playBeats(beats: String, file: String) {
    ...
}
```

The suspend prefix tells the compiler that the function is allowed to suspend.

We'll show you the full code for the project on the next page.

When you call a suspendable function (such as delay) from another function, that function must be marked with suspend.

The full project code

Here's the full code for the Drum Machine project—update your version of *Beats.kt* to include our changes (in bold):

```
import java.io.File
import javax.sound.sampled.AudioSystem
import kotlinx.coroutines.*

suspend fun playBeats(beats: String, file: String) {
    val parts = beats.split("x")
    var count = 0
    for (part in parts) {
        count += part.length + 1
        if (part == "") {
            playSound(file)
        } else {
            Thread.sleep delay(100 * (part.length + 1L))
            if (count < beats.length) {
                playSound(file)
            }
        }
    }
}

fun playSound(file: String) {
    val clip = AudioSystem.getClip()
    val audioInputStream = AudioSystem.getAudioInputStream(
        File(
            file
        )
    )
    clip.open(audioInputStream)
    clip.start()
}

suspend fun main() {
    runBlocking {
        launch { playBeats("x-x-x-x-x-x-", "toms.aiff") }
        playBeats("x-----x-----", "crash_cymbal.aiff")
    }
}
```

Mark playBeats with suspend so that it can call the delay function.

Replace Thread.sleep with delay.

Mark main with suspend so that it can call the playBeats function.

Drum Machine
src/main/kotlin
Beats.kt

Let's see what happens when the code runs.

Test drive

When we run the code, it plays the toms and cymbals in parallel as before. This time, however, the sound files run in separate coroutines in the same thread.

Bam! Bam! Bam! Bam! Bam! Bam!
Tish! Tish!

The toms and cymbals still play in parallel, but this time we're using a more efficient way of playing the sound files.

You can find out more about using coroutines here:

https://kotlinlang.org/docs/reference/coroutines-overview.html

BULLET POINTS

- Coroutines let you run code asynchronously. They are useful for running background tasks.
- A coroutine is like a lightweight thread. Coroutines run on a shared pool of threads by default, and the same thread can run many coroutines.
- To use coroutines, create a Gradle project and add the coroutines library to *build.gradle* as a dependency.
- Use the `launch` function to launch a new coroutine.
- The `runBlocking` function blocks the current thread until the code it contains has finished running.
- The `delay` function suspends the code for a specified length of time. It can be used inside a coroutine, or inside a function that's marked using `suspend`.

You can download the full code for this appendix from https://tinyurl.com/HFKotlin.

appendix ii: testing

Hold Your Code to Account

Everybody knows that good code needs to work.

But each code change that you make runs the risk of introducing fresh bugs that stop your code from working as it should. That's why *thorough testing* is so important: it means you get to know about any problems in your code *before it's deployed to the live environment*. In this appendix, we'll discuss ***JUnit*** and ***KotlinTest***, two libraries which you can use to **unit test your code** so that you *always have a safety net*.

Kotlin can use existing testing libraries

As you already know, Kotlin code can be compiled down to Java, JavaScript or native code, so you can use existing libraries on its target platform. When it comes to testing, this means that you can test Kotlin code using the most popular testing libraries in Java and JavaScript.

Let's see how to use JUnit to unit test your Kotlin code.

Add the JUnit library

Unit testing is used to test individual units of source code, such as classes or functions.

The **JUnit** library (*https://junit.org*) is the most frequently used Java testing library.

To use JUnit in your Kotlin project, you first need to add the JUnit libraries to your project. You can add libraries to your project by going to the File menu and choosing Project Structure → Libraries, or, if you have a Gradle project, you can add these lines to your *build.gradle* file:

```
dependencies {
    ....
    testImplementation 'org.junit.jupiter:junit-jupiter-api:5.3.1'
    testRuntimeOnly 'org.junit.jupiter:junit-jupiter-engine:5.3.1'
    test { useJUnitPlatform() }
    ....
}
```

These lines add version 5.3.1 of the JUnit libraries to the project. Change the numbers if you want to use a different version.

Once the code is compiled, you can then run the tests by right-clicking the class or function name, and then selecting the Run option.

To see how to use JUnit with Kotlin, we're going to write a test for the following class named `Totaller`: the class is initialized with an `Int` value, and it keeps a running total of the values which are added to it using its `add` function:

```
class Totaller(var total: Int = 0) {
    fun add(num: Int): Int {
        total += num
        return total
    }
}
```

Let's see what a JUnit test might look like for this class.

Create a JUnit test class

Here's an example JUnit test class named `TotallerTest` that's used to test `Totaller`:

```
import org.junit.jupiter.api.Assertions.*
import org.junit.jupiter.api.Test

class TotallerTest {
    @Test
    fun shouldBeAbleToAdd3And4() {
        val totaller = Totaller()

        assertEquals(3, totaller.add(3))
        assertEquals(7, totaller.add(4))
        assertEquals(7, totaller.total)
    }
}
```

We're using code from the JUnit packages, so we need to import them. You can find out more about import statements in Appendix III.

The TotallerTest class is used to test Totaller.

This is an annotation that marks the following function as a test.

Create a Totaller object.

Check that if we add 3, the return value is 3.

If we now add 4, the return value should be 7.

Check that the return value matches the value of the total variable.

Each test is held in a function, prefixed with the annotation `@Test`. Annotations are used to add programmatic information about your code, and the `@Test` annotation is a way of telling tools "This is a test function".

Tests are made up of *actions* and *assertions*. Actions are pieces of code that *do* stuff, while assertions are pieces of code that *check* stuff. In the above code, we're using an assertion named `assertEquals` which checks that the two values it's given are equal. If they're not, `assertEquals` will throw an exception and the test will fail.

You can find out more about using JUnit here:

https://junit.org

In the above example, we've named our test function `shouldBeAbleToAdd3And4`. We can, however, use a rarely used feature of Kotlin which allows us to wrap function names in back-ticks (`), and then add spaces and other symbols to the function name to make it more descriptive. Here's an example:

```
....
@Test
fun `should be able to add 3 and 4 - and it mustn't go wrong`() {
    val totaller = Totaller()
...
```

This looks weird, but it's a valid Kotlin function name.

For the most part, you use JUnit on Kotlin in almost the same way you might use it with a Java project. But if you want something a bit more Kotliny, there's another library you can use, named KotlinTest.

Using KotlinTest

The **KotlinTest** library (*https://github.com/kotlintest/kotlintest*) has been designed to use the full breadth of the Kotlin language to write tests in a more expressive way. Just like JUnit, it's a separate library which needs to be added to your project if you want to use it.

KotlinTest is pretty vast, and it allows you to write tests in many different styles, but here's one way of writing a KotlinTest version of the JUnit code we wrote earlier:

```
import io.kotlintest.shouldBe
import io.kotlintest.specs.StringSpec

class AnotherTotallerTest : StringSpec({
    "should be able to add 3 and 4 - and it mustn't go wrong" {
        val totaller = Totaller()

        totaller.add(3) shouldBe 3
        totaller.add(4) shouldBe 7
        totaller.total shouldBe 7
    }
})
```

We're using these functions from the KotlinTest libraries, so we need to import them.

The JUnit test function is replaced with a String.

We're using shouldBe instead of assertEquals.

The above test looks similar to the JUnit test you saw earlier, except that the `test` function is replaced with a `String`, and the calls to `assertEquals` have been rewritten as `shouldBe` expressions. This is an example of KotlinTest's **String Specification**—or **StringSpec**—style. There are several testing styles available in KotlinTest, and you should choose the one which is best suited to your code.

But KotlinTest isn't just a rewrite of JUnit (in fact, KotlinTest uses JUnit under the hood). KotlinTest has many more features that can allow you to create tests more easily, and with less code, than you can do with a simple Java library. You can, for example, use rows to test your code against entire sets of data. Let's look at an example.

Use rows to test against sets of data

Here's an example of a second test which uses rows to add lots of different numbers together (our changes are in bold):

```
import io.kotlintest.data.forall
import io.kotlintest.shouldBe
import io.kotlintest.specs.StringSpec
import io.kotlintest.tables.row

class AnotherTotallerTest : StringSpec({
    "should be able to add 3 and 4 - and it mustn't go wrong" {
        val totaller = Totaller()

        totaller.add(3) shouldBe 3
        totaller.add(4) shouldBe 7
        totaller.total shouldBe 7
    }

    "should be able to add lots of different numbers" {
        forall(
                row(1, 2, 3),
                row(19, 47, 66),
                row(11, 21, 32)
        ) { x, y, expectedTotal ->
            val totaller = Totaller(x)
            totaller.add(y) shouldBe expectedTotal
        }
    }
})
```

We're using these two extra functions from the KotlinTest libraries.

This is the second test.

We'll run the test for each row of data.

The values in each row will be assigned to the x, y and expectedTotal variables.

These two lines will run for each row.

You can also use KotlinTest to:

 Run tests in parallel.

 Create tests with generated properties.

 Enable/disable tests dynamically. You may, for example, want some tests to run only on Linux, and others to run on Mac.

 Put tests in groups.

and lots, lots more. If you're planning on writing a lot of Kotlin code, then KotlinTest is definitely worth a look.

You can find out more about KotlinTest here:

https://github.com/kotlintest/kotlintest

appendix iii: leftovers

The Top Ten Things (We Didn't Cover)

Even after all that, there's still a little more.

There are just a few more things we think you need to know. We wouldn't feel right about ignoring them, and we really wanted to give you a book you'd be able to lift without training at the local gym. Before you put down the book, **read through these tidbits**.

1. Packages and imports

As we said in Chapter 9, classes and functions in the Kotlin Standard Library are grouped into packages. What we *didn't* say is that you can group your *own* code into packages.

Putting your code into packages is useful for two main reasons:

- **It lets you organize your code.**
  You can use packages to group your code into specific kinds of functionality, like data structures or database stuff.

- **It prevents name conflicts.**
  If you write a class named `Duck`, putting it into a package lets you differentiate it from any other `Duck` class that may have been added to your project.

How to add a package

You add a package to your Kotlin project by highlighting the *src* folder, and choosing File→New→Package. When prompted, enter the package name (for example, *com.hfkotlin.mypackage*), then click on OK.

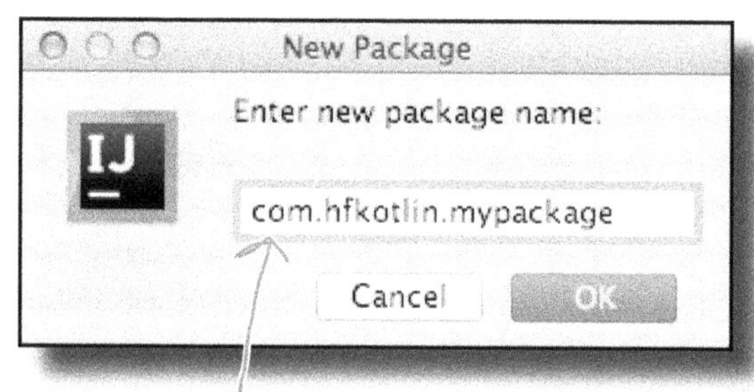

This is the name of the package we're creating.

Package declarations

When you add a Kotlin file to a package (by highlighting the package name and choosing File→New→Kotlin File/Class), a **`package`** declaration is automatically added to the beginning of the source file like this:

```
package com.hfkotlin.mypackage
```

The `package` declaration tells the compiler that everything in the source file belongs in that package. The following code, for example, specifes that *com.hfkotlin.mypackage* contains the `Duck` class and the `doStuff` function:

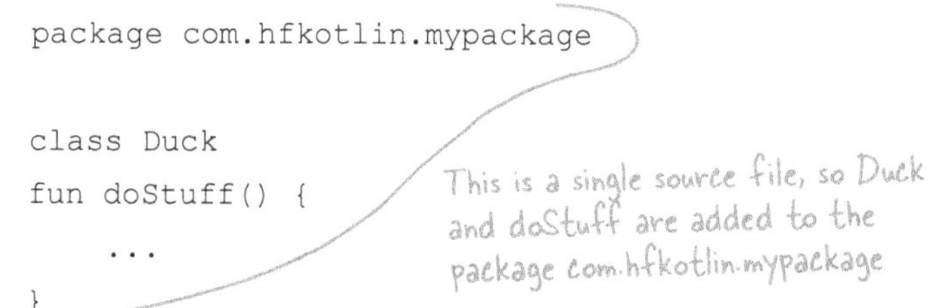

```
package com.hfkotlin.mypackage

class Duck
fun doStuff() {
    ...
}
```


If the source file has no package declaration, the code is added to a nameless default package.

Your project can contain multiple packages, and each package can have multiple source files. Each source file, however, can only have one package declaration.

The fully qualified name

When you add a class to a package, it's full—or *fully qualified*—name is the name of the class prefixed with the name of the package. So if *com.hfkotlin.mypackage* contains a class named `Duck`, the fully qualified name of the `Duck` class is `com.hfkotlin.mypackage.Duck`. You can still refer to it as `Duck` in any code within the same package, but if you want to use the class in another package, you have to provide the compiler with its full name.

There are two ways of providing a fully qualified class name: by using its full name everywhere in your code, or by importing it.

Type the fully qualified name...

The first option is to type the full class name each time you use it outside its package, for example:

```
package com.hfkotlin.myotherpackage

fun main(args: Array<String>) {
    val duck = com.hfkotlin.mypackage.Duck()
    ...
}
```

This is a different package.

This is the fully qualified name.

This approach, however, can be cumbersome if you need to refer to the class many times, or refer to multiple items in the same package.

...or import it

An alternative approach is to **import** the class or package so that you can refer to the `Duck` class without typing the fully qualified name each time. Here's an example:

```
package com.hfkotlin.myotherpackage
import com.hfkotlin.mypackage.Duck

fun main(args: Array<String>) {
    val duck = Duck()
    ...
}
```

This line imports the Duck class...

...so we can refer to it without typing its fully qualified name.

You can also use the following code to import an entire package:

```
import com.hfkotlin.mypackage.*
```

The * means "import everything from this package".

And if there's a class name conflict, you can use the **as** keyword:

```
import com.hfkotlin.mypackage.Duck
import com.hfKotlin.mypackage2.Duck as Duck2
```

Here, you can refer to the Duck class in mypackage2 using "Duck2".

Default Imports

The following packages are automatically imported into each Kotlin file by default:

- *kotlin.**
- *kotlin.annotation.**
- *kotlin.collections.**
- *kotlin.comparisons.**
- *kotlin.io.**
- *kotlin.ranges.**
- *kotlin.sequences.**
- *kotlin.text.**

If your target platform is the JVM, the following are also imported:

- *java.lang.**
- *kotlin.jvm.**

And if you're targeting JavaScript, the following gets imported instead:

- *kotlin.js.**

2. Visibility modifiers

Visibility modifiers let you set the visibility of any code that you create, such as classes and functions. You can declare, for example, that a class can only be used by the code in its source file, or that a member function can only be used inside its class.

Kotlin has four visibility modifiers: **`public`**, **`private`**, **`protected`** and **`internal`**. Let's see how these work.

Visibility modifiers and top level code

As you already know, code such as classes, variables and functions can be declared directly inside a source file or package. By default, all of this code is publicly visible, and it can be used in any package that imports it. You can change this behavior, however, by prefixing declarations with one of the following visibility modifiers:

Remember: if you don't specify a package, the code is automatically added to a nameless package by default.

Modifier:	What it does:
public	Makes the declaration visible everywhere. This is applied by default, so it can be omitted.
private	Makes the declaration visible to code inside its source file, but invisible elsewhere.
internal	Makes the declaration visible inside the same module, but invisible elsewhere. A module is a set of Kotlin files that are compiled together, such as an IntelliJ IDEA module.

Note that protected isn't available for declarations at the top level of a source file or package.

The following code, for example, specifies that the `Duck` class is `public` and can be seen anywhere, while the `doStuff` function is `private`, and is only visible inside its source file:

```
package com.hfkotlin.mypackage

class Duck

private fun doStuff() {
    println("hello")
}
```

Duck has no visibility modifier, which means that it's public.

doStuff() is marked as private, so it can only be used inside the source file where it's defined.

Visibility modifiers can also be applied to members of classes and interfaces. Let's see how these work.

Visibility modifiers and classes/interfaces

The following visibility modifiers can be applied to the properties, functions and other members that belong to a class or interface:

Modifier:	What it does:
public	Makes the member visible everywhere that the class is visible. This is applied by default, so it can be omitted.
private	Makes the member visible inside the class, and invisible elsewhere.
protected	Makes the member visible inside the class, and any of its subclasses.
internal	Makes the member visible to anything in the module that can see the class.

Here's an example of a class with visibility modifiers on its properties, and a subclass which overrides it:

```
open class Parent {
    var a = 1
    private var b = 2
    protected open var c = 3
    internal var d = 4
}

class Child: Parent() {
    override var c = 6
}
```

As b is private, it can **only** be used inside this class. It can't be seen by any subclasses of Parent.

The Child class can see the a and c properties, and can also access the d property if Parent and Child are defined in the same module. Child can't, however, see the b property as it's visibility modifier is private.

Note that if you override a `protected` member, as in the above example, the subclass version of that member will also be `protected` by default. You can, however, change its visibility, as in this example:

```
class Child: Parent() {
    public override var c = 6
}
```

The c property can now be seen anywhere that the Child class is visible.

By default, class constructors are `public`, so they are visible everywhere that the class is visible. You can, however, change a constructor's visibility by specifying a visibility modifier, and prefixing the constructor with the `constructor` keyword. If, for example, you have a class defined as:

```
class MyClass(x: Int)
```

By default, the MyClass primary constructor is public.

you can make its constructor `private` using the following code:

```
class MyClass private constructor(x: Int)
```

This code makes the primary constructor private.

3. Enum classes

An **enum class** lets you create a set of values that represent the ***only*** valid values for a variable.

Suppose you want to create an application for a band, and you want to make sure that a variable, `selectedBandMember`, can only be assigned a value for a valid band member. To perform this kind of task, we can create an enum class named `BandMember` that contains the valid values:

```
enum class BandMember { JERRY, BOBBY, PHIL }
```

The enum class has three values: JERRY, BOBBY and PHIL.

We can then restrict the `selectedBandMember` variable to one of these values by specifying its type as `BandMember` like so:

```
fun main(args: Array<String>) {
    var selectedBandMember: BandMember
    selectedBandMember = BandMember.JERRY
}
```

The variable's type is BandMember...

...so we can assign one of BandMember's values to it.

Each value in an enum class is a constant.

Each enum constant exists as a single instance of that enum class.

Enum constructors

An enum class can have a constructor, used to initialize each enum value. This works because **each value defined by the enum class is an instance of that class**.

To see how this works, suppose that we want to specify the instrument played by each band member. To do this, we can add a `String` variable named `instrument` to the `BandMember` constructor, and initialize each value in the class with an appropriate value. Here's the code:

```
enum class BandMember(val instrument: String) {
    JERRY("lead guitar"),
    BOBBY("rhythm guitar"),
    PHIL("bass")
}
```

This defines a property named instrument in the BandMember constructor. Each value in the enum class is an instance of BandMember, so each value has this property.

We can then find out which instrument the selected band member plays by accessing its `instrument` property like this:

```
fun main(args: Array<String>) {
    var selectedBandMember: BandMember
    selectedBandMember = BandMember.JERRY
    println(selectedBandMember.instrument)
}
```

This produces the output "lead guitar".

enum properties and functions

In the previous example, we added a property to the `BandMember` class by including it in the enum class constructor. You can also add properties and functions to the main body of the class. The following code, for example, adds a `sings` function to the `BandMember` enum class:

```
enum class BandMember(val instrument: String) {
    JERRY("lead guitar"),
    BOBBY("rhythm guitar"),
    PHIL("bass");

    fun sings() = "occasionally"
}
```

Note that we need a ";" to separate the sings() function from the enum values.

Each enum value has a function named sings() which returns the String "occasionally".

Each value defined in an enum class can override the properties and functions it inherits from the class definition. Here's how, for example, you can override the `sings` function for `JERRY` and `BOBBY`:

```
enum class BandMember(val instrument: String) {
    JERRY("lead guitar") {
        override fun sings() = "plaintively"
    },
    BOBBY("rhythm guitar") {
        override fun sings() = "hoarsely"
    },
    PHIL("bass");

    open fun sings() = "occasionally"
}
```

JERRY and BOBBY have their own implementation of sings().

As we're overriding sings() for two values, we need to mark it as open.

We can then find out how the selected band member sings by calling its `sings` function like this:

```
fun main(args: Array<String>) {
    var selectedBandMember: BandMember
    selectedBandMember = BandMember.JERRY
    println(selectedBandMember.instrument)
    println(selectedBandMember.sings())
}
```

This line calls JERRY's sings() function, and produces the output "plaintively".

4. Sealed classes

You've already seen that enum classes let you create a restricted set of values, but there are some situations where you need a little more flexibility.

Suppose that you want to be able to use two different message types in your application: one for "success", and another for "failure". You want to be able to restrict messages to these two types.

If you were to model this using an enum class, your code might look like this:

```
enum class MessageType(var msg: String) {
    SUCCESS("Yay!"),
    FAILURE("Boo!")
}
```

The MessageType enum class has two values: SUCCESS and FAILURE.

But there are a couple of problems with this approach:

- **Each value is a constant which only exists as a single instance.**
  You can't, say, change the `msg` property of the `SUCCESS` value in one situation, as this change will be seen everywhere else in your application.

- **Each value must have the same properties and functions.**
  It might be useful to add an `Exception` property to the `FAILURE` value so that you can examine what went wrong, but an enum class won't let you.

So what's the solution?

Sealed classes to the rescue!

A solution to this kind of problem is to use a **sealed class**. A sealed class is like a souped-up version of an enum class. It lets you restrict your class hierarchy to a specific set of subtypes, each one of which can define its own properties and functions. And unlike an enum class, you can create multiple instances of each type.

You create a sealed class by prefixing the class name with **`sealed`**. The following code, for example, creates a sealed class named `MessageType`, with two subtypes named `MessageSuccess` and `MessageFailure`. Each subtype has a `String` property named `msg`, and the `MessageFailure` subtype has an extra `Exception` property named `e`:

```
sealed class MessageType
class MessageSuccess(var msg: String) : MessageType()
class MessageFailure(var msg: String, var e: Exception) : MessageType()
```

MessageType is sealed.

MessageSuccess and MessageFailure inherit from MessageType, and define their own properties in their constructors

How to use sealed classes

As we said, a sealed class lets you create multiple instances of each subtype. The following code, for example, creates two instances of `MessageSuccess`, and a single instance of `MessageFailure`:

```
fun main(args: Array<String>) {
    val messageSuccess = MessageSuccess("Yay!")
    val messageSuccess2 = MessageSuccess("It worked!")
    val messageFailure = MessageFailure("Boo!", Exception("Gone wrong."))
}
```

You can then create a `MessageType` variable, and assign one of these messages to it:

```
fun main(args: Array<String>) {
    val messageSuccess = MessageSuccess("Yay!")
    val messageSuccess2 = MessageSuccess("It worked!")
    val messageFailure = MessageFailure("Boo!", Exception("Gone wrong."))

    var myMessageType: MessageType = messageFailure
}
```

messageFailure is a subtype of MessageType, so we can assign it to myMessageType.

And as `MessageType` is a sealed class with a limited set of subtypes, you can use `when` to check for each subtype without requiring an extra `else` clause using code like this:

```
fun main(args: Array<String>) {
    val messageSuccess = MessageSuccess("Yay!")
    val messageSuccess2 = MessageSuccess("It worked!")
    val messageFailure = MessageFailure("Boo!", Exception("Gone wrong."))

    var myMessageType: MessageType = messageFailure
    val myMessage = when (myMessageType) {
        is MessageSuccess -> myMessageType.msg
        is MessageFailure -> myMessageType.msg + " " + myMessageType.e.message
    }
    println(myMessage)
}
```

myMessageType can **only** have a type of MessageSuccess or MessageFailure, so there's no need for an extra else clause.

You can find out more about creating and using sealed classes here:

https://kotlinlang.org/docs/reference/sealed-classes.html

5. Nested and inner classes

A **nested class** is a class that's defined inside another class. This can be useful if you want to provide the outer class with extra functionality that's outside its main purpose, or bring code closer to where it's being used.

A nested class in Kotlin is like a static nested class in Java.

You define a nested class by putting it inside the curly braces of the outer class. The following code, for example, defines a class named `Outer` which has a nested class named `Nested`:

```
class Outer {
    val x = "This is in the Outer class"

    class Nested {
        val y = "This is in the Nested class"
        fun myFun() = "This is the Nested function"
    }
}
```

This is the nested class. It's fully enclosed by the outer class.

You can then refer to the `Nested` class, and its properties and functions, using code like this:

```
fun main(args: Array<String>) {
    val nested = Outer.Nested()
    println(nested.y)
    println(nested.myFun())
}
```

Creates an instance of Nested, and assigns it to a variable.

Note that you can't access a nested class from an instance of the outer class without first creating a property of that type inside the outer class. The following code, for example, won't compile:

```
val nested = Outer().Nested()
```

This won't compile as we're using Outer(), not Outer.

Another restriction is that a nested class doesn't have access to an instance of the outer class, so it can't access its members. You can't access `Outer`'s `x` property from the `Nested` class, for example, so the following code won't compile:

```
class Outer {
    val x = "This is in the Outer class"

    class Nested {
        fun getX() = "Value of x is: $x"
    }
}
```

Nested can't see x as it's defined in the Outer class, so this line won't compile.

An inner class can access the outer class members

If you want a nested class to be able to access the properties and functions defined by its outer class, you can do so by making it an **inner class**. You do this by prefixing the nested class with **`inner`**. Here's an example:

```
class Outer {
    val x = "This is in the Outer class"

    inner class Inner {
        val y = "This is in the Inner class"
        fun myFun() = "This is the Inner function"
        fun getX() = "The value of x is: $x"
    }
}
```

An inner class is a nested class that has access to the outer class members. So in this example, the Inner class has access to Outer's x property.

You can access an inner class by creating an instance of the outer class, and then using this to create an instance of the inner class. Here's an example, using the `Outer` and `Inner` classes defined above:

```
fun main(args: Array<String>) {
    val inner = Outer().Inner()
    println(inner.y)
    println(inner.myFun())
    println(inner.getX())
}
```

As Inner is an inner class, we have to use Outer(), not Outer.

Alternatively, you can access the inner class by instantiating a property of that type in the outer class, as in this example:

```
class Outer {
    val myInner = Inner()

    inner class Inner {
        ...
    }
}

fun main(args: Array<String>) {
    val inner = Outer().myInner
}
```

Outer's myInner property holds a reference to an instance of its Inner class.

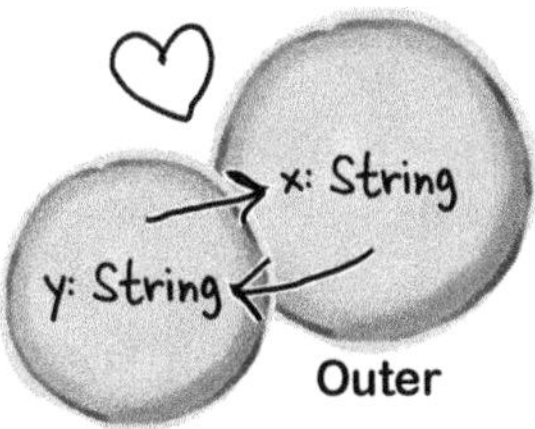

The Inner and Outer objects share a special bond. The Inner can use the Outer's variables, and vice versa.

The key thing is that an inner class instance is *always* tied to a specific instance of the outer class, so you can't create an `Inner` object without first creating an `Outer` object.

6. Object declarations and expressions

There are times where you want to make sure that only a single instance of a given type can be created, such as if you want to use a single object to coordinate actions across an entire application. In these situations, you can use the `object` keyword to make an **object declaration**.

If you're familiar with design patterns, an object declaration is the Kotlin equivalent of a Singleton.

An object declaration defines a class declaration and creates an instance of it in a single statement. And when you include it in the top level of a source file or package, only one instance of that type will ever be created.

Here's what an object declaration looks like:

```
package com.hfkotlin.mypackage

object DuckManager {
    val allDucks = mutableListOf<Duck>()

    fun herdDucks() {
        //Code to herd the Ducks
    }
}
```

DuckManager is an object.

It has a property named allDucks, and a function named herdDucks().

An object declaration defines a class and creates an instance of it in a single statement.

As you can can see, an object declaration looks like a class definition except that it's prefixed with `object`, not `class`. Just like a class, it can have properties, functions and initializer blocks, and it can inherit from classes or interfaces. You can't, however, add a constructor to an object declaration. This is because the object is automatically created as soon as it's accessed, so having a constructor would be redundant.

You refer to an object that's created using an object declaration by calling its name directly, and this allows you to access its members. If you wanted to call the `DuckManager`'s `herdDucks` function, for example, you could do so using code like this:

```
DuckManager.herdDucks()
```

As well as adding an object declaration to the top level of a source file or package, you can also add one to a class. Let's see how.

Class objects...

The following code adds an object declaration—DuckFactory—to a class named Duck:

```
class Duck {
    object DuckFactory {
        fun create(): Duck = Duck()
    }
}
```

The object declaration goes in the main body of the class.

When you add an object declaration to a class, it creates an object that belongs to that class. One instance of the object is created per class, and it's shared by all instances of that class.

Once you've added an object declaration, you can access the object from the class using the dot notation. The following code, for example, calls the DuckFactory's create function, and assigns the result to a new variable named newDuck:

```
val newDuck = Duck.DuckFactory.create()
```

Note that you access the object using Duck, not Duck().

Add an object declaration to a class to create a single instance of that type which belongs to the class.

...and companion objects

One object per class can be marked as a **companion** object using the **companion** prefix. A companion object is like a class object, except that you can omit the object's name. The following code, for example, turns above DuckFactory object into an unnamed companion object:

```
class Duck {
    companion object ~~DuckFactory~~ {
        fun create(): Duck = Duck()
    }
}
```

If you prefix an object declaration with companion, you no longer need to provide an object name. You can, however, include the name if you want to.

When you create a companion object, you access it by simply referring to the class name. The following code, for example, calls the create() function that's defined by Duck's companion object:

```
val newDuck = Duck.create()
```

To get a reference to a nameless companion object, you use the Companion keyword. The following code, for example, creates a new variable named x, and assigns to it a reference to Duck's companion object:

```
val x = Duck.Companion
```

Now that you've learned about object declarations and companion objects, let's look at object expressions.

A companion object can be used as the Kotlin equivalent to static methods in Java.
Any functions you add to a companion object are shared by all class instances.

Object expressions

An **object expression** is an expression that creates an anonymous object on the fly with no predefined type.

Suppose that you want to create an object that holds an initial value for x and y coordinates. Instead of defining a `Coordinate` class and creating an instance of it, you could instead create an object that uses properties to hold the values of the x and y coordinates. The following code, for example, creates a new variable named `startingPoint`, and assigns such an object to it:

```
val startingPoint = object {
    val x = 0
    val y = 0
}
```

This creates an object with two properties, x and y.

You can then refer to the object's members using code like this:

```
println("starting point is ${startingPoint.x}, ${startingPoint.y}")
```

Object expressions are mainly used as the equivalent of anonymous inner classes in Java. If you're writing some GUI code, and you suddenly realize that you need an instance of a class that implements a `MouseAdapter` abstract class, you can use an object expression to create that instance on the fly. The following code, for example, passes an object to a function named `addMouseListener`; the object implements `MouseAdapter`, and overrides its `mouseClicked` and `mouseReleased` functions:

This statement...

```
window.addMouseListener(object : MouseAdapter() {
    override fun mouseClicked(e: MouseEvent) {
        //Code that runs when the mouse is clicked
    }

    override fun mouseReleased(e: MouseEvent) {
        //Code that runs when the mouse is released
    }
})
```

...ends down here.

The object expression in bold is like saying "create an instance of a class (with no name) that implements MouseAdapter, and by the way, here's the implementation of the mouseClicked and mouseReleased functions". In other words, we're providing the addMouseListener function with a class implementation, and an instance of that class, right where we need it.

You can find out more about object declarations and expressions here:

https://kotlinlang.org/docs/reference/object-declarations.html

7. Extensions

Extensions let you add new functions and properties to an existing type without you having to create a whole new subtype. ← There are also Kotlin extension libraries you can use to make your coding life easier, such as Anko and Android KTX for Android app development.

Imagine you're writing an application where you frequently need to prefix a `Double` with "$" in order to format it as dollars. Instead of performing the same action over and over again, you can write an extension function named `toDollar` that you can use with `Doubles`. Here's the code to do this:

Defines a function named toDollar(), which extends Double.

```
fun Double.toDollar(): String {
    return "$$this"    ← Return the current value, prefixed with $.
}
```

The above code specifies that a function named `toDollar`, which returns a `String`, can be used with `Double` values. The function takes the current object (referred to using `this`), prefixes it with "$", and returns the result.

Once you've created an extension function, you can use it in the same way that you'd use any other function. The following code, for example, calls the `toDollar` function on a `Double` variable that has a value of 45.25:

```
var dbl = 45.25
println(dbl.toDollar())    //prints $45.25
```

You can create extension properties in a similar way to how you create extension functions. The following code, for example, creates an extension property for `Strings` named `halfLength` which returns the length of the current `String` divided by 2.0:

```
val String.halfLength    ← Defines a halfLength property
   get() = length / 2.0      that can be used with Strings.
```

And here's some example code that uses the new property:

```
val test = "This is a test"
println(test.halfLength)    //prints 7.0
```

You can find out more about how to use extensions—including how to add them to companion objects—here:

https://kotlinlang.org/docs/reference/extensions.html

And you can find out more about using `this` here:

https://kotlinlang.org/docs/reference/this-expressions.html

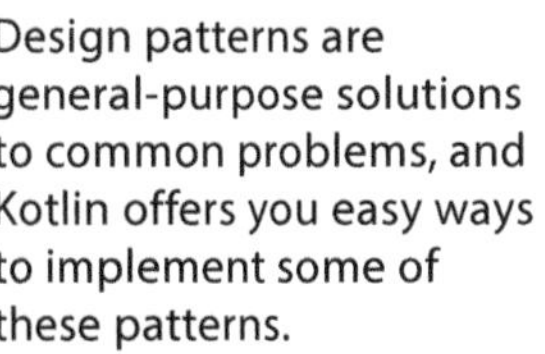

Design patterns are general-purpose solutions to common problems, and Kotlin offers you easy ways to implement some of these patterns.

Object declarations provide a way of implementing the **Singleton** pattern, as each declaration creates a single instance of that object. **Extensions** may be used in place of the **Decorator** pattern as they allow you to extend the behavior of classes and objects. And if you're interested in using the **Delegation** pattern as an alternative to inheritance, you can find out more here:

https://kotlinlang.org/docs/reference/delegation.html

8. Return, break and continue

Kotlin has three ways of jumping out of a loop. These are:

return
As you already know, this returns from the enclosing function.

break
This terminates (or jumps to the end of) the enclosing loop, for example:

```
var x = 0
var y = 0
while (x < 10) {
    x++
    break
    y++
}
```

This code increments x, then terminates the loop without executing the line y++. x has a final value of 1, and y's value remains 0.

continue
This moves to the next iteration of the enclosing loop, for example:

```
var x = 0
var y = 0
while (x < 10) {
    x++
    continue
    y++
}
```

This increments x, then moves back to the line while (x < 10) without executing the line y++. It keeps incrementing x until the while's condition (x < 10) is false. x has a final value of 10, and y's value remains 0.

Using labels with break and continue

If you have nested loops, you can explicitly specify which loop you want to jump out of by prefixing it with a **label**. A label is comprised of a name, followed by the @ symbol. The following code, for example, features two loops, where one loop is nested inside another. The outer loop has a label named `myloop@`, which is used by a `break` expression:

```
myloop@ while (x < 20) {
    while (y < 20) {
        x++
        break@myloop
    }
}
```

This is like saying "break out of the loop labeled myloop@ (the outer loop)".

When you use `break` with a label, it jumps to the end of the enclosing loop with this label, so in the above example, it terminates the outer loop. When you use `continue` with a label, it jumps to the next iteration of that loop.

Using labels with return

You can also use labels to control your code's behavior in nested functions, including higher order functions.

Suppose you have the following function, which includes a call to `forEach`, which is a built-in higher order function that accepts a lambda:

```
fun myFun() {
    listOf("A", "B", "C", "D").forEach {
        if (it == "C") return
        println(it)
    }
    println("Finished myFun()")
}
```

Here, we're using return inside a lambda. When we reach the return, it exits the myFun() function.

In this example, the code exits the `myFun` function when it reaches the `return` expression, so the line:

```
println("Finished myFun()")
```

never runs.

If you want to exit the lambda but continue running `myFun`, you can add a label to the lambda, which the `return` can then reference. Here's an example:

```
fun myFun() {
    listOf("A", "B", "C", "D").forEach myloop@{
        if (it == "C") return@myloop
        println(it)
    }
    println("Finished myFun()")
}
```

The lambda that we're passing to the forEach function is labeled myloop@. The lambda's return expression uses this label, so when it's reached, it exits lambda, and returns to its caller (the forEach loop).

This can be replaced with an **implicit** label, whose name matches the function to which the lambda is passed:

```
fun myFun() {
    listOf("A", "B", "C", "D").forEach {
        if (it == "C") return@forEach
        println(it)
    }
    println("Finished myFun()")
}
```

Here, we're using an implicit label to tell the code to exit the lambda, and return to its caller (the forEach loop).

You can find out more about how to use labels to control your code jumps here:

https://kotlinlang.org/docs/reference/returns.html

9. More fun with functions

You've learned a lot about functions over the course of the book, but there are just a few more things that we thought you should know about.

vararg

If you want a function to accept multiple arguments of the same type but you don't know how many, you can prefix the parameter with **vararg**. This tells the compiler that the parameter can accept a variable number of arguments. Here's an example:

Only one parameter can be marked with vararg. This parameter is usually the last.

The vararg prefix means that we can pass multiple values for ints parameter.

```
fun <T> valuesToList(vararg vals: T): MutableList<T> {
    val list: MutableList<T> = mutableListOf()
    for (i in vals) {
        list.add(i)
    }
    return list
}
```

vararg values are passed to the function as an array, so we can loop through each value. Here, we're adding each value to a MutableList.

You call a function with a `vararg` parameter by passing values to it, just as you would any other sort of function. The following code, for example, passes five `Int` values to the `valuesToList` function:

```
val mList = valuesToList(1, 2, 3, 4, 5)
```

If you have an existing array of values, you can pass these to the function by prefixing the array name with *. This is known as the **spread operator**, and here are a couple of examples of it in use:

```
val myArray = arrayOf(1, 2, 3, 4, 5)
val mList = valuesToList(*myArray)
val mList2 = valuesToList(0, *myArray, 6, 7)
```

This passes the values held in myArray to the valuesToList function.

Pass 0 to the function... ...followed by the contents of myArray... ...followed by 6 and 7.

infix

If you prefix a function with **infix**, you can call it without using the dot notation. Here's an example of an infix function:

```
class Dog {
    infix fun bark(x: Int): String {
        //Code to make the Dog bark x times
    }
}
```

We've marked the bark() function with infix.

As the function has been marked using infix, you can call it using:

```
Dog() bark 6
```

This creates a Dog and calls its bark() function, passing the function a value of 6.

A function can be marked with infix if it's a member or extension function, and has a single parameter which has no default value, and isn't marked with vararg.

inline

Higher order functions can sometimes be slightly slower to run, but a lot of the time, you can improve their performance by prefixing the function with **inline**, for example:

```
inline fun convert(x: Double, converter: (Double) -> Double) : Double {
    val result = converter(x)
    println("$x is converted to $result")
    return result
}
```

This is a function we created in Chapter 11, but here, we've marked it as an inline function.

When you inline a function in this way, the generated code removes the function call, and replaces it with the contents of the function. It removes the overhead of calling the function, which will often make the code run faster, but behind the scenes, it generates more code.

You can find additional information about using these techniques, and more, here:

https://kotlinlang.org/docs/reference/functions.html

10. Interoperability

As we said at the beginning of the book, Kotlin is interoperable with Java, and Kotlin code can be transpiled into JavaScript. If you plan to use your Kotlin code with other languages, we recommend that you read the interoperability sections of Kotlin's online documentation.

Interoperability with Java

You can call nearly all Java code from Kotlin without any problems. Simply import any libraries that haven't been imported automatically, and use them. You can read about any extra considerations—such as how Kotlin deals with null values coming from Java—here:

https://kotlinlang.org/docs/reference/java-interop.html

Similarly, you can find out more about using your Kotlin code from inside Java here:

https://kotlinlang.org/docs/reference/java-to-kotlin-interop.html

Using Kotlin with JavaScript

The online documentation also includes a wealth of information on using Kotlin with JavaScript. If your application targets JavaScript, for example, you can use Kotlin's `dynamic` type which effectively switches off Kotlin's type checker:

```
val myDynamicVariable: dynamic = ...
```

You can find out more about the dynamic type here:

https://kotlinlang.org/docs/reference/dynamic-type.html

Similarly, the following page gives you information about using JavaScript from Kotlin:

https://kotlinlang.org/docs/reference/js-interop.html

And you can find out about accessing your Kotlin code from JavaScript here:

https://kotlinlang.org/docs/reference/js-to-kotlin-interop.html

Writing native code with Kotlin

You can also use Kotlin/Native to compile Kotlin code to native binaries. To find out more about how to do this, see here:

https://kotlinlang.org/docs/reference/native-overview.html

If you want to be able to share your code across multiple target platforms, we suggest you look at Kotlin's support for multiplatform projects. You can find out more about multiplatform projects here:

https://kotlinlang.org/docs/reference/multiplatform.html

Index

Symbols

A

B

C

D

E

F

N

O

P

Q

R

S

U

V

Milton Keynes UK
Ingram Content Group UK Ltd.
UKHW030337171024
449723UK00004B/10